D1449118

PHUKET &
KO SAMUI

SUZANNE NAM

Contents

DISCOVER

Phuket & Ko Samui

Phuket and Ko Samui are Thailand's most popular resort islands, and for good reason. The azure water and soft sand are the stuff of legends. Palm trees, lush green rainforests, paddy fields, and mountain ranges are never far away.

You'll also find reasonably priced accommodations, a good variety of places to eat, drink, and shop, and plenty of outdoor activities that take advantage of the stunning natural landscape. Here you can sleep in a thatched roof bungalow, hike through the lush forests of a national park, or snorkel in the clear blue waters of the Andaman Sea, all in the same day.

Though Thai is a tough language to master on vacation, and the script looks completely undecipherable to most Westerners, you will find at least a little English spoken in almost every corner of Phuket and Ko Samui (as well as Russian and Chinese). With so many tourists visiting, you'll never be far from someone who can help you find what you need or where you're going.

More than anything else, you'll find paradise. With a little bit of effort, you can discover that tranquil patch of sand under a coconut tree that you've been dreaming about.

Clockwise from top left: Rai Le Beach, Krabi; Phuket Town market wares; boating in the Samui Archepelago; Ko Phi Phi; Phuket Aquarium; offshore from Ko Samui.

Planning Your Trip

Where to Go

Phuket

Phuket is Thailand's number one beach destination, and for good reason. The country's largest island has almost a dozen beautiful beaches covered with soft sand and backed by swaying palm trees. The Andaman Sea, with its warm, turquoise waters, is beautiful and inviting. But if you look past the beaches for a moment it becomes clear why Phuket is so popular. There are hundreds of restaurants to eat at, over a thousand hotels, resorts, and guesthouses to choose from, and plenty of shops to peruse.

The Andaman Coast

The peninsula's west coast is undoubtedly the most beautiful region in the country, with postcard-perfect islands and lush rainforests and mountain ranges. The warm, clear waters offer excellent opportunities to snorkel and scuba dive, with stunning limestone rock formations, waterfalls, and caves to explore. Travel north or south from Phuket and you'll find some of the best beaches in the world. The rest of the region is still supported by agriculture and a thriving fishing industry, and it remains relatively undeveloped.

Ko Samui and the Samui Archipelago

Ko Samui, Ko Pha-Ngan, and Ko Tao, once a group of barely inhabited islands known better for coconut trees than anything else, now provide visitors with everything from luxury resorts to thatched beach bungalows. But despite their conveniences, even Samui still feels like a laid-back beach destination. If you want a relaxing beach vacation where you can enjoy good food and great accommodations, head to Samui. Party animals will enjoy Ko Pha-Ngan's famous full-moon raves. And if you're a diver, or aspire to be one, head to Ko Tao for some of the best diving in the region.

Southern Gulf of Thailand

Coconut groves, rubber plantations, and forested mountains characterize Thailand's lower southern gulf. Once a bustling entrepôt, this region is still a significant commercial center for southern Thailand. The largest province, Nakhon Si Thammarat, offers a tutorial of the region's cultural history. The remains of the ancient walled city of Ligor, Buddhist temples, Hindu shrines, and Muslim mosques are all easily accessible here.

When to Go

In general, Thailand's best weather is in the cool season, from November to February. This is when temperatures drop into the 70s and the humidity becomes far less oppressive. This is the most popular time to visit; you'll see plenty of other travelers and peak pricing, especially around Christmas or New Year's. Although people visit Thailand year-round, the low season is generally July-October, when most of the country is subject to monsoon rains. Don't write off this season completely, as it doesn't rain all day or even every day. If you don't mind a few rainy days, you'll pay significantly less for accommodations, and most destinations will be far less crowded. The hot season (March-May) has higher temperatures and lots of humidity. If you don't mind the heat, there are fewer visitors and lower prices.

The best time to go to Phuket is November-March, when the weather cools off a little and the Andaman Sea is at its calmest. This is peak

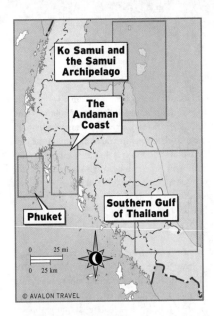

Ko Samui and the Samui Archipelago

The Andaman Coast

Southern Gulf of Thailand

Phuket

0   25 mi
0   25 km

© AVALON TRAVEL

are based on peak season. In the **two-week period** starting **before Christmas and ending January 2,** most hotels and guesthouses will tack on an additional 20 percent or more above peak prices. Even with these higher prices, the choicest places will often be fully booked months in advance. If you are in the area during Christmas or New Year's, many resorts will also require that you pay for a compulsory holiday dinner.

May-October is Phuket's **rainy season,** and while it rains often, the showers generally end quickly. If you can tolerate getting a little wet, it can be pleasantly cool, the island is a little quieter, and prices can be half of peak season. This is the **best time for surfing,** as the waves can be quite dramatic. **Divers and snorkelers** should go during **high season,** when visibility is at its best.

In Samui, there is increased rain from July to November, but the **wettest months** are **September, October, and November**—making for a short and late rainy season. **November-February** is the **cool season,** though not by much. Average daily temperatures don't vary by more than a few degrees month to month.

tourist season, though, so expect lots of other international tourists sharing the beach with you. All accommodations prices in this guide

Before You Go

Passports and Visas

Visitors from most countries do not need to apply for a visa before arriving in Thailand and are granted a **30-day visa exemption,** for free, on arrival. Make sure you have a **valid passport** with at least six months before it expires. If you are planning on staying for more than 30 days, you can apply for a **60-day tourist visa** at the Thai embassy or consulate in your home country before leaving.

Transportation

If you're traveling to Phuket, you may be flying directly to **Phuket International Airport.** Though the airport is quite small, there are international flights from Asia and Europe, especially during high season.

Samui International Airport, quite small as well, also has international flights, but only from nearby Asian cities including Hong Kong and Singapore. Most visitors who arrive on either island fly through Bangkok's **Suvarnabhumi International Airport,** just outside of Bangkok.

The Best of Phuket and Ko Samui

Most visitors pick either Phuket or Samui, but each offers something a little different, and there's no reason you can't see both on vacation. This itinerary will begin in Phuket, where you'll get a chance to tour waterfalls, snorkel, dive, explore the world-famous beaches, and do some island-hopping, too. After that, you'll take a flight to Samui, where you'll visit not only the main island but also neighboring Ko Pha-Ngan.

Day 1

You'll arrive in Phuket on the first day, whether you transited through Bangkok or got a direct flight from another Asian city. During high season, **Air China, Cathay Pacific, China Eastern, Emirates, Korean Air,** and **Singapore Airlines** all fly to Phuket, so if you're flying from a large U.S. city, you should be able to avoid more than one flight change. After you arrive in Phuket, grab a taxi to your hotel on one

of the island's many beaches, drop off your stuff, and take a refreshing swim in the Indian Ocean. Back at your hotel, arrange a **snorkeling** or **scuba diving** tour (if you're already scuba certified) of Ko Phi Phi and the surrounding islands for the next day. Then head to **Patong Beach** for a seafood meal on the water and experience a little nightlife. You could also head to **Surin Beach** for a quieter evening.

Day 2

Wake up early to make sure you don't miss your ride to the pier for the tour of **Ko Phi Phi** and the surrounding islands; most tours start their pickups at 7am. After you've arrived at the boat, hang on for some island-hopping. Spend the day snorkeling or diving around some of **Phang Nga Bay's most beautiful islands.** Don't worry about lunch; it's always included in these day tours. When you get back to your

Mu Ko Ang Thong National Park, near Ko Samui

Best Beaches

Whether you're looking for a quiet place to relax under a palm tree or a chance to lie out all day and party all night, you'll find it on Samui and Phuket.

Surin Beach, Phuket

PHUKET

- **Kata Beach:** One of Phuket's most popular beaches is a great place for families because it's got something for everyone and it's also one of the prettiest beaches on the island. You'll find a wide variety of places to stay on Kata Beach, from resorts with kids' clubs to inexpensive guesthouses. And if you want to grab a meal, or just explore the area, you can do almost everything on foot, as the village, which connects to neighboring Karon Village, is just behind the beach. There's no intense partying going on here, but if you want to grab a drink and listen to some music after the kids are asleep, you'll find plenty of places to do so.

- **Surin Beach:** The small, curved beach on northwest Phuket, on the Andaman Sea, is another great choice for families. It's surrounded by pine trees and hotels, with none of the party scene of the island's southern beaches.

- **Patong Beach:** It's not just the long, wide beach, soft sand, and warm water that make Patong a great choice for those who want to party; it also has the most vibrant nightlife scene on the island of Phuket. Scores of bars and discos are usually filled with visitors and locals 'til all hours of the night.

THE ANDAMAN COAST

- **West Rai Le Beach:** Surrounded by limestone cliffs, this small stretch of beach in Krabi on the Andaman coast has some of the best scenery in the country. Kayak rental on the beach, plenty of rock-climbing routes, and easy day trips to snorkeling spots make West Rai Le a great choice if you're looking for some adventure, too.

- **Ton Sai Bay:** Crystal-clear blue waters surrounded by limestone mountains characterize this bay on Ko Phi Phi, one of Thailand's most popular small islands. The breathtaking scenery and inexpensive bungalows make Ton Sai Bay a popular spot.

KO SAMUI AND THE SAMUI ARCHIPELAGO

- **Bo Phut Beach:** This beach is home to Samui's popular Fisherman's Village and offers a little bit of everything—a pretty beach, good accommodations, and plenty of places to eat, drink, and shop.

- **Chaweng:** Samui's most popular beach attracts the crowds. The wide, pretty beach has lots of hotels and restaurants right on the water, and the nightlife is probably the best on the island.

- **Hat Rin Beach:** This beach, on the erstwhile idyllic Ko Pha-Ngan, is home to the infamous drug- and drink-fueled full-moon parties that seem to be getting more and more popular every year.

hotel, relax for a while by the water before getting ready for dinner.

Day 3

Spend the day lounging and relaxing on the beach. Arrange a ride into **Phuket Town** for dinner; stop at **Raya Thai** if you can get a table.

Day 4

If you're feeling like you've already seen enough, spend another day on the beach. If you've had enough beach time, head to **Rawai Beach** to walk through the small fishing village. You won't be able to do any swimming or sunbathing there, so don't worry about packing a towel. During the evening, ditch the flip-flops and bathing suit for something a little more formal and have dinner at one of the fancier restaurants in **Kata Beach.**

Day 5

In the morning, head for the airport and take a short flight to **Ko Samui.** The only airline offering direct flights is **Bangkok Airways,** and there are limited flights per day, so make sure to book ahead. Once you arrive in Samui, take a moment to enjoy the charming little airport before you grab a taxi and head to your hotel. After you check in to your hotel, spend a couple of hours exploring some of the island's tourist attractions, such as the **Big Buddha** and **Grandfather and Grandmother Rocks,** before retiring to the beach for some more relaxation.

Day 6

As you did in Phuket, you'll spend a day exploring the region on a guided tour. This time, you'll spend your time in **Mu Ko Ang Thong National Park,** essentially the islands surrounding Ko Samui, on a kayaking tour. Wake up early and catch a ride with your tour group to Nathon pier, where your boat will depart after a quick breakfast. Don't worry if you've never kayaked before, as most good outfitters will offer basic instruction and plenty of help during the tour. After paddling to some of the park's most amazing sights, including the emerald lake, **Thale Nai,** enjoy a basic Thai lunch on the beach before kayaking through and around some of the gorgeous islands (and somewhat scary caves!). You'll be back at your hotel by around 6pm, just in time to either collapse from exhaustion or take a quick shower and head out to **Chaweng Beach** for some dinner.

Day 7

Spend your last full day in Samui relaxing by the beach. For dinner, head to **Bo Phut Beach,** where you can pick from a number of restaurants overlooking the water. If you happen to be there on a Friday night, enjoy the **Fisherman's Village Night Market,** full of lots of fun stuff to buy as well as good, cheap food and drink.

Day 8

Take a last dip in the waters of the **Gulf of Thailand** before packing up and heading to the airport for your return home.

Best Places to Stay

Thailand's beaches and islands are home to some of the best resorts and hotels in the world. And while none of these are cheap, thanks to the relative strength of the dollar, they aren't all budget busters, either. In fact, you'll spend as much per night on some of these five-star resorts in Thailand as you would for a run-of-the-mill hotel in many large U.S. cities.

- **Trisara, Nai Thon Beach, Phuket:** One of the country's most beautiful and most luxurious resorts, which says a lot. Rooms are larger than most apartments, and some of the villas come with their own swimming pools and staff.

- **Mom Tri's Villa Royale, Kata Beach, Phuket:** This stunning resort takes full advantage of the amazing natural surroundings, but because it's right in Kata, guests won't feel isolated at all.

- **The Naka Island, Ko Naka Yai:** Looking for a secluded island to relax on, but don't feel like roughing it? This Starwoods luxury resort has everything you could possibly want and is totally removed from the crowds.

- **Six Senses Yao Noi, Ko Yao Noi:** This sprawling property on part of a small island in Ko Phang Nga Bay has massive, understated villas and some of the best service in the world.

- **Rayavadee Premier, Rai Le Beach, Krabi:** You can't go wrong with luxury beach bungalows set on one of the most beautiful beaches in Southeast Asia.

- **The Library, Chaweng Beach, Ko Samui:** This striking modern resort in otherwise middle-of-the-road Chaweng will make you feel like a member of the jet set, even if you aren't. The red-tiled swimming pool and gorgeous view of the Gulf will impress even the most jaded traveler.

Diving Thailand's Coasts

The waters surrounding the Andaman coast and the Samui Archipelago offer an amazing diversity of marine life and dive sites from beginner to advanced, some considered among the best in the world. Along Thailand's two coasts, hundreds of dive shops offer courses, equipment rental, day trips, and live-aboards. If you're planning on diving in the region, don't worry too much about where you are staying relative to the areas where you want to dive; most diving shops (especially in Phuket) offer dives to all of the most popular sites in the region.

Phuket
KO RACHA NOI
Ko Racha Noi is a popular place to visit on a day trip and has a nice mix of both **colorful coral** and **challenging, rocky terrain.**

SHARK POINT
Another very popular destination is Shark Point, about 32 kilometers (20 mi) east of Chalong Bay. There are three **rock outcroppings** that attract sharks, including **leopard sharks.**

ANEMONE REEF
Just under one kilometer (0.6 mi) away from Shark Point is Anemone Reef, with lots of **anemone, coral,** and plenty of **colorful small fish.**

KING CRUISER WRECK
If you're interested in wreck diving, close by is King Cruiser Wreck, a **sunken car ferry** in Phang Nga Bay. This site is appropriate for most divers and attracts lots of fish.

diver with feather sea stars in the Andaman Sea

snorkeling at Ko Phi Phi

The Andaman Coast

KO PHI PHI

The waters surrounding Ko Phi Phi offer both nice diving and **excellent snorkeling.** The biggest attraction here is the **colorful coral** and **vibrant fish.** Most of the dives are not difficult, but divers looking for more of a challenge can check out the wall diving at **Ao Nui.**

KO LANTA

South of Ko Lanta are some excellent (and convenient) dive sites. The **Mu Ko Lanta National Park** is a group of 15 small islands, many with good diving in surrounding areas. You'll find lots of rocky terrain attracting colorful fish, some **underwater caves** to explore, and beautiful coral. The **Ko Kradan Wreck** is now an **artificial reef.**

SURIN ISLANDS

These islands are part of the **Mu Ko Surin National Park** and are best known for the excellent coral surrounding them. The biggest draw is **Richelieu Rock,** a rock pinnacle jutting out of the ocean that's known to attract giant, gentle **whale sharks.** These islands are accessible by live-aboard trips from Phuket, but if you're staying in Khao Lak, you can visit on a day trip.

SIMILAN ISLANDS

These nine **granite islands** make up the **Mu Ko Similan National Park** and are considered by most to offer the best diving in Thailand and some of the best diving in the world. Here you'll find plenty of colorful reefs and **plankton blooms** attracting sharks, rays, and plenty of **tropical fish.** Other parts of the island grouping are more rugged, with **boulder formations** offering more adventurous diving. There are also **great night-diving spots** where you'll see **squid, crustaceans,** and other creatures. These islands can be visited on day trips from Phuket and Khao Lak, but many people choose multiday live-aboards.

Ko Samui and the Samui Archipelago

SAIL ROCK

This **rock pinnacle** between Ko Tao and Ko

Pha-Ngan is the region's **most popular dive spot** and is appropriate for all levels of divers. The pinnacle, which towers about nine meters (10 yd) above the surface, is a magnet for fish, so there's plenty of **colorful marinelife** to be spotted. The **swim-through chimney,** a cavernous tunnel through the pinnacle, is a must-do for anyone visiting Sail Rock.

CHUMPHON PINNACLE

Just under 10 kilometers (6 mi) northwest of Ko Tao is Chumphon Pinnacle, a very popular **granite pinnacle** that does not break the surface. The base is covered with **colorful anemones** and attracts plenty of large and small fish. Large **whale sharks** are often spotted here, as are **leopard sharks.**

SHARK ISLAND

Southeast of Ko Tao is a grouping of rocks surrounded by colorful **coral and anemones.** Snappers, rays, and angelfish congregate in the rocks and, as you might suspect from the name, so do **sharks.**

KO MA

Just north of Ko Pha-Ngan (connected by a strip of sand at low tide) is Ko Ma, which has some vibrant and healthy **hard and soft coral** as well as lots of vivid marinelife. Given its proximity to the main island and its suitability for **divers of all levels,** this is often where beginning divers are taken when they are getting certified.

KO NANG YUAN

The **three interconnected islands** also offer some nice snorkeling and diving opportunities. The **coral reef** attracts plenty of smaller fish and is a nice place for **beginning divers** and for snorkelers. Nang Yuan Pinnacle, a small **granite pinnacle** below the surface, attracts larger fish that have come to feed.

Dive Shops, Courses, and Certification

In Thailand most diving instruction courses offer **PADI** (www.padi.com) open-water diver certification. These courses take 3-4 days, at the end of which you'll be certified to dive all over the world. You'll spend time in the classroom first learning

snorkeling by one of the Ko Nang Yuan islands

Spas and Wellness

There are probably more spas in Thailand, per capita, than in any other country in the world. In most parts of Phuket and Ko Samui, you will be able to find inexpensive massage parlors offering Thai and oil massage, usually for the equivalent of less than $20 per hour. These outfits are often not much more than a shop house with a handful of staff, but they are more than adequate if you just need a massage and don't mind the fact that you might have to share a room with another client.

If you want something a little more luxurious, there are numerous stand-alone spas on both Ko Samui and Phuket. The best service tends to be at the resort spas. You don't need to stay at a resort to enjoy its spa, but it does make it harder to get a convenient booking (many reserve the best slots for their guests), so make sure to book treatments ahead. Resort spas can be very expensive: An hour-long massage can run as much as 6,000 baht (about $200).

PHUKET

- **Trisara** (60/1 Mu 6, Srisoonthorn Rd., Nai Thon Beach, tel. 07/631-0100, www.trisara.com), one of Phuket's absolute best luxury resorts, also has an

Spa at Anantara Phuket Villas

amazing spa. The location is a bit out of the way if you're not staying in the area, but it's worth the trip for a private yoga class, a consult with one of its holistic healers, or an indulgent massage with three therapists.

- **Sun Spa** (106/46 Mu 3, Srisoonthorn Rd., Surin Beach, tel. 07/631-6500, www.twinpalms-phuket.com) is a lovely, modern spa at the chic Twin Palms resort on Surin Beach. It has almost a dozen different facials to choose from, plus standard massages and treatments.

- The **Spa at Anantara Phuket Villas** (888 Mu 3, Mai Khao Beach, tel. 07/633-6100, www.phuket.anantara.com) offers a variety of treatments using mainly local herbs. Treatment rooms are luxuriously decorated with Thai furnishings; you won't forget you're on an exotic holiday while you're here.

KO SAMUI

- **Is Spa** (14/1 Mu 2, Chaweng Beach, tel. 07/742-2767, www.thelibrary.co.th) at the Library on Chaweng is a modern, luxurious spa offering traditional spa treatments such as Thai massage, Thai herbal wraps, and Swedish massage. The setting, with its minimalist treatment rooms, is sure to be Zen inducing. Another bonus: It's very convenient to everything.

- **Banyan Tree Spa Samui** (99/9 Mu 4, Lamai Beach, tel. 07/791-5333, www.banyantree.com) offers a full range of facial, body, and massage treatments, including some ayurvedic options. There is also an area called the Rainforest, which looks like a rainforest, with herbal steams, mud treatments, and other water therapies. Treatment suites are gorgeously decorated with regional woodwork and textiles and are very private, so you won't be sitting in the waiting room wearing your robe with other guests around.

about safety and dive theory, take your first dive in a swimming pool, and advance to supervised open-water dives. Expect to pay 10,000-15,000 baht for the full course, including equipment and dives. If you can't imagine wasting hours inside a classroom while you're on vacation, and assuming there is a PADI training center where you live, you can do the classroom and pool-diving components of your training at home and bring your referral paperwork with you to Thailand, where you'll be able to complete the open-water portion of the certification.

Certified divers looking to advance their skills can also take **dive master** courses, become certified diving instructors, and arrange training internships at some of the larger training centers. These programs are at least two weeks long and cost 30,000-75,000 baht.

There are many dive shops in the area, especially on Ko Tao, which has dozens. Safety records across Thailand's diving industry are good, but make sure to inspect equipment and talk to the instructors and dive masters you'll be with before signing up to make sure you're comfortable with them. Also ask about environmental awareness. PADI divers should follow a strict no-hands rule, but some dive shops have been known to be somewhat lax about it (touching or even brushing up against coral can damage it).

On Ko Tao, especially, many dive shops also have small guesthouses, and you'll get a discounted rate (sometimes just a few hundred baht) if you're taking lessons or going out on dives with them. Accommodations run the gamut from basic and clean to luxurious. You'll be surrounded by fellow divers if you choose to stay in one of these guesthouses.

There are also plenty of dive shops on Ko Samui and Ko Pha-Ngan that offer diving trips and equipment. You can also take 3-4-day PADI diving certification courses at shops on the islands. Live-aboards tend to be less popular in this part of the country; instead, most diving is done on day trips or multiday trips where divers sleep in basic accommodations on one of the islands in Ang Thong National Marine Park.

Phuket

It's no wonder millions of people visit Phuket each year. If you're in the market for the perfect beach vacation and don't mind sharing your space with others, nothing can beat it. The landscape, with its hilly, green, forested interior and clean, sandy

beaches, is awe-inspiring. The vibes of the beaches and their surrounding areas vary from spring break fun to secluded romantic getaway to family-friendly. The accommodations range from unbelievably cheap to unbelievably luxurious. The tourism infrastructure is solid, and anything you want—perhaps a spur-of-the-moment diving trip, a midday massage on the beach, or a bespoke suit made in 24 hours—is available with no hassle. As if that weren't enough, nearly all of the sweeping, inviting beaches face west, so picture-perfect sunsets are a given. On an island this popular and this built-up, there are no more absolutely deserted places, but the northern and southern parts of the west coast offer some surprisingly quiet, quaint, and relaxed places to pull up a beach chair and chill out.

Thailand's largest island is about 48 kilometers (30 mi) long and 16 kilometers (10 mi) across. Imagine an elongated star with extra points and you'll have a rough idea of what

Phuket looks like from above. The points are promontories, rock formations jutting out into the ocean and separating the island into numerous individual beaches with curving coasts. The road system on the island is very well maintained, and there is both a coastal road that encircles nearly the whole island and large multilane inland roads. Off the main island, the Andaman Sea is littered with small islands and elegant rock formations jutting out from the sea. Many of the surrounding islands could be destinations in their own right, if not overshadowed by the main island.

Phuket and the surrounding areas rebuilt quickly after the 2004 tsunami, but the momentum from the redevelopment seems not to have slowed once all of the damage was repaired. There are new resorts and villas popping up in every corner, new shopping malls, bars and restaurants opening just off the beach and further inland, and more visitors coming every year to stay, eat, drink, and

Previous: sunset on Phuket's west coast; Phuket Town. **Above:** monkeys on a beach in Phuket.

Look for ★ to find recommended
sights, activities, dining, and lodging.

Highlights

★ **Mai Khao Beach:** This quiet beach is fast becoming a favorite among families and local visitors, thanks to the ever-increasing selection of decent resorts and lack of crowds (page 24).

★ **Surin Beach:** This beautiful beach is quiet and relaxed, but offers plenty to do and great accommodations options (page 25).

★ **Patong Beach:** This busy, bustling beach is where you'll find all the action. Whether you're looking to shop, jet ski, parasail, or drink and dance the night away, you'll find it here (page 26).

★ **Kata Yai and Kata Noi Beaches:** These two beaches have clean, white sand and beautiful views, without the big crowds (page 26).

★ **Ko Mai Thon:** This little island is surrounded by stunning coral, making it a great place for snorkeling (page 29).

Phuket coastline

Phuket

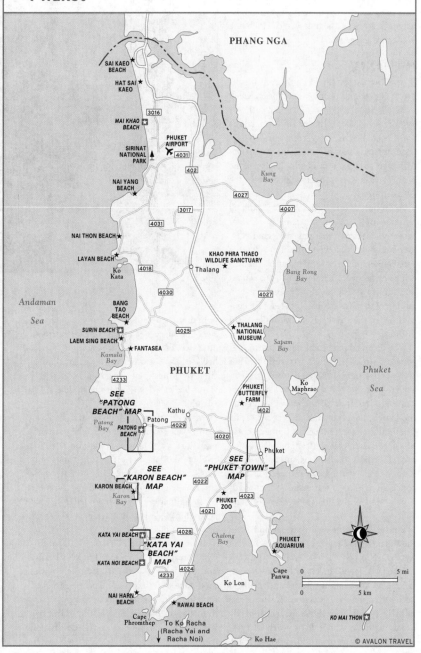

shop in those new places. If you want to experience some of what Phuket became famous for, hurry up and come now: Even the most remote beaches and islands won't be the same in the next few years.

HISTORY

During prehistoric times, Phuket was inhabited by indigenous people sometimes referred to as Negritos, a group of hunter-gatherer pygmies who were, like many indigenous Southeast Asians, displaced and assimilated during waves of successive migration. Although no clear records exist, the last of the pygmy tribes was probably wiped out in the 19th century.

Although Phuket, then called Jang Si Lang or Junk Ceylon, shows up in some of Ptolemy's maps and writings, the island's history is largely unknown until about 800 years ago. Phuket's main natural resource, tin, was mined by prehistoric inhabitants, but what is now known as Phuket didn't come to the attention of the Thai people until the 13th century, when they arrived for trading and tin mining.

Word spread of the abundant natural resources, which included not only tin but also pearls, and by the 15th-16th centuries Thalang, as the island was then known, became a popular trading center, attracting the Dutch, Portuguese, and French. While Thailand has never technically been colonized, the Dutch set up trading posts in the region in the 16th century, and parts of the island were governed by tin traders under a concession. Phuket was even under the administration of the French between 1681 and 1685.

At the end of the Ayutthaya period, after the Burmese had sacked the capital city and were pushed back by General Taksin, they set their sights on Phuket and the surrounding region, invading the island and trying to take it over in 1785. The island's governor was killed by the intruders, but Phuket did not fall, according to the story told by nearly every islander. The governor's widow and her sister,

rubber tapping

both disguised as men, led a force against the siege and succeeded in repelling the Burmese after weeks of fighting. In recognition of their heroism, the two women were granted noble titles by King Rama I, and today there is a statue dedicated to them in the middle of the island.

After that dramatic high point in Phuket's history, the island continued to be used primarily as a tin-mining area, and later for rubber plantations, attracting thousands of Chinese immigrants in the 19th century, many of whom remained and, with the Muslim fisherfolk who immigrated from what is now Malaysia, constitute much of the modern indigenous population.

It wasn't until the 1970s that intrepid foreign travelers "discovered" Phuket's beauty and began to visit the island to enjoy the mountainous rainforests and pristine beaches. Starting with some small bungalow developments on Patong Beach, the island has boomed into a world-class tourist destination over the past three decades. Urban Thais in their 50s and 60s will often laugh and reminisce about what the Andaman coast used to be like before travelers and developers realized it was a natural tourist destination, when they'd head down on motorcycles to the largely untouched island for some adventure. Fast-forward 30 years, and the dirt roads and simple local folks have since been replaced by an exceptionally sophisticated infrastructure with easily navigable roads, hospitals, shopping malls, and an international airport.

Nowadays Phuket's "local" population is not just the Chinese immigrants and Muslim fisherfolk but thousands of Thais who've moved here to open hotels, restaurants, and other tourism-related businesses. The mining industry is virtually gone, but rubber tapping remains one of the island's income generators. The island's identity is tourism, attracting millions of visitors each year and accounting for the majority of the island's revenues.

PLANNING YOUR TIME

Phuket is filled with opportunities to relax on beautiful beaches, explore the stunning physical landscape, enjoy local foods, and pamper yourself in a bit of luxury. You can spend three weeks island-hopping, diving, hiking, and playing golf, or spend just a few days lying on the beach without even touring the neighboring areas, and you'll still have something of value from your trip.

While it may be tempting to idle your days away in the immediate vicinity of your hotel, make sure to set aside at least one day to explore the surrounding islands by boat. The small islands you'll pass on the way create scenery that's enchanting and like nothing in North America. Off the smaller islands is some of the best scuba and snorkeling in the world.

If you've never dived before, Phuket is the place to start. There are numerous dive schools that offer PADI certification, and the courses are inexpensive and a lot of fun. Even if you're not interested in diving, set aside a couple of hours to snorkel above some of the shallow coral reefs.

ORIENTATION

Patong functions as the center of the most popular and developed part of Phuket, though it's not in the middle of the island, but farther south. The northernmost part of the island, once almost totally ignored, is slowly becoming developed.

Beaches and Islands

While there are plenty of other sights that can fill your day, Phuket really is all about hanging out on the beaches and exploring the surrounding islands. Phuket is ringed with beaches, each with its own distinct personality. If you don't like one, go up a kilometer or two to the next one to find your perfect spot. Almost all of the sandy beaches on the island face west and look out onto the clear blue Andaman Sea, they are all clean, and they all offer at least minimum amenities (restrooms and small shops or food vendors for drinks and snacks) close by. Due to the island's topography, most of the beaches are separated from each other by rocky outcroppings, creating a natural curving bay at each. What really sets the beaches apart aside from size is what's going on behind them. A cozy beach chair with a great view will feel a lot different depending on whether there are copses of pine and palm trees behind you or a big street lined with shops, cafés, and restaurants. Luckily, whether you're looking for some action or just want peace and quiet, Phuket has both.

For most people, it's a good idea to pick the beach first, then the accommodations. Phuket has a main road running down the west coast, making all beaches easily accessible by car or scooter. On the island, the *sabai sabai* attitude tends to take hold quickly, and although all of the beaches are easy to access, it's a lot nicer to be able to walk to your favorite spot in a few minutes instead of taking a taxi or driving.

SAI KAEO BEACH
หาดทรายแก้ว

The northernmost beach on the island, **Sai Kaeo Beach** is one of the least developed and least populated, with just a few casual shacks selling seafood on the southern part of the beach and no hotels or other commercial enterprises to speak of. The golden coarse sand beach is backed by pine trees and gently curves before becoming Mai Khao to the south.

★ MAI KHAO BEACH
หาดไม้ขาว

Just below Sai Kaeo Beach is **Mai Khao Beach,** home to endangered giant leatherback turtles that lay their eggs in the sand during the cool season. When they hatch a few months later, usually in April, the babies make their way to the ocean en masse, a fascinating spectacle if you happen to be around when it happens. In recent years, community groups have beefed up protection of the turtles, restricting access to the beach during nesting and hatching periods. Although much of it is still a part of the national park and therefore undeveloped, not all is protected. There are a handful of resorts on this stretch of beach, although accommodations are spread out and options are limited. There are two coral reefs 1.5 kilometers (1 mi) out that can easily be seen with just a snorkel.

NAI YANG BEACH
หาดในยาง

Just south of the airport and Sirinat National Park is **Nai Yang Beach,** a small, gently curving bay with golden sand and surrounding pine and palm trees. Like other northern beaches, there is no large access road running parallel to the coast (the main road is inland about a quarter of a mile), so it is still relatively undeveloped and feels a little out of the way. There are a handful of resorts within walking distance of the beach, though so far nowhere right on the water.

NAI THON BEACH
หาดในทอน

This half-mile stretch of coastline, called **Nai Thon Beach,** is surrounded on either side by rocky promontories and forested hills. It has a wide beach area covered in soft, light-colored sand. Though there are a few mostly high-end

Mai Khao Beach

resorts on Nai Thon, even during high season it is a very quiet beach. No Jet Skis or parasails, but you can rent a beach chair with umbrella, and there are places to eat and drink along the beach.

LAYAN BEACH
หาดลายัน

Layan Beach, really just the northern tip of Bang Tao Beach, is small and quiet. During the April-October low season, this pristine beach is nearly deserted, and it may be as close to the desert-island experience as you'll find on Phuket. There's really nothing in the area aside from a couple of simple beachfront restaurants serving local food. Behind the beach is a more residential area, although there are numerous villas being built in the vicinity.

BANG TAO BEACH
หาดบางเทา

South of the airport but north of Patong and the island's central beaches is **Bang Tao Beach,** the longest beach on Phuket. Lagoons, resort and villa developments on the beach, and a main road far from the water make this a relatively quiet and uncrowded beach, though it does have its share of touts and Jet Skis. The largest group of resorts is in a development called Laguna, which has seven different resorts spread out over 1,000 acres. Those resorts and the shared grounds take up most of the central part of Bang Tao Beach.

★ SURIN BEACH
หาดสุรินทร์

The perfect balance of secluded and interesting, **Surin Beach** has plenty to do, but none of the fast-paced activity you'll find on other popular beaches. The small, clean beach is backed by large green lawns and tall trees with only a small road behind it. Although there's no boardwalk, a pedestrian lane between the palms and pine trees is lined with small beach shops and restaurants, many of which set up dining areas right at the edge of the sand. Surrounding the beach area are some nice modern luxury resorts and some good dining options.

What makes Surin special is that it still feels like a local family beach, and it still feels like Thailand. There's a small town-meets-Miami Beach vibe here—local school kids playing volleyball on the lawn behind you while you sip a glass of wine on a comfy beach chair and watch the sun set. Surin is small, though, and if you're looking for a place where you can wander around on foot for more than a

Nai Thon Beach

few minutes, you will be disappointed here. The main road that runs perpendicular to the beach is too busy and fast to allow for much pedestrian activity, and there isn't much to see or do aside from right in the center near the beach anyway.

LAEM SING BEACH
หาดแหลมสิงห์

Tiny **Laem Sing Beach** was once a bit of a secret but is now a little more crowded and popular. It feels worlds away from the bustle of the area's other beaches. To access the small, curved beach, you'll have to walk down a steep path, and the shore is hidden from the main road. There are still some vendors selling fruit, snacks, and random souvenirs at Laem Sing, places to rent chairs, and even a few casual shops to grab lunch, so don't worry about amenities. Laem Sing also has some granite rock formations along the shore, making it a nice place to do a little casual snorkeling.

KAMALA BAY
อ่าวกมลา

Not quite like Karon or Kata to the south, but with a little more going on than Surin, the relatively undeveloped stretch of wide **Kamala Bay,** shaded by trees, is pleasant and relaxed. There are a few larger resorts right on the beach, and in the hills above the bay are a handful of small upscale hotels. Part of the beach is bordered by protected lands. Right behind the southern part of Kamala Bay is Kamala Village, a former fishing village that is still home to some who ply the ocean in their colorful longtail boats. The village isn't large but has a number of inexpensive guesthouses and places to get fresh seafood and other meals.

★ PATONG BEACH
หาดป่าตอง

Not quite the desert-island paradise you may have imagined, **Patong Beach** is a built-up, bustling beach community filled with Starbucks, McDonald's, scores of hotels and restaurants, a full-fledged shopping mall within walking distance of the beach, and a vibrant nightlife scene. For some, Patong is the only place to go in Phuket; for others, it's the worst-case scenario for a tropical vacation. If going out 'til the wee hours of the morning then rolling onto the beach to sleep it off with your fellow revelers is your thing, pick Patong. If you're looking for a quiet place to relax away from the hustle and bustle of urban life, stay away. The white-sand beach is generally covered with beach chairs and umbrellas by day but, despite being crowded, is a wide, clean beach with soft sand and clear water. It is one of the island's nicest beaches, if you don't mind lots of people or Jet Skis. The beach is one of the largest in the area, and the wide sidewalk has some small playgrounds and some interesting sculptures, too, if you get bored of the natural scenery.

KARON BEACH
หาดกะรน

Karon Beach is big and wide, another popular spot for visitors, but much less built up than Patong. For some it's a perfect balance between amenities and quiet. Karon is one of the largest beaches on the island, and instead of being bordered by trees or a quiet street, there is a fairly main road adjacent and numerous shops across the street. There will still be some loud water sports such as Jet Skis, but the beach is large enough that noisy activities are confined to the southern end. The village behind the beach is attached to Kata Village, so there is plenty to explore on foot.

★ KATA YAI AND KATA NOI BEACHES
หาดกะตะใหญ่และกะตะน้อย

Kata Beach divides itself into **Kata Yai Beach** and **Kata Noi Beach.** What's so great about Kata Beach is what's missing. Most of the land directly in front of Kata Yai, separated by a narrow lane, is used by an enormous but discreet Club Med, virtually ensuring that there will be no high-rise hotels or other development on the spot

Patong Beach

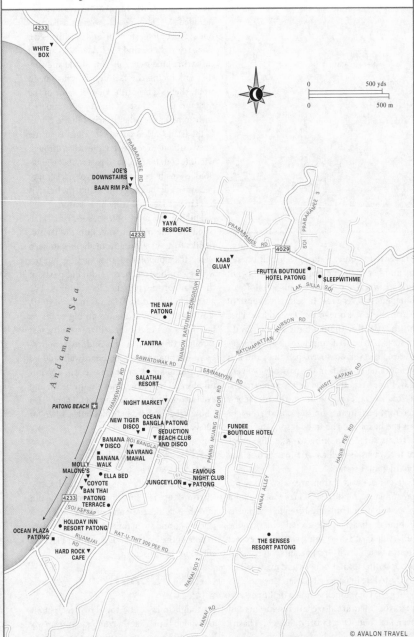

4233

WHITE
BOX

PRABARAMEE RD

JOE'S
DOWNSTAIRS
BAAN RIM PA

YAYA
RESIDENCE

4233

PRABARAMEE RD

SOI PRABARAMEE 3

4029

KAAB
GLUAY

FRUTTA BOUTIQUE
HOTEL PATONG
SLEEPWITHME

LAK SILLA SOI

THE NAP
PATONG

THANON RATUTHIT SONGROIPI RD

NURSON RD

Andaman Sea

TANTRA

SAWATDIRAK RD

RATCHAPATTAN

SAINAMYEN RD

PHISIT KAPANI RD

SALATHAI
RESORT

THAVEWONG RD

NIGHT MARKET

PATONG BEACH

PHANG MUANG SAI GOR RD

New Tiger
Disco

OCEAN
BANGLA PATONG

FUNDEE
BOUTIQUE HOTEL

SEDUCTION
BEACH CLUB
AND DISCO

BANANA
DISCO

SOI BANGLA

HA5IB PEE RD

NAVRANG
MAHAL

BANANA
WALK

MOLLY
MALONE'S

ELLA BED

FAMOUS
NIGHT CLUB
PATONG

COYOTE

JUNGCEYLON

BAN THAI

NANAI ALLEY

4233

PATONG
TERRACE

SOI KEPSAP

HOLIDAY INN
RESORT PATONG

OCEAN PLAZA
PATONG

RUAMJAI
RD

RAT-U-THIT 200 PEE RD

THE SENSES
RESORT PATONG

HARD ROCK
CAFE

NANAI SOI 2

NANAI RD

© AVALON TRAVEL

0   500 yds
0   500 m

Karon Beach

LE MERIDIEN
PHUKET BEACH RESORT

WISET RD

PATAK RD,
SOI 24

PHUNAWA RESORT

CENTARA GRAND
BEACH RESORT PHUKET

MANDARAVA
RESORT AND SPA

PATAK
SOI 20

TWO CHEFS
BAR AND GRILL

KANITA
RESORT &
CAMPING

*Andaman
Sea*

Karon Beach

SIMPLITEL
HOTEL

PATAK

PATAK
SOI 18

PATAK
RD

0   500 yds

0   500 m

© AVALON TRAVEL

for years to come. Kata Yai's beach is used by another high-end hotel (the beach is not private, but some access points are only for hotel guests). As a result, Kata, just south of Karon Beach, is one of the few large beaches on the island without a built-up boardwalk of sorts. That doesn't mean there are no amenities, however. *Som tam,* pad thai, and roti vendors set up stalls in the parking lot every day, there are public showers and restrooms across the lane, and some of the nicest waterfront restaurants on the island are right on the beach. In the low season, the beach attracts surfers looking to take advantage of the waves as well as surf instructors and board-rental stands.

The Kata and Karon area also has some great relaxed nightlife if you're looking for a place to have a drink and listen to live music. Behind the beach area is a small village in the hills, filled with everything you would expect from a beach town—restaurants, cafés, small shops selling local products, and many tailors trying to lure in passing travelers. In fact, Kata Village has developed so much in the past few years that there are also chain restaurants and even fast food. Don't worry, though, it hasn't lost its charm or beach town feeling.

NAI HARN BEACH
หาดในหาน

Nearly at the southern tip of the island is the secluded **Nai Harn Beach,** with a small coastline set off by long strips of land on either side. The area right behind the beach is a patch of casuarina pine trees, offering shade and further enhancing the feeling of seclusion. In front, there's a beautiful view of some of the rock formations just off the coast. Compared with some of the other beaches in the center of the island's west coast, Nai Harn is a little more difficult to access, but the drive, through winding country roads and past rubber plantations, is worth the extra time involved. Perhaps because it's at the end of the island, the beach is less crowded, even during high season.

During the monsoon season, Nai Harn often has the biggest waves on the island, thanks to a quick drop from shallow to deep water. It's a popular spot for surfing, but the waves can be treacherous during parts of the year for inexperienced swimmers. The area right behind Nai Harn is made of steep, stony cliffs, and there are no big roads or built-up areas in the immediate vicinity, just a couple of resorts and a Buddhist monastery. Although there's no boardwalk and no nightlife to speak of, there are still a handful of small shops right next to the beach and even a couple of little restaurants. There's also a bus that goes directly from Phuket Town for 100 baht.

CAPE PHROMTHEP
แหลมพรหมเทพ

The southernmost point of the island, **Cape Phromthep,** is a small headland jutting out into the sea like the point of a star. It's not a place to go and swim for the day, rather a place to take in the view. This is a popular place for enjoying the sunset.

RAWAI BEACH
หาดราไวย์

It's tough to lay out a towel or beach chair and spend the day at **Rawai Beach,** as many longtail fishing boats are moored here during

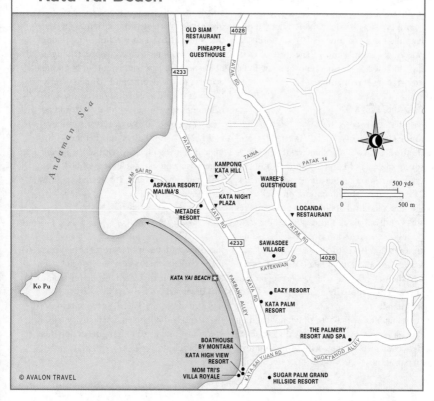

Kata Yai Beach

the day, and the coral fragments on the coast make it really uncomfortable on bare feet for wading in the water. But the area surrounding it is a small fishing village with a wet market selling lots of fresh seafood as well as some touristy souvenirs made from shells, making it a pleasant little excursion if you happen to be in the neighborhood. This is one of the few beaches not facing west, something to keep in mind if you're looking for a sunset view.

CHALONG BAY

อ่าวฉลอง

Chalong Bay is not suitable for swimming, but it serves as the launching point for a number of charter and tour boats heading to different islands off the coast. In the morning the pier is filled with visitors getting ready for excursions, and in the afternoon you'll see the same folks heading back. The little streets surrounding the bay have a relaxed atmosphere and some inexpensive guesthouses, as well as diving and other marine-activity supply shops. In the afternoon and at night, there are a couple of modern restaurants with outdoor seating and great views, perfect if you've just returned from an excursion and are looking for a place to unwind and watch the sunset.

★ KO MAI THON

เกาะไม้ท่อน

Ko Mai Thon is known for some excellent

coral formations within snorkeling distance of the shore and can be reached from the mainland in less than an hour. This small island is home to the private Honeymoon Island Resort, so any visits have to be arranged through them. At the time of writing, the resort was under renovation, with no known date of reopening.

KO RACHA

เกาะราชา

Made up of two islands, **Racha Yai** and **Racha Noi,** about 13 kilometers (8 mi) off the southern coast of Phuket, **Ko Racha** is generally visited on diving and snorkeling trips. There are no accommodations on Racha Noi, but now a handful of little bungalows and resorts dot Racha Yai. On Racha Yai the most popular spot to go is Tawan Tok Bay, sometimes called **Ao Bungalow.** The sand here is very fine and soft. When the seas are calm and the water is clear, this is a great place for snorkeling, especially as it's so close to the mainland.

Racha Noi, which can only be visited on day trips, has some excellent diving at the hard coral reefs off the northern and southern coasts of the island, and it is not uncommon for divers to see manta rays and even occasional whales. There's also a relatively new **shipwreck** off the southwest coast. Not yet overgrown with sea life, it nonetheless attracts lots of fish and is a fun thing to do if you've never wreck-dived before. Diving off of Racha Noi, however, is not for beginners because of the depths and strong currents. Newbies should stick with Racha Yai, which has some great coral reefs of its own and can easily be viewed by novice divers and even snorkelers. Many dive, snorkel, and touring companies offer day trips to the islands; otherwise, you can get a longtail boat from Chalong Bay if you're interested in going there on your own.

KO LON

เกาะโหลน

Just a few minutes by boat from the mainland is the chilled-out **Ko Lon.** There's not a ton to do here, but if you're looking for a bit of that desert-island feeling that's easy to get to, it is a good option. There's just one resort on the island, although you can take day trips if you're just interested in hanging out on their sandy beach.

Sights

If you can drag yourself away from the beautiful beaches, Phuket has a number of interesting places to see. Aside from sights geared for visiting tourists, Phuket and the surrounding islands are home to some amazing natural sights, including rainforests, mangrove swamps, karst rock formations rising out of the ocean, and marine areas with colorful fish and coral. Since it is a vacation town, there are tons of fun or silly ways to spend your afternoons, whether taking in a cabaret show or visiting a nature conservation center. They may not be all that culturally significant, but they'll certainly keep you distracted on a rainy day.

INLAND PHUKET
Thalang National Museum

พิพิธภัณฑสถานแห่งชาติถลาง

The **Thalang National Museum** (Mu 3, Si Sumthon, Thalang, tel. 07/631-1426, 8:30am-4:30pm daily except national holidays, 30B, free under age 7), eponymous with one of Phuket's historical names, houses a number of exhibitions demonstrating Phuket's history and includes some prehistoric artifacts such as stone tools as well as religious items. The museum isn't vast or particularly comprehensive, but there are some entertaining displays reenacting life on the island throughout the ages, including a reenactment of the famous Battle

Phuket Town

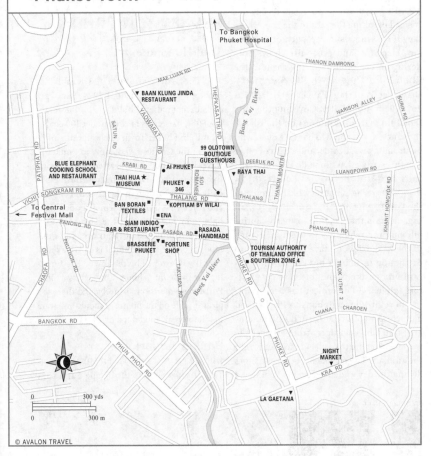

To Bangkok
Phuket Hospital

THANON DAMRONG

MAE LUAN RD.

BAAN KLUNG JINDA
RESTAURANT

YAOWARAJ

SATUN RD.

NARISON ALLEY

SURIN RD.

THEPKASATTRI RD.

Bang Yai River

99 OLDTOWN
BOUTIQUE
GUESTHOUSE

DEEBUK RD.

LUANGPOHW RD.

PATIPHAT RD.

BLUE ELEPHANT
COOKING SCHOOL
AND RESTAURANT

KRABI RD.

AI PHUKET

RAYA THAI

THANON MONTRI

THAI HUA ★
MUSEUM

PHUKET ●
346

SOI
ROMANEE

THALANG RD.

THALANG

VICHIT SONGKRAM RD.

To Central
Festival Mall

BAN BORAN
TEXTILES

KOPITIAM BY WILAI

KHANIT HONGYOK RD.

RANONG RD.

■ENA

SIAM INDIGO
BAR & RESTAURANT

RASADA RD.

RASADA
HANDMADE

PHANGNGA RD.

PHUTHON RD.

BRASSERIE
PHUKET

FORTUNE
SHOP

TOURISM AUTHORITY
OF THAILAND OFFICE
■ SOUTHERN ZONE 4

CHAOFA RD.

TAKUAPA RD.

Bang Yai River

PHUKET RD.

TILOK UTHIT 2

CHANA

CHAROEN

BANGKOK RD.

PHUN PHON RD.

NIGHT
MARKET

PHUKET RD.

KRA RD.

0   300 yds
0   300 m

LA GAETANA

© AVALON TRAVEL

of Thalang, involving the two sister-heroines. The highlight of the museum might be a 9th-century statue of the Hindu god Vishnu, discovered in the forests of Phang Nga about 200 years ago.

Kathu Mining Museum
พิพิธภัณฑ์เหมืองแร่ภูเก็ต

The **Kathu Mining Museum** (Mu 5, Kathu Ko Kaew Rd., Kathu, tel. 08/8766-0962, 9am-4pm daily except national holidays, 100B foreigners, 50B Thais, 50B for foreign children, 20B for Thai children) showcases Phuket's

past as a tin mining hub. The museum, in a massive former mansion, has some interesting exhibits that illustrate the daily lives of tin miners and their families, as well as the nuts and bolts, so to speak, of tin mining. Like other museums in Phuket, some of the execution of exhibits seems to miss the mark, and it's not a particularly crowded place, so it can feel a little deserted or aged despite that it's only been open since 2009. Still, since it's relatively close to Patong Beach, it's worth visiting if you're looking for a little information about the island's history.

Khao Phra Thaeo Wildlife Sanctuary

เขตอนุรักษ์พันธุ์ สัตว์ป่าเขาพระแทว

Instead of taking the kids to the zoo, where they'll see animals in captivity, or to monkey, elephant, and crocodile shows bordering on exploitation, bring them to the **Khao Phra Thaeo Wildlife Sanctuary** (Bang Pae Waterfall, Pa Khao, tel. 02/896-2672, 9am-4pm daily). Covering the only remaining virgin rainforest on the island, the sanctuary is home to barking deer, wild boars, monkeys, lizards, and a host of other creatures as well as some lovely waterfalls such as **Namtok Ton Sai** and **Namtok Bang Pae.** The sanctuary is also home to the **Gibbon Rehabilitation Project,** an organization that takes in formerly captive gibbons and rehabilitates them for return to the wild. Gibbons have been poached to extinction in Phuket but are now kept in captivity on the island, often to lure visitors into bars. The project has been working to reintroduce gibbons to Phuket and has set up a facility at the wildlife sanctuary staffed by volunteers from all over the world who come to feed, care for, and train the animals. The project is open for visitors during the day and also accepts volunteers year-round. There's no admission fee, but they do accept donations.

PHUKET TOWN AND THE EAST COAST

Thai Hua Museum

พิพิธภัณฑ์ภูเก็ตไทยหัว

The **Thai Hua Museum** (28 Krabi Rd., Muang District, tel. 07/621-1224, 9am-7pm daily except national holidays, 200B foreigners, 50B Thais, free children under 100 cm [40 in] tall) in Phuket Town celebrates the influence of the Chinese who came to Phuket in waves before, during, and after the tin boom. Exhibits focus on everything from business to daily life, and although the museum is small and somewhat limited in scope, it does highlight an important part of the island's history. The museum is one of the nicest and most modern on the island, and it is worth a quick visit if you are in Phuket Town. The building the museum is housed in, a classic Sino-Portuguese mansion, is lovely, and there is a pleasant café on the premises should you want to take a break and have a drink.

Phuket Aquarium

สถานแสดงพันธุ์สัตว์น้ำภูเก็ต

The **Phuket Aquarium** (Cape Panwa, 51

Phuket Aquarium

Sakdi Det Rd., Phuket Town, tel. 07/639-1126, 9am-5pm daily, 100B adults, 50B children), a part of the Phuket Marine Biological Center, has a collection of ocean and saltwater fish as well as sharks, rays, and sea turtles housed in over 30 tanks. It's a great opportunity to see some of the exotic tropical fish that might have swum by you in the ocean (except for the gigantic cod, which you'll be hoping aren't swimming anywhere near you). The coolest part of the aquarium is a clear tunnel through one of the large tanks, which you can walk through to see the sharks, fish, and rays. For kids, there's a touch pool where they can experience firsthand what a sea cucumber feels like. The center, located at Cape Panwa on the southeast part of the island, also has a research vessel you can visit when it's not out at sea. Although the aquarium is not quite on par with what you may be used to at home, and it's a far drive if you're not close to Cape Panwa to start, children seem to enjoy it quite a bit.

Phuket Butterfly Farm
สวนผีเสื้อและโลกแมลงภูเก็ต

If you can't get enough of flying insects during your tropical vacation, check out the **Phuket Butterfly Farm** (71/6 Samkong, Phuket Town, tel. 07/621-5616, www.phuketbutterfly.com, 9am-5:30pm daily, 300B adults, 150B under age 10), which is home to tens of thousands of butterflies fluttering around its outdoor garden. There's also an insectarium, with bugs of all types to see, including giant grasshoppers, bugs that look like leaves and sticks, and even tarantulas. The farm is also home to a domesticated otter the staff adopted from its former owner and keeps on the grounds to protect it from the wild. The butterfly farm can arrange to pick you up from your hotel for a small fee.

Entertainment and Events

SHOWS
Fantasea
ภูเก็ตแฟนตาซี

More a Las Vegas spectacle than a mellow evening, **Fantasea** (99 Mu 3, Kamala Beach, tel. 07/638-5000, www.phuket-fantasea.com, 5:30pm-11:30pm Fri.-Wed., dinner 6pm-8:30pm, show begins 9pm, show and dinner 1,200B) can put on a show: Special effects, scores of acrobats and other performers in costume, and even dancing elephants make for quite an event. There's also a buffet dinner, carnival games, and shopping to keep you busy after the program. It's not quite a romantic night out, but it's great for families with children.

NIGHTLIFE

Much of the island's nightlife is centered on Patong Beach, which becomes a sort of red-light district meets frat party come nightfall. There are scores of bars and discos packing in the travelers, and music and people seem to pour out of every doorway into the streets surrounding Bangla Road. The music is almost always pop, Top 40, or techno. If that's not your scene, it can be tough to find live music venues or sophisticated places to hang your hat, get your drink on, or do a little dancing. Although there are plenty of high-end accommodations, this trend historically has not spilled over into the nightlife choices, and many visitors not interested in extreme partying tend to spend their nights hanging out at the bars in their hotel or resort. That may be changing, as small bars sans working women or eardrum-bursting music are beginning to appear in small numbers.

The nightlife scene in Phuket is very fluid, and bars and clubs that were popular a year ago may already be closed down, or reincarnated with a different name, by the time you visit. Bars generally close at 1am, nightclubs at

2am, although those rules are sometimes less strictly enforced in Phuket.

Patong Beach

New Tiger Disco (Bangla Rd., tel. 07/634-5112, 7pm-2am daily, no cover), which opened in 2013 after the old Tiger Disco burned down in 2012, is one of the most popular places to go at night in Patong. The tiger theme is over the top, with statues of roaring tigers all over the massive three-story complex that literally shakes because the music is so loud at night. There are multiple independent bars in the complex, and though all are welcome at these establishments, with explicit names and lots of scantily clad women, there is definitely a target market.

Seduction Beach Club and Disco (39/1 Bangla Rd., tel. 08/2776-7949, 10pm-late daily, cover 200B) attracts a young crowd of mostly travelers who like to dance and drink. Ibiza-style electronic dance music with a little hip-hop thrown in seems to be the music of choice here, which seems to work well for the crowd it attracts. The ambiance is much less seedy than other bars on this *soi*.

Famous Night Club Patong (Jungceylon Shopping Complex, tel. 07/636-6717, 1pm-late daily, no cover) on the roof of the Jungceylon mall, positions itself as a classy, upscale nightclub and for the most part delivers, though with a crowd of mostly young travelers it's hard to keep the promise entirely. Aside from the swanky interior, the big attraction is the glass-bottom swimming pool: From the dance floor below you can watch people swimming above. And if you feel like taking a swim, know you're being watched, too!

Banana Disco (96 Thawewong Rd., tel. 08/1271-2469, 7pm-2am daily, cover 200B) is one of the area's most popular nightclubs. Despite (or maybe because of) the name, it seems to attract lots of young, single local women. Though it is known as a pickup joint, it doesn't feel too sleazy, especially compared to the choices on Bangla Road. The music selection is techno and pop, and the cover charge includes one drink.

If you're looking for some nightlife that doesn't involve loud music and dressing up, there are some good pubs and bars in Patong, too. **Molly Malone's** (94/1 Thawewong Rd., tel. 07/629-2771, 10am-late daily, no cover) is your standard Irish bar, which means you'll find decent Western food, beer, and lots of football on television. There is also live music most nights and pool tables.

Hard Rock Cafe (48/1 Ruamjai Rd., tel. 07/636-6381, 11am-2am daily, no cover) has live music, nachos, cheeseburgers, and lots of music memorabilia. It's also quite expensive compared to other live music venues on the island, but if you are looking for a reliable, no-surprises place to go, it might be worth the cost.

FESTIVALS AND EVENTS

Most events are scheduled according to the lunar calendar, so dates change from year to year. Make sure to check with the **Tourism Authority of Thailand** (tel. 02/250-5500, www.tourismthailand.org) for specific dates when you are visiting.

Chinese New Year

In Phuket, **Chinese New Year** (Jan. or Feb.) is celebrated with the Phuket Old Town Festival, which celebrates the island's Chinese heritage. The locus of the celebration is in Phuket's Old Town, and the main streets are closed off for three days to make room for song and dance performances. There are also art exhibits and other events around the city. Although everyone in the Old Town will be celebrating, the beach areas will have fewer events.

Songkran

Phuket, and just about every other place in Thailand, goes wild during the traditional new year celebration of **Songkran** (Apr.). For three full days, locals and visitors pour out into the streets to pour water on each other. The ritual was probably originally intended to symbolically wash away sins and bad luck. Nowadays, in all popular beach areas, people bring out big water guns and buckets of water, so expect to get soaked. If you're visiting during this time, some businesses will be closed.

Phuket Vegetarian Festival

For nine days each year, during the **Phuket Vegetarian Festival** (Sept.), vegetarian food dominates the city. Special vegetarian fare can be found everywhere, from street stalls to high-end restaurants. Even carnivores will enjoy trying their favorite Thai dishes without meat. You'll be able to find them at any restaurant or stall adorned with yellow flags. The festival, which has roots in Chinese traditions but also some elements of Hinduism, originated in Phuket and later spread to other parts of the country. The island is the place it is most intensely celebrated, and during the festival there are ceremonies at many of Phuket's Chinese temples, plus street processions where participants engage in what can only be described as physical torture. Walking on hot coals and piercing oneself with spears and hooks are common activities among participants, so spectating is definitely not for the fainthearted or children.

Loi Krathong

One of Thailand's most beautiful celebrations, **Loi Krathong** (Oct.-Nov.) takes place each year on the evening of the 12th full moon of the Thai lunar year (usually October or November). At all major beaches in Phuket, thousands of people launch small floats covered in flowers and candles. The floats, or *krathong,* symbolize the letting go of bad luck and bad feelings, and the holiday is usually celebrated by couples. Don't worry if you didn't bring your own float; there will be plenty of vendors selling them.

Laguna Phuket Triathlon

The popular **Laguna Phuket Triathlon** (Nov.) attracts people from all over the region. Set in the Laguna Phuket complex of resorts, it has triathletes swimming through a lagoon, into the Andaman Sea, then biking the hills of Phuket and finishing with a flat run around the large Laguna complex. The distances, a 1.8-kilometer (1 mi) swim, 55-kilometer (34 mi) bike ride, and 12 km (7.5 mi) run, are not regulation, but they are a bit longer than an Olympic triathlon. The event has been going on for two decades and is very popular, so sign up well in advance if you are considering competing.

King's Cup Regatta

Billed as Asia's biggest and most popular regatta, the **King's Cup Regatta** (Dec.) takes place over the course of a week in December. It has been going on since 1987 and continues to grow in size and popularity. Even if you're not competing, you can enjoy watching and try to crash (or snag an invite to) one of the many parties surrounding the event.

Shopping

If you're just looking for small souvenirs to take home, every village near every beach has small items such as seashells or Thai-styled handicrafts. There are some small shops throughout the island selling items that are a little more authentic, as well as some high-end antiques stores, some gem stores, and even full-fledged shopping malls.

If you're shopping for gems or antiques on the island, it's difficult to ensure you are getting a good deal unless you have some amount of expertise to evaluate the merchandise. Although there are some good deals to be had, there is no redress should you get home and realize you are unhappy with your purchase.

There are a couple of large shopping malls on the island, serving both visitors and the year-round folks—a real convenience if you find you've forgotten something from home.

PATONG AND VICINITY

Patong's shopping scene has gotten increasingly sophisticated and increasingly convenient. Aside from the massive Jungceylon shopping mall, the main beach road has more and more places to spend money every year.

Jungceylon (181 Rat-U-Thit 200 Pee Rd., Patong, tel. 07/660-0111, 11am-midnight daily) is about a 10-minute walk from Patong Beach up Soi Bangla. The mall, which opened in 2007, is a considerable step up from the shopping that was previously available in the area. There's a full-sized **Robinson Department Store,** a **Carrefour** hypermarket stocked with food, appliances, electronics, and everything in between, and many other stores to fulfill your shopping needs. The mall also has a nice little food court in the basement, serving up noodle and rice dishes, smoothies, and even fresh seafood. Aside from the food court, the bottom level also houses **That's Siam.** This shop, really a group of small shops, carries scores of Thai handicrafts and other decorative items, including home textiles, silk products, and delicious-smelling bath and body goodies.

Banana Walk (124/11 Taweewong Rd., Patong, tel. 08/1987-1148, 10am-10pm daily), right on the main beach road in Patong, is a small, upscale shopping mall with some clothing stores, gift shops, a couple of electronics stores, and plenty of restaurants. There is also a Boots drugstore and a small Villa supermarket on the premises. Hours of individual shops may vary.

The Ocean Group has two midsize shopping malls in Patong, **Ocean Plaza Patong** (48 Taweewong Rd., Patong, tel. 07/634-1297, 10am-10pm daily) and **Ocean Bangla Patong** (31 Bangla Rd., Patong, tel. 07/634-1163, 10am-10pm daily). These midmarket malls are a little hectic and less modern than the newest shopping malls in the area, but in addition to all the stand-alone stores, both have lots of market carts and stalls selling souvenirs, clothes, and shoes, plus good food courts with mostly Thai dishes.

NORTHERN WEST COAST

This area is where you'll find lots of antiques shops and galleries, catering mainly to people who are furnishing villas they've purchased on the island.

Oriental Fine Art (106/19-20 Bangtao Rd., Thalang, tel. 07/632-5141, 9am-8pm daily) is a large multistory shop that feels more like a gallery for Asian sculpture, except that you

Jungceylon shopping mall

can buy everything on display. They also carry furniture, mainly with classic Chinese styling, and will arrange worldwide shipping.

Songtique (8/48-49 Srisoontorn Rd., Cherngtalay, tel. 08/1668-2555, 9am-6pm Mon.-Sat.) carries mostly original-period Buddha images and reproductions. Some of the pieces are stunningly larger than life, although the owner also stocks images small enough to take home with you. There is also a selection of antique Chinese furniture. This store is worth dropping by just to see the beautiful Buddhas.

On the road to Laguna Phuket, there are a handful of furniture and antiques stores. **Heritage Collection** (60 Phuket Laguna Rd., tel. 07/632-5818, 9am-8pm daily) has an inventory of beautiful antiques from China and Southeast Asia. There are Chinese chests, paintings, sculptures, and plenty of Buddhist objects in this large shop.

For more contemporary items, **Ceramics of Phuket** (185/6 Mu 7, Srisoontorn Rd., Thalang, tel. 07/627-2151, 8am-5pm Mon.-Sat.) carries vases, display bowls, and decorative figures, all from a local designer.

Located in the swanky Plaza Surin, **Ginger Shop** (Plaza Surin, 5/50 Mu 3, Cherngtalay, Thalang, tel. 07/627-1616, 10am-8pm daily) is a fun shop carrying everything from cushions to glassware and even spa products. What really sets the shop apart, though, is the clothing and women's accessories. There's a lot of beading going on in their collection of tops, dresses, bags, and scarves, but since they design their clothes with contemporary lines, the result looks modern and just a little funky.

PHUKET TOWN

Just outside of the center of Phuket Town is the large, convenient **Central Festival Mall** (74/75 Mu 5, 5 Vichitsongkram Rd., tel. 07/629-1111, 10:30am-11pm daily), which has a large high-end department store, a sports store, a bookstore, and plenty of other shops carrying both local and international products. The mall also has a large movie theater, multiple restaurants, and a food court. In 2014, it underwent a major renovation to upgrade the facilities.

Ban Boran Textiles (51 Yaworat Rd., tel. 07/621-1563, 10:30am-6:30pm Mon.-Sat.), a funky little shop in Phuket Town, sells a nice selection of mostly handwoven textiles from Thailand and other countries in the region. Offerings include wall hangings as well as clothing, and prices are quite reasonable. There are also some curios and decorative jewelry.

Phuket Town's fashionable shopping scene

ENA (52 Yaworat Rd., tel. 08/9651-9973, 10:30am-6:30pm Mon.-Sat.) is a lovely little textiles shop that specializes in clothing, scarves, handbags, and home decor made from fabrics produced in the region. Prices are reasonable, and this shop usually has a good stock of inventory despite its small size. Rasada Handmade (29 Rasada Rd., tel. 07/635-5439, 9:30am-7pm Mon.-Sat.) is another little shop specializing in textiles and small objects for the home that stocks items such as bedcovers, tablecloths, and Buddhist figures.

For more upscale decorator objects, stop in at Fine Orient (51/20 Chaofa West Rd., tel. 07/652-1552, 10:30am-5:30pm Thurs.-Tues.). The shop specializes in reproduction and antique furniture from China but also carries furniture and other items from neighboring countries. Many of the things sold here are beautiful, expensive, and too big to fit in a suitcase. The shop will arrange shipping for anything you buy there.

Kai Tak Interior Designs (Royal Phuket Marina, 63/202 Thep Kasattri Rd., tel. 07/636-0891, 9am-7pm Mon.-Sat.) carries some beautiful furniture and decorator items from all over the region. The prices here are on the high to very high end, but the shop is worth visiting if only to look at what they've got.

Fortune Shop (12-16 Rasada Rd., tel. 07/621-6238, 9:30am-7pm Mon.-Sat., 10am-3pm Sun.) has lots of small Thai souvenir items, including Thai silk decorative pillows and wall hangings, pottery, jewelry, and spa products. This is a great one-stop shop if you're looking to pick up some nice gifts to bring home.

Sports and Recreation

DIVING

The waters surrounding Phuket offer an amazing diversity of marinelife and dive sites from beginner to advanced. Some of these sites are considered among the best in the world. Hundreds of dive shops offer courses, equipment rental, day trips, and live-aboards (where you live aboard a boat for a few days). If you're planning on diving in the region, don't worry too much about where you are staying relative to the areas where you want to dive; most diving shops offer dives to all of the most popular sites in the region.

The area surrounding the main island offers some good diving day trips. Ko Racha Noi is a popular place to visit on a day trip and has a nice mix of both colorful coral and challenging, rocky terrain. Another very popular destination is Shark Point, about 32 kilometers (20 mi) east of Chalong Bay. There are three rock outcroppings that attract—as the name implies—sharks (mostly leopard sharks). Just under one kilometer (0.6 mi) away is Anemone Reef, with lots of anemone, coral, and plenty of colorful small fish.

If you're interested in wreck diving, close by is King Cruiser Wreck, a sunken car ferry in Phang Nga Bay. This site is appropriate for most divers and attracts lots of fish. Other wrecks near Phuket, including SS Petaling, HMS Squirrel, and HMS Vestal, are considered technical dives and can only be visited by experienced divers.

Certification

In Thailand most diving instruction courses offer PADI (www.padi.com) open-water diver certification. These courses take 3-4 days, at the end of which you'll be certified to dive all over the world. You'll spend time in the classroom first learning about safety and dive theory, take your first dive in a swimming pool, and advance to supervised open-water dives. Expect to pay 10,000-15,000 baht for the full course, including equipment and dives. If you can't imagine wasting hours inside a classroom while you're on vacation, and assuming there is a PADI training center where you live, you can do the classroom and pool-diving components of your training at home and bring your referral paperwork with you to Thailand, where you'll be able to complete the open-water portion of the certification.

Certified divers looking to advance their skills can also take dive master courses, become certified diving instructors, and arrange training internships at some of the larger training centers. These programs are at least two weeks long and cost 30,000-75,000 baht.

Recompression Chambers

Although accidents and the bends are quite rare, **Badalveda Diving Medical Center at Bangkok Hospital Phuket** (2/1 Thanon Hongyok Utis, Phuket Town, tel. 07/625-4425, 24-hour emergency hotline tel. 08/1989-9482) has a hyperbaric chamber and medical staff who specialize in diving injuries.

Dive Shops and Centers

When choosing a company to go diving with, first check the PADI website, which lists all of the PADI-certified dive shops across the globe and is searchable by country. There are many excellent dive shops and training centers throughout the Andaman region, and Thailand in general has an excellent safety record when it comes to diving. Instructors and dive masters are both local and foreign, and all are fluent in English. To pick a dive shop, it's best to drop in to some in your vicinity and spend a few minutes talking to staff before deciding who to dive or train with. The following dive centers are all certified by PADI to offer open-water diving certification, dive master training, and instructor training. All also offer one-day trips and multiday liveaboard diving trips.

- **Dive Asia** (24 Thanon Karon, Kata Beach, tel. 07/633-0598, www.diveasia.com)

- **Kata Diving Service** (Kata Garden Resort, 121/1 Mu 4, Thanon Patak, Karon Beach, tel. 07/633-0392)

- **Marina Divers** (45 Thanon Karon, Karon Beach, tel. 07/633-0272)

- **Oceanic Divecenter** (30 Thanon Karon, Karon Beach, tel. 07/633-3043, www.oceanicdivecenter.com)

- **Pro-Tech Dive College** (389 Thanon Patak, Karon Beach, tel. 07/628-6112, www.protechdivers.com)

- **Sea Dragon Dive Center** (5/51 Mu 7, Thanon Khuek Khak, Khao Lak, Phang Nga, tel. 07/648-5420, www.seadragondivecenter.com)

- **Sea Fun Divers** (Katathani Beach Resort, 14 Kata Noi Rd., Kata Noi Beach, tel. 07/633-0124, www.seafundivers.com)

- **Sea World Dive Team** (177/23 Soi Sansabai, Patong Beach, tel. 07/634-1595, www.seaworld-phuket.com)

- **Sunrise Diving** (49 Thanon Thawewong, Patong Beach, tel. 07/629-2052)

- **Visa Diving** (77 Mu 7, Ko Phi Phi, tel. 07/560-1157, www.visadiving.com)

- **Warm Water Divers** (229 Thanon Rat-U-Thit 200 Pee Rd., Patong Beach, tel. 07/629-2201, www.warmwaterdivers.com)

- **West Coast Divers** (120/1-3 Rat-U-Thit 200 Pee Rd., Patong Beach, tel. 07/634-1673, www.westcoastdivers.com)

SNORKELING

If you're not a diver, there is still a lot to see in relatively shallow waters if you're armed with a snorkel and a mask. The north end of **Patong Beach,** the north end of **Kata Beach,** the south end of **Karon Beach,** and the north end of **Kamala Beach** have lovely coral or rocks just off the coast, and you'll definitely see some tropical fish around most of the beaches even if the bottom of the sea is sandy. Otherwise, you can arrange a day trip to tour some of the islands in **Phang Nga Bay,** which will include

Drowning Hazards

During high season, the Andaman Sea is often calm and clear, with few waves and no dangerous tides. But during the April-October monsoon season in the low season, the sea can become deadly, especially if there is a storm in the surrounding area. Dozens of people drown in Phuket every year, both locals and visitors.

Phuket has a flag system on all of its beaches, and anytime you see a red flag, it means authorities have decided that the waves and undercurrent are too dangerous. Swimming is not advised at these times, although during low season there are generally no lifeguards around to enforce this rule on even the most popular beaches.

For surfers, this is the best time of year to be in Phuket, as the waves are great, particularly on Nai Harn and Kata Beaches. It's also a great time to learn how to surf, as you can rent a board for a few hundred baht at Kata and even take some lessons at one of the many casual surf schools that set up shop on the south end of the beach. But if you are not a strong swimmer, stay out of the water or remain very close to shore.

some snorkeling time. Most tour providers will rent snorkels and fins, too. These tours are almost exclusively sold through travel agents, and there are scores of them in Phuket. Some outfitters offering tours are **Oceanic Divecenter** (30 Thanon Karon, Karon Beach, Phuket, tel. 07/633-3043, www.oceanicdivecenter.com), **Sea World Dive Team** (177/23 Soi Sansabai, Patong Beach, tel. 07/634-1595, www.seaworld-phuket.com), and **Warm Water Divers** (229 Thanon Rat-U-Thit 200 Pee, Patong Beach, Phuket, tel. 07/629-2201, www.warm-waterdivers.com). If you're buying a snorkeling trip, make sure to ask how much time you'll spend on the boat versus in the water, the type of boat you'll travel on, and the islands you'll visit.

SEA KAYAKING

Most of the sea kayaking and sea canoeing trips that originate in Phuket will involve taking a motorboat to **Phang Nga Bay,** where you'll explore the smaller islands, lagoons, and caves for the day before being shuttled back to the big island. Paddling around Phang Nga Bay is a spectacular way to see the area. You can get up close to many of the smaller islands with no beaches to land on, and as opposed to a speedboat tour, you'll be traveling slowly enough to look closely at the nature

around you. Most guides will require only that you are in reasonably good shape to participate. Some will also even paddle for you, should you wish to just sit back and enjoy the scenery. If you're already an experienced paddler, these group tours may feel a little slow, but all of the tour guides can arrange personalized itineraries if you give them enough notice. **Sea Canoe** (367/4 Yaowarat Rd., Phuket Town, tel. 07/621-2172, www.seacanoe.net) has trips that run from one day to one week and has been running trips in the Andaman every day for nearly 20 years.

Andaman Sea Kayak (tel. 07/623-5353, www.andamanseakayak.com) also has one-day and multiday trips from Phuket, which they combine with camping in a national park. Day trips start around 3,200 baht per person.

Experienced paddlers may want to rent their own kayaks to explore the islands. **Paddle Asia** (tel. 07/624-0952, www.paddlea-sia.com) rents well-maintained, high-quality kayaks, although they will only rent to experienced kayakers. If you are not experienced or familiar with the area, unguided kayaking is not recommended unless you're paddling around close to the shore. Many area beaches are filled with Jet Skis and speedboats, and fishing boats travel frequently between beaches and islands.

PADDLE BOARDING

Paddle boarding, or stand-up paddling, has become a very popular sport in Phuket over the past few years. The high season, when there are very few waves, is the best time of year to do it. During rainy season the sea is too choppy (though it's a good time to surf if you're looking for an alternative board sport). There are paddle board schools and rental shops opening all over the island, though some will only be open during high season.

Stand Up Paddle Thailand (131/34 Mu 4, Thalang, Phuket, tel. 07/662-0201, www.standuppaddlethai.com), close to Layan Beach, rents and sells equipment and can suggest places in the area to take lessons. **Starboard Stand Up Paddle Board** (at Phuket Windsurfing Shop, 37/10 Mu 1, Rawai, Phuket, tel. 087/888-8244, www.isup. asia/index.php/paddle-phuket) rents and sells equipment, does repairs, and offers individual and group lessons. They will deliver equipment to you.

If you are in the Karon Beach area, visit **SSS Phuket** (122/1 Patak Rd., Karon Beach, Phuket, tel. 07/628-4070, www.sssphuket. com) for rentals and lessons. For lessons, rentals, and tours, plus cocktails, Thai food, and a cool place to hang out on Kamala Beach, visit **Skyla's Surf and SUP Club** (Kamala Beach, North End, Phuket, tel. 082/519-3282, www. skylaphuket.com).

SAILING AND SPEEDBOAT CHARTERS

There are a number of sailing companies that offer everything from just the sailboat to a whole crew. If you have the time and money, spending a week sailing around the Andaman coast is a luxury adventure you'll never forget. For large groups, the cost of chartering a sailboat and doing some private island-hopping can be even cheaper than staying on a resort, and all the charter companies will take care of food, supplies, and fuel. Chartering a sailboat or speedboat will cost 15,000-100,000 baht per day, depending on the type of vessel and whether it has a crew.

Phuket Sailing (20/28 Soi Suksan 2, Mu 4, Tambon Rawai, Amphoe Muang, tel. 07/628-9656 or 08/1895-1826, www.phuket-sailing. com) offers both crewed and noncrewed boats and will help you design an itinerary. **Yacht Pro** (adjacent to Yacht Haven Marina, tel. 07/634-8117 to 07/634-8119, www.sailing-thailand.com) has day sailing trips and also offers lessons.

Speed boat tours from Phuket are popular.

If you're interested in sailing in the area around Phuket and you have your own boat, there are three separate marinas, the **Phuket Boat Lagoon, Royal Phuket Marina,** and **Yacht Haven Phuket Marina,** with year-round anchorage.

GOLF

Phuket boasts a handful of well-maintained golf courses open to visitors. Playing on courses surrounded by palm trees and over-looking the ocean is a real treat. Although you can walk on during the low season, it is essential to make reservations as far in advance as possible during the high season, when the cooler weather makes a day on the greens that much more enjoyable. Caddies are obligatory at all of the clubs.

Located closer to the east coast near Phuket Town, the **Phuket Country Club** (80/1 Mu 7, Vichitsongkram Rd., Kathu, tel. 07/631-9200, www.phuketcountryclub.com, 3,000B) has an 18-hole par-72 course over a former tin mine. The course is great for less-experienced players, although it's not as challenging for low-handicappers.

Set between Phuket Town and Patong Beach in the middle of the island, the **Loch Palm Golf Club** (38 Mu 5, Vichitsongkram Rd., Kathu, tel. 07/632-1929, www.lochpalm. com, 3,000B) is a hilly course but otherwise good for beginner golfers.

One of the island's newest courses, **Red Mountain Golf Course** (38 Mu 5, Vichitsongkram Rd., Kathu, tel. 07/632-1929, 4,500B), in the middle of the island, opened in 2007 on another former tin mine. This course is well designed for shorter hitters, and there are lots of slopes and water to contend with.

Located at the Laguna Phuket, home to a handful of luxury resorts, the **Laguna Phuket Golf Club** (34 Mu 4, Srisoonthorn Rd., Cherngtalay, tel. 07/627-0991, www.la-gunaphuket.com/golfclub, 3,400B) has an 18-hole par-71 course with great views of the Andaman Sea.

Although **Thai Muang Golf** (157/12 Mu 9, Limdul Rd., Thai Muang, Phang Nga, tel.

07/657-1533, www.thaimuanggolfcourse.com, 2,200B) isn't the fanciest course in the area, it does have the only course set right next to the beach. But for the view, you'll have to travel a bit, as the course is actually about an hour's drive off the island in Phang Nga.

Blue Canyon (165 Mu 1, Thep Kasattri Rd., Thalang, tel. 07/632-8088, www.blue-canyonclub.com, canyon course 5,600B, lakes course 4,000B) has two separate 18-hole courses. The lakes course, as the name implies, is surrounded by small water hazards on 17 of the 18 holes. The canyon course, home to the Johnnie Walker Classic, is the nicest in Phuket and has been played by the likes of Tiger Woods and Ernie Els.

The Nicklaus Design **Mission Hills Phuket Golf Club** (195 Mu 4, Pla Khlock, Thalang, tel. 07/631-0888, www.missionhill-sphuket.com, 3,800B) has both an 18-hole and a separate 9-hole course and is located in the northeast part of the island. This is a favorite course among regular golfers on the island, with not only great views of the ocean but also challenging sea breezes to contend with.

GO-KARTS

If you get really bored staring at the beautiful views or island-hopping and want to try something a little more adventurous on land, check out the **Patong Go Kart Speedway** (118/5 Vichitsongkram Rd., Mu 7, Kathu, tel. 07/632-1949, 10am-7pm daily Nov.-May, from 1,000B). You can spend your time circling the course or practice a few times before you compete in a Grand Prix race with other participants. Kids have to be at least age 16 unless they're participating in one of the kids-only races. Make sure to book ahead, as the course is very popular.

CYCLING

If you're interested in touring the island on two wheels, **Action Holidays Phuket** (10/195 Jomthong Thani 5/4 Kwang Rd., Phuket Town, tel. 07/626-3575, www.bike-toursthailand.com) offers full-day (2,400B) and half-day (1,400B) bike tours around the island. Most of the tours will keep you in the less-touristed eastern part of the island and are a great way to see some smaller villages and rubber plantations. They also offer tours of a neighboring island, Ko Yao Noi, that start in Phuket and involve a short boat ride.

Accommodations

Phuket already has over a thousand accommodations options along the coast, and new ones are being built every year. While it may be hard to find that secluded beach ambiance when all you can see around you are hotels, guesthouses, and cranes building them, the competition keeps costs very competitive, especially during the low season. If you're willing to pay for it, there are still quiet places on the island, and some of the high-end resorts even have small private or semiprivate beaches. And if you stay in the northern part of the island, around the airport, you'll find the beaches much less crowded. If you're traveling with children, bear in mind that Patong Beach can get pretty seedy at night. There are plenty of discos and clubs catering to both gay and straight clientele, and passing through the nightlife neighborhood at night is difficult to avoid if you're staying here.

While you'll still be able to find a few inexpensive bungalows on the beaches in the northern part of the island, if you're basing yourself in the southern part of Phuket or anywhere around Patong Beach, inexpensive accommodations are almost exclusively guesthouses set inland from the beach, and you'll need to walk at least a few minutes to get to the water. In those areas, waterfront rooms are only available at midrange and high-end resorts.

MAI KHAO BEACH
Under 1,500B

With all of the development going on, it's surprising that cheap, simple beach bungalows such as **Mai Khao Beach Seaside Cottages** (Mai Khao Beach, tel. 08/1895-1233, www. mai-khao-beach.com, 600B) still exist. The very basic thatched-roof huts have mattresses on the floor, no air-conditioning—only fans—and have shared bathrooms with cold-water showers. Mai Khao Beach is a very quiet spot with limited amenities, but there is a beachfront restaurant on the premises serving good inexpensive Thai food. There are also nicer, fan-cooled beachside cottages with en-suite bathrooms if you want to spend a little more. There is a two-night minimum at this property.

Though it's not on the beach (it's about a mile inland), **Phuket Camp Ground** (137/7 Mu 3, Baan Dan Yit, Mai Khao Beach, tel. 08/1370-1579, www.phuketcampground. com, 500B) is set on a lake and offers a very pretty location to either pitch a tent or rent one of the property's tents. There are also air-conditioned bungalows available for those who like the surroundings but prefer not to camp. There is a restaurant and canteen on the premises.

The bungalows at **Bungalow@Maikhao** (128 Mu 3, Mai Khao Beach, tel. 08/3391-3960, 1,200B) aren't fancy but do offer en-suite bathrooms and air-conditioning, a step above the typical beach bungalow experience. Mai Khao in general is not very crowded, but because there is not too much development around this property in particular, it can feel very remote. The on-site restaurant serves Thai food and drinks, but closes early. Take the long walk to the neighboring Holiday Inn if you want something late at night.

1,500-3,000B

Near Bungalow@Maikhao, but almost twice the price, is the large **Holiday Inn Phuket Mai Khao Beach Resort** (81 Mu 3, Mai Khao Beach, tel. 07/660-3699, www.ihg.com, 2,800B), which offers guests comfortable, modern rooms, a massive swimming pool that spreads out from one end of the resort to the other, and plenty of other facilities, including a kids' club. Though the resort is popular among couples and groups of adults, it is very family-friendly and there are family suites with rooms designed specially for young children. The resort is right on the beach, and there is a small sunbathing area set up with chairs and towels for guests. There are limited places to eat within walking distance, but plenty of hotel restaurants and bars.

Over 4,500B

Repeat visitors to Phuket often say the **JW Marriott** (231 Mu 3, Mai Khao Beach, tel. 07/633-8000, www.marriott.com, 4,500B) is their favorite hotel on the island, perhaps because of the top-notch facilities and quiet, scenic location on Mai Khao Beach. The upscale resort has numerous swimming pools, including a children's pool and a pool with waterslide, a tennis court, a full-service spa, plus plenty of planned activities every week, including bicycle tours and sailing lessons. The kids' club, and suites and villas with plenty of space for little ones, make this a great choice for families.

The **Anantara Phuket Villas** (888 Mu 3, Mai Khao Beach, tel. 07/633-6100, www.phuket.anantara.com, 15,000B), on the relatively quiet and peaceful Mai Khao Beach, has luxurious large villas with private pools. The lush property is unmistakably Thai; all the villas are filled with traditional Thai furnishings but are still modern and stylish. The Anantara spa is likewise luxurious and traditional, and though treatments can be pricey, the surroundings make it worth the cost. Service is discreet, but staffers are very focused on making sure guests are well taken care of. For an indulgent, romantic vacation in a secluded spot on a beautiful beach, the Anantara will not disappoint.

NAI YANG BEACH
Under 1,500B

If you can manage to snag one of the six bungalows at **Tanamas House** (57/16 Mu 1, Nai Yang Beach, tel. 07/620-5218, www.tanamashouse.com, 1,200B), within walking distance of Nai Yang Beach, consider yourself lucky. Tanamas House is a true value property and a great choice for those who want some resort amenities but don't want to pay hundreds of dollars per night for them. The lovely bed-and-breakfast has lush landscaping and a nice swimming pool, and the rooms are small but very clean and comfortable. There is a restaurant on the grounds; if you are looking for something fancier, you can walk to the Indigo Pearl, which has more upscale food and drink options.

Seapines Villa Liberg (111 Mu 5, Soi Bang Malao 2, Nai Yang Beach, tel. 08/1814-4883, www.villalibergphuket.com, 1,200B) offers pretty Thai-style rooms set around a pleasant swimming pool, which is surrounded by a lush, green garden. Rooms have basic decorations and furnishings but are tasteful, clean, and large for the price. Facilities are limited to the swimming pool and a small café that serves a very limited breakfast. On the plus side, the beach is just a hundred meters away.

Panpen Bungalows (65/11 Mu 5, Nai Yang Beach, tel. 08/7469-4797, www.panpenbungalowphuket.com, 1,000B) is very close to Nai Yang Beach and has clean, modern cottages with air-conditioning and private bathrooms. Though it might lack the rustic charm of thatched-roof bungalows, it's definitely going to be cleaner and more comfortable. The property is close to the airport and offers free transfers to and from between 6am and midnight. Many visitors choose to stay here before an early flight out, and the cost of a night's stay in one of the bungalows is just a little more than the cost of an airport transfer from another part of the island.

Chez Charly Bungalow (65/6 Mu 1, Tambon Sakoo, Nai Yang Beach, tel. 07/620-5124, 1,000B) is a small, homey, family-run operation with just a handful of bungalows and studios for rent. Rooms won't win any design awards, but they are far better fitted, and more comfortable, than anything else you'll find in this price range. Plus, the couple who run it are friendly and helpful. It's a 15-minute walk to the beach from here, and food and drink options in the surrounding area are very limited.

1,500-3,000B

Near a quiet, pretty beach is the comfy **Golddigger's Resort** (74/12 Surin Rd., Nai Yang Beach, tel. 07/632-8424, www.golddigger-resort.com, 2,100B). This very small resort has clean, basically furnished guest rooms and some larger family accommodations that can sleep four people. There's also a nice swimming pool on the grounds, but if you want to go to the beach, it's only a five-minute walk. The decor leaves a lot to be desired, but this is an excellent deal in the off-season, when rates are just over half price.

3,000-4,500B

Dewa Phuket Resort (65 Mu 1, Tambon Sakoo, Nai Yang Beach, tel. 07/637-2300, www.dewaphuketresort.com, 4,000B) has pool villas, suites, and apartments with kitchens and multiple bedrooms for those traveling in larger groups or with children. The pretty, modern Thai-style resort has a massive swimming pool and plenty of activities, such as yoga, to keep guests busy. Like other properties on Nai Yang, Dewa Phuket Resort is not right on the beach; rather, you have to cross a road and walk about five minutes. Though the property bills itself as a boutique property, with nearly 100 rooms it's a bit too large to truly qualify.

Over 4,500B

The Bill Bensley-designed **Indigo Pearl** (Nai Yang Beach, tel. 07/632-7006, www.indigo-pearl.com, 5,500B) is a standout in the luxury-resort category. Designed to convey Phuket's mining history, the property has cement flooring, exposed beams, and thatched roofs juxtaposed against colorful, modern design elements in addition to verdant landscaping throughout. The guest rooms are as funky as the common space. Expect modern modular furniture and color combinations not often seen in generic hotel rooms. There are also tennis courts, a library, and activities for children. The only drawback is that the resort is not right on the beach; it's a five-minute walk.

NAI THON BEACH

Perhaps the most beautiful and luxurious resort on the island is **Trisara** (60/1 Mu 6, Srisoonthorn Rd., Nai Thon Beach, tel. 07/631-0100, www.trisara.com, 22,500B). The guest rooms are larger than most city apartments and furnished with impressive teakwood pieces. The multibedroom villas are pricey but come with their own waitstaff, private pools, and amazing views of the ocean. There is also a larger pool at the resort right on the edge of the coast, and a very small private beach for guests.

Nai Thon Mansion (424 Mu 4, Nai Thon Beach, tel. 08/1894-5344, www.naithonbeachhotelphuket.com, 800B) hits above its weight when it comes to value for money. The rooms at this budget guesthouse are clean, modern, and comfortable, and it's just a few minutes on foot to the beach. If a stand-alone, four-story building is too far off from the thatched-roof beach bungalow you've been imagining, though, you might want to consider another option. However, it is one of the only inexpensive places to stay on tiny Nai Thon.

BANG TAO BEACH AND LAGUNA

Laguna Phuket (390/1 Mu 1, Srisoonthorn Rd., tel. 07/636-2300, www.lagunaphuket.com, 4,000B) is an expansive compound with six separate resorts set around a small lagoon just off the coast. With about 240 hectares of shared space along with private beaches, the resort feels like a large village of its own instead of part of the rest of the island. The land it sits on, now prime property on Bang Tao Bay, was once a tin mine that had been abandoned, the land left fallow for years. In the 1980s the land was reclaimed at a cost of

US$200 million. There's also an 18-hole golf course, tennis courts, activities for children, and even a wedding chapel, should you choose to tie the knot on a romantic vacation. The upside of Laguna Phuket is that it's completely enclosed and has everything you'll need for a relaxing vacation. But that can be a downside, too, as there's little chance to experience Thailand when you're there unless you venture off the compound.

The swankiest, and most expensive, of the resorts is **Banyan Tree Laguna** (33, 33/27 Mu 4, Srisoonthorn Rd., Nai Yang Beach, tel. 07/632-4374, www.banyantree.com, 14,000B), filled with large luxury villas with small private pools and beautifully manicured grounds. Individual Thai-style villas are decorated with modern furnishings and have separate sitting and sleeping areas. The villas are exceptionally well maintained and feel more like five-star hotel rooms than beach bungalows.

The **Allamanda Laguna Phuket** (29 Mu 4, Srisoonthorn Rd., tel. 07/632-4359, www.allamandaphuket.com, 3,000B) is a more down-to-earth property and has very spacious suites that are perfect for families or larger groups traveling together. There are three large pools on the property and three separate pools for children; it's hard to get bored hanging out on the property. Although the Allamanda is not directly on the beach, it offers a shuttle to its own beach area with sun chairs and changing rooms.

Outside of the Laguna complex is the **Sunwing Resort and Spa** (22 Mu 2, Chern Thalay, tel. 07/631-4263, www.sunwingphuket.com, 3,000B), a large, self-contained resort with nearly 300 rooms and suites right on a quiet stretch of beach south of Laguna. The four-star property has clean, modern facilities, a spa, and multiple bars and restaurants. This is a very family-friendly property, with an extensive kids' club and activities for children, rooms and suites designed for families, and multiple swimming pools. It tends to be popular with Scandinavian tourists but attracts guests from all over the world.

SURIN BEACH
Under 1,500B

Surin doesn't have too many budget options, but the **Surin Bay Inn** (106/11 Mu 3, Surin Beach, tel. 07/627-1601, www.surinbayinn.com, 1,000B) is a good choice if you want clean, basic accommodations a bit nicer than a backpacker guesthouse. All rooms have modern fittings, and bathrooms are more than decent by any standard. Decor is inoffensive, which is an achievement in this price category. The inn is just a few minutes from Surin Beach, across the main road.

1,500-3,000B

The **Surintra Resort** (106/11 Mu 3, Surin Beach, tel. 07/627-1601, www.surinbayinn.com, 1,500B) is a small property with just enough facilities to call itself a resort, though because the common spaces are very limited and the swimming pool quite small, it would be better called a "micro-resort." Still, for the price and location, just a few minutes on foot to Surin Beach, you can't really expect much more. Rooms are stylish and modern, though there isn't a particular design theme that permeates the whole property.

3,000-4,500B

Right next door to the Twin Palms is the **Manathai** (121 Srisoonthorn Rd., Surin Beach, tel. 07/627-0900, www.manathai.com, 4,000B). Not quite as swanky or expansive, the Manathai still has pleasant, well-designed, modern guest rooms and excellent, friendly service. Neither of the two pools is large, but they are beautifully laid out with indigo-blue tiles. The common lobby and bar area, which has soaring ceilings and plenty of plush and comfortable sitting areas, almost makes up for the fact that the pools and other common areas are just too small for the number of guest rooms.

In the hills above Surin is **Ayara Hilltops** (125 Mu 3, Surin Beach, tel. 07/627-1271, www.ayarahilltops.com, 4,000B), an adults-only resort with large, nicely designed Thai-style suites and villas overlooking Surin Bay. The lush, green landscaping and beautiful swimming pool make the resort feel much farther away from the rest of the world than it is, as it's just a five-minute walk down to Surin Beach. Some of the more expensive suites have their own whirlpools or plunge pools. No one under 18 is allowed on the property, and it's a very popular destination for couples on romantic holidays.

Over 4,500B

Situated in Surin, just across the main road from the beach, ★ Twin Palms (106/46 Mu 3, Srisoonthorn Rd., Surin Beach, tel. 07/631-6500, www.twinpalms-phuket.com, 5,000B) is the perfect blend of urban chic and tropical resort. The guest rooms look out onto two big, beautiful pools and perfectly landscaped grounds, and inside is a blend of dark woods and clean whites—it's definitely designed for the jet-set crowd. What really makes the property stand out is the location. Though you could spend all your time lazing around the pool and eating at its restaurants, it's two minutes to the shore, and the resort has a small area reserved for guests, so you can enjoy comfortable chairs and great service on the beach, too.

KAMALA BEACH
Under 1,500B

The Print Kamala Resort (74/8 Mu 3, Kamala Beach, tel. 07/638-5396, www.print-kamalaresort.net, 1,400B), a few minutes by foot to Kamala Beach, is a good-value property for travelers who want to stay in a resort but don't want to pay five-star prices. Rooms have a neutral Thai decor and modern amenities but are a bit dated. The high density of rooms to common space and the fact that most rooms face the swimming pool mean you'll never feel total peace and quiet here, but the convenience the proximity to the beach and to Kamala Village bring may make up for that fact.

1,500-3,000B

Kamala Dreams (96/42-74/1 Mu 3, Kamala Beach, tel. 07/627-9131, www.kamaladreams.net, 2,000B) is another good-value property if you are looking for a resort right on the beach. The property is very small—just under 20 rooms and suites—but there is a nice swimming pool and a restaurant on the premises. The rooms are large and come equipped with kitchenettes (microwaves and refrigerators) but are a little dated, as is the whole property. Kamala Village is directly behind Kamala Dreams, so there is plenty of eating and shopping close by.

Kamala Beach Resort—A Sunprime Resort (96/42-3 Mu 3, Kamala Beach, tel. 07/627-9580, www.kamalabeach.com, 2,700B) is a large, adults-only, midrange resort right on Kamala Beach. The massive common grounds have multiple swimming pools, bars, and restaurants, but if your room is at the far end of the resort, you'll be walking for a few minutes to get to the property's stretch of beach. Guest rooms are clean and modern and share the same subtle Thai style seen in most hotels in this price range. The decor isn't particularly charming, but it is inoffensive and practical. This is not a five-star luxury resort but has most high-end amenities, including minibars, satellite TV, and high-speed Internet in the guest rooms. No one under 15 is allowed at this resort.

Sunwing Resort Kamala Beach (96/66 Mu 3, Kamala Beach, tel. 07/637-1650, www.sunwingkamala.com, 2,700B) is a massive self-contained resort right in the center of Kamala Beach. Rooms are modern and comfortable, and even the smallest are designed with families in mind, as they have pull-out couches, refrigerators, and microwaves. The resort is full of families, so if the idea of kids running around is not appealing to you on vacation, look elsewhere! Those who have small kids will love the extensive activities for children, the waterslides, and the mascots that roam the grounds. For travelers looking for a one-stop shop, the resort has bars and restaurants on the premises, though it is so close to Kamala Village that it's easy to walk out to find other food and drink.

3,000-4,500B

Another great option for families is the **Swissotel Phuket Kamala Beach** (100/10 Mu 3, Kamala Beach, tel. 07/630-3000, www. swissotel.com, 3,200B), as the smallest rooms available are one-bedroom apartments with full living rooms and kitchenettes. All rooms overlook the large swimming pool in the center of the resort, and are modern and very large. Two-bedroom suites can be set up to accommodate families with children or groups of adults, and staff will bring in toys and play furniture as well. The kids' club has daily activities as well as a ball pit for children to play in. The only drawback is the fact that there is no direct beach access, guests must walk through an underpass to cross the road to get to Kamala Beach.

Over 4,500B

Set in the hills above Kamala Beach, the **Paresa** (49 Mu 6, Layi-Nakalay Rd., Kamala Beach, tel. 07/630-2000, www.paresaresorts. com, 20,000B) offers guests high-end, jet-set luxury in a convenient central location. The property's style—modern and minimalist—isn't oozing Thai character, but since the views of the island and the ocean are so stunning, guests won't be able to forget they are on Phuket. The large main infinity pool is set right in the cliffs over Kamala Beach. Villas and suites are spacious, and many have private pools as well as indoor and outdoor areas for entertaining.

PATONG BEACH
Under 1,500B

The Frutta Boutique Hotel Patong (86/14 Prabaramee Rd., Patong Beach, tel. 07/634-5092, www.frutta-boutique.com, 1,200B) is a fun, quirky little hotel with excellent-quality rooms and facilities for the money. The theme of the property is fruit, and every room and common space is decorated to embrace that theme. The result is colorful and playful; the rooms themselves are very clean and modern. There is a small, pretty swimming pool and a restaurant on the premises. Be warned that some of the cheaper rooms do not have windows.

Cheap and chic **Me Hotel** (39/119 Prabaramee Rd., Patong Beach, tel. 07/634-3044, 1,200B) has small, stylish guest rooms and very cheap prices. Beds are decked out with crisp white sheets and duvets, and the modern baths are equally minimalist and stylish. The lobby area is very small but so well decorated it looks totally out of place in the neighborhood. The downside is that you'll have to walk about 20 minutes to the beach (or take a taxi or *tuk tuk*), but for those who would rather save their money for martinis, it's not such a bad trade-off.

If you don't need a swimming pool or a gym, **Patong Terrace** (209-12/13 Rat-U-Thit 200 Pee Rd., Patong Beach, tel. 07/629-2159, www.patongterrace.com, 750B) is a good-value guesthouse in Patong. The modern decor is a nice change from the drab interiors that are so common among other guesthouses in this price range; bathrooms are much nicer than the competition. Located on a main road parallel to the beach road, the location is very central and can be loud at night, especially if your room faces the street. Service at this guesthouse is far better than most, and it tends to attract a loyal following of repeat customers.

YaYa Residence Phuket (187-187/1 Phra Bar Ram Mee Rd., Patong Beach, tel. 07/634-5191, www.yayaresidencephuket.com, 750B) is cheap, clean, and convenient. The guesthouse is on the northern end of Phuket, about 5 minutes on foot to the beach but about 20 minutes to the center of the nightlife scene. This is a good option if you're looking to save some cash and don't want to be in the middle of Patong.

The small, cheap, pleasant **FunDee Boutique Hotel** (232/3 Phung Muang Sai Gor Rd., Patong Beach, tel. 07/636-6780, www.fundee.co.th, 1,200B) is a few blocks from Patong Beach but worth the walk if you're looking for something a little nicer than the average guesthouse. The property is only a few years old, spotlessly clean, and somewhat stylishly decorated with modern Thai furnishings and textiles. It's not really a boutique hotel and doesn't have a pool, but there is a very small bar and café as well as plenty of food and drink options just outside the door.

1,500-3,000B

ELLA Bed (100/19-20 Soi Perm Pong Pattana, Thawewong Rd., Patong Beach, tel. 07/634-4253, www.theellagroup.com, 2,200B) might be the most stylish small hotel in Patong. The industrial decor, which mixes carefully chosen furnishings with poured concrete and clean, white walls, is a refreshing break from the typical, play-it-safe decor in most hotels and resorts. Beach and bars are just a few minutes away on foot, but because ELLA Bed is tucked away in a side *soi*, it feels a little less hectic than the rest of Patong. There is a lovely café-bar on the first floor that's worth visiting even if you're not staying at the property. Service is great, too, and it's clear that the owner really cares about this place.

Salathai Resort Phuket (10/4 Sawasdirak Rd., Patong Beach, tel. 07/629-6631, www.phuketsalathai.com, 2,200B) is centrally located between Patong Beach and Jungceylon mall for those who want to enjoy the beach and the area's shopping and nightlife. Though it rates itself a three-star property, the fact that there is a decent swimming pool and a small restaurant-bar makes this resort more appealing than typical properties with that rating. Rooms are clean and comfortable, though the Thai-style decor seems a little dated. For the money, though, it would be hard to find a better property.

Over 4,500B

Holiday Inn Resort Patong (52 Taweewong Rd., Patong Beach, tel. 07/637-0200, www.ihg.com, 5,000B), on the southern part of Patong Beach, is a massive property with more than 400 guest rooms. Rooms, suites, and villas are tastefully decorated with subdued Thai accents, and the grounds are green and pretty. There are six swimming pools, and two

restaurants and bars, though it's easy to get out to Patong from here, too. Families traveling together will appreciate the family suites, with multiple bedrooms and kitchenettes, as well as the kids' club and children's swimming pool.

A block in from the beach is **The Nap Patong** (5/55 Hat Patong Rd., Patong Beach, tel. 07/634-3111, www.thenappatong.com, 4,500B), a midsize, stylish boutique hotel. The minimalist design, with lots of stark white walls and poured concrete, is consistent throughout the guest rooms and the common areas, and although the property is only a four star, it does feel more upscale than most. The swimming pool is small, as are the rest of the facilities, though rooms are well sized considering the location.

If you want to enjoy ocean views but remove yourself from the hustle and bustle of Patong, consider the **Senses Resort Patong** (111/7 Nanai Rd., Patong Beach, tel. 07/633-6600, www.thesensesresort.com, 5,000B), located in the hills about a kilometer (0.6 mi) from the beach. Even basic rooms are spacious (over 500 square feet), and they are also tastefully fitted with sleek, modern furniture. The large infinity pool has a beautiful view of Patong below, and the property is designed in general to take advantage of the views and natural light. Though the property feels very grown-up, children are welcome and there is even a small kids' playroom.

KARON BEACH
Under 1,500B

A great budget option in Karon is the **Pineapple Guesthouse** (261/1 Patak Rd., Karon Plaza, tel. 07/639-6223, www.pineapplephuket.com, 700B), with very clean, basic guest rooms just a few minutes' walk from the beach. The outside is unimpressive and blends in with the overly aggressive signage in Karon Plaza, but the owners have added some little extras inside, including colorful walls and decorations, to make the guest rooms stand out among so many competitors in the area. There are also shared dorms for those who want to save some cash or solo travelers looking to meet people.

1,500-3,000B

Simplitel Hotel (470/4 Patak Rd., Karon Beach, tel. 07/639-6531, www.simplitelphuket.com, 2,500B) offers modern, clean, comfortable hotel rooms in the middle of Karon Village. Aside from the nicely decorated rooms, the biggest draw here is the location, very convenient if you want to hang out at the beach during the day and go out in Karon Village at night. There is no swimming pool on this property, but the beach is walking distance away.

Sugar Palm Grand Hillside Resort (1 Soi Khoktanod Soi 3, Kata Rd., Karon Beach, tel. 07/633-0388, www.sugarpalmgrand.com, 2,500B) is a big, modern, attractive resort in the hills above Kata and Karon Beaches. Chic European-style rooms are large (standard ones start at about 450 square feet), and many have nice views of the surrounding hills. The infinity swimming pool, which cascades down in a series of steps, is very cool, and there is a fitness room and spa on the premises. This property is just a few minutes on foot to Kata and Karon Villages.

Kanita Resort & Camping (23/2 Soi Patak, Karon Beach, tel. 07/651-0233, www.phuketkanita.com, 1,500B) offers guests a more secluded, less urban location than most places in Karon, plus modern, new rooms (the resort opened in 2013) and even camping facilities. There is a small swimming pool and restaurant on the premises, too. The lush grounds, and surrounding neighborhood, will let you enjoy the natural beauty of Phuket, but the downside is that it is a very long walk to the beach and a tougher walk back, as the resort is in the hills.

3,000-4,500B

Phunawa Resort (16/1 Patak Rd. Soi 24, Karon Beach, tel. 07/636-3000, www.phunawa.com, 3,500B) is an all-suites resort with large one- and two-bedroom suites, perfect for families, groups, or those staying for long stretches of time. Larger suites have full kitchens instead of kitchenettes. Inside, rooms are modern and very bright, with light furniture and textiles. The large, circular pool, around which most guest suites are located, makes up for the fact that the grounds are not extensive. The resort is in the Karon hills, close enough to walk for those in good shape and if the weather isn't too hot, but otherwise you'll need to arrange transport through the resort or on your own.

Mandarava Resort and Spa (14/2 Patak Rd. Soi 24, Karon Beach, tel. 07/668-1800, www.mandaravaresort.com, 3,500B) is a beautiful, modern, Thai-style resort in the hills of Karon. Rooms, suites, and villas are big and comfortable, and decor is subdued and modern. As the property is in the hills, the three swimming pools and various decks scattered throughout the property really take advantage of the views. The resort has dining and drinking options, but if you want to go into town you'll have to take the free shuttle or arrange other transportation, as it's just too far to walk comfortably. Children under 12 are not allowed at the Mandarava Resort and Spa.

Over 4,500B

Centara Grand Beach Resort Phuket (683 Patak Rd., Karon Beach, tel. 07/620-1234, www.centarahotelsresorts.com, 5,500B) has every amenity and facility one could possibly want on vacation—restaurants, bars, a fitness center, multiple swimming pools, waterslides and a lazy river worthy of a water park, a kids' club, a fancy spa, the list goes on. It's also right on the beach, so you could arrive at the Centara, unpack your bags, and never leave the resort for your whole vacation. If you do want to venture out, though, you are right near the center of the action and can get to Patong in 10 minutes or Karon Village in just a few. Though most large resorts offer good buffet breakfasts, the Centara's is just a little bigger and a little better. A great choice for families, though you will pay for all the amenities and conveniences. During high season, though, this resort can be very crowded.

Le Meridien Phuket Beach Resort (29 Soi Karon Nui, Karon Beach, tel. 07/637-0100, www.lemeridienphuketbeachresort.com, 6,500B) is one of the best-located resorts in all of Phuket. It's on a small stretch of beach in northern Karon, and though it technically isn't private, as there's nothing on either side and limited access, there are few people other than guests and hotel employees around. Like the Centara Grand, it's also very close to Karon and Patong, so you won't spend too much time or money getting out if you want to. Amenities and facilities are excellent, with multiple restaurants, a massive swimming pool, a kids' club and large outdoor playground, and a spa. Most guest rooms have been recently renovated and are simple and modern with some Thai decor. With almost 500 rooms, this is a very large property, but service still feels personal and friendly.

KATA BEACH
Under 1,500B

Waree's Guesthouse (40 Patak Rd. Soi 7, Karon Beach, tel. 07/633-1016, 1,200B) is a basic, old-fashioned guesthouse with comfortable, clean rooms and a small but pleasant garden area. With just a handful of rooms, service at this family-run property is very personal, and it tends to attract repeat visitors. The residential neighborhood this guesthouse is located in is about 10 minutes from the beach.

Eazy Resort (64/22-37 Kata Rd., Kata Beach, tel. 07/628-4401, www.eazyresort.com, 1,200B) has everything a traveler needs—clean rooms, a swimming pool, a small restaurant, and a good location within walking distance of the beach. It opened in 2013, so everything is new and in good repair. Eazy Resort really is more a motel than a resort, though, and the only grounds to speak of are the swimming pool and the restaurant.

Kata High View Resort (233 Koketanode Rd., Kata, tel. 07/633-0660, www.katahiviewresort.com, 1,200B) is a lovely, inexpensive small resort with a nice swimming pool, modern, well-designed rooms, and a location

about 10 minutes on foot from Kata Beach. This is a budget property, and there is no restaurant on the premises, not too much of a problem as it is so close to Kata Village and all the food and drink offerings there. The resort is set in the hills above Kata, which makes for great views from some of the common areas. You'll need to climb up stairs to get to your room, though, which would be challenging for small children or anyone with limited mobility.

1,500-3,000B

The Palmery Resort and Spa (82/20 Koketanode Rd., Kata Beach, tel. 07/633-3171, www.thepalmery.com, 2,200B) is a good-value resort in the hills behind Kata Beach. The property, which opened in 2013, has spacious rooms that are comfortably equipped. The clean, modern design of this midsize resort seems to appeal to younger couples, which seems to be the biggest demographic at the resort. Like most resorts of this size, the "heart" of the property is the swimming pool, in this case a sleek, minimalist one with pretty blue tiles.

Some may find the overt Thai decor at **Sawasdee Village** (65 Katekwan Rd., Kata Beach, tel. 07/633-0979, www.phuketsawasdee.com, 3,000B) a bit over the top, but once inside this small, upscale resort, most suspend their cynicism and embrace it for what it is. In fact, many find that the lush landscaping, Khmer-style architecture, and regional art that decorates Sawasdee Village create a beautiful, exotic environment. Aside from aesthetics, the resort has plenty going for it. Service at the resort is very friendly, and the location can't be beat—it's about 150 meters (492 ft) from the beach, and Kata Village is at its doorstep.

Aspasia Resort (1/3 Laem Sai Rd., Kata Beach, tel. 07/628-4430, www.aspasiaphuket.com, 2,900B) isn't quite a five-star luxury resort, but it offers guests an experience that comes quite close, for a much lower price. The location in the hills between Karon and Kata Beaches, overlooking the water, feels remote and secluded but is in fact very central. The rooms have a modern Asian aesthetic, with simple but high-end wooden furniture. Large suites with full kitchens are great for long stays and big groups. The stepped grounds are lovely, though they might not be that suitable for families with small children.

3,000-4,500B

Metadee Resort (66 Kata Rd., Kata Beach, tel. 07/633-7888, www.metadeephuket.com, 3,500B), a modern, full-service resort a 10-minute walk from the beach, has a stunning, massive, free-form central swimming pool. The modern, spacious villas and guest rooms are clustered around the pool, and some have direct access from their balconies, though some have their own smaller, private pools. The overall design at the resort is clean, light, and minimalist, with some small Thai details. There is a fitness center, a spa, and a restaurant on the premises, and it's just a short walk to town. This is not quite a five-star property, but if you're able to book it at a discount, it's a great value in a great location.

For a larger family-friendly property near Kata Beach, try **Kata Palm Resort** (60 Kata Rd., Karon, tel. 07/628-4334, www.katapalmresort.com, 3,500B). The resort is just a few minutes on foot to Kata Beach but also has a very large pool area with a funky little artificial waterfall and a bar in one of the pools, should you wish to remain at the resort for the day. Guest rooms are a mix of traditional Thai with a nondescript large hotel; it's nothing stunning from a design point of view but definitely nice-looking, clean, and comfortable.

Over 4,500B

Boathouse by Montara (Kata Beach, tel. 07/633-0015 to 07/633-0017, www.boathousephuket.com, 6,500B), formerly called Mom Tri's Boathouse, is a beautiful small hotel in a fantastic spot right at the end of Kata Beach. The comfortably appointed guest rooms are decorated in a modern Thai style, and many have views looking right out onto the ocean. After extensive renovations

in 2012, the property feels fresh and modern. There is an excellent restaurant on the premises, and a spa and small swimming pool, too. This is a great place to stay if you're looking for something a little more upscale right on Kata Beach.

Perhaps one of the highest-rated resorts on Kata Beach, by any standard, is **Mom Tri's Villa Royale** (12 Kata Noi Rd., Kata Beach, tel. 07/633-3586, www.villaroyalephuket.com, 9,500B). Set on Kata Noi, the resort scales the cliffs behind the shore. All rooms and suites are very large and include sitting areas. Decor is very low-key and elegant—clearly the architect who designed and owns this property didn't want to compete with the gorgeous natural surroundings. With just 35 rooms and suites, the resort is very small, and the service level is very high. Though the resort is very close to everything going on in Kata and Karon, the premises feels very private and secluded, a real luxury in Phuket.

NAI HARN

The Royal Phuket Yacht Club (23/3 Mu 1, Viset Rd., Nai Harn, tel. 07/638-0200, www.theroyalphuketyachtclub.com, 4,000B) on Nai Harn Beach is a well-established, large luxury resort with beautiful views of the Andaman Sea, nice facilities, and comfortable rooms. The facilities and common areas are pretty and well designed, with the large swimming pool overlooking the ocean. The property underwent renovations in 2014.

The very popular **U Sunsiri Phuket** (11/5 Mu 1, Rawai, tel. 07/633-6400, www.uhotelsresorts.com, 3,000B) resort, a few hundred meters inland from Nai Harn Beach, opened in 2013. The eclectic design choices—a bit of industrial chic, some Asian furnishings, and even some old-world opulence—come together to create a very modern, aesthetically pleasing resort. The kids' club and waterslide make this a family-friendly property, as do the large suites with kitchenettes. As for food and drink, the hotel has multiple bars and restaurants, but you can also walk out to the beach for inexpensive Thai and Western food.

RAWAI BEACH

Le Piman Resort (43/148 Mu 7, Viset Rd., Rawai, tel. 07/661-3732, www.lepimanresort.com, 1,500B) is a nice small midmarket resort and a good value for those who want to stay in the area. The very pretty grounds, comfortable villas and guest rooms, and friendly service almost make up for the fact that the property isn't near any swimmable beaches, though that's a problem in all of Rawai.

Navatara Phuket Resort (90/28 Mu 6, Viset Rd., Rawai, tel. 07/661-3879, www.navataraResort.com, 1,500B) is another great property on the wrong side of the tracks. The small resort, centered on a wide, pretty swimming pool, designed with subtle Thai architectural elements, is pretty and neutral. Basic rooms are comfortably sized at around 350 square feet and are modern and fitted with everything from hair dryers to Wi-Fi. There's nothing to speak of in the area, though the resort provides a free shuttle bus to nearby attractions.

Serenity Resort and Residences Phuket (14 Mu 5, Viset Rd., Rawai, tel. 07/637-1900, www.serenityphuket.com, 3,000B), a midsize luxury resort on the coast of Rawai Beach, has comfortable, modern rooms and some very large suites for families and large groups. The small island of Ko Lon is directly across the water from the resort, making for a beautiful view. You can kayak and do other ocean activities. The beach itself is not swimmable or fit for sunbathing, though; it's essentially a tidal mud flat.

PHUKET TOWN

If there ever was a reason to stay in Phuket Town, it would have to be **Phuket 346** (15 Soi Romanee, Thalang Rd., Phuket Town, tel. 07/625-8108, www.phuket346.com, 1,300B), an art gallery-guesthouse in an old Sino-Portuguese shophouse in the center of the city. Each of Phuket 346's three guest rooms are quirky and funky but have big, comfortable beds, TVs, and Wi-Fi. The lobby, gallery, and attached café are very modern but have incorporated Phuket Town's historic architecture.

99 Oldtown Boutique Guesthouse (99 Thalang Rd., Phuket Town, tel. 081/797-4311, 800B) is another wonderful place to stay in Phuket Town. The perfect location in the center of the historic district, charming, authentic rooms, and very modern bathrooms mean you'll be talking about this place long after you head home from Phuket. The price, less than US$25 per night most times of the year, is unbeatable for what you get.

More of a hostel than a guesthouse or hotel, **Ai Phuket** (88 Yawolat Rd., Phuket Town, www.aiphukethostel.com, tel. 081/721-2881, 300B) is cheap, clean, and fun, plus it's in a historic Sino-Portuguese building in the center of town. Shared dorm rooms have a typical bunk bed setup, but they are very colorful and well decorated, a surprise at this price range. Shared bathrooms are modern and very cool, nothing like the typical hostel. The lobby and other common areas are also filled with funky art and comfortable places to sit and read.

NEARBY ISLANDS

Coral Island Resort (Coral Island, tel. 07/628-1060, www.coralislandresort.com, 2,500B) is the only option you have if you want to stay on this beautiful little island just off Phuket. The resort is basic, with decent but aging rooms, a restaurant, and even a swimming pool, but the reason people come here is not for the accommodations so much as the island itself. If you're interested in snorkeling or diving off Coral Island, adjust your expectations for this resort, relish in the fact that it's so inexpensive for the location, and enjoy your trip.

Bungalow Raya Resort (Ko Racha, tel. 07/638-3136, www.rayaresort.net, 1,200B) has basic, old-fashioned beach bungalows on Ko Racha. Fan cooling, cold water, and basic bedding are on offer, but even if you're past your backpacking days, the location overlooking the beach is worth any amount of inconvenience or discomfort. There is also a small restaurant-bar on the premises.

The Racha Phuket Resort (Ko Racha, tel. 07/635-5455, www.theracha.com, 7,000B) is a small five-star luxury resort on the secluded island of Ko Racha. Stark white interiors and minimalist, Mediterranean-inspired design make the resort feel very modern inside and out. The large central swimming pool overlooks the ocean, and the resort itself is just steps away from the sand. Day-trippers, though, can make the beach feel crowded and hectic, so it's best to spend your time there in the early morning or late afternoon.

Tenta Nakara Resort (31/1 Mu 5, Ko Naka Yai, tel. 081/398-6515, www.tentana-kara.com, 1,700B) is all about getting back to nature. There's no electricity, and the old-fashioned thatched-roof bungalows and tents are designed to remove as many barriers to the outdoors as possible. It's not all about roughing it, though, as bathrooms are modern and there is even a small place to get massages on the premises. The restaurant on the premises runs on generator power in the evening, but things shut down pretty early here, so don't expect a big party. Large, multibedroom bungalows are very family-friendly, too.

The Naka Island (32 Mu 5, Ko Naka Yai, tel. 07/637-1400, www.nakaislandphuket. com, 13,000B), part of the Starwoods Luxury Collection, is an all-villa property on a semi-private stretch of beach on Ko Naka Yai. Even basic villas are over 4,000 square feet and have small private plunge pools. The decor is very tropical, with thatched roofs, adobelike structures, and plenty of natural materials. The main swimming pool has a beautiful view of Phang Nga Bay. There are two restaurants and a bar, though you may feel a little captive to the (expensive) food and drinks on offer. The resort includes pickup from the airport and transfer to the island by private boat; it's a very exciting and exclusive experience.

Food

You'll find that although the island is packed full of beautiful resorts and beaches, food offerings are simply not up to par with what you'll find in Bangkok and other urban areas in the country. Things are definitely improving, and there are some great restaurants on Phuket, though. Many restaurants in tourist areas offer some sort of hybrid menu combining Thai food and Western food, whether it's German, French, Italian, Swiss, or just cheeseburgers and french fries to go with your pad thai or fried rice. Unfortunately, most places do neither cuisine particularly well but manage to stay in business because they're located on the beach or because visitors are happy enough to be in such beautiful surroundings that they're not so bothered by the lack of excellent food. Though hotel restaurants are usually less interesting than stand-alone ones, on Phuket they are often where you will find the best meals (casual Thai food excepted).

MAI KHAO BEACH

Kin Dee Restaurant (71/6 Mai Khao Beach, tel. 082/814-8482, 10:30am-10pm daily, 100B), a beach restaurant serving good Thai food, has become a favorite among tourists in Mai Khao. The relaxed atmosphere, inexpensive prices, and friendly service make it a really pleasant experience. This is a very casual place—just an open-air dining area filled with bamboo furniture. They also deliver and even have a Thai cooking class.

The comfortable but modern and stylish dining room at **Cinnamon** (53/3-4 Mu 4, Mai Khao, tel. 07/661-6253, 11am-11pm Wed.-Mon., 300B) serves good, straightforward Thai dishes plus pasta and sandwiches. Though it is out of the way if you're not staying in the area, if you're at a nearby resort it's worth the trip for a little change of scenery.

NAI YANG BEACH

Tatonka (382/19 Mu 1, Srisoontorn Rd., Cherngtalay, Thalang, tel. 07/632-4399,

6pm-midnight Thurs.-Tues., 600B) just outside of the Laguna Resort area, offers innovative global cuisine in a Native American-themed restaurant with an open kitchen where you can watch chefs prepare your Thai bouillabaisse or Peking duck pizza. This is some of the best fusion food you'll find on the island, and the dining room and outdoor dining areas have a casual elegance to them.

The attractive, high-end Thai@Siam (82/17 Mu 5, Nai Yang Beach, tel. 07/632-8290, 11:30am-11pm daily, 450B) features mostly Thai seafood dishes served in a lovely setting—an expansive old wooden Thai house surrounded by lush gardens. In addition to Thai classics such as fried spring rolls and *yam talay* (seafood salad), there are also some Western dishes and fusion dishes. This is really a restaurant for travelers, so those who want more intense flavors should make that clear when ordering.

The casual but sophisticated Siam Supper Club (36/40 Lagoon Rd., Cherntalay, tel. 07/627-0936, 11:30am-6pm daily, 800B) serves a high-end, European-heavy menu with some local cuisine. The atmosphere, reminiscent of an old speakeasy, is even more convincing when there is live jazz music playing (call for the schedule). Even without live music, this place exudes the type of sophisticated charm you rarely see on a tropical island. Prices, especially for imported wines, can be quite high, but many visitors find it a worthwhile splurge.

SURIN BEACH

Right on Surin Beach, there are a number of small restaurants serving up seaside meals and offering menus of both Thai and Western food. Everything is pretty much predictably decent and inexpensive. If you come around dusk and sit at one of the tables on the beach, you'll feel like you're dining like royalty regardless of what you're eating—the view from the tables is magnificent during sunset. In the parking lot of the beach, a number of street vendors begin setting up in the late afternoon, and there is plenty to choose from there if you're looking for something more casual.

Twin Brothers (Surin Beach, tel. 09/591-1274, 11am-10pm daily, 200B) is a little fancier than most of the choices on the beach. They have a mixed Thai and Western menu, including pizza. In addition to the food, they've set up a free Wi-Fi zone, so you can surf the Net and eat at the same time.

For something a little more upscale right on the beach, ★ Catch Beach Club (Surin Beach, directly across from Twin Palms, tel. 07/631-6500, 11am-11pm daily, 500B), the beach restaurant of the Twin Palms, has indoor and outdoor seating that opens right onto the beach. The restaurant, done in stark white with an amazing array of cocktails and a good wine list, is more Miami Beach than Surin. They also have live-music performances on the weekends. It's a jet-set spot on an otherwise totally unpretentious beach. But despite appearances, it is a laid-back and friendly place to have food or drinks.

In keeping with the upscale urban trendiness that characterizes many of the best resorts in Surin, Kindee (71/6 Mu 5, Mai Khao Beach, tel. 07/634-8478, www.kindeerestaurant.com, noon-11pm daily, 250B) offers authentic, flavorful Thai dishes in an unpretentious, relaxed outdoor restaurant. The atmosphere, basic bamboo furniture in lush surroundings, is casual but very pretty. The vast menu includes familiar dishes such as pad thai and some, such as banana flower salad, that new visitors to Thailand may not have tried before. The owner also offers cooking classes.

KAMALA BEACH

At the southern end of Kamala Beach is ★ Rockfish (33/6 Kamala Beach Rd., tel. 07/627-9732, 8am-10pm daily, 500B), one of the most popular restaurants on the islands. No wonder it gets kudos: The menu, split into Thai, Western, and fusion sections, has something for everyone but does everything well, apparently a difficult task considering the quality of fare served up at many tourist-oriented restaurants in the area. The restaurant-bar also has a nice casual atmosphere and, set right on the beach, a beautiful view of the Andaman Sea.

White Orchid (18/40 Mu 6, Kamala Beach, tel. 08/1892-9757, 11:30am-11pm daily, 250B) offers inexpensive but well-prepared classic Thai dishes in a pleasant setting on the beach. The restaurant, essentially a large thatched-roof roadside shack on Kamala Beach, also has tables on the sand. Service is very friendly and relaxed. Eating here feels a little like Phuket used to be—full of character and less crowded and commercialized.

★ **Silk** (Andara Resort and Villas, 15 Mu 6, Kamala Beach, tel. 07/633-8777, www.silk-phuket.com, 6pm-1am daily, 600B) recently relocated from its Surin Plaza location to more central Kamala Beach, but it's still as swanky and chic as ever. No wonder: It's owned by the same group that owns the popular bar area Lan Kwai Fong in Hong Kong. The interior is stunning, with soaring ceilings, red silk, and dark wood throughout, and you can have your meal served at one of the dining tables or, if you're feeling indulgent, lounging on one of the opium beds. The menu has many typical Thai dishes with a little extra flair, such as the panang curry with duck and asparagus.

PATONG BEACH

Patong Beach has everything, and lots of it. Hundreds of guesthouses, hotels, and resorts, hundreds of little shops to spend your money in, and hundreds of places—from small street stalls to sit-down restaurants and familiar Western-brand fast food—to find something to eat. Quantity aside, Patong is unfortunately not known for quality dining. To find the best places, you'll have to venture out a little bit. If you're looking for some authentic Thai food and are not too picky about where you eat, venture over to the **night market** on Rat-U-Thit Road, parallel to the beach, between Soi Bangla and Sawatdirak Road. You'll find plenty of seafood and other stalls set up, catering to hungry visitors and locals alike.

Right in the center of all the action, across the street from the beach, is the **Ban Thai Restaurant** (94 Thaveewong Rd., Patong Beach, tel. 07/634-0850, 11am-1am daily, 500B). The outdoor dining area is lovelier than one would expect in the middle of Patong Beach, and the seafood is fresh and well prepared. The restaurant is great for people-watching, but it's not a place for a quiet romantic dinner: There's often loud live music playing in the background and plenty of commotion to be heard from the streets of Patong.

Unpretentiously serving up solid Thai food, **Kaab Gluay** (58/3 Phrabaramee Rd., Patong Beach, tel. 07/634-0562, 5am-2:30pm daily, 200B) is always a favorite among local residents. The simple restaurant up the road from Patong Beach has many of the Thai dishes you'll see all over the country, including *tom yam kung,* but also fresh local fish dishes, all for very reasonable prices.

An excellent choice for high Thai cuisine is **Baan Rim Pa** (223 Prabaramee Rd., Patong, tel. 07/634-0789, noon-10pm daily, 600B), in the cliffs adjacent to Patong Beach, overlooking the ocean. The view is wonderful, and the food is solid, although the menu may feel a little touristy. The atmosphere is relaxed but much more formal than most beachfront restaurants. It's not the type of place to walk into in flip-flops after a day at the beach, but it's a great choice for a special night out on the island.

If you're in the mood for Indian, **Navrang Mahal** (58/11 Bangla Rd., Soi Patong Resort, tel. 07/629-2280, noon-midnight daily, 300B) off Soi Bangla is unpretentious and relaxed but has fantastic food. They have both northern and southern dishes on the menu, and you'll find good curries and dals as well as many dishes with fresh seafood.

Another excellent Indian choice is **Tantra** (186/5-6 Taweewong Rd., tel. 07/629-6016, noon-midnight daily, 300B), right on the main beach road. The modern Indian decor feels very loungy, helped by the floor seating. The menu is unsurprising, but it includes favorites such as tandoori chicken, saag paneer, and samosas.

For something a little more chic, with a great view and a relaxed vibe, ★ **Joe's Downstairs** (223 Prabaramee Rd., Patong, tel. 07/634-4254, noon-1am daily, 600B), right below Baan Rim Pa, is a fun tapas bar-cocktail lounge-restaurant with an international menu. The modern white interior is a nice backdrop to the view of the ocean and the colorful, artfully arranged dishes.

White Box (247/5 Prabaramee Rd., Kalim Beach, Patong, tel. 07/634-6271, noon-11pm daily, 800B), a slick modern restaurant just north of Patong Beach on the beach side, has great views of the ocean from the glass-enclosed indoor dining room or the terrace. The trendy restaurant's menu, which includes French, Thai, and fusion dishes, is a bit pricey, but the atmosphere, views, and attentive service make it worth the price. Those who don't want to dine here can stop in for rooftop cocktails and live jazz instead.

Sure, you're not in Cabo, but if you're in the mood for some Mexican food, head to **Coyote** (94 Beach Rd., Patong Beach, tel. 07/634-4366, 11:30am-11pm daily, 350B) on Patong. Like their locations in Bangkok, the decor is bright and colorful, the margarita menu huge, and the food surprisingly good considering how far you are from Mexico.

KARON BEACH AND KATA BEACH

Karon and Kata, listed together because the two villages are connected, have a great variety of food and drink options within walking distance of the beach, one of the reasons the area is such a popular place to stay. For high-end dining, stick with one of the resort restaurants, as there are so far no excellent stand-alone restaurants in the area. But, for casual lunches and dinners, there are plenty of options.

The **Kata Night Plaza** (100 Rd., Kata Beach, Kata, tel. 080/087-3475, hours vary), a small outdoor mall that opened in 2013, has a number of restaurants, including a pizza place, La Piazzetta, a sushi restaurant, Big Fish, and a few other small places to eat. It also has a number of chain restaurants, including a Pizza Company, a Coffee Club, a Swensen's, and a Wine Connection.

Set inside the Aspasia Phuket, **Malina's** (1/3 Laem Sai Rd., Kata Beach, Karon, tel. 07/633-3033, 7am-11pm daily, 500B) has a chic contemporary feeling thanks to lots of stainless steel and glass, and it offers a Thai menu as well as Mediterranean fare. The food is less edgy than the decor, but expect the Thai dishes, such as seafood in tamarind soup, to be more interpretive than what you'll find at traditional restaurants. The best part of the place, aside from the view to the sea from the outdoor seats, is the desserts.

The Boathouse (Kata Beach, tel. 07/633-0015, www.boathousephuket.com, 10:30am-11pm daily, 800B), right on Kata Beach, is the restaurant next to Mom Tri's and has one of the best wine selections on the island. This is definitely a place to trade the flip-flops for nicer garb. The kitchen serves both Thai and Western food, and although the restaurant is technically indoors, it opens out onto the beach, and there's a wonderful view to accompany your meal.

Locanda (Bougainvillea Terrace Resort, 86 Patak Rd., Kata Beach, tel. 07/633-0139, www.locanda-phuket.com, 2pm-2am daily, 1,000B) in Kata is part Argentinean *churrascaria,* part Thai restaurant that is owned by Swiss people and has an Italian name, but the combination works well. It's one of the best places on the island to get a steak. A big plus for those balking at the sorry selection of wines on the island, there's also a wine cellar with Old World and New World wines to choose from. If you're not totally stuffed by the grilled meats, the restaurant has a small but well-prepared Thai menu.

The entrance to **Kampong Kata Hill** (4 Karon Rd., Kata, tel. 07/633-0103, 6pm-11pm daily, 500B), in the center of Kata, is easy to miss, but if you walk up the hill on the (many) outdoor stairs, you'll find one of the nicest Thai restaurants in the area. The decor, filled with Thai antiques and Buddha images, might seem a bit over-the-top to some, but it's pretty and pleasant. The menu includes just about every Thai dish imaginable, from Thai salads to curries plus plenty of seafood. **Two Chefs Bar and Grill** (526/7-8 Patak Rd., Karon Beach, tel. 07/628-6479, www. twochefs-phuket.com, 8am-11pm daily, 450B) probably comes the closest to American chain-restaurant dining on Phuket. The restaurant serves a mixed menu of Tex-Mex, Thai food, sandwiches, and burgers in a comfortable, modern setting. Though the Thai food is definitely toned down for Western palates, it's consistent, and most find the flavors plenty intense. They also serve some hearty breakfast dishes in the morning. In addition to the Karon location, there are two locations in Kata.

Old Siam Restaurant (Thavorn Palm Beach Resort, 311 Patak Rd., Karon Beach, tel. 07/639-6090, www.thavornpalmbeach.com, noon-10:30pm daily, 650B) in the Thavorn Palm Beach Resort, has good Thai food, including the usual *tom yam kung* and Thai curries, but the location, an outdoor dining room with views of the beach, makes it worth visiting. It's more casual than some of the other, higher-end hotel restaurants.

PHUKET TOWN

The **night market** in Phuket Town, on Ong Sim Fai Road near the bus station, probably has the best casual food in the vicinity. Although Phuket Town attracts a number of travelers, the diners here are mostly locals, and the food is consequently reasonably priced and freshly prepared.

Phuket Town's historic center has a handful of lovely cafés. ★ **Kopitiam by Wilai** (18 Thalang Rd., Phuket Town, tel. 083/606-9776, 11am-10pm daily, 300B) might not be the chicest or most modern, but it's a contender for most interesting. The little café is filled with cool photos of Phuket from decades past, and the old Chinese furnishings and decorations are that much more convincing given the old Thai-Chinese men that hang out here

on occasion. Aside from coffee, Malaysian-style tea, and snacks, there is also a full lunch and dinner menu.

★ **Raya Thai** (48 Deebuk Rd., Phuket Town, tel. 07/621-8155, 10am-11pm daily, 300B) is a must if you're anywhere near Phuket Town around lunch or dinnertime and prefer excellent local food and charming atmosphere to Westernized menus and slick decor. The elegant yet unpretentious restaurant is in an old Chinese-style home, and there's also outdoor seating in the small courtyard. Madam Rose (as the restaurant is sometimes called) has been running things for decades, and she offers deliciously prepared traditional Thai cuisine, with lots of fresh seafood on the menu. The *tom yam kung* is particularly good. This is one of those gems that's more popular with out-of-town Thais on vacation than with hordes of Westerners. It is a very family-friendly restaurant, too.

Even if you're not staying in Phuket Town, **Siam Indigo Bar & Restaurant** (8 Phang Nga Rd., Phuket Town, tel. 07/625-6697, www. siamindigo.com, 6:30am-11pm daily, 500B) is reason enough to make the trip. The restaurant, set in a nicely restored old Sino-Portuguese building, offers a mixed menu of Thai and French fusion dishes as well as creative cocktails. The decor is fresh and modern, and the space also doubles as a modern art gallery to showcase local artists' work.

The stately, expansive **Baan Klung Jinda Restaurant** (158 Yaowarat Rd., Phuket Town, tel. 07/622-1777, 11am-2pm and 5pm-10pm Mon.-Sat., 350B) is set in an old colonial-style house, complete with porticos and shuttered windows, a definite step up from most of the dining options on the island. Inside, the menu is deliberately traditional and typical, although there are some more exotic ingredients such as venison. Expect to find lots of curry and seafood dishes, all well prepared and presented. The restaurant also has a good wine selection, another plus if you're looking for a special place to dine.

Blue Elephant Cooking School and

Restaurant (96 Krabi Rd., Phuket Town, tel. 07/635-4355, 11:30am-10:30pm daily, 650B), set in the old Phuket governor's mansion, has been serving royal Thai cuisine to patrons for years. Dishes, including curries and *tom yam kung,* will seem familiar to most who know Thai food, but presentation here is meticulous. The physical setting, another old colonial mansion, is stunning and makes for a very special spot for lunch or dinner. Like the Bangkok location, the Blue Elephant in Phuket also offers cooking classes.

La Gaetana (352 Phuket Rd., Phuket Town, tel. 07/625-0523, 6pm-11pm Thurs.-Tues., 700B) offers classic Italian cooking in a homey, friendly environment in Phuket Town. The full menu includes antipasti, pastas, meat dishes, and some yummy Italian desserts. The owner is around most nights, and service can be a bit stereotypically attentive, though from the reactions of diners most seem to enjoy it. Make sure to book for dinner as the place can fill up.

Another European favorite in Phuket Town is Brasserie Phuket (18 Rassada Rd., Phuket Town, tel. 07/621-0511, 11am-midnight daily, 1,100B), a Belgian restaurant with a seafood-heavy menu and imported Belgian beers. The

dining room is pretty and modern, though perhaps not as opulent as you'd expect given the prices, which can be high. Still, the fresh seafood, including lots of salmon and even fresh oysters, are worth it and at such high quality are hard to find in Phuket.

There are several seafood restaurants along Chalong Bay, but Kan-Eang Seafood (9/3 Chofa Rd., Chalong Bay, tel. 07/638-1323, 10am-midnight daily, 400B) is a favorite among returning visitors to the island. Originally opened in the 1970s as a small fish stand, Kan-Eang has grown into a large open-air restaurant facing the bay. Try the steamed fish with lime and chili sauce and crab-fried rice for an authentic local seafood meal. This restaurant is insanely popular with large tour groups, but don't be put off by the big buses in the parking lot.

Wood-fired pizza, fresh seafood, Thai food, and a great view are what draw travelers and expats to Nikita's (Rawai Beach Rd., tel. 07/628-8703, 10am-1am daily, 250B) night after night. You might not get that cultural experience you've been craving if you come for dinner, but you'll definitely satisfy any pizza urges. The view from the tables on Rawai beach, the cold beer on tap, and the relaxed atmosphere only add to the experience.

Information and Services

TOURIST AND TRAVEL INFORMATION

The main island tourist office (191 Thalang Rd., Phuket Town, tel. 07/621-2213 or 07/621-1036, www.tourismthailand.org) is located in Phuket Town and offers maps and general information about the island. There's also a Tourism Authority of Thailand office right in the airport, and it's a convenient place to grab some maps and get general information.

There is also a noticeable presence of tourist police in Phuket, especially during the high season. If there's ever a need, dial tel.

02/678-6800, 02/678-6809, or toll-free 1699 from any phone in Thailand.

BANKS AND CURRENCY EXCHANGE

As long as your local bank is on one of the international networks, such as Cirrus, you should have no problems getting access to money anywhere on Phuket, although some of the outlying islands don't have ATMs or banks. There are ATMs and currency-exchange kiosks in the Phuket International Airport.

You will get the best rate if you use your

ATM card instead of changing currency or travelers checks, but all Thai banks charge a 180 baht fee in addition to any fee your own bank may charge, so you have to factor that in when deciding on the best way to handle your money (they also charge a 150 baht fee to cash travelers checks, so it may be a wash). Thai ATMs all have an English-language option. Remember that Phuket is a pretty casual place, and you'll most likely be spending a lot of time swimming, away from your valuables, or on a boat with other travelers you don't know, so it's better not to carry wads of cash with you. If your hotel doesn't have a safe that you feel confident with (and most casual bungalows don't), take out only as much money as you need for a day or two.

Branches of all of the major banks offer currency-exchange services in Phuket Town, Patong, and the other large beach areas. Rates are always posted, and after you calculate in fees and commissions, they will be better than anything you'll get from someone offering to exchange money for you on the street or out of a shop front. You may be required to show your passport, so make sure to bring it with you. If you want to exchange travelers checks, you will be able to do so at any of the bank branches as well.

International hotels and restaurants will take American Express, MasterCard, and Visa cards, but smaller guesthouses and virtually all casual restaurants are cash-only. You may be asked to pay an additional fee, usually 2-3 percent, to use a credit card. Though all major credit card companies prohibit the practice, it's rampant in Thailand.

EMERGENCY AND MEDICAL SERVICES

Phuket has two major private hospitals with English-speaking staff. While the level of service may not be as high as in the swanky international hospitals in Bangkok, these institutions do cater to foreigners, and staff are well trained and professional. If there is an emergency or you need to be

seen by a doctor before you head off the island, do not hesitate to stop into one of these hospitals. Both have 24-hour walk-in services for a fraction of what you'd pay back home. **Bangkok Hospital Phuket** (2/1 Hongyok Utis Rd., Phuket Town, tel. 07/625-4425) is located in Phuket Town. **Phuket International Hospital** (44 Chalermprakiat Ror 9 Rd., tel. 07/624-9400) is on the airport bypass road. Both hospitals have emergency services. If you want help from Bangkok Hospital, dial 1719 from any local phone. The Bangkok Hospital has a 24-hour emergency response, including ambulance service. The emergency number for Phuket International Hospital is 07/621-0935, and they also have 24-hour emergency service. If you are using Phuket as a base and heading out to one of the surrounding islands, remember that you may be hours away from medical care.

There are small **pharmacies** all over the island if you need medications, many of which are available here without a prescription, though if you need something that isn't commonly used in Thailand, you may have trouble getting it. Antibiotics and oral contraceptives are very easy to find, but make sure you know the generic name of the drug you need, as many pharmaceutical companies brand their products differently in different countries.

VISAS AND OFFICIALDOM

Neither the **American embassy** (tel. 02/205-4000), the **British embassy** (tel. 08/1854-7362), nor the **Australian embassy** (tel. 02/344-6300) has a consular office on the island, but each can be reached by phone in case of emergency or to provide guidance.

COMMUNICATIONS

The best place to get stamps is at your hotel, and even the smallest guesthouses will arrange to send postcards home for you.

While there are still Internet cafés in the region, these days they have been superseded by businesses that offer **free Wi-Fi** with the expectation that you have a device to take advantage of it. Many restaurants and coffee shops have Wi-Fi, as well as spas and massage parlors. Even if you're staying in an 800 baht-per-night guesthouse, you may find a solid Wi-Fi signal in your guest room.

LAUNDRY SERVICES

There are no real wash-and-dry launderettes on the island, but there are plenty of places to get your laundry done inexpensively. If you are staying in any of the popular beach towns, including Patong, Kamala, Kata, or Karon, there will be plenty of shops offering laundry services, sometimes as a side business to a convenience store or even a coffee shop, so keep an eye out for little signs, and ask if necessary. Nearly every hotel, even cheap bungalows, will have some laundry services, too. Take advantage of this when planning your packing. Expect to pay 50-100 baht per kilogram. Prices will be substantially higher in larger resorts, which often charge by the piece.

LUGGAGE STORAGE

There is luggage storage at the Phuket airport at a rate of 60 baht per day per item; it's to the left just after you exit the baggage-claim area. Many hotels and guesthouses will also store your luggage for a small fee.

Transportation

GETTING THERE

Although Phuket is an island, it is connected to the mainland by a short bridge, making boat travel unnecessary unless you are coming from one of the smaller islands in the region (such as Phi Phi or Lanta). Many people take advantage of the inexpensive flights from Bangkok, but it is also easy to travel overland to the island.

Air

Phuket has one international airport, the **Phuket International Airport** (tel. 07/632-7230 to 07/632-7237, http://phuketairportthai.com) located in the northwest part of the island on Thep Kasattri Road, serving passengers arriving from all over the world.

If you're coming from Bangkok, it's cheap and easy to get to Phuket by air. Between regular and low-cost airlines, there are more than 20 flights per day, and even during peak travel it is unlikely you won't be able to find a flight on the day you want to leave (although you're better off making reservations in advance if you are traveling in December-January). The low-cost carriers, including **Nok Air** and **Air Asia,** often have same-day flights available for less than 2,000 baht each way. Unless it's peak season or Sunday night (when Bangkok residents are returning from weekend getaways), you can literally show up at the airport and ask for the next available flight. Flights are just over an hour from the city, making Phuket an easy place to go even for a weekend.

Flights from Bangkok to Phuket and Krabi are still running from both the new Suvarnabhumi airport and the old airport, Don Muang, which was supposed to be decommissioned after the new airport was built, but was reopened for domestic flights while repair work was being done on the new airport and seems to be lingering. The situation is supposed to be temporary, and the old airport feels makeshift, with very limited food or modern airport comforts. There is only one terminal open, so you won't have to worry about going to the wrong place, but if you're taking a taxi to the airport in Bangkok, make sure the driver understands which one you are going to. Make sure you understand, too. It's not uncommon for carriers to book you on a flight from Don Muang going to Phuket but returning to Suvarnabhumi.

Train

Phuket does not have rail service, but you can take a train to Surat Thani (actually Phun Phin, about 10 minutes by car outside of Surat Thani), and then switch to a bus for the remainder of the journey. An overnight second-class sleeper to Surat Thani will cost around 650 baht, and there are also a couple of trains leaving during the day. The train ride is around 14 hours, then you'll switch to a bus, which you need to pick up in town, although there are cheap buses from the train station to Surat Thani. The bus from Surat Thani to Phuket is about five hours and costs under 200 baht. The whole journey will take around 20 hours, making taking a bus directly from Bangkok a little more appealing (and less expensive).

Bus

There are frequent buses to Phuket from Bangkok and other parts of the country. If you're coming from Bangkok, you can take a bus straight from the **Southern Bus Terminal** into Phuket. The journey takes around 12 hours and costs 625 baht for the air-conditioned luxury bus run by **Phuket Central Tour** (tel. 02/434-3233 or 07/621-3615). Other air-conditioned government express buses cost around 500 baht.

If you're heading to Phuket from Bangkok, watch out for tour companies running their own buses, especially those originating in the Khao San Road area. They can be cheaper than government buses and seem more convenient since they leave from the center of the city. But oftentimes you'll arrive at the departure point at the scheduled time only to have to wait another hour or more as other passengers arrive. Government buses leaving from the Southern Bus Terminal are generally prompt, and the air-conditioned buses are surprisingly pleasant. Seats are comfortable and recline, there is a bathroom on board, and you'll be given a blanket if you take an overnight bus.

If you're coming from Krabi, there are frequent daily buses to Phuket; the cost is less than 200 baht, and they take about four hours. You can also travel between Phuket and Phang Nga by bus. The ride is about 2.5 hours and it costs under 150 baht.

Car

Depending on where you're coming from, it's easy to drive into Phuket (the island is connected by bridge to Phang Nga), and since getting around once you're there can be expensive, a car could come in handy. Phuket

Phuket bus

is best reached from Highway 4, which runs north-south down the peninsula. To get to Phuket, you have to travel through Phang Nga Province to get to the Surin Bridge, and the turnoff from the highway is at Route 402, which is well signed in English indicating that it's the route to take to get to Phuket. Route 402 is called Thep Kasattri Road; it runs inland down the island and is where the airport is located.

GETTING AROUND
Taxi

Over the past few years, taxi service on Phuket has become more expensive and less regulated, leading many to refer to Phuket taxi drivers and companies as the "taxi mafia." Metered taxis are generally hard to come by in Phuket, but drivers are supposed to follow a regulated price list for trips between common areas. Expect to pay 400-800 baht to get from the airport to your hotel. The official taxi stand is on the right of the arrivals terminal once you exit the building. Although there will be many people offering you taxis the minute you step out of the terminal, just walk to the taxi stand and take one from there, as it's almost always a better deal.

In every beach village, there are taxi stands for unmetered taxis with prices posted. Expect to pay at least 300 baht for any trip you take with one of these cars. If you're traveling farther than the next beach town, prices will be higher. To get back to the airport from your hotel will generally run around 800 baht if you're in the southern part of the island and slightly less the closer you are to the airport.

Tuk Tuk

The most common way to get around the island is by *tuk tuk*. Not quite like the three-wheeled version seen all over Bangkok and Chiang Mai, the Phuket version is more like a small pickup truck with seats in the back facing backward and forward. They're often painted in bright colors or carry advertisements for local businesses, and some of them also have bright neon lights. You can't miss

them—they look like mini disco buses. In Patong, you'll find rows of *tuk tuks* lined up on the main road waiting for customers. When none are waiting, you can just flag one down. It's best to settle on a price before you get into the *tuk tuk,* and generally it's around 200 baht to get to a nearby beach, more for farther destinations. They don't have seat belts—or doors, for that matter—so if you're traveling with small kids, be advised.

Motorcycle Taxi

Motorcycles are less common in Phuket than in Bangkok, but they can be found in very developed areas such as Phuket Town and Patong. Drivers wear brightly colored vests, often with white numbers on the back, and will negotiate fares to take you where you need to go. Prices range anywhere from 50 baht to get from one part of a beach to another to a few hundred baht if you are traveling farther.

Motorcycle Rental

Many people rent motorcycles to get around Phuket. Mostly you'll find 100 cc and 110 cc bikes, which have a clutchless shift system (you still have to change gears with your left foot, but you don't need to squeeze a clutch to do so), but there are also lots of places renting newer scooters that are totally automatic.

At around 250 baht per day (slightly more in high season or if you're in a remote area), it's the cheapest form of transportation you'll be able to find on the island. It's also a great way to see Phuket, since you're totally mobile and you can come and go as you please. The downside is that some of the roads are windy and hilly, which can be challenging or scary for new riders, and that some parts of Phuket are as congested as large cities. Also, riding a motorcycle anywhere is dangerous. If you rent one, make sure you know what you are doing, and always wear your helmet. You may feel like the only person on the island with one on, but you'll avoid potentially expensive and inconvenient traffic tickets, as the Phuket police occasionally crack down on helmetless riders.

Car Rental

There are numerous international and local car rental companies on the island. While a car isn't necessary, this is a great option if you have children. Although not all of the agencies will require this, it's best to go to an auto club office at home to get an international driver's license before arriving. You can legally drive in Thailand without one, but for insurance reasons some companies will ask that you have it anyway. Brush up on your skills driving a car with a manual transmission before you arrive, as there are few automatic transmission cars available on Phuket.

Avis (arrival terminal, Phuket International Airport, tel. 07/635-1243, www.avisthailand.com, 8am-9pm daily) has a rental counter right at the airport, and you can book online and pick up your car when you arrive.

Andaman Car Rent (51/11 Mu 3, Cherngtalay Rd., Surin Beach, tel. 07/632-4422, www.andamancarrent.com, 9am-9pm daily) is located on Surin Beach and has a good selection of Jeeps and other sport vehicles as well as regular cars. They'll pick you up from the airport if you arrange it ahead of time.

Via Phuket (120/18 Rat-U-Thit Rd., Patong Beach, tel. 07/634-1660, www.via-phuket.com, 8am-5pm Mon.-Sat.) has off-road vehicles in addition to normal cars and will pick you up and drop you off wherever you are staying.

Braun Car Rental (66/29 Soi Veerakit, Nanai Rd., Patong Beach, tel. 07/629-6619, www.braun-rentacar.com, 9am-9pm daily) is on Patong Beach and will do pickup and drop-off at the airport or at your hotel. Braun also rents car seats for a small fee.

The Andaman Coast

Look for ★ to find recommended
sights, activities, dining, and lodging.

Highlights

★ **Mu Ko Similan National Park:** This group of small islands offers some of the best diving opportunities in the world (page 79).

★ **Rai Le Beach:** Dramatic limestone cliffs along with warm, clear, emerald-colored water and plenty of outdoor activities make the beach on the west side of Rai Le in Krabi perhaps Thailand's best beach destination (page 83).

★ **Ton Sai Bay:** This is the most popular area of Ko Phi Phi, drawing crowds of day-trippers. The scenery is amazing, as are the diving and snorkeling options surrounding it (page 92).

★ **Khlong Dao Beach:** This beach is beautiful and quiet, and it has just enough amenities and accommodations choices, with none of the overcrowding found at some of the more popular island destinations (page 99).

★ **Ko Kradan:** Arguably the prettiest island in Trang, Ko Kradan offers amazing views of neighboring islands and accessible reefs for snorkelers (page 106).

If paradise were a place on earth, it would be somewhere on the Andaman coast of Thailand. The region is astoundingly beautiful—bright, clear, warm water teeming with wildlife from tropical fish to magnificent coral, even occasional sea cows

and reef sharks (the kind that don't eat people). The coast and islands have sandy beaches, and there are hundreds of small islands and limestone rock formations rising up out of the ocean. Inland, there are tropical rainforests, mangrove swamps, mountains, and waterfalls. If it's an active vacation you're looking for, there are abundant opportunities to snorkel, dive, sea kayak, or hike, especially in the numerous national parks.

But it's not just the physical beauty and activities that make the area such a great traveling experience. The region still offers a chance to glimpse rural and small-city life in Thailand. While Phuket has attracted residents from all over the world as well as transplants from Bangkok and other parts of the country, and largely feels like a commercialized tourist destination, if you travel north to Phang Nga Province, you'll find small fishing villages along the coast where fishing families can often be found clearing nets at the end of

the day or setting out squid to dry in the sun. To the south, in Satun, you'll find a largely Muslim population and a fascinating blend of Islam and Buddhism evidenced in the houses of worship and the dress of the local people.

In the past few decades, Phuket has really blossomed into a world-class destination for vacationers from all over the world, with all of the pros and cons that go with it. But traveling either north to Phang Nga or south to Krabi and Trang, things slow down again, although even in Trang there are more and more bungalows, resorts, and hotels for visitors being built every year. Though many travelers go to one spot on the Andaman and plant themselves there for the duration, if you want to both indulge and explore, it's an easy place to be a little more adventurous. Public and private buses can take you from Phuket or Krabi either north or south along the coast, and if you rent a car, you'll find the highway system exceptionally well maintained and generally

Previous: Ao Nang; Maya Bay in Phang Nga Bay; Rai Le Beach. **Above:** kayaking off the coast of Krabi.

The Andaman Coast

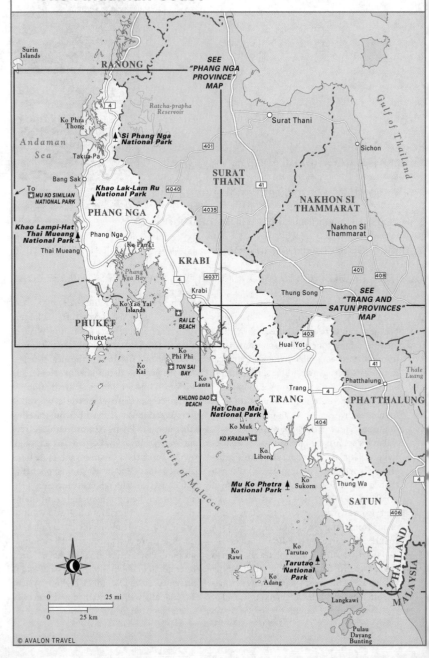

RANONG

SEE "PHANG NGA PROVINCE" MAP

Surin Islands

Ratcha-prapha Reservoir

Surat Thani

Ko Phra Thong

Si Phang Nga National Park

Andaman Sea

Sichon

Takua Pa

401

SURAT THANI

Bang Sak

41

NAKHON SI THAMMARAT

To MU KO SIMILIAN NATIONAL PARK

Khao Lak-Lam Ru National Park

4040

PHANG NGA

4035

Nakhon Si Thammarat

Khao Lampi-Hat Thai Mueang National Park

Phang Nga

Ko PanYi

KRABI

401 408

Thai Mueang

4037

SEE "TRANG AND SATUN PROVINCES" MAP

Phang Nga Bay

4 Krabi

Thung Song

Ko Yao Yai Islands

PHUKET

RAI LE BEACH

Huai Yot

Phuket

403

Thale Luang

Ko Phi Phi

Ko Kai

TON SAI BAY

Ko Lanta

Trang 4 Phatthalung

PHATTHALUNG

KHLONG DAO BEACH

Hat Chao Mai National Park

TRANG

Straits of Malacca

Ko Muk

404

KO KRADAN

Ko Libong

Mu Ko Phetra National Park

Ko Sukorn

Thung Wa

SATUN

406

4

Ko Rawi

Ko Tarutao

Tarutao National Park

THAILAND MALAYSIA

Ko Adang

Langkawi

Pulau Dayang Bunting

Gulf of Thailand

N

0   25 mi

0   25 km

© AVALON TRAVEL

navigable, even if you can't read a word of Thai.

The Andaman coast is also perfect for island-hopping, and the best way to do that is by boat. There are plenty of ferries, speedboats, and longtails to take you from island to island and beach to beach. You can fly into Phuket, spend a few days on one of the nearby beaches, then take a boat to Phi Phi, Ko Lanta, or one of the other numerous islands in Phang Nga Bay, or hit 3-4 islands in one trip; there are hundreds of islands in the region to choose from. Some, such as Phi Phi, are arguably overpopulated with travelers and resorts. But there are still some beautiful islands you can stay on that feel less exploited by tourism and kinder to the natural surroundings.

Prices are still amazingly reasonable considering the physical landscape. Even in the most coveted areas, you'll be able to find simple accommodations, sometimes right on the beach, for less than US$40 per night, even cheaper the farther away from Phuket you are. Of course, if you're looking for five-star luxury, you'll be able to find that, too. Some of the best resorts in the world have Andaman coast addresses.

PLANNING YOUR TIME

How you plan your time depends mostly on what you want to get out of your vacation. If you're hoping to pick a beach on the Andaman coast, grab a chair, and sit and relax for the duration of your time in Thailand, you won't need to do much planning at all.

If you do choose to explore some of the region's surrounding islands, remember that getting from one place to another can often take a few hours and involve taking land transportation to a pier and then a sometimes-long boat ride, especially if you are relying on public transportation. Many tour operators offer day trips to surrounding islands from Krabi or Phuket, and these can be an excellent way to see many different places at once, although you won't have any control over the schedule or itinerary.

If you really want to explore each island (or stay overnight), your best bet is to take one of the large ferries from Phuket to Ko Phi Phi, Ko Lanta, or Krabi and then use the smaller longtail boats to take you to other islands in the vicinity. Some people prefer to base themselves on one of the more built-up islands (Ko Lanta or Ko Phi Phi) and explore the surrounding islands on day trips, but it's just as easy to sleep on different islands or even camp at one of the island national parks. If you plan on island-hopping, make sure to pack light. Longtail boats, which are colorful wooden boats used for short trips, are small, usually not covered, and sometimes a little leaky. There's no room for a large suitcase or even a very large backpack. It is also possible to charter a sailboat or speedboat to island-hop, but the cost is in the thousands of dollars for a multiday trip.

If you've come to the region primarily to dive, you'll actually find it much easier to get around, as there are numerous large dive boats offering live-aboard, multiday dive trips that will take you to some of the best diving sites in the country. Trips generally depart from Phuket, Krabi, and Khao Lak.

Phang Nga Province จังหวัดพังงา

Phang Nga Province, north of Phuket on the mainland, is home to the spectacular Phang Nga Bay, which overlaps with Phuket and Krabi. But aside from this well-known tourist spot, traveling north along the west coast, the region has beautiful beaches and a mountainous, forested interior. It's also home to the Surin and Similan National Marine Parks off the coast. With plentiful coral, this is some of the best diving and snorkeling in the country. The mainland beaches are arguably as top-notch as those in Phuket and Krabi, and the area is more visited by travelers every year. Although there are world-class resorts, and the lower part of the region is easily reached from the Phuket airport (to Khao Lak it's about the same drive as to parts of southern Phuket), it's definitely quieter. There's nothing even close to the density of Phuket's Patong Beach, so it is perfect for those looking for a slightly off-the-beaten-track experience without having to cut out any amenities.

PHANG NGA BAY

Surrounded by Phuket to the west, Phang Nga Province to the north, and Krabi to the east, Phang Nga Bay is filled with small islands and rock formations rising out of the sea, creating breathtaking scenery that, for many, is what the Andaman coast is all about. There are more than 100 islands in the bay; some, such as Ko Yao Noi, are large enough for accommodations, and some, such as "James Bond Island," are so small that they're barely more than rocks. In addition to some sandy beaches, the bay's islands and surrounding coasts are also home to verdant mangrove swamps. You may be able to sight egrets, kingfishers, and herons. There are hidden lagoons inside some of the islands where you can snorkel or swim in sheltered waters, and caves on some of the islands from the continued erosion of the limestone material they're primarily made of. The relatively shallow waters create amazing ocean colors, from light blue when the sun is shining to deep emerald, and despite the fact that you'll probably be plying the waters and exploring the caves with thousands of visitors from all over the world, it's worth the crowds and the slightly commercialized feeling of the area just to enjoy the physical landscape.

There is only one public ferry to the bay, traveling from the east side of Phuket to Ko Yao Noi. To tour the bay, you'll either need to arrange a group tour with one of the many travel agents in the region or hire a private boat from Phang Nga. There are many agencies offering tours, and it can be a convenient way to see the area.

Islands

Ko Pan Yi (เกาะปันหยี, Sea Gypsy Island) is really a large cluster of houses, shops, and even a mosque built on stilts right over the water next to a small rocky island, a sort of Water World-esque village in the middle of the sea. The people living in the village are primarily Muslim fisherfolk, who used to make their living plying the surrounding waters but now have seen much of their existence subsidized by the thousands of tourists who visit each day and who buy food and drinks on the island. The island is quite picturesque, but it's not inhabited by the traditional sea gypsies of the region, called Moken, a nomadic people who spend months at a time at sea.

About one hour by boat from Krabi, the **Mu Ko Hong Islands** (หมู่เกาะห้อง) are made up of stunning limestone formations surrounded by coral reefs with some sandy beaches. Although the islands are too small to have any accommodations, they can be visited during day trips and for snorkeling, canoeing, or kayaking. One of the larger islands in the group, Ko Hong, has a small hiking trail.

The islands of **Ko Yao** (เกาะยาว) are the largest in Phang Nga Bay and comprise the

Phang Nga Province

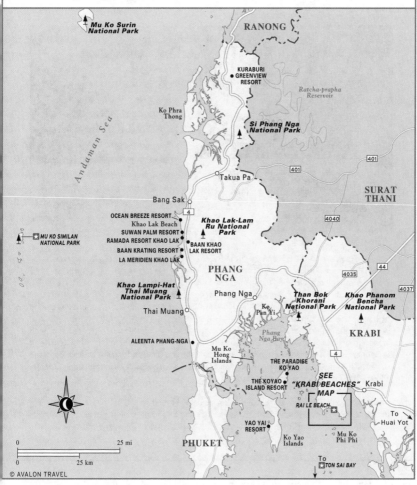

larger **Ko Yao Yai** and the smaller **Ko Yao Noi** to the north. Just a couple of hours by ferry from the mainland, the Ko Yao islands are amazingly untouched by the rampant tourism that seems to have changed even the smallest islands from places supported by local industry and quiet refuges for indigenous animals to bungalow- and bar-laden resort spots. Here it's dirt roads, water buffalo, and dense green forest. Perhaps this is because the beaches are not as beautiful as some of the others in the area—at low tide it's just too rocky to swim. Still, if you are looking to get away somewhere quiet and feel like you're actually in Thailand, these islands provide a truly special experience. The local culture is primarily Muslim Thai, and there's much less of a party scene; it can even be hard to find a beer at the handful of small restaurants. Both islands have accommodations, even a couple of luxury resorts, although the smaller Ko Yao Noi has the most options for

James Bond Island

Ko Phing Kan

When the James Bond thriller *The Man with the Golden Gun* came out in 1974, Phang Nga Bay was barely known by anyone outside Thailand. The tiny island where Roger Moore stood is formally called Ko Phing Kan, but it's often referred to as James Bond Island. Like many of the islands in Phang Nga Bay, it has spectacular karst topography and a small but beautiful beach.

Fast-forward three decades, and little Ko Phing Kan has become a staple on the tourist trail. During high season, literally hundreds of people visit the island each day, a trip that's often combined with a visit to Ko Pan Yi to see the "sea gypsies" of Thailand. Instead of a deserted beach in paradise, as seen in the film, the beach is now crammed full of vendors selling postcards and other tourist items. And everyone, it seems, wants to have his or her picture taken on the island, against a backdrop of the spectacular Ko Tapu. Ko Tapu, which means "nail island" in Thai, is a beautiful karst formation towering about 180 meters (591 ft) straight out of the water; it can also be seen in the film.

Many tour companies will encourage visitors to take this day trip, and if you're a big James Bond movie buff, you might enjoy it despite the crowds being herded on and off the island. But bear in mind that although the islands of Phang Nga Bay are beautiful and worth visiting, marine ecosystems are fragile. There are plenty of stunning islands to see, and it's better to spread the impact of our visits around instead of piling it all onto one tiny island.

places to stay. So far, there are no ATMs on the island (although this may be changing soon), so bring plenty of cash from the mainland if you're planning on hanging out here. To get to Ko Yao, you can take a longtail boat from the Bang Rong pier on the east coast of Phuket. There are daily ferries at 9:30am, noon, and 5pm.

Sea Kayaking

Phang Nga Bay is a great kayaking destination. You can explore the smaller islands that have lagoons, caves, and no beaches to land on. Many kayaking trips originate from Phuket, where you can make arrangements for a daylong or multiple-day trip to the area.

Accommodations and Food

If you want to stay on Ko Yao but are looking for something in the budget category, the **Yao Yai Resort** (Mu 7, Ban Lopareh, tel. 08/5784-3043, www.yaoyairesort.com, 1,000B) has some very cheap little wooden bungalows with their own small outdoor sitting areas. The guest rooms are not spectacular, but they are clean, and many of them have air-conditioning. There's no pool, but there is a small restaurant on the premises and a nice beach.

The Paradise Ko Yao (24 Mu 4, Ko Yao Noi, tel. 07/623-8081 or 08/1892-4878, www.theparadise.biz, 7,500B) is a contemporary but casual bungalow resort with very well-designed, open, airy guest rooms, many with their own sitting rooms that open to the surrounding landscape of Phang Nga Bay. Some of the guest rooms even have whirlpool tubs. The grounds are set in the hills, which are speckled with the thatched roofs of the bungalows, and they also have a very chic infinity swimming pool.

This is the place to go if you want to experience that secluded desert-island feeling with a little luxury. **The Koyao Island Resort** (24/2 Mu 5, Ko Yao Noi, tel. 07/659-7474 to 07/659-7476, www.koyao.com, 8,000B) has some beautiful villas set right on the beach, each with a charming rustic feeling but without compromising on amenities such as air-conditioning or nice baths. There's also a small spa and a beautiful swimming pool.

Few properties in the world, let alone in Thailand, can compete with the reputation the **Six Senses Yao Noi** (56 Mu 5, Ko Yao Noi, www.sixsenses.com, 15,000B) has built up over the years. The sprawling property offers only private villas, and each is located far enough away from the rest to feel totally secluded. The understated decor, with mostly natural materials, allows the amazing views and natural surroundings to take center stage. Service is impeccable, and many who stay here say they have never been better cared for. Although Ko Yao Noi is not a private island, the resort feels very much like a secret hideaway of the rich and famous; perhaps it helps that you can arrive by private seaplane or helicopter if you choose.

Since most of these islands are visited as day trips, the only food you'll find is very casual beach dining. Ko Pan Yi, a popular lunch stop for boat tours, has some reasonable restaurants right on the water, serving seafood and other Thai dishes, and Ko Yao has some similar spots to eat.

If you're staying at one of the resorts, meals are not included, but each of the accommodations listed has a reasonable restaurant on-site.

Transportation

As Phang Nga Bay is bordered by Phuket, Krabi, Phang Nga, and Trang to the south, there are a number of different launching points from which to see the islands. If you are flying into Phuket airport, it's actually easier to get a boat from Phuket than to drive to Phang Nga and seek sea transportation from there. Phuket is so heavily visited that many of the tours around Phang Nga Bay will originate at one of the Phuket marinas. Krabi is also a very popular launch point, and if you fly into Krabi, you'll most likely be taking a boat from Ao Nang.

If you are staying at one of the island resorts, they will advise you of the best way to get there (the nicer ones will arrange transportation for you). If you're going for a day trip, you'll most likely do it as part of an organized tour leaving from Phuket or Krabi; these tours almost always pick you up from your hotel and bring you back in the evening. Tours advertising trips to Ko Pan Yi or "James Bond Island" are good for viewing the bay, and if they don't include snorkeling or other activities, they will cost around 500 baht per person. Many of the small islands don't have consistent ferry service, so if you want to spend the day on one of them without a tour, you will have to hire a boat to take you out. You can hire a boat from Phuket marina, but you'll probably pay hundreds of dollars, since the only boats that can access the bay from there are speedboats. If you're coming from Phang Nga, you'll be able to hire a private boat for a couple of hours from the Ao Phang Nga National Park visitors center in Tha Dan. Expect to pay around 1,000 baht for two hours.

If you're driving, the only island in the bay you'll be able to access is Ko Lanta. Otherwise, plan on driving to Tha Dan, Krabi, or Phuket and leaving your car there to switch to sea transportation.

KHAO LAMPI-HAT THAI MUANG NATIONAL PARK
อุทยานแห่งชาติ เขาลำ
ปี –หาดท้ายเหมือง

The **Khao Lampi-Hat Thai Muang National Park** (Mu 5, Amphoe Thai Muang, Phang Nga, tel. 08/4059-7879 or 07/641-7206, 8:30am-6pm daily, 400B) is a small national park on just over 7,200 hectares of land and water that is best known for some spectacular waterfalls, including the **Namtok Lampi,** a three-tiered waterfall that runs all year. The waterfall is about 13 kilometers (8 mi) from the park headquarters on the beach; to get there you'll need to drive most of the way along the main road (there are plenty of signs for the waterfall) and then take a short walk to the falls.

Another great waterfall to explore is **Namtok Ton Phrai,** the largest in the park (although like most waterfalls in the country, it will be less impressive during dry season). These falls are about 11 kilometers (7 mi) from the park's headquarters on the beach, and there are marked roads from there. There is also a ranger station here and a canteen, as it is one of the most popular spots in the park. If you're looking for a quiet beach, **Hat Thai Muang** is a 13-kilometer (8 mi) stretch of sandy beach with clear blue waters. If you visit November-February, you may see **sea turtles** coming to lay their eggs on shore at night, and park rangers collecting the eggs to incubate them safe from poachers or predators in their nursery (this is the main reason the beach is a protected national park). In March there's a festival in which locals and visitors watch the little baby turtles make their way to the sea after hatching.

The park has both bungalows for rent and camping areas where you can pitch a tent. There are some small food vendors around during the day in addition to the canteen at Namtok Lampi.

Transportation

By car from Phuket airport or anywhere on Highway 4, head straight north to Phang Nga on Highway 4 for about 56 kilometers (35 mi) to the Tai Muang Market, where you'll see a sign for the national park. Turn off the main road onto Route 401 for about 6.5 kilometers (4 mi).

There are frequent buses from Bangkok to Phang Nga, which often traverse the popular Highway 4 and terminate in Phuket; they cost 400-500 baht for an air-conditioned bus. From Phang Nga to the park, you can pick up a normal local bus for about 30 baht or an air-conditioned bus for 45 baht.

KHAO LAK
ตะกั่วป่า

Just an hour's drive from the Phuket airport is Takua Pa Province, although it's often referred to as Khao Lak (the name of a part of the province). Despite being literally washed away by the 2004 tsunami, the area is once again an up-and-coming resort area with beautiful beaches, scenic mountain ranges with rainforest in the background, and some luxurious resorts and quaint bungalows. Although more travelers are visiting the area every year, especially in Khao Lak, and you'll see some big brand-name accommodations, it still feels much quieter and more relaxed than any beach you'll find on Phuket.

Khao Lak-Lam Ru National Park
อุทยานแห่งชาติ เขาหลัก–ลำรู้

Spanning four provinces, the **Khao Lak-Lam Ru National Park** (Mu 7, Khuk Khak, Takua Pa, tel. 07/648-5243, 8:30am-6pm daily, 400B), named after the large mountain within its borders, Khao Lak, has kilometers of pristine beach and thick forest. There are a number of small waterfalls, including the Lam Ru waterfall, a five-tiered waterfall hidden amid thick trees. During the day the park is populated not only with visitors but also with beautiful butterflies and exotic birds. If you feel like camping, there is a campground with some limited facilities and just a few bungalows available for rent. Khao Lak Beach is also part of the park, and although parts of the beach are too rocky for swimming, there are some sandy patches where you can lay out a towel and enjoy the view of the Andaman Sea.

Beaches and Islands

The **Khao Lak Beach** region, close to the bridge connecting Phuket with the mainland, offers clean, quiet stretches of beach with amazing crystal-clear waters. From north to south, there are three beaches: **Bang Niang, Nang Thong,** and **Sunset.** Together they take up about eight kilometers (5 mi) of coastline. Khao Lak has traditionally been a hangout for divers, since it's an easy place to set off to the Similan or Surin Islands, and thus remains a laid-back, rustic place to visit. There are lots of dive shops, a handful of restaurants, and the Andaman Sea to keep you occupied.

About 32 kilometers (20 mi) north of Khao Lak is **Bang Sak,** even less developed than its neighbor to the north, which has attracted some luxury resorts in the past few years. There's no nightlife in the area, but if you're looking for a place to be based for some diving or looking to enjoy the water and the convenience of the Phuket airport without dealing with crowds, this is a great spot. The beach is really spectacular: The shore is wide and flat, and the white sands are smooth and relatively unmarred by rocks.

Diving and Snorkeling

Divers in Khao Lak will be able to get to many of the places listed in the Phuket chapter. The waters surrounding the Andaman coast and its islands offer diverse marinelife and dive sites from beginner to advanced, some considered among the best in the world. The biggest draws for trips out of Khao Lak are the **Similan Islands** and the **Surin Islands,** as they are farther north and therefore easier to get to from Khao Lak. However, you can still get trips from Phuket and Phuket dive shops will also drive guests from Phuket to Khao Lak and then put them onto boats there. Most dive shops offer dives to all of the most popular sites in the region.

Diving is really Khao Lak's reason for being a tourist destination, so it's no surprise that there are so many diving shops in the area. The following outfitters are PADI certified. Check the PADI website (www.padi.com) for more.

• **Wicked Diving** (4/17 Mu 7, Khao Lak, tel. 07/648-5868, www.wickeddiving.com)

• **Khao Lak Explorer** (13/43 Mu 7, Petchkasem Rd., Khao Lak, tel. 07/648-5308, www.khaolakexplorer.com)

• **Liquid Liveboards** (13/43 Mu 7, Khao Lak, tel. 07/648-5069, www.liquid-adventure.com)

• **Sea Dragon Dive Center** (5/51 Mu 7, Petchkasem Rd., Khao Lak, tel. 07/648-5420, www.seadragondivecenter.com)

Accommodations

Ocean Breeze Resort (26/3 Mu 7, Khuk Khak, Takua Pa, www.gerdnoi.com, tel. 07/648-5145, 1,800B), formerly called Gerd & Noi Bungalows, isn't very fancy, but it is located right on the beach and has clean, very family-friendly accommodations. The larger bungalows can easily sleep a small family, and there's a small swimming pool and a restaurant serving Thai and European food. The vibe is like old Khao Lak—laid-back and unpretentious.

If you plan to spend some time doing a liveaboard diving trip to the outer islands, the **Kuraburi Greenview Resort** (140/89 Mu 3, Kura, Kuraburi, tel. 07/640-1400, www.kuraburigreenviewresort.com, 1,900B) has some charming cabins in which to base yourself at superbudget prices. The cabins and guest rooms look like they would be more appropriate in New England than Southeast Asia, with lots of exposed wood and rocks along with views of the grounds. The hotel runs lots of dive and snorkeling trips and can arrange live-aboards on their boats, but the hotel itself is not right on the water.

Just south of Bang Sak, **Baan Khao Lak Resort** (26/16 Mu 7, Petchkasem Rd., Khuk Khak, Takua Pa, tel. 07/648-5198, www.baankhaolak.com, 3,500B) is a great value, even during the high season. All of the guest rooms and villas are modern, stylish, and well maintained, and the grounds of this resort on the beach are lushly landscaped and have lots of amenities you wouldn't expect for the price, including a pool right on the beach, restaurants, and an outdoor beach bar. This is a family-friendly property and also one of the rare resorts in the country that have wheelchair-accessible rooms and grounds.

Set on Bang Niang, **La Flora Resort and Spa** (59/1 Mu 5, Khuk Khak Rd., Takua Pa, tel. 07/642-8000, 5,500B) is a surprisingly large resort, with over 100 guest rooms and villas set on a quiet stretch of beach. The guest rooms are spacious and designed with a modern Thai theme, and the best are the villas on the beach. While the area may be quiet, the resort's restaurants, spa, gorgeous swimming pool, and even free Wi-Fi will keep you occupied.

For a smaller resort experience, **Baan Krating Resort** (28 Mu 7, Khuk Khak, Takua Pa, tel. 07/648-5188 or 07/648-5189, www.baankrating.com, 2,000B), next to Khao Lak-Lam Ru National Park, has rustic grounds set in the cliffs overlooking the ocean and peppered with wooden bungalows connected via walkway. Each of the guest rooms is individually decorated, but you won't have to do without nice sheets and decent baths if you decide to stay here, as the bungalows, although not brand new, are definitely not in the budget category. The pool and common areas are small, as is the resort, but there's a restaurant on the premises, and the view of Khao Lak Bay is amazing. This is definitely a place for the young and agile: Depending on where your bungalow is, you may be climbing stairs.

The **Suwan Palm Resort** (30/27 Mu 7, Khuk Khak, Takua Pa, tel. 07/648-5830, www.suwanpalm.com, 3,000B) is on the same beach as some of Khao Lak's most expensive properties, and although it's not a luxury chain, it does offer guests clean, modern guest rooms, a nice swimming pool, a bar and restaurant on the premises, and even a small spa. The facilities are small but sufficient for those whose primary goal is to enjoy the beach. Low-season rates can be an excellent value.

The **Ramada Resort Khao Lak** (59 Mu 5, Khuk Khak, Takua Pa, tel. 07/642-7777, www.ramadakhaolak.com, 3,500B), though not quite as nice as Le Meridien, is a nice new resort set on a beautiful strip of beach. The guest rooms are large and modern, and some have unobstructed views of the Andaman Sea. Pool villas are compact but a great value for those who want some privacy. The property's main swimming pool, which is just behind the beach, is massive. There is also a spa, a fitness center, and an activity program for kids.

The JW Marriott Khao Lak (41/12 Mu 3, Khuk Khak, Khao Lak, tel. 081/270-9760, www.marriott.com, 4,000B) is a gorgeous, massive luxury resort with expansive grounds and a prime location right on the beach. Rooms are large, modern, and tastefully decorated with regional art and textiles. The central swimming pool is enormous. Additional facilities include a fitness center, full-service spa, and a kids' club. You definitely will not want for anything at this resort, and though it isn't cheap by any means, it's a good value considering what you get for your money. There is a good variety of food and drink on the premises, or you can walk out for local food. This resort is very popular with families and has good facilities and rooms for small children.

★ **Le Meridien Khao Lak** (9/9 Mu 1, Khuk Khak, Takua Pa, tel. 07/642-7500, www.starwoodhotels.com, 5,000B) is one of the nicest resorts in the area. The nine-hectare grounds are lush and well manicured, with a large child-friendly pool and direct beach access. The guest rooms are modern, airy, and comfortable, with dark-wood details and crisp linens. The villas are spacious, although they can cost significantly more than the rooms. There's a beautiful spa on the premises and a charming Thai restaurant. Although this is a large chain resort, there's no generic feeling here.

The small, luxurious **Sarojin** (60 Mu 2, Khuk Khak, Takua Pa, tel. 07/648-5830, www.sarojin.com, 7,000B) resort, located right on the beach, has large, comfortable guest rooms and suites filled with modern Thai-style furnishings. The grounds are lush and spacious and include shaded *salas* (pavilions) for lounging at the large modern pool as well as a high-end spa. The resort's restaurant and bar options are a little pricey, but the breakfast, included in most rates, has lots of variety and is served 'til late. Service in general is excellent and attentive, and this is a great choice for a romantic getaway or honeymoon.

Casa de La Flora (67/213 Mu 5, Khuk Khak, Takua Pa, tel. 07/642-8999, www.casadelaflora.com, 7,000B), not to be confused with the larger, less expensive La Flora Resort and Spa, is a modern, minimalist, high-end, small boutique resort on the beach. All accommodations are suites or villas, and most have fantastic views of the beach. The architecture, simple materials, and very basic shapes are striking. Stand-alone villas are basic concrete boxes with ample windows to allow in plenty of natural light. There is also a large, beautiful swimming pool on the grounds, as well as a spa, fitness center, and restaurant.

Just south of the Khao Lak area, and only a few kilometers from the Sarasin Bridge to Phuket, is the ★ **Aleenta Phang-Nga** (33 Mu 5, Khok Kloi, Takua Pa, tel. 02/508-5333, www.aleenta.com, 12,000B), at the top of the class of small boutique resorts in Thailand. The villas are swanky and contemporary, with a blend of Mediterranean and Thai styling; some are full apartments with living areas and small private pools. The common areas are small, but the restaurant has an excellent East-West menu. Little touches, including iPods in every guest room and scented oil burners, will make you feel pampered. This is definitely a place you're likely to find incognito movie stars.

Food

For a little bit of everything, and cocktails, too, head to the superpopular **Smile Khaolak Restaurant** (5/15 Mu 3, Petchkasem Rd., tel. 083/391-2600, 11am-10pm daily, 200B). The menu features mostly standard Thai dishes, including basics such as spring rolls and curries, but it also has an extensive vegetarian menu. The setting is casual but pretty—lots of bamboo and Thai art fill the dining room. Smile is more than a few steps above a shophouse restaurant; make sure to call for reservations. The restaurant is filled with mostly foreign tourists, not a particularly authentic place but a good choice nonetheless.

For straightforward Thai food, head to **Everyday Lazy House** (89 Mu 3, Petchkasem Rd. at Bang Niang Market, tel. 081/397-2802, 4pm-11pm daily, 300B). The menu features lots of fresh seafood, and also traditional Thai favorites and some very yummy desserts. There is live music many nights, and of course lots of cold beer. This is another very popular restaurant with tourists. There are also cooking classes taught by the staff; call ahead to arrange one.

Hill Tribe Restaurant (13/22 Mu 6, Petchkasem Rd., Khao Lak, tel. 086/283-0933, 1pm-10pm daily, 200B) isn't entirely authentic northern Thai food, but it is a lot more interesting than the basic, tourist-friendly Thai food you'll find at resorts and guesthouses all over the region. Dishes such as banana flower salad and baked duck are worth trying; they also offer a *khan toke* meal, which is essentially a set meal served on a single tray featuring sticky rice and Burmese curry. The dining room here is very casual—triangle pillows, mats, and low tables so you can sit on the floor and eat, though you can choose to sit at a conventional table, too.

Enzo, Bistro Fusion Japanese (62/2 Mu 5, Khuk Khak, Khao Lak, tel. 07/648-6671, 1pm-11pm daily during high season, opens at 3pm during low season, 600B) specializes in fresh sushi and sashimi but also offers other Japanese items, such as tempura and grilled fish and meat. There is a very popular sushi buffet on many evenings during high season. The restaurant is comfortable and homey, and there is nice outdoor seating, too.

Every town needs at least one English pub, and in Khao Lak that's **Mars Bar** (19/12 Mu 6, Khuk Khak, Khao Lak, tel. 084/746-5951, 8am-11pm daily, 200B). Quiz nights, beer, chips, and kidney pies are all to be found here. The dining room itself isn't much more than a typical Thai shophouse, and the vibe here is very friendly and unpretentious.

The pizza at **La Piccola Maria Pizzeria** (30/27 Mu 7, Petchkasem Rd., Khao Lak, tel. 087/803-3919, 8am-9pm daily, 250B) isn't going to blow you away, but considering that you are in the middle of a tropical beach area in Asia, these guys do a credible job. They also serve pasta, salad, and some grilled meat, and all food is available for takeout. The little corner restaurant can get very crowded, though with indoor and outdoor seating it can accommodate dozens of people at once.

Transportation

The easiest way to get to Phang Nga is to fly into **Phuket International Airport** (tel. 07/632-7230 to 07/632-7237, www.phuket-airportthai.com). Since the airport is in the northern part of the island, it's less than an hour's drive from the Sarasin Bridge to Phang Nga. Metered taxis from the airport will drive you to Phang Nga for 300-1,000 baht, depending on where you're going. If you're heading for Khao Lak, expect to pay around 700 baht.

If you're driving, Phang Nga is best reached by car by driving along Highway 4 until you reach Phang Nga, which will be well signed in English.

Buses running from Bangkok to Phuket will always stop in Phang Nga along the way as long as you let the driver know that's where you're going (since Phang Nga is the only land crossing to the island).

KO PHRA THONG

เกาะพระทอง

Separated from the mainland by a channel, mudflats, and mangroves, this little island, just 90 square kilometers (35 sq mi), is named Phra Thong, or golden Buddha, based on a legend that shipwrecked pirates buried a gold statue of the Buddha somewhere on the island. These days, there are no pirates around, and the treasure has never been found, but the island is home to a handful of fishing villages and just a couple of ecofriendly resorts. The beaches on the west side of the island are beautiful, serene, and relatively untouched by commercialism. In addition to the mangroves, sea grass, and patches of rainforest, the island is home to macaques, otters, and lemurs, to name just a few of the small animals you might run into. It's also home to sea turtles that come to bury their eggs on the shore every year. Although the island and neighboring Ko Ra together form one of the newest national parks in the country, there are no national park amenities.

Sports and Recreation

There are plentiful opportunities to hike and walk the island, although there are no established marked trails. If you are staying on the island, the resort will provide you with a map of the areas you can safely explore.

Accommodations

The **Golden Buddha Resort** (131 Mu 2, Ko Phra Thong, tel. 08/7055-4099, www.goldenbuddharesort.com, 3,500B) is a small, quiet, ecofriendly resort on the west coast of the island. Here you'll find beach yoga and wooden bungalows close to the water, without the typical crowds or prices. You have to forgo luxuries such as air-conditioning and reliable Internet access, but if you're looking for a quiet, remote place on the shore, this is a beautiful spot to relax and unwind. There are also larger houses available for groups.

You can also camp on the island, as it's a national park, although right now there are no bungalows, tent rentals, or canteens, so you have to bring everything you need with you, including water.

Food

There's really no tourism infrastructure set up on the island, so finding food is challenging. If you're staying at the island's resort, they'll make sure to feed you. Otherwise, you may be able to find someone to prepare a meal for you in the villages, slightly inland. If you're coming for the day or camping, pack food and water.

Transportation

To get to Ko Phra Thong, you'll first have to find your way to the Kuraburi pier. If you're driving, take Highway 4 to the Kuraburi district, which is south of Ranong Province and north of Takua Pa and Si Phang Nga National Park. From the pier in Kuraburi, there are no scheduled boats. You can either negotiate with a longtail captain to take you, or if you are staying at the Golden Buddha Resort, they will arrange to have someone pick you up. Expect to pay 1,000-1,500 baht each way, even if you arrange it through the hotel.

★ MU KO SIMILAN NATIONAL PARK

The **Similan Islands** are a group of nine islands located about 50 miles off the coast of Thailand, west of Khao Lak. They are considered to have the best diving in all of Thailand and some of the best in the world. Here you'll find plenty of colorful reefs and plankton blooms (during the hot season) attracting sharks, rays, and tropical fish. Other parts of the island grouping are more rugged, with boulder formations offering more adventurous diving. There are also great night-diving spots where you'll see squid, crustaceans, and other creatures. These islands can be visited on day trips from Phuket and Khao Lak, but many people choose multiday live-aboards.

Because the Similan Islands are part of a national marine park, **Mu Ko Similan National Park** (tel. 07/645-3272), and are far from the mainland, access to them is restricted. Depending on the time of year you visit, you will be able to visit some of the islands, but not all, and you'll have to visit them as part of an organized diving or day tour. Though it is frustrating not to have free access to these islands, it is probably for the better, as they (and the coral that has made them so popular) are already starting to show signs of wear and tear from the hundreds of tourists who visit each week.

Beaches and Islands

As islands go, the Similans initially seem less stunning than some of the islands in Phang Nga Bay, with their dramatic limestone formations and beautiful surrounding waters. The Similans are covered in foliage and boulders and are completely uninhabited. But those islands that do have sandy beaches (some do not) have gorgeous light sand thanks to the abundant coral reefs in the area. And once you go below the surface of the water, you'll discover not only coral reefs but underwater rock formations that attract an astounding diversity of marinelife.

The largest and most popular of the islands in this archipelago is **Ko Similan.** It and **Ko Miang** are the only two islands visitors are allowed to land on. Both are run by the National Parks of Thailand, which provides very limited accommodations and food service on each.

However you plan your trip, the islands are only open for visitors between November and May; they close completely during the rainy season.

Day Trips

Many of the diving companies listed in Phuket and Khao Lak offer day trips for either diving or snorkeling. It's a long day, as the trip is either 3 hours on a ferryboat or 90 minutes by speedboat, but if you only have a day and want to see this amazing area, it's a great opportunity. Four companies that offer day trips are **Wicked Diving** (4/17 Mu 7, Khao Lak, tel. 07/648-5868, www.wickeddiving.com), **Khao Lak Explorer** (13/43 Mu 7, Petchkasem Rd., Khao Lak, tel. 07/648-5308, www.khaolak-explorer.com), **Liquid Liveboards** (13/43 Mu 7, Khao Lak, tel. 07/648-5069, www.

liquid-adventure.com), and **Sea Dragon Dive Center** (5/51 Mu 7, Petchkasem Rd., Khao Lak, tel. 07/648-5420, www.seadragon-divecenter.com).

Trips generally include transfer from your hotel or guesthouse, breakfast, boat to the Similans, and diving or snorkeling equipment. Rates start at 2,500 baht for snorkeling or 4,800 baht for diving, plus national park fees (700B pp).

Overnight Trips and Camping

The only way to stay overnight on Ko Similan or Ko Miang is to stay at one of the park's bungalows or campsites. These are basic bungalows and cabins with running water and electricity. Costs are between 1,000 and 2,000 baht per night, per room. Book accommodations with the Department of National Parks (tel. 02/562-0760, np_income@dnp.go.th). Once the reservation is booked, you must transfer full payment to the National Parks by bank wire (or at a Krung Thai Bank or ATM in Thailand).

Tour companies that offer overnight trips to the islands will make arrangements in advance for you. Even if you do make your own arrangements, there is no ferry between these islands and the mainland or Phuket, so you must contact a tour company for transportation.

Live-Aboards

The most common way to see the Similan Islands, and the world below them, is on a live-aboard boat, where you'll dive during the day and eat, sleep, and hang out on the boat the rest of the time. The quality and size of live-aboards vary tremendously from tour company to tour company (and the type of boat a tour company uses is not necessarily indicative of the quality of dive instruction or supervision you will get). Nearly all of the dive companies listed in Phuket and Khao Lak do live-aboard trips to the Similan Islands. Four companies that offer live-aboard trips are **Wicked Diving** (4/17 Mu 7, Khao Lak, tel. 07/648-5868, www.wickeddiving.com), **Khao**

Lak Explorer (13/43 Mu 7, Petchkasem Rd., Khao Lak, tel. 07/648-5308, www.khaolakex-plorer.com), **Liquid Liveboards** (13/43 Mu 7, Khao Lak, tel. 07/648-5069, www.liquid-adventure.com), and **Sea Dragon Dive Center** (5/51 Mu 7, Petchkasem Rd., Khao Lak, tel. 07/648-5420, www.seadragondivecenter.com).

Transportation

If you're not going to the islands on a live-aboard, you can take one of the **National Parks ferries,** which run from September to May. The boat leaves the Thap Lamu Port at 8:30am and takes about 1.5 hours to get to the National Parks headquarters on Similan Island. Boats returning to the mainland depart at 1:30pm. Round-trip fare is 2,700 baht per person.

MU KO SURIN NATIONAL PARK

Mu Ko Surin National Park (tel. 07/647-2145), a group of five islands called the **Surin Islands,** is about 35 miles from the mainland, due west from Kuraburi. It is known for its impressive coral reefs and **Richelieu Rock,** a rock pinnacle jutting out of the ocean that attracts whale sharks. These islands are accessible only by live-aboard trips from Phuket, but if you're staying in Khao Lak, you can visit on a day trip.

Beaches and Islands

Ko Surin Nua and **Ko Surin Tai,** adjacent to each other, are the largest and the most popular of this group of islands. Ko Surin Tai is where the national park office is located, as well as some camping facilities, bungalows, and canteens. Some of the Surin Islands are inhabited by small groups of Moken people who live in a larger group on Ko Surin Tai.

The group of islands is hilly and covered in vegetation. Aside from the excellent coral reefs that fringe some of the islands, they are close enough to each other, and the surrounding waters are shallow enough, that it's possible to walk from Ko Surin Nua to Ko Surin Tai during certain times. **Chong Chark Bay,** which connects the two, offers stunning views of the islands and surrounding clear water.

Access to both islands is very limited. Visitors are not permitted to wander the island freely. There are no similar restrictions on the open water, though, so your best bet for exploration is by longtail boat tour, which can be arranged through the national park office. You can also rent snorkeling equipment there if you didn't bring your own.

These islands are only open for visitors between November and May; they close completely during the rainy season.

Day Trips

Because the islands are farther north than the Similans, it's only possible to do day trips from Khao Lak. Many diving shops in Khao Lak offer daylong diving and snorkeling trips, including **Wicked Diving** (4/17 Mu 7, Khao Lak, tel. 07/648-5868, www. wickeddiving.com), **Khao Lak Explorer** (13/43 Mu 7, Petchkasem Rd., Khao Lak, tel. 07/648-5308, www.khaolakexplorer.com), **Liquid Liveboards** (13/43 Mu 7, Khao Lak, tel. 07/648-5069, www.liquid-adventure. com), and **Sea Dragon Dive Center** (5/51 Petchkasem Rd., Mu 7, Khao Lak, tel. 07/648-5420, www.seadragondivecenter.com). These trips will include transport from your hotel to the pier, speedboat or slow boat to the Surin Islands (about 1 hour or about 4 hours), snorkeling and diving, lunch, more snorkeling and diving, and transport back. Rates with most companies start at 3,000 baht for snorkeling and 5,500 baht for diving.

Overnight Trips and Camping

Many diving shops also organize overnight trips to the islands. Accommodations, available through the Department of National Parks, are basic wooden bungalows and cabins with running water and fan cooling. All are located on Ko Surin Tai. Prices are 2,000-3,000 baht per night. Book accommodations with the Department of National Parks (tel. 02/562-0760, np_income@dnp.go.th). Once the reservation is booked, you must transfer full payment to the National Parks by bank wire (or at a Krung Thai Bank or ATM in Thailand).

Tour companies that offer overnight trips to the islands will make arrangements in advance for you. Even if you do make your own arrangements, there is no ferry between these islands and the mainland or Phuket, so you must contact a tour company for transportation.

Live-Aboards

Live-aboards are the best way to see as much of the Surin Islands as possible, especially if you are an experienced diver. The quality and size of live-aboards vary tremendously from tour company to tour company (and the type of boat a tour company uses is not necessarily indicative of the quality of dive instruction or supervision you will get). There are fewer dive companies doing live-aboards to the Surin Islands than the Similan Islands, and nearly all of them are based in Khao Lak. Four such outfitters are **Wicked Diving** (4/17 Mu 7, Khao Lak, tel. 07/648-5868, www.wickeddiving.com), **Khao Lak Explorer** (13/43 Mu 7, Petchkasem Rd., Khao Lak, tel. 07/648-5308, www.khaolakexplorer. com), **Liquid Liveboards** (13/43 Mu 7, Khao Lak, tel. 07/648-5069, www.liquid-adventure. com), and **Sea Dragon Dive Center** (5/51 Petchkasem Rd., Mu 7, Khao Lak, tel. 07/648-5420, www.seadragondivecenter.com).

Transportation

If you're going through a tour company or travel agent, they will arrange transportation for you and will likely even include transfer from your hotel. If you are trying to get to the Surin Islands on your own, there is a **ferry** run by the national parks department that runs from September to mid-May and departs daily at 9am from Kuraburi Port, which is about 60 miles north of Khao Lak. The trip takes about 2.5 hours to get to the National Parks headquarters on Ko Surin Nua. Tickets cost 1,500 baht. Boats returning to the mainland depart at 1pm. Round-trip fare is 1,100-1,700 baht per person. If you go this route, make sure you contact the Department of National Parks (tel. 07/647-2145) to confirm that it is still running before making your plans around it.

In Kuraburi, there are some travel agents who can arrange passage on a speedboat or another vessel making the journey. One such agency is **Kuraburi Greenview Travel** (www.toursurinislands.com), part of the Kuraburi Greenview Resort (140/89 Mu 3, Kura, Kuraburi, tel. 07/640-1400, www.kuraburigreenviewresort.com).

SI PHANG NGA NATIONAL PARK

อุทยานแห่งชาติศรีพังงา

Mostly rainforest on a rugged mountain range, **Si Phang Nga National Park** (8:30am-6pm daily, 400B) has the 60-meter-high (197 ft-high) **Namtok Tam Nang** waterfall and a number of smaller waterfalls. There are a limited number of marked trails in the park; on them are ample opportunities to spot rare birds, including hornbills. There are small bungalows for rent as well as a campground, but this park, unlike most others in the region, does not have a beach. Although the names are similar, this is not the same park as Ao Phang Nga National Park.

Sports and Recreation

There are a few short marked **hiking trails** in the park. The nicest is actually the shortest, at just over 1.5 kilometers (1 mi), starting at the **Tam Nang waterfall**. From there, you head up to a viewpoint in the forest where you can see the mangrove swamps edging out into the sea.

Transportation

The national park is located between Kuraburi and Takua Pa on Highway 4. If you're driving, you'll see signs from the highway for the national park and the Tam Nang waterfall. Follow signs for either, as the park's headquarters are right next to the waterfall. The park is east of Highway 4.

Krabi   กระบี่

With a rugged coastline and white-sand beaches, the former fishing area of Krabi is probably the most beautiful province on the mainland of Thailand if you're looking for a beach destination. Like the island of Phuket, Krabi has a mountainous green interior broken up by highlands and some plains as well as an irregular coastline creating lots of small bays and beaches. Right off the coast of Krabi are some of the most beautiful limestone rock formations in the Andaman Sea, which offer great opportunities for rock climbing, if you're feeling adventurous, or sea kayaking through some of the caves worn into the rocks, if you prefer a less strenuous approach. The best beaches in Krabi are located in the center of the province, around Rai Le and Nang, and you'll have to see them to understand just how beautiful a simple beach can be. It's not just the water and the sand, although the crystal-clear blue Andaman Sea and clean, fine sand certainly help. It's the surrounding cliffs and luxuriant tree greenery as well as the view to the small islands off the coast that create a landscape like nowhere else in the world. Krabi Province is also technically home to some of the best islands in region—Ko Phi Phi and Ko Lanta—although many people will travel to these from Phuket or Trang, as they are about halfway between those locations and Krabi. Although Krabi certainly has its share of luxury resorts catering to vacationers' every whim, the region is nowhere near as built up as Phuket is. Getting to some of the popular beaches involves taking a boat from the mainland—although Krabi is not an island, there are many spots where no roads go. Maybe because it is slightly less accessible, Krabi also has a more rugged feel to it.

KRABI TOWN
เมืองกระบี่

Most people pass through Krabi Town on their way to the beaches or skirt it entirely on their way from the Krabi airport to the boat pier. While there's no reason to stay in Krabi Town unless you're on a really tight budget, as it's not close to the beach and the available accommodations are not quite up to international standards, it's an interesting place to spend a few hours, if only to see what life is like away from the beaches. The town is set on the Krabi River, an estuary that empties into the Andaman Sea farther down, and there are some picturesque wooden houses built on stilts, although you may find some of the town less charming and appealing due to its urbanized feel. Krabi Town does have some of the most interesting and creative statues-cum-traffic lights in Thailand. If that's not enough to hold your attention for very long (they're not *that* interesting), there's also a **night market** (Khong Kha Rd., right next to the Chao Fa pier, 6pm-10pm daily) where visitors often stop to take photos or grab a snack from one of the curry stalls or *satay* vendors. The **Maharat Market,** on Maharat Soi 9, opens at 3am and closes by midday daily. It's one of the largest indoor markets in the country, and although you probably won't be taking home any of the seafood or produce on offer, it's worth looking at.

BEACHES
Ao Nang Bay
อ่าวนาง

The large, sweeping **Ao Nang Bay** is the most popular beach area in Krabi, with scores of accommodations, including many large international chains. Although nowhere near as hopping as Patong, Ao Nang is nonetheless a very touristy, slightly generic resort area. Still, the physical landscape surrounding the bay is impressive—there are scores of different small islands and rock formations in view. Ao Nang also serves as a jumping-off point for day trips to the surrounding islands. Unfortunately, the beach itself is not great for swimming. There is substantial boat traffic, and also no sun chairs or umbrellas available.

Noppharat Thara Beach
หาดนพรัตน์ธารา

Just adjacent to Ao Nang is **Noppharat Thara Beach,** a long sandy beach that's technically part of a national park. Lined with casuarina trees, the beach used to be quiet and relatively undeveloped, but in recent years it has become increasingly busy and built up. Much of the overflow from Ao Nang spills out onto the southern part of this beach, but the development is creeping north, too. There are accommodations and places to eat here, though it's just a quick ride to Ao Nang. Like Ao Nang, it's not a great beach for sunbathing or swimming, though more and more people seem to be doing it. There are no sun chairs or umbrellas available to rent, and at low tide it can be a long, long walk to the water.

Klong Muang Beach
หาดคลองม่วง

The newest destination beach in Krabi is **Klong Muang Beach,** north of Ao Nang and Noppharat Thara. The beach is more remote than either, but that is changing quickly, as high-end hoteliers have "discovered" it and are building luxury resorts in the area. The beach itself isn't great for swimming. It can be very shallow depending on the tides and is also rocky in places. Still, if you want to be on the water and enjoy a relatively secluded experience, take a look at some of the accommodations options here.

★ Rai Le Beach
หาดไร่เลย์

The small **Rai Le Beach,** surrounded by limestone cliffs behind and large rock formations rising from the sea in front, is the most beautiful of the beaches in Krabi and arguably one of the most beautiful in all of Thailand. Since Rai Le is an isthmus jutting off the mainland,

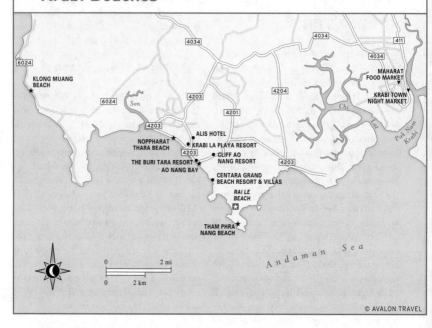

Krabi Beaches

there are actually two Rai Le beaches, one to the east and one to the west. With crystal-clear blue waters and soft sand, **West Rai Le** is both breathtaking and totally relaxed. **East Rai Le** also has lovely surrounding scenery, but it's actually mostly mudflats, and there's no sand and nowhere to lay out a towel. But that's not a problem, as you can easily walk to sandy West Rai Le in 10-15 minutes if you're staying on the east side, where accommodations are generally less expensive. Rai Le's beauty has not escaped the rest of the world's attention. More hotels have sprung up in spots where it seemed impossible to build, and it has become a destination for day-trippers doing tours of the region. Although it is still as beautiful as it always was, it's much less peaceful, especially during midday.

Tham Phra Nang Beach
หาดถ้ำพระนาง

Just a short walk from Rai Le at the end of the peninsula, the small, secluded **Tham**

Phra Nang Beach is bordered by a rocky headland on one side and limestone cliffs on the other. There's also a mystical cave here—**Tham Phra Nang Nok,** or Princess Cave—believed by local fisherfolk to house a sea princess. Although so far she hasn't been sighted by any travelers, you can check out the interesting offerings that are left for her in the cave. This beach is also a day trip destination, and during the day it can be literally overrun.

SPORTS AND RECREATION
Rock Climbing

Krabi has the best rock climbing in the country, thanks to the beautiful limestone mountains and the built-up rock-climbing industry. There are hundreds of bolted routes that will take you as high as 300 meters (984 ft) at varying levels of difficulty. This is not a sport to try without some training or proper equipment, but fortunately there are at least half a dozen rock-climbing shops offering lessons, rentals, and guided tours. Total beginners can take either full-day (2,000 baht) or half-day (1,000 baht) lessons, which include on-the-ground training and climbing. Those with experience can either hire a guide to explore the many routes in the area or just rent the necessary equipment and pick up a map from any of the shops.

Wee and Elke of **Basecamp Tonsai** (Ton Sai Beach, next to Ton Sai Bay Resort, www.basecamptonsai.com), formerly Wee's Climbing School, literally wrote the book on rock climbing in Krabi. You can buy their newly updated guide at their shop or take one of the half-day, full-day, or multiday classes they offer. Their shop also sells and rents an extensive selection of equipment. **Hot Rock** (Rai Le Beach West, tel. 07/562-1771, www.railayadventure.com) is also highly recommended because of the professionalism and personalities of their guides. They offer instruction for beginners and tours for advanced climbers. Their shop also sells and rents equipment.

Kayaking

The uneven coastline, mangrove forests, and scores of rock outcroppings and islands make Krabi an excellent area to explore with a kayak. Many guided kayaking tours (around 1,500 baht for a full day) leave from Ao Nang. On a typical tour, you'll spend some time paddling through the nearby mangrove forests and also set out to explore some of the small islands and sea caves that have been created through thousands of years of erosion. **Sea Canoe Thailand** (Ao Nang, tel. 07/569-5387) is one of about half a dozen companies offering daily kayak tours.

On Rai Le Beach West, there are rental kayaks available right on the beach (400 baht for the day). Inexperienced kayakers should be aware that currents can be surprisingly strong and that longtail boats, speedboats, and larger vessels are frequently in the water and may not see you.

Snorkeling

The islands around Krabi, including **Ko Phi Phi,** have some of the best snorkeling in the country, and it's quite possible to see not only amazingly colorful tropical fish and coral gardens with just a snorkel and a mask, but you might even spot some reef sharks. While many people choose to enjoy snorkeling on one of the day tours offered by dive shops and travel agents in Krabi, it is also possible to charter a longtail boat to take you out on

Rai Le Beach, Krabi

your own. If you're going the prepackaged-tour route, **Kon-Tiki Thailand Diving & Snorkeling Center** (61/1 Mu 2, Ao Nang, tel. 07/563-7675, www.kontiki-krabi.com) offers snorkel-only excursions (850 baht) instead of the usual boat tour of the area with snorkeling tacked on. Their tours will take you to Ko Phi Phi and the Mu Ko Hong islands, and since they're focused on snorkeling you'll spend as much time as possible in the water.

If you'd prefer to go out on your own, longtail boats can take you out to the smaller islands around Ao Nang and will generally know where you'll be able to see fish or coral. There are scores of private longtail captains in Ao Nang and West Rai Le available; prices for personalized trips are entirely negotiable, but you should expect to pay at least 1,000 baht for a few hours on the sea. Longtail boats are smaller, less comfortable, and slower than speedboats (and life preservers are generally nonexistent), so if you are planning on going out on one, it's best done for shorter distances.

rock climbing in Krabi

ACCOMMODATIONS
Ao Nang

If you want to avoid the big properties, **The Buri Tara Resort** (159/1 Mu 3, Ao Nang, tel. 07/563-8277, www.buritara.net, 3,500B), with only 69 guest rooms, is a smart, stylish choice in the budget-luxury category. The pool isn't as large as what you'll find at other resorts, and it's a few minutes' walk to the closest beach, but the property opened at the end of 2006 and the guest rooms are nicely decorated in a modern dark-wood style with some Thai touches.

The small, charming **Alis Hotel** (125 Ao Nang, tel. 07/563-8000, www.alisthailand. com, 2,500B) has a unique Mediterranean design and comfortable guest rooms with luxurious baths. For nice guest rooms and a good location about 10 minutes from the beach, it's a good choice. There's a nice rooftop pool and a bar on the premises, but the grounds aren't massive, and the lack of things such as elevators are a reminder that it's not quite a boutique resort but rather a small hotel.

Although not as beautifully kept up as the Centara Grand, the large **Krabi La Playa Resort** (143 Mu 3, Ao Nang, tel. 07/563-7015 to 07/563-7020, www.krabilaplaya.com, 5,100B) has a great pool area and roomy, well-furnished guest rooms done in a modern Thai style. It is right on the beach and an easy walk to town. Some of the guest rooms have swim-up access to the pool.

The **Cliff Ao Nang Resort** (85/2 Mu 2, Ao Nang, tel. 07/563-8117, www.thecliffkrabi. com, 8,000B) is a beautiful property with many design elements from traditional bungalows but completely modern, comfortable guest rooms. Although there are some rustic elements, they're purely aesthetic—there's not a trace of backpacker to be found. The semioutdoor baths are spacious and have rain showerheads, the restaurant is elegant, and the pool is large and minimalist so as not to detract from the natural beauty found in the surrounding cliffs and ocean. This is definitely a hip, romantic resort designed for couples, although kids are welcome.

The **Centara Grand Beach Resort and Villas** (396-396/1 Mu 2, Ao Nang, tel. 07/563-7789, www.centralhotelsresorts.com, 8,000B) has large, beautiful guest rooms with stunning ocean views, top-class resort amenities, and excellent service, all set on its own small private bay with a small beach right next to Ao Nang. If you don't feel like leaving the compound, there are five different places to eat within Centara as well as a spa and multiple swimming pools. If you're looking for a big resort experience in Krabi, this is probably the best price you'll find in the category, and especially in the off-season, when you'll pay about half the price; it's a bargain.

Noppharat Thara

Sunda Resort (19 Mu 3, Noppharat Thara, tel. 07/566-1262, www.sundaresort.com, 1,200B) has all the basics a traveler would want in a small resort—a swimming pool, small on-site restaurant, decent buffet breakfasts, and clean, modern rooms. The Sunda Resort is surprisingly stylish for a three-star resort, though because of limited facilities it is not in any way a luxury property. To get to the beach, you'll need to walk about 15 minutes; there is also a hotel shuttle available.

For a slightly more upscale resort, try the **Baan Habeebee** (25 Mu 5, Noppharat Thara, tel. 07/566-1210, www.baanhabeebee.com, 4,000B), also about 10 minutes on foot to the beach and a short shuttle bus ride to Ao Nang. The mostly wooden structures on this leafy resort have a tropical island feel, as does the pretty swimming pool. Most of the stand-alone bungalows have big sitting porches, too. This is a halal resort, so there is no beer served. It is also close to a local mosque, so you will hear the call to prayer starting early in the morning.

Klong Muang

Nakamanda Resort (126 Mu 3, Klong Muang, tel. 07/756-8200, www.nakamanda.com, 4,000B) is a new all-villas resort on Klong Muang. It has a great location on the beach, right across from a small uninhabited island (you can even walk there during low tide). The villas and common areas are designed in a Mediterranean-meets-Balinese style, with clean, white buildings topped with terraced roofs. Inside the rooms, the decor is subtly tropical and inoffensive. The large swimming pool looks out onto the beach, though it's not a great one for swimming. Staff is attentive and friendly.

The **Phulay Bay, A Ritz-Carlton Reserve** (111 Mu 3, Klong Muang, tel. 07/562-8111, www.ritzcarlton.com, 10,000B) is undoubtedly the most luxurious resort in the area. Rooms are palatial (the smallest are about 800 square feet) and include all the amenities one would expect at a Ritz-Carlton—flat-screen TVs, massive bathrooms, DVD players, free Wi-Fi, and minibars. Some have small private pools overlooking the ocean. The rooms are bright and airy with lots of traditional Thai elements. The common spaces make full use of the region's beautiful woodwork. The location, on a small bump of beach on Klong Muang, is very secluded, though it's still only 10 minutes by car to Ao Nang.

Rai Le Beach

Since it's set on the mudflats side of Rai Le, you'll have to walk about 15 minutes to get to the good part of the beach from **Sunrise Tropical Resort** (39 Mu 2, Ao Nang, Rai Le Beach, tel. 07/562-2599, www.sunrisetropical.com, 3,500B), but it is a great value if you want to stay in a well-appointed beach bungalow without paying five-star resort prices. The bungalows are modern, spacious, and clean, the baths have outdoor showers and are nicely fitted, and the grounds are leafy. The larger villas are enormous for the price. Although it's a small property with only 28 bungalows, there's a pool, a small restaurant, and an Internet café.

If you can get one of the bungalows at ★ **Railei Beach Club** (Rai Le Beach, Ao Nang, tel. 07/562-2582, www.raileibeachclub.com, 5,000B), consider yourself lucky. A cluster of houses set right on the beach, this is neither a resort nor a hotel. Each of the homes is individually owned and rented out by owners when they're not in town, and they vary in size from cozy bungalow to four-bedroom house. The design of each is a little different, but they're all wooden bungalow houses with clean, comfortable bedrooms and baths. Some have elegant dark-wood furnishings; others are a little more rustic. The larger buildings have their own kitchens and entertaining space, perfect for a family or larger group, or a couple that wants to spend an extended time. There's no pool, although it is set on what is arguably the most beautiful part of the beach. Although it's not a resort, there's daily maid service, and if you want, they'll arrange to have someone come to your bungalow and cook dinner for you.

"Beach bungalow" doesn't do the **Rayavadee Premier** (214 Mu 2, Ao Nang, tel. 02/301-1850, www.rayavadee.com, 15,000B) justice. The individual accommodations are more like small luxury homes set in a quiet, secluded part of the beach. This is one of the most indulgent places to stay on Rai Le, as is clear from the hefty rates you'll pay. The property has nearly 100 bungalows, so there are lots of amenities, including tennis courts, a fitness center, and a handful of restaurants. While most people staying on Rai Le have to arrive at the pier on the east side of the beach and walk to their resort, the Rayavadee will arrange to have a private boat pick you up from Krabi Town and deliver you straight to the resort. Despite the high prices, peak season fills up months in advance, so book quickly if you're interested in staying here.

FOOD
Krabi Town

Hands down the best Thai restaurant in Krabi Town, both for food and ambience, is ★ **Ruen Mai** (315/5 Maharat Rd., tel. 07/563-1797, 11am-10pm daily, 200B). It may be filled with travelers, but don't be put off. It's worth feeling like a lemming to enjoy a meal in this verdant garden setting. The curries and other typical Thai dishes are well executed, but for something different, try the crunchy *plai sai* fried fish snacks or *kaeng som* sour curry with fish. This is also a great place for vegetarians. Although there aren't many straight veggie offerings on the menu, the kitchen will prepare just about anything you want without meat.

For a distinctly southern-Thailand breakfast dish, head to **Kanom Jin Mae Weaw** (137 Krabi-Khao Thong Rd., next to the PTT gas station, tel. 07/561-2666, 7am-noon daily, 50B) for some *kanom chin*—curry served over thin rice noodles. This very casual place has three different varieties and serves them spicy. For Western palates it may feel more appropriate to have this for dinner, but it's a morning meal, so get there early to try it.

Ao Nang

For seafood on the beach, **Wangsai Seafood Restaurant** (98 Mu 3, Ao Nang, tel. 07/563-8128, 10am-10pm daily, 300B) is a good relaxed restaurant with a view of the ocean and a large deck right on the beach. The large sign is in Thai (it's the only place with no English sign), but the menu has English translations for all the typical Thai seafood dishes, including seafood fried rice and braised fish in lime, chilies, and garlic. The restaurant is quite popular among foreign visitors.

Another popular, solid choice for seafood on the beach is the **Salathai Restaurant** (32 Mu 2, Ao Nang, tel. 07/563-7024, 9am-10pm daily, 300B). The menu has both traditional Thai dishes with seafood and some Western fare. Better to stick with the local food and seafood, which you can select yourself, and enjoy the view at this charming thatched-roof restaurant right on the water. It's not very fancy, by any standard, but the food and location are just right.

Krua Thara (82 Mu 5, Ao Nang, tel. 07/563-7361, 11am-9:30pm daily, 200B) has great seafood dishes, whether part of a traditional Thai meal or just plain grilled or fried with Thai sauce. Like most of the places to eat in Krabi, it's nothing fancy to look at, but the food is good.

Rai Le Beach

While Rai Le has some of the best beachfront property in Thailand, it's definitely not a contender for best dining options; Krabi Town and Ao Nang have much better dining. That's not to say the food is bad, but there isn't much selection—most of it is from bungalow and resort restaurants and the roti vendors on the beach in the afternoon.

TRANSPORTATION

When planning your trip, remember that Krabi Town is more than 16 kilometers (10 mi) away from the area's main attraction—the beaches. You'll likely want to head to Ao Nang, as that's where most accommodations are and where you can catch a longtail boat to one of the outer beaches or islands.

Air

The **Krabi Airport** (tel. 07/563-6541) has frequent flights from Bangkok and is served by **Thai Airways** and **Bangkok Airways** as well as the budget airlines **Nok Air, Air Asia,** and **One-Two-Go.** If you're coming in from Singapore, **Tiger Airways** also has direct flights from that city. Although the airport is comfortable and modern, it's very small, and the services inside, including food, are very limited.

From the airport, it's about a 30-minute drive to Ao Nang; there are plenty of taxis on hand to take you (400-600 baht). There is also a private airport shuttle that runs at least every hour (more frequently during high season) between the airport and Ao Nang. The fare is 150 baht, so if you're traveling with a group, it can be more economical (and faster if you happen to be staying at the last hotel on the route) to take a taxi.

It's also possible to fly into Phuket International Airport and then make the three-hour drive to Krabi. There is a minibus from the Phuket airport that goes to Krabi Town. It leaves three times daily 9am-1pm for 350 baht per person.

Boat

From Phuket, there is a boat that heads to the Noppharat Thara pier next to Ao Nang at 8am daily and goes back to Phuket at 3pm. The ride is about two hours and costs 350 baht.

Boat connections between Phi Phi and Krabi are frequent, especially during high season. There are **ferries** from Noppharat Thara pier that are currently running once daily at 3pm. The ride is about three hours and costs 550 baht. To get to Krabi from Phi Phi, there are frequent boats during high season, leaving at 9am, 10:30am, and 2:30pm.

If you're on Phi Phi, there are also ferries that leave Phi Phi at 9am for Ao Nang in Krabi and take a little under three hours.

If you are coming from Ko Lanta, boats only run during high season; otherwise, you'll have to take a minivan, which involves two short ferry crossings. During high season, ferries from Ko Lanta to Krabi leave at 8am and 1pm daily, returning at 10:30am and 2:30pm. The cost is 300 baht per person and takes about 1.5 hours.

Even if you're coming by air or ground transportation to Krabi, if you're staying in Rai Le, you'll have to take a boat to get to your ultimate destination. Although Krabi is on the mainland, there are no roads to Rai Le; you have to take a longtail boat from Ao Nang or Krabi Town. There are frequent boats from the Saphan Chaofa pier that should run around 80 baht per person (unless you arrive after the scheduled boats have stopped running, in which case you will have to negotiate with the owner of the boat). Your hotel in Rai Le will be able to arrange the transfer for you. The short trip to Rai Le can be a little treacherous, depending on the weather conditions and what you're carrying. The boats stop on East Rai Le beach, and if the tides are in when you arrive, the pier may be partially submerged in water. You have to walk, carrying your luggage, through sometimes knee-deep water, so it is essential that you pack only what you can comfortably lift over your head while walking. Once you get onto dry land, if you're staying on West Rai Le, you'll need to walk about 15 minutes to get to your final location. There are no cars or motorcycles—another reason to pack light. If you happen to be staying at the Rayavadee, they'll arrange a private boat to take you directly to the hotel—they'll even carry your stuff for you.

Bus

There are overnight buses leaving from Bangkok's Southern Bus Terminal at 5:30pm daily for the 12-hour overnight drive to Krabi. Tickets on air-conditioned luxury buses cost 850 baht and terminate in Krabi Town. Regular air-conditioned buses leave Bangkok at 7am, 4pm, and 5:30pm daily and cost 450-600 baht. There are also frequent buses to Krabi from Phuket, Ko Pha-Ngan, Surat Thani, Trang, and Hat Yai.

Car

It's relatively easy to drive to Krabi. Highway 4, which runs south down the peninsula, is the best way to go and is well signed in English for the correct turnoff to Ao Nang. Once you're in the area, many people find cars totally unnecessary, as most time is spent either on the beach or at one of the many marine sights that can't be reached by road anyway.

THAN BOK KHORANI NATIONAL PARK

อุทยานแห่งชาติธารโบกขรณี

Mostly mountainous rainforests and mangroves, the small **Than Bok Khorani National Park** (8:30am-6pm daily, 400B) also has a number of ponds, caves, and streams that seem to disappear under the limestone mountains as well as, of course, sandy beaches. There are also more than 20 small islands, really just rocks jutting out of the ocean, that are a part of the park. The best way to visit the islands is by canoe or kayak, but most do not have beaches, so it's difficult to disembark. Camping is allowed in the park, but amenities are very limited, so you'll have to bring everything with you.

Inside the park is the cave **Tham Phi Hua To,** which is believed to have been a shelter for prehistoric people living in the area; it has some prehistoric paintings of people and animals. The cave got its name, which means "big-headed ghost cave," because of the number of abnormally large human skulls found in the cave. It is also used by Buddhist monks as a temple and for meditation retreats. The cave is not accessible by land; to visit you have to take a boat. If you aren't already exploring the area by boat, or just want to visit the cave, you can pick up a longtail boat to take you there from the Bo Tho pier in Ao Luek.

Transportation

If you're staying in Ao Nang, you can get to the park either by land or by sea. It's a one-hour drive to the Bo Tho pier in Ao Luek, where you'll be able to either rent a canoe or kayak or charter one of the local boat captains to take you around. If you don't have a car, you can charter a longtail boat from Ao Nang to take you to the park and tour you around the islands (expect to pay around 1,000 baht for the trip, regardless of the number of passengers), making it a great day trip if you're hanging out in one of the more touristed areas in Krabi.

KHAO PHANOM BENCHA NATIONAL PARK

อุทยานแห่งชาติเขาพนมเบญจา

Another small national park worth visiting for a few hours because of the waterfalls and peaks is **Khao Phanom Bencha National Park** (8:30am-6pm daily, 400B). There are some short hiking trails, including one that will take you to the highest point in the area, at more than 1,200 meters (3,937 ft), and another that will bring you to a three-tiered waterfall called **Namtok Huay To,** where the water collects into 11 large pools at the base. The Tham Khao Phueng cave has stalagmites and stalactites typical of caves in the region. You can pick up a map of the park at the ranger station; the trails are easy to moderate.

Transportation

Less than 32 kilometers (20 mi) from Krabi Town, Khao Phanom Bencha National Park is best accessed either by car, *tuk tuk,* or motorcycle. If you get a ride from Krabi Town or Ao Nang, it's better to arrange round-trip transport, since when you're done exploring the park, there may not be anyone around to bring you back. If you are driving, take Pracha U Thit Road north out of Krabi Town, until you see Ban Thap Prik Health Center, where you take a left and continue heading north to the ranger station.

KHLONG THOM

คลองท่อม

Sights

The **Khlong Thom hot spring** (10B pp) is worth a visit if you happen to be in the area, particularly for the so-called **Emerald Pool,** where springwater collects in the forest, creating a strangely deep emerald or turquoise color, depending on the time of day. To see the pool at its best, come when the light is soft, either very early in the morning or just before dusk.

Right near the Emerald Pool is the **Ron Khlong Thom waterfall,** in a part of the forest with lots of small hot springs that flow into cold streams, creating a warm-water waterfall.

The **Khao Pra-Bang Khram Wildlife Sanctuary** (เขตรักษาพันธุ์สัตว์ป่า เขาประ-บางคราม, 8:30am-6pm daily, 200B), also commonly referred to as Khao Nor Chuchi, has some small trails through lowland forests and past the Emerald Pool. The sanctuary is considered the single richest site for birds in the whole region, and you're likely to spot black hornbills and kingfishers. Gurney's Pitta, of which there are less than 100 pairs estimated to exist on the planet, are known

to nest in this area. There is also camping in the sanctuary, although unlike the national parks, there are no tent rentals, so you have to come equipped.

If you're interested in archaeology, the **Wat Khlong Thom Museum** (Mu 2, Petchkasem Rd., Khlong Thom, tel. 07/562-2163, 8:30am-4:30pm daily, free) at Wat Khlong Thom houses numerous items found during an excavation of Kuan Luk Pat, commonly referred to in English as the bead mound. Items on display include tools from the Stone and Bronze Ages, pieces of pottery, coins, and colored beads said to be more than 5,000 years old.

Transportation

To get to Khlong Thom, drive on Highway 4 heading south from Krabi Town; Khlong Thom will be marked at the junction of Highway 4 and Route 4038. From there, you will see well-marked signs directing you to the Emerald Pool or the wildlife sanctuary. You can also take a public bus headed for Trang from the bus terminal outside Krabi Town and tell the driver when you board that you want to get off at Khlong Thom. These buses run nearly hourly during the day, and you'll spend less than 30 baht to get to Khlong Thom. You'll end up in a small town area and will have to find transport to the surrounding sights, but during the day there are plenty of motorcycles that will take you. Although you can sometimes find a ride back from the sanctuary or the Emerald Pool, it's best to arrange round-trip transport at least back to Khlong Thom, where you can catch a bus heading for Krabi or Trang for the rest of your journey.

Mu Ko Phi Phi

In recent decades it seems the rest of the world has discovered what residents and intrepid travelers knew all along—the Ko Phi Phi islands, a small group of islands in Krabi Province about 40 kilometers (25 mi) off of the west coast of the mainland and just south of Phang Nga Bay, are lush and beautiful, the surrounding waters warm and clear, and the marinelife astounding. The discovery may have something to do with the Leonardo DiCaprio movie *The Beach,* which was filmed in the area. Certainly the movie helped put the islands on the map, but it's the physical beauty and ease with which you can go from lazing around on the beach to snorkeling or scuba diving that will make sure it stands the test of time.

The largest island of the group and the only one with tourist accommodations, Ko Phi Phi Don is shaped like two separate islands connected together by a thin strip of land with sandy beaches on each side. The beaches along that isthmus, Ton Sai Bay on the south and Loh Dalam Bay on the north, have become very popular for day-trippers and those staying on the island. The island is only about 16 kilometers (10 mi) long, and there are no roads or motorized transportation to take you from one part to another. Instead, there are plenty of longtail boats that function like shuttle buses and taxis. The rest of the islands in the group can easily be visited via a short ride on a longtail boat taxi from Phi Phi Don, or on a longer two-hour ferry or tour boat if you're coming from Phuket or Krabi.

Originally inhabited by Muslim fisherfolk, Phi Phi Don has changed dramatically in recent years. Ton Sai Bay is jam-packed with restaurants and small shops selling everything from sunglasses to T-shirts. Where there were once only a few simple bungalows, there are now full-scale resorts with swimming pools, spas, and anything else a traveler might be interested in, although in a much lower-key manner than you'll see on Phuket. If you're visiting Phi Phi or one of the surrounding islands for the day, you'll notice scores of speedboats and ferries moored close to the shore, all bringing in visitors who can crowd the beaches during high season. Residents and enlightened guests do their best to keep the island clean, but at times you will notice some wear and tear from the hundreds of visitors who come to the island every day. It's a shame, because Phi Phi is probably one of the most beautiful islands in the Andaman region, and it increasingly feels like its beauty is on the edge of being spoiled by overly eager tour operators and irresponsible visitors.

Neighboring, smaller Ko Phi Phi Le is a stunning limestone island encircling emerald-green Maya Bay. There are no accommodations on Phi Phi Le, but it has become a huge tourist draw, with day-trippers visiting by the hundreds per day during high season. With the throngs of other people and scores of motorboats in the bay, it's amazing that the island continues to look as beautiful as it does.

BEACHES
★ Ton Sai Bay
หาดต้นไทร

The beaches along **Ton Sai Bay,** including **Hin Khom Beach** and **Long Beach** (Hat Yao), are stunningly beautiful, with white sand and mountain ranges off in the distance as well as some great opportunities for viewing the coral just off the coast. This beach area, however, is the most popular, and right behind the beach there are scores of guesthouses, bungalows, and even some bars and shops. If you want a budget backpacker experience in paradise, this is where you'll probably end up. This is also a popular place for day visitors to hang out, meaning it can become very crowded during high season.

Ranti Beach
อ่าวรันตี

Off the east coast of the larger part of Phi Phi Don, **Ranti Beach** has fewer accommodations and can only be reached from Ton Sai Bay on foot, or by speedboat or longtail, so pack light if you are planning on staying here. The beach itself is as beautiful as the rest of the island, and there is plentiful coral to view right off the coast. If you're looking for budget bungalows but want to avoid Ton Sai, Ranti is a great place to stay.

Phak Nam Beach
อ่าวผักหนาม

Phak Nam Beach has the same clear blue water and soft sand as Ranti, but is even more secluded, with very few accommodations, though this will probably be changing soon in light of all the development going on in the region. To get to this beach, you can either hike to the east side of the island or take a water taxi.

Laem Thong Beach
หาดแหลมตง

Way at the northern tip of the island, **Laem Thong Beach** is one of the quieter areas, with a long white-sand beach and only a few accommodations. This area, at a point when the island thins out to only about 200 meters (656 ft) wide, has a quiet, peaceful atmosphere and a handful of high-end resorts. It can be a little difficult to get to if you're coming from Ton Sai Bay, as it's too far to walk, and you have to travel by water, but the beach has its own pier, so you can skip the crowds and commotion and head straight here from the mainland instead.

Ko Phi Phi Le
เกาะพีพีเล

On **Ko Phi Phi Le** there are no accommodations but some beautiful places to visit either from the mainland or from Phi Phi Don. Amazing emerald water and large rock formations characterize **Maya Bay** (อ่าวมาหยา), a tiny bay on the east side of Phi Phi Le. Once you enter the bay, you'll be astounded by the beauty of the surrounding physical landscape. There's a small beach for swimming with rocky outcroppings overhead and even a tiny bit of rainforest to walk around in. There are no overnight accommodations on Maya Bay, but the place gets packed with day-trippers, so try to arrive early to enjoy a bit of the beauty without the crowds. You can go by longtail boat or speedboat, or paddle over on

view from Ko Phi Phi

your own. The bay itself is not great for snorkeling (especially because it's usually filled with boats), but if you walk across the island and through a small cave (you can't miss it, as there's only one path you can walk on), there's some better snorkeling off of that coast, including views of sea urchins and tropical fish.

Monkey Beach (Hat Ling, หาดลิง) is a fun place to visit if you want to hang out with the scores of monkeys populating this pretty little strip of sandy coast that can be reached by canoe, speedboat, or longtail boat. If you go, make sure you bring something for the monkeys to snack on—as a result of thousands of tourists visiting every year, they've grown to expect some compensation in exchange for the entertainment they're providing, and they can get a little surly and even aggressive if you disappoint them.

SPORTS AND RECREATION
Diving

Phi Phi has some of the best diving in Thailand, made even better by the fact that it's so accessible and inexpensive. There's no need to set out on a boat for days or even to stay on Phi Phi. With all of the organized dive trips from Phuket, you can easily schedule full-day trips and return to the main island at night. Most of the outfitters listed for the Andaman coast offer trips to Phi Phi. There are more than a dozen certified PADI dive shops on Phi Phi; check the PADI website (www.padi.com) for information about them. Four companies that offer diving trips off Ko Phi Phi are **Wicked Diving** (4/17 Mu 7, Khao Lak, tel. 07/648-5868, www.wickeddiving.com), **Khao Lak Explorer** (13/43 Mu 7, Petchkasem Rd., Khao Lak, tel. 07/648-5308, www.khaolakexplorer.com), **Liquid Liveboards** (13/43 Mu 7, Khao Lak, tel. 07/648-5069, www.liquid-adventure.com), and **Sea Dragon Dive Center** (5/51 Mu 7, Petchkasem Rd., Khao Lak, tel. 07/648-5420, www.seadragondivecenter.com).

Boating

Most of the boating that goes on around Phi Phi is through chartered speedboats that take visitors from island to island during the day. These trips are hugely popular, as evidenced by the number of charter boats that line the coast of Phi Phi. Many of these tours include some snorkeling as well as lunch and depart from either Phi Phi or Phuket. There are a handful of companies that offer tours, although they sell almost exclusively through third-party tour agents, and you can arrange a tour through any travel agency on the mainland or Phi Phi, or from your hotel. Because of the intermediaries, prices for the trips can vary and are negotiable, although the agent may not tell you that it's not actually their company putting together the package. Prices for a day trip around Phi Phi should run about 1,200-2,000 baht, depending on the type of vessel you're on and the number of other passengers.

If you want to cruise around the surrounding islands at your own pace, at almost any beach you can hire a longtail boat to take you from one place to another. It's quite an experience to sit back and take in the view of the Andaman Sea from one of the long, thin, colorful boats while the captain steers from behind. Compared to speedboats, longtail boats are a lot smaller and less agile in choppy waters, so they're best enjoyed if you're only doing limited island-hopping. When longtail boats are used as taxis, prices are usually fixed, and you should expect to pay 40-100 baht per trip. Chartering a boat for a fixed amount of time can cost anywhere from 400 baht, depending on the number of people and the time of year.

Kayaking

The area around the Phi Phi islands offers excellent opportunities for sea kayaking to explore the hidden bays and mangrove forests surrounding the islands. If you're just looking to paddle around close to shore, there are plenty of kayaks on the beaches available for rent. Experienced kayakers can rent kayaks and arrange to have them pulled by longtail from Phi Phi Don to Maya Bay on Phi Phi Le, which costs around 300-500 baht. You can also request that the boat's captain pick you up at a designated time and place when you're ready to return. It's possible to cross from one island to another by kayak, but weather conditions can change rapidly, and only experienced kayakers should attempt the venture.

If you're kayaking, bear in mind that Phi Phi is a very popular destination for speedboats and larger tour boats, and by midday in high season the whole area can get very crowded with larger vessels. What may seem like just an annoyance can become dangerous if you're not seen by another boat, so pay close attention to the waters around you. The quietest time for kayaking is early in the morning, before the rest of the world arrives.

ACCOMMODATIONS

Phi Phi Don was long a favorite of travelers on a budget, thanks to the cheap bungalows, especially along Ton Sai Bay, that had few amenities but the prime real estate on the island. The island was devastated during the tsunami in 2004, and most of the bungalows, resorts, and hotels have had to rebuild. Like everywhere else in Thailand, tourism is moving upscale, and the rebuilding seems to have shifted the island's focus from budget backpacker upward. Although there are still opportunities to sleep in a small shack on the beach without air-conditioning or hot water for just a few hundred baht per night, you'll find those accommodations increasingly packed together in smaller and smaller areas (namely Ton Sai), with midrange hotels and more expensive resorts popping up on the island in their place. On the luxury front, the island is increasingly getting its share of high-end resorts, too. Perhaps because Phi Phi is so beautiful and so popular, hoteliers don't seem to be trying too hard to compete with one another or to woo guests. The most common complaint that travelers have about the island is that where they stayed was overpriced and mediocre, regardless of whether it was a cheap bungalow or a high-end resort.

Ton Sai Bay

With scores of guesthouses in the area, Ton Sai Village, the small strip of flat land in the middle of the island, is a popular spot for visitors to stay. Here's where you'll find most conveniences; the majority of the island's restaurants and small shops are here, but you'll find less peace and calm.

J. J. Guesthouse (Ton Sai Village, tel. 07/560-1090, www.jjbungalow.com, 700B) offers very basic fan-cooled guest rooms in its small guesthouse. Guest rooms are clean and comfortable, and definitely good value for the money. There is a small restaurant on the property. For a little more money, you can stay at one of the bungalows, which are all air-conditioned and spacious, though simple.

Viking Natures Resort (222 Mu 7, tel. 07/581-9399, www.vikingnaturesresort.com, 1,200B) has old-fashioned wooden bungalows in a rustic, lush setting about 20 minutes on foot from Ton Sai Village. Rooms are basic wooden structures nestled in the trees. They are fan-cooled and because they're not airtight, you have to rely on a mosquito net at night to keep critters out. Larger bungalows have space for lounging and can sleep up to six people. Some parts of this resort are louder than others at night, so make sure you state your preference when you reserve.

JJ Residence (95 Mu 7, tel. 07/560-1090, www.jjresidence.com, 1,500B) is a small hotel in Ton Sai Village on the side farthest from Ton Sai Bay. Rooms are modern, clean, and comfortable, and there is a nice small swimming pool on the grounds. This is a good choice for those who want to stay right in the center of the action, but it can get loud and hectic here even during the day as it is right next to the market.

If you want to stay right near Ton Sai Bay but still feel a little pampered, the **Phi Phi Island Cabana Hotel** (58 Mu 7, tel. 07/560-1170, www.phiphi-cabana.com, 4,200B) is a nice choice for a not-too-expensive resort. The guest rooms are well maintained, and the grounds are nicely designed. The guest rooms are all decorated in a modern Thai style and feel much less rustic than bungalows you'll find scattered along the beach, and there's a nice large swimming pool with comfortable chairs. The hotel is also very well located on Ton Sai between two beaches, so visitors can take advantage of the more inexpensive longtail boats in the area to hop from place to place. The only trade-off is that with more than 150 guest rooms, it's not quite a small resort.

Laem Thong Beach

At the northern tip of the island, in secluded Laem Thong Beach, is **Phi Phi Natural Resort** (Mu 8, Laem Thong Beach, tel. 07/561-3010, www.phiphinatural.com, 3,300B). The standard guest rooms and cottages have a rustic feel to them, with lots of exposed wood and simple, basic furnishings. It's nothing luxurious or fancy, but there's air-conditioning and a small swimming pool with an ocean view. The resort is tucked away from any crowds and feels secluded and relaxed, more like a summer vacation at camp. There are also larger cottages that are great for families.

For something a little more predictable, if with slightly less personality, the **Holiday Inn Phi Phi Island** (Mu 8, Laem Thong Beach, tel. 07/562-7300, www.phiphi.holidayinn.com, 4,000B) has nice individual bungalows, many with ocean views. The swimming pool is not huge but opens onto the beach. Bungalows are decorated in a modern, somewhat generic style but have some small Thai details. Many have their own small balconies or porches.

The least expensive option on this part of the island is the three-star **P.P. Erawan Palms Resort** (Mu 8, Laem Thong Beach, tel. 07/562-7500, www.pperawanpalms.com, 2,500B), a pretty, midsize resort with standard rooms and stand-alone bungalows. Rooms are modern, clean, and pretty, with basic wood furnishings and modern bathrooms. The little swimming pool overlooks the beach, which is usually quiet and uncrowded.

Ao Lo Bakao

This beach's only resort, **Outrigger Phi Phi Island Resort and Spa** (Ao Lo Bakao, tel. 07/562-8900, www.outrigger.com, 6,500B), is definitely on the higher end of the beach bungalow experience, although it's not quite a five-star luxury resort. The bungalows and villas are done in a traditional Thai design with thatched roofs that fade into the surrounding palm trees and are designed to let in as much light and ocean view as possible. There are a spa and a few restaurants on the premises as well as a fantastic swimming pool looking out onto the Andaman Sea. This is a great place to stay if you're looking for seclusion and are happy to idle your vacation away reading books and listening to the waves, although at low tide the shore is too rocky and shallow to swim. Getting off the resort during the day can be a little tricky—the resort has infrequent shuttle boats running to Ton Sai Bay, but if you miss them and need to charter a private boat from the hotel, the prices are steep.

Ao Toh Ko

Ao Toh Ko Bungalows (Ao Toh Ko, Phi Phi Island, tel. 08/1731-9470, 350B) offers supercheap, basic sleeping accommodations with lovely beach views in a quiet, secluded beach on the east coast of the island. If you're on a budget, or just want to experience what Phi Phi was like before all the other travelers came, these little bungalows will feel charming and quaint, and the little bar and inexpensive restaurant on the premises will feel like an added extra. If you're higher maintenance, this is not the place for you, however: There's no air-conditioning or hot water in most of the guest rooms.

FOOD

Come nighttime, Ton Sai Bay is ground zero for food and entertainment, and if you're staying on one of the more remote beaches, the action can be a welcome change from all that peace and quiet. Almost all of the resorts on the island have small restaurants serving Thai food. Western food tends to be more than well represented at the stand-alone shops, perhaps to feed all the hungry Americans, Europeans, and Australians who flock here.

Even if you'll feel a little guilty eating baked goods on a tropical island, ★ **Pee Pee Bakery** (Ton Sai Bay, 7am-8pm daily, 40B) is hard to resist. The shop's glass display cases of doughnuts, breads, and cakes seem to beckon every traveler, especially around breakfast time. The bakery also serves Thai food, sandwiches, and pizza, all of which are well prepared.

During the day, the seafood restaurants right on the edge of the beach overlooking Ton Sai Bay are usually filled with day-trippers on arranged tours. At night, these restaurants feel less like food conveyer belts and are pleasant places to drink a cold Singha over dinner and enjoy the view. **Chao Koh** (tel. 07/560-1083, 11am-9pm daily, 250B) is one with good seafood and a nice view. Cuisine here is traditional Thai seafood dishes. The food is good, but don't expect anything too creative.

Anna's Restaurant (111 Mu 7, tel. 085/923-2596, 7:30am-9pm daily, 250B) in Ton Sai Village is something of an institution in Phi Phi, though the menu is just basic Thai food, with some Western/European dishes, and drinks (nothing out of the ordinary for Thailand). Service is consistent and reliable, and it's a big enough restaurant that you can almost always get a table. If you just want an easy place to sit and eat decent food, you won't be disappointed here.

Hidden behind the Outrigger Resort in Loh Ba Gao is this tiny casual Thai place, **Knock Out Bar** (Loh Ba Gao, tel. 087/278-7901, 11am-9pm daily, 200B), owned by a family that also runs longtail boat tours of the island. The bamboo bar and thatched roof feel just right after a long day of island-hopping, and the food is mostly good, basic Thai food that's freshly prepared. This is also a fun place to hang out and have a drink, as everyone is very friendly and relaxed.

Le Grande Blu (Ton Sai Village, tel. 081/979-9739, 11am-10pm daily, 600B), a small French and Thai fusion restaurant, is considered by some to be the best restaurant on the island. The pretty, all-wood dining room is just a step nicer than most nonresort restaurants here. And whether you want to try the excellent European fare or prefer to stick with Thai food, the quality of the food and service are also a step above. Western desserts, including profiteroles and crème brûlée, will really hit the spot if you are craving a bit of non-Thai food! This is Ko Phi Phi, so don't expect a fine dining experience; you won't be refused service if you show up in shorts.

Although some visitors, particularly the over-30 crowd, seem perplexed as to the reason, **Hippies** (Hin Khom Beach, tel. 08/1970-5483, 8am-late daily, 200B) is a wildly popular restaurant, bar, and party spot right on Hin Khom Beach. The menu, which features Middle Eastern food, pizza, and plenty of Thai dishes, seems designed to offer something for everyone. The food is actually pretty good (although if you want authentic Thai food, make sure to ask for it extra spicy), but it's really the beachfront location, charming thatched roofs and bamboo furniture, and laid-back vibe that are the draws here.

TRANSPORTATION
Getting There

The only way to get to the island is by water. In the past, intrepid tour operators have tried using seaplanes for the short flight from Phuket airport, but they have not managed to make that business model work.

Phi Phi Don is easily reached by ferryboat or speedboat from Phuket or Krabi. There are no public ferries per se, only private operators, and when you buy a ticket, most will include a ride from your hotel in Phuket or Krabi to the pier. Schedules change frequently, especially in the low season, but during high season there are at least two boats from Chalong Bay in Phuket to Ton Sai Bay on Phi Phi Don, one in the morning and another in the afternoon, and returning boats on a similar schedule.

The trip should take around two hours, depending on the weather conditions. From Krabi, there are boats leaving from Ao Nang and Rai Le Beaches daily, also in the morning and afternoon. Fares run from 350 baht upward, depending on the time of day and the season. If you're with a large group of people, it can sometimes be more economical to charter your own speedboat from Chalong Bay or Krabi to Phi Phi. In a small, fast vessel, the trip can take half as long as the larger boats, but you should expect to pay a few thousand baht per journey.

Given the cost of the trip, if you have some time to spare, it may be worthwhile to take one of the package tours that will not only bring you to Phi Phi but also provide a tour of neighboring islands and sights while you're on the way. Just make sure the boat will stop at Ton Sai Bay (if that's where you're going), as some tours skip this spot entirely.

Many of the hotels on Phi Phi can arrange your transport from either Krabi or Phuket for you if you're staying on their property. Otherwise, you can buy tickets from any travel agent, but when purchasing, make sure to ask about the size of the boat and the number of passengers if you have a preference for the type of vessel. Larger ferries and speedboats generally take 90 minutes from either Krabi or Phuket. During the low season, it's fine just to show up at the pier and buy a ticket, but during high season ferries can sometimes sell out, so the best bet is to find a travel agency and buy a ticket as soon as you can.

Getting Around

There are no taxis or *tuk tuks* on Phi Phi; for the most part there aren't even any roads. Most of the getting-around involves walking or traveling from Ton Sai Bay to other spots on the island by longtail boat, the area's taxi service. You'll pay 40-100 baht per person per trip from one part of the island to another, depending on the distance and whether you are traveling alone. From one island to another, expect to pay around 100 baht per person for the boat trip. Your hotel will be able to arrange a boat for you, but if you're picking one up from the beach, make sure you agree on the cost in advance.

Ko Lanta
เกาะลันตา

Just off the coast of Krabi is Ko Lanta, really two adjacent islands—**Ko Lanta Yai** and **Ko Lanta Noi.** Ko Lanta Yai, generally referred to just as Ko Lanta, is a large, thin island with limestone cliffs, a jungly interior, mangroves, and some good coral beaches. Although there are mangroves along much of the coast, there are also some great sandy beaches on the west side of the island, and that's where you'll find plenty of bungalows and small resorts. The interior has some great hiking trails through rainforests and some waterfalls worth checking out in Lanta's national park, which covers nearly half the island. Ko Lanta is arguably nearly as blissfully beautiful as Phi Phi, but Ko Lanta has yet to explode with the same popularity as its neighbor, and it has a strange half-backpacker, half-luxury vibe to it that some visitors find a perfect balance. You'll see this interesting dichotomy in the choice of accommodations as well—there are some great choices at both the upper and lower ends. Ban Saladan, a small village on the northeast corner of the island, functions as Ko Lanta's Main Street. This is where many of the ferries arrive, and there are also some limited amenities such as ATMs, Internet cafés, and supermarkets, but some of the more popular beach areas will have similar amenities as well. Ko Lanta Noi, adjacent to Ko Lanta Yai, has no beaches and has therefore not become a big destination, but depending on how you get to Ko Lanta, you may end up passing through the island.

SIGHTS
Lanta Old Town
หมู่บ้านเก่าแก่เกาะลันตา

Located on the east side of southern Ko Lanta, **Lanta Old Town** is a quaint fishing village that now serves as the island's capital. It's picturesque, with little teakwood houses on stilts above the water and brightly colored fishing boats set against the backdrop of an enticing blue ocean speckled with islands that seem to emerge as you watch. But Lanta Old Town is also a fascinating place to observe the cultural diversity in southern Thailand that's often difficult to discern in heavily touristed areas. The town, once a major fishing port in the middle part of the 20th century, is home to Chinese immigrants, descendants of nomadic seafarers, and Thai Muslims who've created a comfortable, peaceful town blending all of their cultures together.

BEACHES AND SURROUNDING ISLANDS
★ Khlong Dao Beach
หาดคลองดาว

Khlong Dao Beach, closest to Ban Saladan, is a long stretch of wide, sandy beach on the southwest tip of the island backed by casuarina and palm trees. The waters in this crescent-shaped beach are generally quite calm, but this is the island's most popular tourist spot, so expect more of everything—more accommodations, more places to eat, and more people. It's still Ko Lanta, though, so even during peak season, you won't see any overcrowding at Khlong Dao.

Pra Ae Beach
หาดพระแอะ

Pra Ae Beach (also called **Long Beach**) is another stretch of wide, sandy beach, with a nice selection of bungalows and resorts right on the water nestled among the trees. Just a few kilometers down from Khlong Dao, Long Beach is rarely crowded.

Khlong Khong and Khlong Nin Beaches
หาดคลองโขง และ หาดคลองนิน

As you move farther down the island, there are still plenty of bungalows right on the coast, but the beaches become less crowded with accommodations and people. Both **Khlong Khong** and **Khlong Nin Beaches** are served by a little village called Ban Khlong Nin, where you'll find all the basics, including an ATM, some places to eat, and small shops.

Kan Tiang Bay and the Southwest Coast
อ่าวกันเตียง

With less usable beach in relation to mangrove or rocky shore, this is where the island starts to feel remote. **Kan Tiang Beach,** located within the bay of the same name, with its white sands and just a scattering of resorts, is nearly deserted in the low season, making it a great choice if you're looking for a quiet, romantic getaway. **Mai Pay Bay** is sometimes nicknamed "Last Beach" because it's at the end of the island and feels like the last beach in Thailand that hasn't been discovered. With simple bungalows and little going on other than the beautiful scenery and warm blue waters, Mai Pay Bay feels off the beaten path, and it attracts the backpacker crowd and other adventurers seeking scenery as well as peace and quiet.

Ko Ha
เกาะห้า

A group of five small rocky islands off the coast of Ko Lanta, **Ko Ha** is a popular place for diving and snorkeling due to the abundant coral and exotic sealife surrounding the islands as well as the excellent visibility in the water. There are no accommodations on the island, but it's often visited on day trips. To get to Ko Ha, you'll need to charter a speedboat or sailboat or go with an organized tour.

Ko Hai (Ngai) Lanta
เกาะไหง

With just a handful of resorts and very limited amenities, **Ko Hai Lanta** offers the quintessential desert-island experience if you're willing to give up a few luxuries in exchange. The small island, mostly hilly rainforest, has a stretch of beautiful beach with views of karst rock formations rising from the sea and some great coral snorkeling just off the coast. The island is in Krabi Province just south of Ko Lanta Yai, but it's more convenient to get there by taking a boat from Trang instead. If you're staying on the island, the resort will arrange transportation for you.

Ko Ta Lebeng and Ko Bu Bu
เกาะตะละเบ็ง และ เกาะบุบุ

Off the east coast of Ko Lanta, **Ko Ta Lebeng** is a limestone island with dramatic limestone cliffs and lush mangroves as well as a small bit of sandy beach. The island is very popular among sea kayakers and is a great place to go if you're not confident in open waters—the smaller Ko Ta Lebeng is protected by the main island, and the waters are a little calmer.

If you want to stay on a small island, **Ko Bu Bu** has only one resort with a handful of bungalows and clear warm waters for snorkeling. "Chilled-out" might be too exciting to describe the place—there's some great sandy beach and not much else to occupy your time other than sitting in a hammock and reading a book. The island is even too small for any long hiking.

NIGHTLIFE

Club Ibark (Khlong Nin Beach, Ko Lanta Yai, tel. 08/3507-9237, 6pm-late daily, no cover) bills itself as the country's freshest and funkiest club and, while that's definitely not true, it is the hottest thing going on Ko Lanta. Of course, Ko Lanta is a small island, and the nightlife pickings are pretty slim. Still, during high season the club pulls in a good crowd, and the DJs spin music that's head and shoulders above the typical Western pop classics you'll hear at most venues. There's a casual, fun vibe at this open-air dance club, and since everyone is on vacation, the partying can go on 'til late at night.

SPORTS AND RECREATION
Ko Lanta National Park

Ko Lanta National Park covers Hat Hin Ngam and Hat Tanod Beaches at the southern tip of Ko Lanta as well as a handful of surrounding small islands and rock formations. There are no resorts on the beaches, and like the other national parks with beaches, there are some camping amenities. **Tanod Beach,** at the bottom of Ko Lanta, is covered in rugged mountain terrain and sugar palms, giving way to a beautiful beach. There are hiking trails throughout this area filled with birdlife, and at the end is the Lanta lighthouse, where you can climb up and view the island from above.

There are campgrounds as well as many bungalows that can be rented from the parks authority. Approaching the lighthouse and surrounding area by road can be really tough without a 4WD vehicle, and depending on the weather, it may be easier to charter a longtail boat to take you.

Snorkeling

If you're looking to do some serious snorkeling, the area surrounding Ko Lanta has some great coral reefs and marinelife to see. You can swim out on your own, but to really see what's going on in the sea, arrange a boat trip around the island and neighboring islands. **Freedom Adventures** (70 Mu 6, Khlong Nin Beach, Ko Lanta Yai, tel. 08/4910-9132 or 08/1077-5025, www.freedom-adventures. net) runs group day trips for about 1,500 baht from Ko Lanta on its charming wooden motorboat and can also create a personalized itinerary for you depending on your interests and abilities. This is a great excursion for nondivers who are interested in seeing the coral and tropical fish, as these folks specialize in snorkeling and not diving, so they'll only take you places you can enjoy viewing the underwater world without need of breathing gear.

ACCOMMODATIONS
Under 1,500B

Bu Bu Island Resort (Ko Bu Bu, tel. 07/561-8066, 350B) is a throwback to the days when simple bungalows on quiet beaches dominated the now mostly built-up Andaman coast. Guest rooms are very basic thatched-roof bungalows with private cold-water baths. There's also a small restaurant here, making it a great place to just chill out and enjoy the view.

1,500-3,000B

If you want to pay backpacker prices but don't want to forgo things such as a swimming pool and a restaurant on the premises, the **Andaman Lanta Resort** (142 Mu 3, Khlong Dao Beach, Ko Lanta, tel. 07/568-4200, www.andamanlanta.com, 2,100B) is a decent midrange option. The guest rooms are clean, if a little weary, but the resort is relaxed and child-friendly. Located on the north part of the island, it's definitely in a more crowded neighborhood, but the nearby beach stays mellow even during high season. It sort of looks like a group of IHOP restaurants, since all of the buildings have similar blue roofs.

Right nearby, at the southern end of Khlong Dao Beach, **Lanta Villa Resort** (14 Mu 3 Saladan, Ko Lanta, tel. 07/568-4129 or 08/1536-2527, www.lantavillaresort.com, 1,900B) is a similar property with clean, basic guest rooms and a nice swimming pool right on the popular beach. The bungalow-style rooms are a little too close together to feel secluded, but for this price and this location, it really is a bargain.

Ancient Realm Resort & Spa (364 Mu 3 Saladan, Ko Lanta, tel. 08/7998-1336, www.ancientrealmresort.com, 1,800B) is a solid midrange beach resort with excellent service and good-value guest rooms. Some might be aesthetically offended by the liberal use of Buddhist and Southeast Asian images in the decor, but if you can get past that, the guest rooms are very comfortable and clean, and the beach location is excellent. All guest rooms have air-conditioning and hot water. The resort also feels less businesslike than some other properties, so staff and guests are more relaxed and friendly.

LaLaanta Hideaway (188 Mu 5, Ko Lanta, tel. 07/566-5066, www.lalaanta.

com, 2,800B) is quiet, secluded, and relaxing, and though the bungalows are not at the five-star level, they are clean, nicely furnished, and comfortable enough that you won't miss much. There is a hotel restaurant and bar, plus a large swimming pool overlooking the Andaman Sea. The beach the resort is located on feels very secluded, and those who are looking for a place that feels like a deserted island will enjoy their time here.

3,000-4,500B

The small **Baan Laanta** (72 Mu 5, Kan Tiang Bay, Ko Lanta Yai, tel. 07/566-5091, www.baanlaanta.com, 3,500B) resort has only 15 bungalows, which straddle the line between rustic and luxurious. Terra-cotta tiles and lots of wood and bamboo give the guest rooms a very natural feeling, but things like a minibar, bathrobes, and private balconies with excellent views add bits of pampering and indulgence. The dark-tiled pool, spa *sala* (pavilion), and outdoor bar are small but swanky-feeling and well maintained.

A boutique resort of the best kind, ★ **Sri Lanta** (111 Mu 6, Khlong Nin Beach, Ko Lanta Yai, tel. 07/566-2688, 3,800B) is both aesthetically pleasing and geared toward connecting visitors to the beautiful surroundings of Ko Lanta. This is not a place designed to make you forget where you are: The individual thatched-roof villas have wall-length shutters that you can open out onto the grounds, and the interiors are rustic but comfortable and deliberately don't have TVs. But things like the amazing black-tiled swimming pool, Wi-Fi, and good iced coffee mean you won't feel like you're missing out on much during vacation.

Over 4,500B

With bright, beautiful guest rooms set on a property that creeps into the surrounding rainforest along with lots of things to do, the **Rawi Warin Resort & Spa** (139 Mu 8, Ko Lanta, tel. 07/560-7400, www.rawiwarin.com, 7,800B) has more personality and charm than most large resorts. The guest rooms are modern but have an airy, clean tropical style to them, and the stucco exteriors give the resort a more Mediterranean feel than a Southeast Asian island feel. Some of the gigantic villas have their own swimming pools, but the common areas, which include multiple swimming pools, tennis courts, and a gym, are more than sufficient to keep you occupied. One of the restaurants also has free Wi-Fi. The property is very child-friendly, although some of the guest rooms are located up in the hills and will require a little bit of walking.

If you're looking for more amenities, the ★ Pimalai Resort (99 Mu 5, Ba Kan Tiang Beach, Ko Lanta, tel. 07/560-7999, www.pimalai.com, 12,000B) is a larger property with more than 100 guest rooms nestled in the hilly rainforest above a beautiful, quiet stretch of white-sand beach. All of the guest rooms are in small bungalow buildings, giving the property a less crowded feeling despite the fact that there may be hundreds of guests and staff around during peak season. Inside, the guest rooms are a little more generic but still have some nice Thai design elements. The 35-meter (115 ft) infinity swimming pool overlooking the ocean is nearly as beautiful as the beach below.

FOOD

If you're just looking for casual food, you'll find lots of roti vendors around, selling the traditional Muslim rolled and flattened pancakes. They're traditionally served with savory curries, but these guys will stuff them with all sorts of sweet treats, including chocolate and bananas, for around 30 baht.

Gong Grit Bar (Khlong Dao Beach, 176 Mu 3, Saladan, Ko Lanta, tel. 08/9592-5844, 8am-10pm daily, 300B) is one of the many places you'll find on Khlong Dao Beach serving up local fare and seafood dishes on the beach. This one isn't very fancy—none of them are—but the food is well done and the service is good. Gong Grit is at the southern end of the beach.

TRANSPORTATION
Getting There
Boat

During high season, there is a twice-daily ferry from Krabi's new pier on Tharua Road, just outside Krabi Town. Remember that there are two piers in Krabi: Chao Fah pier, which is now used for travel immediately around Krabi, and the new pier, which is used for larger vessels. The ferry for Lanta leaves at 8am and 1pm, takes about 90 minutes, and costs 300 baht. It's best to arrange transport to the pier through your hotel in Krabi. There are also daily boats during high season from Ko Phi Phi to Ko Lanta, departing at 11:30am and 2pm daily. That trip takes 90 minutes and also costs 300 baht.

Bus

Although Ko Lanta is an island, you can do much of the journey there by land, using two ferry crossings that can accommodate vehicles. In the low season, this is the only option, and there are numerous minivan services that will take you from Krabi to Ko Lanta. If you take one of the scheduled vans with Lanta Transport (tel. 07/568-4121), which run every few hours and take about 90 minutes, you'll pay 250 baht per person. You can also arrange to have a private minivan with any tour company, which should cost around 1,000 baht.

Car

If you're driving to Ko Lanta, head south on Highway 4 toward Trang (if you're coming from the Phang Nga area). Turn off at Route 4206 at Khlong Thom, about 32 kilometers (20 mi) from Krabi Town, and follow that road heading south all the way to the Hua Hin pier on the mainland. That leg of the journey is about 29 kilometers (18 mi). From there you'll take your first ferry crossing to Ko Lanta Noi. The second ferry, about 8 kilometers (5 mi) after the first, will bring you to Ko Lanta Yai; each will cost 100 baht.

Getting Around
Ko Lanta does not have a public

transportation system; to get around you'll have to rely on occasional motorcycle taxis and the shuttle buses and trucks run by the island's resorts. If you're driving on your own, by car or motorcycle, the island has a main road on the west coast that runs north-south and will allow you access to those beaches.

Trang and Satun Provinces
จังหวัดตรัง และ จังหวัดสตูล

The two southernmost provinces on the Andaman coast before Thailand becomes Malaysia, Trang and Satun have not yet become popular tourism destinations, although direct flights from Bangkok to Krabi and Trang make them readily accessible for those looking for something off the beaten path. Both share much of the topography of neighboring Krabi—limestone cliffs, beautiful beaches, mangrove swamps, and a verdant interior—but are less commonly visited by travelers, most likely due to the plethora of amazing places to see so close to Phuket and its well-maintained tourism infrastructure. If the idea of flying into a big international airport and staying in a place where you'll most definitely see other foreign travelers is unappealing, these two provinces are worth the extra effort it takes to get here, if only for the chance to see what Thailand is really like while at the same time enjoying beautiful beaches and islands. The provinces are home to some spectacular small islands off the coast, most protected by two large national marine parks and easily accessible from the mainland either for day trips, if you're in a hurry, or extended stays, if you're looking for a desert-island experience. Off the coast of Trang is the Mu Ko Phetra National Park, comprising about 30 islands you can dive and snorkel around, or enjoy the gray-white sandy beaches and do some bird-watching. Off the coast of Satun are the Tarutao Islands, which, compared to their northern neighbors, are more visited, although still nothing like what you'll see in Phang Nga Bay. The national park comprises more than 50 islands where you can see coral and go snorkeling and scuba diving.

The mainland also has its share of natural beauty, and although there are scant tourist sights to see, there's still plenty to keep you busy should you decide to stay here for more than a day or two. Trang was the first area in Thailand where rubber trees, now an important part of the economy of the south, were planted, and Satun is home to a majority Muslim population, making both provinces culturally and historically interesting places to visit in addition to their physical beauty.

Compared to Phuket or Krabi, you won't find the same number or quality of accommodations on the mainland of either Trang or Satun, although a couple of resorts have sprung up in the area as well as some very budget, very simple beach bungalows.

TRANG
Trang Town
เมืองตรัง

Trang Town isn't so much a tourist town as just a small town going about its daily business: Although there are travel agencies that can set up dive expeditions to the nearby islands, hardware stores and noodle shops are the rule instead of tailor shops and bars. It's not a physically beautiful town, and most travelers will see it only in transit from the mainland to the beaches, but if you're interested in what semiurban life looks like in this part of the world, it's a pedestrian-friendly place where you can wander around for a while observing the mundane without fear of getting lost. While it's sometimes difficult to discern small cultural differences among regions in

Trang and Satun Provinces

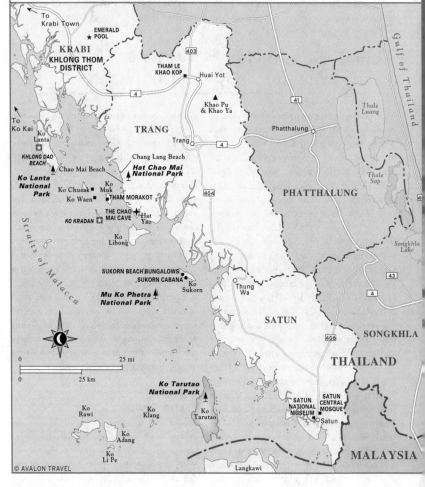

foreign countries, Trang feels distinctly different from more northern areas of Thailand. Like other parts of southern Thailand, the distinct mix of Thai-Chinese and Malay cultures can be fascinating to observe, plus there is some Sino-Portuguese architecture. Other than that, there isn't too much to see except for the markets and the governor's house, set on one of the area's hills.

Here you'll also find some of the best coffee shops. Say goodbye to instant and order a *kopi* instead. Just like the coffee you'll find in cafés in Malaysia and Singapore, this is the strong cloth bag-filtered version with a generous helping of sweetened condensed milk to make it go down smoothly. Trang is also known for two other culinary specialties—dim sum, which you can find at many coffee shops and which is especially popular for breakfast, and *mu yang Trang,* Trang-style crispy roasted pork. **Ton Noon Dim Sum** (202 Pad Sathani Rd., 6am-9pm daily, 30B) and **Khao Chong Coffee** (Phatthalung Rd., tel. 07/521-8759, 6am-9pm daily, 30B) are two traditional *kopi* shops with excellent dim sum choices.

Nok Air is the only airline offering flights to Trang from Bangkok, currently leaving from Don Muang airport. If you book far enough in advance on Nok Air, tickets are as cheap as 2,800B round-trip with tax. Otherwise, you may pay a little under 4,000B for a ticket.

There's an **overnight train** from Bangkok to Trang that leaves Hua Lamphong Station at 5:05pm and arrives in Trang at 7:55am the next day. The tickets cost under 800 baht for a first-class sleeper ticket, so if you're comfortable sleeping on trains, it's a really economical and adventurous way to get to the region.

There are buses for Trang that leave the Southern Bus Terminal in Bangkok around 6pm; call tel. 02/435-1199 for the latest schedule. Buses take 12-14 hours. Expect to pay in the neighborhood of 800 baht for a ticket on an air-conditioned luxury bus, less than 550 baht for an unair-conditioned bus.

If you're driving from the surrounding areas, Highway 4 cuts through Trang in a zigzag pattern, making it the most accessible route for inland travel in the province. For the beaches in the southern part of the province, however, you'll have to turn onto secondary road 404. Although Trang is close to Phuket, Krabi, and Phang Nga as the crow flies, the drive can take hours due to the mountainous terrain. The drive from Krabi Town to Trang takes two hours; from Phuket to Trang, it takes 4.5-5 hours, so plan accordingly.

Mu Ko Phetra National Park
อุทยานแห่งชาติหมู่เกาะเภตรา

Mu Ko Phetra National Park, a marine park in Trang, is a small grouping of islands just north of the Ko Tarutao area that feels even more remote than the rest of the province. The scenery, including the craggy limestone rock formations jutting out from the ocean and rainforest-covered islands, is spectacular. Under the surface of the sea surrounding

many of the islands there's coral at relatively shallow depths, making this a great destination for snorkeling. The only way to stay in the national park is either to camp or to rent one of the national park bungalows on Ko Phetra.

Ko Khao Yai means "large mountain island." Although that could adequately define many of the islands in the Andaman Sea, Ko Khao Yai stands out because, thanks to erosion and tectonic forces, one of the large chunks of limestone jutting off the island has been worn through and forms a sort of natural bridge that can be rowed under during low tide.

The much smaller **Ko Lidi,** which covers less than 10 square kilometers (4 sq mi), doesn't have great beaches for swimming, but it has some caves within the limestone cliffs that are nesting grounds for swallows, along with a campground where you can rent tents.

Accommodations through the Department of National Parks are basic bungalows and dormitory-style rooms with running water and fan cooling. Some are located right on the water. There is also a campground where you can pitch a tent. Prices are 600-1,500 baht per night. Book accommodations with the Department of National Parks (tel. 02/562-0760, np_income@dnp.go.th). Once the reservation is booked, you must transfer full payment to the National Parks by bank wire (or at a Krung Thai Bank or ATM in Thailand). There is a small canteen and restaurant at the park headquarters.

The closest major city to Ko Phetra is Hat Yai, which is about 60 miles away. From Satun, the park is about 35 miles. If you are driving from Hat Yai, take Highway 4 north to Route 406. When you hit the beginning of Route 416, follow that road until you see signs for the park. There are also public buses that run from Satun to the park. You'll need to check the schedule at the Satun bus station (intersection of Route 406 and Sulakanukoon Soi 17).

Ko Muk
เกาะมุก

Just off the coast of Trang, across from

Chang Lang Beach, **Ko Muk** is a small inhabited island with some beautiful beaches backed by limestone cliffs on the west coast, coral clusters to snorkel around (particularly nearby Hat Sai Yao), and a scattering of bungalows and resorts catering to travelers. To the south, the eastern part of the island is mainly a fishing village, and the local economy is also dependent on the rubber plantations in the center of the island. But to the north, on the west coast, lies one of the coolest physical attractions in the region—the **Tham Morakot** (Emerald Cave). If you visit during low tide, you can access the cave and interior lagoon by boat, but the more fun way to go is during high tide, when the entrance to the cave is nearly filled with water and you have to swim through the limestone passage. When you reemerge, you'll be in a beautiful emerald lagoon surrounded by cliffs. During high season this is a popular place, so don't expect to have it to yourself.

To get to Ko Muk, you can take a longtail or speedboat from the Kuan Tungku pier, which is about 30 minutes from Trang Town. If you're flying into the Trang airport, there are frequent *song thaew* traveling this route during the day; expect to pay around 50 baht per person. At the pier, you'll have to negotiate with the captain, but a trip to Ko Muk will take around 30 minutes on a longtail boat and will cost around 400 baht.

Hat Chao Mai National Park
อุทยานแห่งชาติหาดเจ้าไหม

The **Hat Chao Mai National Park** (Mu 5, Ban Chang Lang, Amphoe Sikao, tel. 07/521-3260, 8:30am-6pm daily, 200B) is a large protected area covering 19 kilometers (12 mi) of rocky and sandy coastline north of Hat Yao and south of Krabi Province. The interior of the park includes mangrove swamps, mountains, and rivers. The park also technically extends to the adjacent islands of Ko Muk, Ko Kradan, Ko Waen, Ko Cheaung, Ko Pring, and Ko Meng, although you won't necessarily notice that you've entered the park or even

have to pay an entrance fee if you're visiting one of these islands. Although the park is a beautiful nature preserve and includes some amazing coral reef offshore, what Hat Chao Mai is best known for is the **dugong**, or sea cows, that live in the ocean territory covered by the park. This endangered species, similar to a manatee, was once hunted but has now been adopted by the locals as the region's unofficial mascot. The sweet, awkward-looking dugong can sometimes be spotted during snorkeling or diving trips along the coast or islands covered by the park. If you're looking to explore the mainland part of the park, there are simple bungalows for rent as well as areas to camp with restrooms and canteens serving up tasty, casual local food.

★ Ko Kradan
เกาะกระดาน

Partially under the protection of the Hat Chao Mai National Park, **Ko Kradan** is often called the most beautiful island in Trang. It's no surprise, given the beautiful view of Ko Muk and other neighboring islands that seem to emerge magically from the Andaman Sea, the pristine soft-sand beaches, and the surrounding coral reefs. For snorkelers it's particularly alluring: The water is clear, and you'll only need to swim out to shallow depths to see some amazing coral and tropical fish. Although there are some rubber plantations on the island, it's largely undeveloped and usually visited by tourists as part of a tour to Ko Muk. If you want to stay over, there are a few bungalows on the island, and you can also camp on the island through the parks department.

Hat Yao and Surrounding Islands
หาดยาว

The longest stretch of beach in the province, **Hat Yao** has some clear sandy swaths punctuated by rock formations and rocky cliffs backed by pine and palm trees. Off the coast in the warm, clear-blue waters of the Andaman Sea are some islands and rock formations where you'll be able to do some snorkeling and diving away from the crowds a little farther north. There are very limited accommodations on the beach; it's definitely quiet and secluded. For budget travelers it's a great option if you feel like you've been squeezed out of the more popular tourist areas as they've gone upscale—you can still find accommodations for less than US$15 per night in the area.

Just off the coast of Hat Yao is **Ko Libong.** The largest island in Trang is a very short trip by longtail boat from the pier at Yao Beach and has a handful of small fishing villages and rubber plantations populated by the mostly Muslim Thais living in the area. The island itself has some beautiful sandy beaches and rugged, hilly rainforest in the middle, and there is snorkeling right off the coast, although not as much coral to be seen as you'll find in and around Phi Phi. Ko Libong also has a handful of quaint resorts if you're looking to stay on the island overnight.

South of Ko Libong is **Ko Sukorn,** one of the southernmost islands in Trang Province. This island has a handful of small villages mostly engaged in fishing and working on small rubber plantations on the island. The brown sandy beaches are surrounded by clear waters, and the island is mostly flat and without many of the rock formations characteristic of the region. The island is small enough that you can walk around it in a few hours, and close enough that it only takes about 20 minutes in a longtail boat from the mainland; you'll get a chance to see how people in the region make a living while enjoying the laid-back atmosphere on the island.

There are some relaxed bungalow resorts here, although nothing is fancy. If you're looking for an off-the-beaten-path island getaway, this is a great place to stay for a few days. **Sukorn Beach Bungalows** (Ko Sukorn, tel. 07/526-7707, www.sukorn-island-trang.com, 1,000B) is casual and unpretentious. This is definitely a place to stay for the location and the price, and for now you won't have to worry about being overrun by other travelers, since Ko Sukorn hasn't made it big yet. The guest rooms are filled with simple bamboo furniture and are a very short walk to the beach; most have air-conditioning. There aren't many amenities available here, but there is a small restaurant serving Thai food.

Sukorn Cabana (Ko Sukorn, tel. 07/511-5894, www.sukorncabana.com, 1,000B) has airy, basic, but pretty bungalows. This is not a high-end resort—many of the bungalows don't have air-conditioning or hot water—but they're just minutes from the beach.

Ko Chueak and **Ko Waen,** just adjacent to each other off the coast of Trang, are two very small islands with some of the best casual snorkeling in the region. Aside from some exotic, colorful fish, there is plenty of deep- and shallow-water coral to view.

On the mainland, the national park area covers **Khao Pu** and **Khao Ya** mountains, which have thick forest cover, caves, and plenty of waterfalls to hike around in. Tha Le Song Hong—Lake of Two Rooms—is a fascinating and beautiful physical phenomenon to view. The large, clean lake is nearly divided by a mountain rising from the middle, creating two separate bodies of water. To get there by car, take Petchkasem Road (Huai Yot-Krabi) to Ban Phraek, then turn right and drive about 13 kilometers (8 mi). There will be signs in English pointing the way. If you want to rough it a little, there's a Boy Scout campground (tel. 07/522-4294) nearby. When it's not filled with kids, they rent out the houses.

Chang Lang Beach
หาดฉางหลาง

Chang Lang Beach has all of the spectacular scenery typically found along the Andaman coast—limestone cliffs, sandy beaches, and casuarina pine trees. One of the campsites, as well as the main headquarters for Hat Chao Mai National Park, is located on the beach.

At the tip of a forested headland is **Chao Mai Beach,** a wide stretch of sandy beach covering about three kilometers (2 mi) of coastline. Both of these beaches are beautiful and feel much more remote and less populated by visitors than the national parks to the north; if you come during the low season, you may well be the only person around.

The **Chao Mai Cave** is one of the larger caves in the region, with extensive stalactites and stalagmites, fossils, and multilevel chambers. There's also a spring inside one of the chambers, and some of the stalactites and stalagmites have joined, creating strange-looking pillars and an altogether otherworldly feeling inside. Although the cave is on the grounds of the national park, it's easier to access from Yao Beach. From here, you can rent a rowboat to row into the cave from the ocean.

Another cool cave to visit is **Tham Le Khao Kop,** which has pools of water and a stream flowing through it as well as steep interior cliff walls, plus more than three kilometers (2 mi) of stalagmites and stalactites. During the day there are guides who'll row you through the cave in a little boat. At one point the passage is so low you have to lie on your back in the boat, which feels like an adventure. To tour the cave with a boat and guide, the fee is 200 baht per boat or 30 baht per person. Take Highway 4 from the Huai Yot district heading toward the **Wang Wiset district** (อำเภอวังวิเศษ). After about six kilometers (4 mi), you will see Andaman intersection; continue for 460 meters (1,509 ft), and you will see another intersection with a temple on the right; turn left, drive about 640 meters (2,100 ft), and you'll see a bridge to the cave.

SATUN
Satun Town
เมืองสตูล

As untouristed as Trang Town is, **Satun Town** is even more so. The center of the southernmost province on the Andaman coast before Malaysia, the town of Satun, as with the whole province, is primarily Muslim, having been a part of Malaya until the early 19th century. Sectarian violence has infected the three southernmost provinces on the east side of the peninsula, but even though Satun is nearly right next door, there have been no reports of insurgent activity here, and it's a great opportunity to catch a glimpse of a culture

different from what you'll see to the north. To better understand Islam in Thailand, visit the **Ku Den Mansion,** the Satun National Museum. Housed in a colonial-style former palace that once housed King Rama V, this museum for Islamic studies has interesting displays on the lives of Muslims in the area through the ages. There's also the large **Satun Central Mosque.** Although it's not going to win any architectural awards, having been completed in the late 1970s, you can visit to pray or watch others do so.

If you're heading to Satun, you can take a train to Hat Yai (there's no train station in Satun), but then you have to travel by land for the remaining 95 kilometers (59 mi).

Satun is on the same bus line as Trang. Buses leave the Southern Bus Terminal in Bangkok around 6pm; call tel. 02/435-1199 for the latest schedule. Buses will take 12-14 hours to reach Satun. Expect to pay in the neighborhood of 800 baht for a ticket on an air-conditioned luxury bus, less than 550 baht for an unair-conditioned bus.

If you're driving through Satun, Route 416 travels down the coast slightly inland, and from there you'll turn off onto country roads depending on your destination. Although Satun is close to Phuket, Krabi, and Phang Nga, keep in mind that the drive can take hours due to the mountainous terrain. If you are driving from Krabi Town to Satun, it will take three hours. From Phuket to Trang, the drive will take 5.5-6 hours.

Ko Tarutao National Park
อุทยานแห่งชาติหมู่เกาะตะรุเตา

Ko Tarutao National Park in Satun is the highlight of the region if you're looking for a place to do some diving and snorkeling. The park comprises more than 50 islands off the coast of Satun and just north of Malaysian territorial waters, some barely a speck on the map and some, such as Ko Tarutao, covering dozens of square kilometers of land. Within the island group you'll find rainforests, clean quiet beaches, mangroves, coral reefs, and plenty of wildlife. The park headquarters (tel.

07/478-3485) is on the northwest part of the main island, which has a pier, bungalow accommodations, and campgrounds.

Many people visit these islands on chartered tours from the mainland. These tours are generally done on speedboats and include lunch, a chance to enjoy the scenery, and some snorkeling.

The largest island, **Ko Tarutao,** is a mountainous, forested island with limestone cliffs, mangrove swamps, and white-sand beaches. The island formerly housed a detainment center for political and other prisoners, but these days it's home to some of the national park facilities as well as the biggest selection of bungalows and resorts. If you're interested in seeing the darker side of the country's history, you can visit the old prisons at **Talo Udang Bay** in the southernmost part of the island and Talowao Bay in the southeastern part of the island. They're connected by a trail that was built by prisoners before the site was abandoned during World War II.

Mu Ko Adang Rawi comprises two islands, **Ko Adang** and **Ko Rawi,** both characterized by light-sand beaches, verdant interiors with limestone cliffs, and some coral reefs offshore that can be easily viewed when snorkeling or diving. Many people visit these islands as part of a day trip, but if you want to stay overnight, there are some bungalows available through the parks department, or you can rent a tent from them or bring your own to camp on the beach.

Ko Kai and **Ko Klang** in the center of the marine park are also both popular spots for snorkeling and hanging out on the clean sandy beaches. There are no accommodations here, and tour groups will often add these islands to a multiple-island day tour.

On the larger islands, there are a small number of decent accommodations, if you are looking to hang out in the area for a few days as you island-hop from one sight to the other. If you're on a budget or really want to enjoy the natural environment unfettered by modern distractions, try camping at one of the many campgrounds or renting a bungalow from the national parks department. The bungalows and dormitory-style rooms are basic, with running water and fan cooling, and are located on Ko Taratao. There is also a campground on the beach on both Ko Taratao and smaller Ko Adang. Prices are 500-1,500 baht per night. Book accommodations with the Department of National Parks (tel. 02/562-0760, np_income@dnp.go.th). Once the reservation is booked, you must transfer full payment to the National Parks by bank wire (or at a Krung Thai Bank or ATM in Thailand). There is a canteen at the park headquarters and another on smaller Adang Island to the west.

Ko Li Pe
เกาะหลีเป๊ะ

Just below the national park is **Ko Li Pe,** a small, charming island just 40 kilometers (25 mi) from Malaysia's Langkawi Island. Populated by sea gypsies and a smattering of unpretentious resorts and bungalows, every year the island is becoming more popular with adventurous vacationers looking for something a little off the beaten path. Still, it's small enough that you can tour the whole island in two hours, and you won't find any big partying or even ATMs on Ko Li Pe, just a handful of beautiful beaches and some dive shops catering to those who want to enjoy the underwater life around the island.

There are three beaches on Ko Li Pe, which is shaped roughly like a boomerang pointing northeast. The eastern beach is called Sunset Beach, the northern beach is Sunrise Beach, and the southwestern beach (the inside of the boomerang) is called Pattaya Beach. Sunrise Beach and Pattaya Beach are connected to each other by a road that functions as the island's main street.

Many resorts close up shop during low season, but there are some that remain open year-round. **Idyllic Concept Resort** (Sunrise Beach, tel. 08/8227-5389, www.idyllicresort.com, 3,500B) features modern, funky guest rooms and bungalows right on the beach, plus a resort restaurant. The resort opened in 2013 and is very clean and well-maintained.

Sita Beach Resort and Spa Villa (Pattaya Beach, tel. 07/475-0382, www.sitabeachresort.com, 3,500B) is a full-service midrange resort with a swimming pool, a restaurant, a bar, and a small spa. Guest rooms are comfortable and have flat-screen TVs and vaguely Thai decor. The pool area is spacious and surrounded by guest rooms and villas. The resort is very family-friendly, too. The location and the view of the beach, though, are the big attractions here.

The cool, popular, and ecochic **Castaway Resort** (Sunrise Beach, tel. 08/3138-7472, www.castaway-resorts.com, 2,000B) is a collection of stand-alone bamboo bungalows on the beach, plus an outdoor bar and restaurant. The accommodations are basic—there's no air-conditioning or hot water, although because the bungalows are right off the water, ceiling fans keep everything cool enough. Most bungalows have an upstairs and a downstairs plus a small balcony for lounging and enjoying the view.

Ko Samui and the Samui Archipelago

Look for ★ to find recommended sights, activities, dining, and lodging.

Highlights

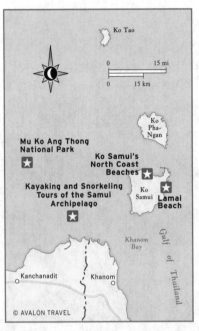

★ **Lamai Beach:** This pretty beach on Thailand's popular resort island offers everything you could ever want, including soft sand, peace and quiet, and five-star resorts (page 116).

★ **Ko Samui's North Coast Beaches:** The small **Bo Phut Beach** is pretty and relaxed, without any of the crowds you'll find at other popular Samui beaches (page 117).

★ **Mu Ko Ang Thong National Park:** These lush, green islands near the Samui Archipelago are easy to visit on a day trip and offer snorkeling, kayaking, and camping (page 119).

★ **Kayaking and Snorkeling Tours of the Samui Archipelago:** Prepare to be amazed by the beauty of the small islands that surround Ko Samui (page 121).

O nce just a quiet island happily going about its business of coconut farming, Ko Samui is now one of the most popular vacation spots in Thailand. Filled with palm trees and rimmed by white-sand beaches, the island has all the ingredients necessary

for a gorgeous holiday retreat. If you're arriving by plane to Ko Samui, the moment you step off the airplane and onto the tarmac you'll understand what the island is all about. There's no steel or glass at the international airport. Instead, it's a group of thatch-roofed huts where you check in and pick up your luggage. To get to and from the planes, passengers are taken by open-air buses akin to large golf carts. If you're arriving by ferry from the mainland, you'll get to enjoy the spectacular view of the surrounding islands during the 90-minute ride.

The island is not all huts and coconut trees, however. Since its debut as a budget destination, Samui has grown up. Although there are still beach bungalows to be found, there is also a large selection of five-star resorts as well as lots of spas and retreats and a dining scene that gets better every year. Thanks to a ring road that circles the entire island, there's plenty of built-up infrastructure, and you'll

have easy access to things such as medical care and rental cars. Every beach has at least one Internet café, and many hotels and cafés in more built-up beach areas have Wi-Fi. The development hasn't come without a price. Although the beaches are still beautiful, parts of the island can seem like a messy, incoherently developed mass of cheap concrete buildings and tangled power lines. Covering nearly 260 square kilometers (100 sq mi), Samui is a large island and can sometimes feel like a small city instead of desert paradise.

Just north of Samui, Ko Pha-Ngan is still mostly a backpacker haven, with a good selection of inexpensive places to stay and plenty of cheap drinks and all-night partying. The island's famous full-moon parties, which seem to take place every weekend regardless of the lunar phase, are what has given Ko Pha-Ngan this reputation, although there are more high-end resorts opening up and attracting a different type of independent traveler. The physical

Previous: the Samui Archipelago; Mu Ko Ang Thong National Park; Chaweng Beach. **Above:** kayaking in Mu Ko Ang Thong National Park.

The Samui Archipelago

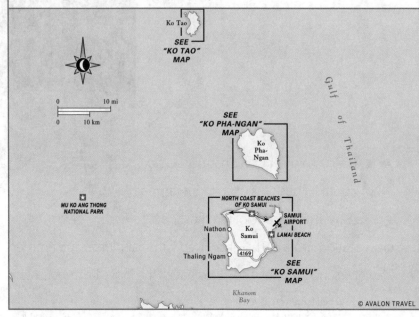

Ko Tao
SEE "KO TAO" MAP

0   10 mi
0   10 km

Gulf of Thailand

SEE "KO PHA-NGAN" MAP
Ko Pha-Ngan

MU KO ANG THONG NATIONAL PARK

NORTH COAST BEACHES OF KO SAMUI

SAMUI AIRPORT

Nathon   Ko Samui   LAMAI BEACH

Thaling Ngam   4169

SEE "KO SAMUI" MAP

Khanom Bay

© AVALON TRAVEL

landscape of the island, with gentle hills covered in trees and white-sand beaches, is as beautiful as Samui, and perhaps even more so, as it's less developed. Part of this is certainly due to the fact that there are no flights to the island. If you are visiting Pha-Ngan, you'll need to take a ferryboat from Surat Thani or Ko Samui, making it a good choice if you have the luxury of time but not money. Ko Tao, the northernmost main island in the archipelago, is still largely a base for divers but shares the same topography as its larger neighbors.

HISTORY

The island of Samui was first officially recorded by the Chinese around 1500 in ancient maps but was probably settled more than 1,000 years ago by mariners from Hainan in southwest China. While the mainland was a part of the Srivijaya Kingdom, Samui and neighboring islands were not a significant part of the kingdom. Until the 1970s, Ko Samui was just a simple island relying on ample coconut trees and fishing for commerce. During World War II, Ko Samui was briefly occupied by the Japanese, but otherwise it stayed below the radar.

Three decades later, the island and neighboring Ko Pha-Ngan arrived on the backpacker trail and slowly grew from quiet tropical refuges to international tourist destinations.

PLANNING YOUR TIME

Many visitors to the gulf spend all of their time on Ko Samui, and it's easy to do so with direct flights to the island from Bangkok. There are few cultural and historical sights to visit, as the island has really only developed around the travelers that have come to visit in recent decades, but there are plenty of beach activities to fill your time. If you plan on seeing more than one of the islands in the archipelago, give yourself at least a week, especially if you want to get some

Ko Samui

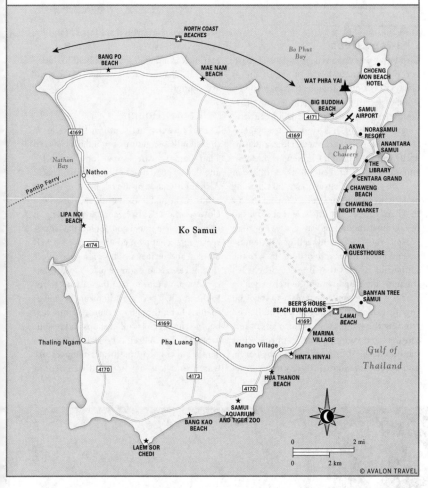

© AVALON TRAVEL

diving in. Hopping from Ko Samui to Ko Pha-Ngan to Ko Tao is simple but time-consuming, and there are frequent ferryboats between the islands.

If you're flying into nearby Surat Thani and taking a ferry to Ko Samui, expect to spend about half a day getting from the airport to the ferry pier and then to the island itself. It's not as convenient as flying into Ko Samui, but you may save yourself quite a few thousand baht. There are only two airlines—Bangkok Airways and Thai Airways—that fly into Ko Samui from Bangkok. Bangkok Airways, which owns the Samui airport, is known for great service and convenient flight schedules, but not cheap prices. Since Thai Airways started flying to Samui a few years ago, many thought prices would go down. So far, they haven't, so travelers on a budget usually opt to take one of the low-cost carriers to Surat Thani and transfer from there.

Beaches

EAST COAST
Chaweng Beach

Chaweng Beach, on the island's east coast, is the most famous beach in Samui, and it always draws more than its fair share of visitors, especially those traveling from other countries. The beach itself is a beautiful, long strip of light, soft sand backed by palm trees, and the water is warm, clear, and generally calm. Although Chaweng is one continuous bay, it's broken into three different sections—North Chaweng, Central Chaweng and Chaweng Noi, and Coral Cove just below it. There's a reef just offshore that serves to break most incoming waves. During high season, you can't avoid feeling a little hustle and bustle here, and visitors flock to the numerous resorts that line the beach. It's the most built-up area on the island, which makes it a very convenient place to stay, and in addition to the bungalows you'll find fronting the shore, there are also lots of restaurants and vendors. The main road runs parallel to the shore just behind the beach, and it feels more like a little city than a quiet

beach town. Here you'll see lots of familiar brands, such as McDonald's, Pizza Hut, and Starbucks. In fact, it might be hard to notice you're in Thailand at all, as most of the signs are in English.

★ Lamai Beach

Lamai Beach, just south of Chaweng, is the island's second most popular beach. In Thai, Lamai means "sweet" and "smooth," and that's a good description of Lamai Beach. Although Chaweng Beach has the softest sand and arguably the best view, Lamai is a close second. It's also second to Chaweng in terms of development and, for lots of visitors, represents a happy medium between development and seclusion. There is a good selection of resorts and ample places to eat, but it's also a bit more *sabai* than its neighbor to the north. There are still plenty of conveniences here, though, as central Lamai just behind the beach is full of shops and restaurants. The beach itself is typical of Samui—a gently curving bay, bathwater-temperature water, and lots of surrounding coconut

Lamai Beach

trees swaying in the wind. Lamai Beach has rougher water, as there's no reef to break the waves as they come in. At the southern end of the beach is the strange rock formation HinTa HinYai, which draws daily crowds of visitors.

SOUTH COAST

Hua Thanon Beach and **Bang Kao Beach** on the south of the island are the least developed on Samui. Some of this part of the coast is rocky, although there are plenty of places were you can comfortably spread out a towel or open a beach chair and enjoy the peace and quiet. There are not many accommodations on this part of the island, but the few that are here are quite nice and have private beaches. The village at Hua Thanon is a picture-perfect, charming little Muslim fishing village with a small market that adds to the overall beauty of the physical surroundings.

WEST COAST

The west coast of the island is dominated by **Nathon Bay,** where most ferries from Ko Pha-Ngan and Surat Thani arrive. The town of Nathon is definitely worth some time, as it's home to many of the local residents of the island and offers a chance to see what life is like in Thailand, but bear in mind that Nathon is the business end of Samui, and the beach itself is much less beautiful than what you'll find at Lamai, Chaweng, or Big Buddha Beaches.

South of Nathon Bay are two wonderful small beaches. **Lipa Noi Beach** is nestled amid coconut trees. The water is shallow for quite a way offshore, making it a great place for kids to play. There are a few cheap bungalows and resorts here, and a handful of places to eat, but otherwise it's a very quiet, almost sleepy beach area. May through November, the water is too shallow for swimming except at high tide. **Thaling Ngam** is a small, secluded beach backed by cliffs and ubiquitous coconut trees. The scenery is beautiful, but parts of the beach are rocky and the sand has lots of coral fragments, so it's not as soft as other beaches on the island.

★ NORTH COAST

On the northern part of the island, the largest stretch of beach is at **Bang Po Beach.** This beach, which is four kilometers (2.5 mi) long, has clear water, soft, light sand, and coconut trees as well as a coral reef just off the coast. It's backed by green hills and has a beautiful, secluded feeling. Despite all the draws, the beach is generally quite quiet, and there are only a handful of resorts and visitor amenities in the area. If you're looking to do a lot of swimming, this is not a great spot, as the water is very shallow until you pass the reef, and this may be why it's less popular. It's a good beach for snorkeling, however, since the reef is in shallow water, and you'll usually see at least a handful of people out looking at the reef and marinelife.

Mae Nam Beach, Bo Phut Beach, and **Big Buddha Beach** (also called Bangrak Beach) are all adjacent to each other on the northern coast, and some consider this the best part of the island. Each of the beaches is in a softly curving cove, and although there's no view of either sunset or sunrise, the beach, the water, and the surrounding greenery are beautiful. There are a handful of inexpensive bungalows here along with some of the nicest resorts on the island and some trendy, upscale places to eat. Although not nearly as busy as Chaweng Beach, there are still dive shops and travel agencies if you're looking to schedule an excursion. Some spots on these beaches won't be easily swimmable April-November due to seasonal tides that make the water too shallow. Mae Nam Beach is the quietest of the three and could be a great choice if you want to feel like you're in a quiet area but have access to more of the action. Plus it has the best selection of cheap bungalows. Bo Phut Beach is particularly charming, especially due to the adjacent fishing village with charming wooden shophouses. If you're looking to Jet Ski, it's one of the places on the island you can rent a Jet Ski on the beach. If you're looking for peace and quiet, however, all the activity can be annoying. Big Buddha Beach, right near the airport, has the most action. Although it's named after the large golden Buddha that sits on a nearby hill overlooking the island, it's not quite the tranquil spot the name would imply. There are scores of cheap bungalows here, and the beach tends to attract a younger crowd. Although there are no discos or true nightclubs, there are plenty of bars with live music lining the beach at night.

Sights

EAST COAST
Wat Phra Yai
วัดพระใหญ่

At the northern tip of the island is **Wat Phra Yai** (Temple of the Big Buddha), an outdoor temple with an immense 10-meter (33 ft) golden statue of Buddha. Although it's right near the eponymous Big Buddha Beach, it's a very peaceful place to visit and hear the resident monks pray and get a nice panoramic view of the surrounding area, especially at sunset (since you'll have to climb quite a few stairs to get to the Buddha). When you visit, you have to toll the bells surrounding the Buddha for good luck. If you're anywhere in the area, you won't be able to miss the big Buddha on the mountain. To get here, you'll need to take Route 4171 heading east, or arrange a ride with an off-duty *song thaew*.

SOUTH COAST
HinTa HinYai
หินตาหินยาย

Near Lamai Beach, **HinTa HinYai** (Grandfather and Grandmother Rocks) is a very famous natural phenomena—strange rocks look like human sex organs when viewed from a certain angle. The locals discreetly refer to them as grandfather and grandmother. Make sure to bring a camera to capture the view.

When you're done, make sure to buy some *kalamae* from one of the nearby vendors. It's a type of Thai toffee and it's creamy, not too sweet, and comes packaged in little triangles. The rocks are just a couple of kilometers south of Lamai Beach off of the ring road. If you are on Lamai, you can either walk there or catch a *song thaew* the short distance (make sure to tell the driver you are going to HinTa HinYai).

Mae Nam Beach, on the north coast of Ko Samui

Samui Aquarium and Tiger Zoo

พิพิธภัณฑ์สัตว์น้ำสมุยและสวนเสือ

The **Samui Aquarium and Tiger Zoo** (33/2 Mu 2, Maret, tel. 07/742-4017, www. samuiorchid.com, 9am-5pm daily, 250B) are part of the private Samui Orchid Resort, and the animals are there as entertainment, not part of a conservation effort or scientific endeavor. In the tanks you'll see lots of colorful coral as well as exotic tropical fish and even a couple of sharks. In the cages are tigers, monkeys, and birds, and you can even have your picture taken with one of the tigers if you're brave enough.

Laem Sor Chedi

เจดีย์แหลมสอ

On the southern tip of the island is **Laem Sor Chedi,** a seldom-visited, peaceful place with a large, ornate *chedi* (pagoda) right adjacent to the beach. Although you won't find much to do here, that's sort of the point. Next to the *chedi* is a small forest clearing often referred to as the meditation forest, where visitors can go and sit and ponder existence (you can even arrange to spend a few days at the *wat* learning how to meditate, but you'll need to work that out in person with the resident abbot). Laem Sor Chedi is about 1.5 kilometers (1 mi) off the main ring road around the island, so it is possible to take a *song thaew* and then walk the rest of the way. You can also take a taxi, but if you do not want to walk the 1.5 kilometers (1 mi) back to the main road, consider asking the driver to wait for you. The round-trip will cost you around 500 baht depending on which beach you are coming from. If you are driving, on the way to the *chedi* is a secret viewpoint. All of the signs are in Thai, so to get there your best bet is to enlist the help of a local (taking a taxi might be even better). You'll have to follow the turnoff to the Rattanakosin Chedi, up an extremely steep road to a beautiful viewpoint where you can see the southern part of the island.

★ MU KO ANG THONG NATIONAL PARK

อุทยานแห่งชาติหมู่เกาะอ่างทอง

The gem of the region, **Mu Ko Ang Thong National Park** spans a cluster of more than 40 small islands in the Samui Archipelago. The relatively small, amazingly green islands are really limestone mountains rising out of the sea, so there are plenty of caves and interesting rock formations to explore while you're there, as well as a handful of sandy beaches, rare birds, and macaques.

What really sets this group of islands apart is that they are virtually undeveloped and uninhabited, something you won't see on the Andaman coast. Before being declared a national park in 1980, the area was used by the Royal Thai Navy, and thus there are no bungalow developments or other commercial activity to disturb the natural environment. Getting to the islands is not a problem, though: There are plenty of tour companies on Samui and in Surat Thani who do daily day trips.

If you're into snorkeling or scuba, this is probably not the place for you, however. The water can be less than crystal clear, and there is only limited coral. This has nothing to do with the cleanliness of the water in the gulf; it's just that the islands are located in relatively shallow waters, and sediment that runs off from mainland rivers into the gulf doesn't settle quickly. If you're planning on visiting the park, remember that it is closed for most of November-December because of the monsoon season.

The national park headquarters (tel. 07/728-6025, 8am-7pm daily) are on the northwest part of the island of **Ko Wua Talap,** and this is a great place to start your tour of the islands (many guided tours stop here for a couple of hours). In addition to a white-sand beach right in front of the headquarters, there is also a hiking trail to a lookout point with a fantastic view of the surrounding islands. If you take the hike, expect to spend at least an hour going up and down, and do not attempt it in flip-flops. At certain points the trail becomes very steep (and very slippery if it has recently rained), and you'll need to rely on the ropes to pull yourself up. Although there are no commercial accommodations on any of the islands in the park, there are simple but charming fan-cooled bungalows and a campground on Ko Wua Talap as well as a drinks concession and a small restaurant.

Ko Mae Ko also has a nice beach to spend some time on, but if you're visiting this island, make sure to hike up to **Thale Nai,** a large emerald-green saltwater lake in the middle of rising cliffs. Much of the path is lined with stairs, which can be very steep at times, and as long as you go slowly, the 10-minute climb is fine even for moderately active people. For clear water, sandy beaches, and good snorkeling by the shore, **Ko Samsoa,** just across from Ko Mae Ko, is also a nice island on which to spend some time. If you're on a tour, you'll be provided with snorkel gear, though many boats don't bring fins.

Most visitors to the national marine park start from Ko Samui, where there are a number of tour operators that do the trip. There is no public ferry to Ko Wua Talap. Those visiting on their own need to arrange a charter speedboat with one of the tour companies on Ko Samui or Ko Phangan.

Shopping

Most of the tourist shopping you'll find on the island is in the **street stalls** surrounding the beaches, which sell everything from sarongs to kitchenware made of coconut shells.

If you're looking to drop a few baht, find that you've forgotten your flip-flops, or want casual and inexpensive beachwear, the best bet is **Chaweng Beach.** The nearby roads are lined with stalls and small shops, and it's an especially vibrant and bustling scene after dark. It's sometimes referred to as the **Chaweng Night Market,** although it is technically open all day. When you buy, make sure to barter, as prices tend to start high. Although there are some more upscale shops in Chaweng as well, prices are generally not that competitive if you're comparing them to what you'll find in Bangkok, or in any major city around the world, for that matter.

Fisherman's Village Walking Street (Hat Bophut Rd.) one block from Bophut Beach, is filled with small shops, restaurants, bars, massage parlors, and travel agencies. Every evening you'll find a handful of folks selling snacks and souvenirs, but on Friday nights the whole street is transformed into the **Fisherman's Village Night Market,** filled with vendors selling everything from knock-off tee shirts to fried squid, pizza, mojitos, and crepes.

The shopping scene for necessities is a little better. Chaweng has a **Tops Market** with international and local groceries, and there are similar shops in Lamai. The **Tesco Lotus** on the ring road between Bo Phut Beach and Chaweng Beach has everything from household appliances to staple groceries, plus fresh meat and produce. It's in a mall surrounded by smaller local shops, pharmacies, restaurants, and a movie theater.

Sports and Recreation

★ KAYAKING AND SNORKELING TOURS

Day tours to **Ang Thong National Park** or neighboring **Ko Tao** and **Ko Nang Yuan** are some of the most popular activities for visitors to Samui. There are a handful of companies offering these tours, which almost always include either snorkeling or kayaking. Some also include elephant trekking. Tickets are almost always sold through tour agents scattered across the island. Tours are very similar to one another and competitively priced, so expect to pay 1,200-1,500 baht for a day tour. Even though many brochures have prices printed on them, agents will almost always offer at least a 10 percent discount, so ask if you haven't been offered it. Also make sure to look over the tour brochure and ask the travel agent what your tour includes. Each usually includes pickup from your hotel or guesthouse; you'll be dropped off at the pier, where you'll board either a **speedboat** or a **ferry** with other passengers. Speedboat tours have the benefit of less time in transit and are a little more adventurous, but a ride on a larger boat allows for more relaxing and lounging. Regardless of the type of vessel, you'll be given a light breakfast (coffee and fruit or pastry) and you'll also be served lunch either on board or on one of the islands you'll stop at. Make sure to bring a swimsuit, towel, and good shoes for hiking, as many tours include stops on islands with good viewpoints.

Samui Island Tour (349 Mu 3, Ang Thong, tel. 07/742-1506, www.samui-island-tour.com) offers daily tours of Ang Thong National Marine Park on large ferries, with stops at Ko Mae Ko and Ko Wua Talap (national park headquarters). It also offers kayaking with a guide on its tours. Expect to pay 400-500 baht extra to use the company's kayaks.

Seahawk Speedboat (14/1 Mu 2, Chaweng Beach, tel. 07/723-1597) offers speedboat tours of both Ang Thong National Marine Park and the islands surrounding Ko Tao. The marine park tours are similar to those offered by Samui Island Tours with the addition of a stop at Ko Paluay, where you can snorkel or use one of the company's kayaks. Its Ko Tao day tour takes you to Ko Tao for snorkeling, then to Ko Nang Yuan (the three connected islands) for sunbathing and sightseeing.

Another speedboat tour is **Grand Sea Discovery** (187 Mu 1, Mae Nam Beach, tel. 07/742-7001, www.grandseatours.com), which offers tours to Ko Tao and Ko Nang Yuan, Ang Thong National Marine Park, or Ko Pha-Ngan. Its Ko Tao trip follows basically the same route as Seahawk Speedboat's, and its marine park tour is similar to that of Samui Island Tour. Grand Sea Discover also offers a one-day tour of Ko Pha-Ngan, where you'll do some sightseeing, visit an elephant camp, have lunch, and swim and snorkel.

Sea Safari by Speed Boat (tel. 07/742-5563, www.islandsafaritour.com) offers a typical tour of Ang Thong National Marine Park, which includes sea canoeing, but also adds elephant trekking or ATV biking in the afternoon, making for a long but full day.

ISLAND TOURS

If you're interested in staying on dry land, there are also a few outfits offering island tours. **Sita Tour 2000** (9/13 Mu 2, Chaweng Beach, tel. 07/748-4834) offers half-day tours of the island's sights, including stops at the Big Buddha, HinTa HinYai rocks, and even a monkey show. These trips cost less than 500 baht for a half day, but they do not include meals, and since the island's sights and attractions aren't all that spectacular, they are probably best left for a rainy day. **Mr. Ung's Safari** (52/4 Mu 3, Chaweng Beach, tel. 07/723-0114, www.ungsafari.com) offers full-day tours of the island's sights but throws in some trekking, four-wheeling, and elephant rides.

BOATING

Lately Samui has become a popular place for sailors—not the type on shore leave from long journeys abroad but the jet-set kind who like to travel in multimillion-dollar yachts. Much of this popularity may be due to the **Samui Regatta** (www.samuiregatta.com), an annual five-day sailboat race held in late May-early June, pulling in competitors from all over the world. If you find yourself without your own boat on Samui, there are a handful of sailboat rental agencies, including **Samui Ocean Sports** (Chaweng Regent Beach Resort, 155/4 Mu 2, Bo Phut Beach, tel. 08/1940-1999, www.sailing-in-samui.com) and **Sunsail Thailand** (Phuket Boat Lagoon, tel. 081/891-4437, www.sunsailasia.com). If you're lucky enough to be staying at the posh Anantara Samui, it has a number of craft available for rent, including Hobbies and Lasers, as well as sailing lessons and other sailing activities.

Accommodations

EAST COAST
Under 1,500B

For a quintessential beach bungalow experience, try **New Huts** (Lamai Beach, tel. 08/9729-8489, 200B). Here you'll get a small, very basic wooden bungalow just a few steps above a shack and share a basic bath with other travelers. Oh, and there's no air-conditioning, but for 200 baht it's hard to complain, especially considering the location a short walk from a nice part of Lamai Beach. If you can't get a room here, **Beer's House Beach Bungalows** (161/4 Mu 4, Lamai Beach, tel. 07/723-0467, www.beerhousebungalow.com, 600B) is another excellent option in the budget category. Here most of the bungalows have private baths with cold-water showers, and there is a small restaurant on the premises.

The ★ **Akwa Guesthouse** (28/12 Chaweng Beach Rd., tel. 08/4660-0551, www.akwaguesthouse.com, 800B) is head and shoulders above the typical guesthouse experience in Thailand, and if you're looking for an edgy, comfortable place on Samui, and there happens to be a room available, you can't go wrong here. The guesthouse, just a two-minute walk from quieter northern Chaweng Beach, is clean, funky, and inexpensive, and the management and staff are excellent. The guest rooms are all decorated with pop art prints and colorful, thoughtfully placed furnishings, starkly contrasting against the white-duvet-covered beds. There's free Wi-Fi throughout, and standard guest rooms come equipped with DVD and MP3 players; some have nicely decorated wooden decks, too. If you want to have an urban palace in the middle of the tropics, the 65-square-meter (700 sq ft) penthouse is also available, and it has an amazing deck. The downstairs restaurant, which offers very reasonably priced Thai and Western dishes all day, has the same design theme and friendly attitude. Aside from the fabulous decor, reasonable prices, and good food, everyone who works at the Akwa is sincere and will go out of their way to make your stay memorable, from arranging airport transfers to setting up excursions. Although there's no pool here and it doesn't have the typical resort amenities, this is the type of place you rarely find in touristy areas and one you'll want to return to again after your first stay.

Beachfront bungalows are tough to find in this price range on this beach, but **Thong Ta Kian Villa** (Thong Ta Kien Bay, 146 Mu 4, Maret, tel. 07/723-0978, 1,300B) offers some exceptionally clean, large, stand-alone guest rooms. Design is simple, and this is certainly not a resort, but extras such as air-conditioning, small fridges to keep your beer cold, and

TVs put this property well above the typical beach bungalow offerings.

NovaSamui Resort (147/3 Mu 2, Chaweng, tel. 07/723-0864, www.novasamui.com, 1,200B) has cheap, clean guest rooms, a large swimming pool, and nicely maintained common areas. Although the NovaSamui has some resort-level amenities, it's not a luxury resort, and it's not right on the water, but just a short walk from Chaweng Beach. For about one-third of the price, however, it's an excellent choice.

Marina Villa (124 Mu 3, Lamai Beach, tel. 07/742-4426, www.marinavilla-samui.com, 1,400B), right on Lamai Beach, is a small, pleasant, family-friendly resort with comfortable, clean guest rooms and a good location. This is not a luxury resort but does have two swimming pools and a restaurant.

1,500-3,000B

Choeng Mon Beach Hotel (24/3 Mu 5, Choeng Mon Beach, Bo Phut, tel. 07/742-5372, www.choengmon.com, 1,500B), on Choeng Mon Beach just northeast of Bo Phut Beach, is a somewhat generic midsize tourist hotel but has amenities and facilities, including a swimming pool, a small gym, and a restaurant that make it a good value for guests who want resort perks but do not want to pay resort prices for them. Guest rooms at this beachfront property are clean, simple, and comfortable. Larger groups can also rent one of the bungalows.

The **Lamai Wanta** (124/264 Mu 3, Lamai Beach, tel. 07/742-4550, www.lamaiwanta.com, 1,800B) is right on Lamai Beach and has modern, comfortable, well-maintained guest rooms and a small but very pretty pool overlooking the ocean. There are both traditional hotel rooms and stand-alone villas, some with two bedrooms. The location, just walking distance from Lamai's restaurants, is convenient, but the hotel is big enough that it still feels quiet and private.

Montien House (5 Mu 2, Chaweng Beach, tel. 07/742-2169, www.montienhouse.com, 2,500B) is another great property on Chaweng

if you're looking for a resort environment but don't want to pay five-star prices. The Montien is right on the beach but far enough away from the center that you'll be able to enjoy some peace and quiet. There's a lovely small pool and a beachside restaurant, and the traditional Thai-style grounds are well maintained. The standard guest rooms are clean and well maintained, if a little Spartan. The beachfront guest rooms, housed in small cottages, are a little more expensive but feel a little more luxurious and are great for small families.

Another inexpensive gem on Chaweng is **Tango Beach Resort** (119 Mu 2, North Chaweng Beach, www.tangobeachsamui.com, 2,700B). This is not five-star luxury, but nonetheless it's an amazing value for the price. The small resort has pretty, simple grounds with a nice, if small, swimming pool, a beachfront bar and restaurant, and its own chair-and-towel service on the sand. The guest rooms are surprisingly well furnished in a modern Thai style, and some even have views of the ocean. Baths are on par with more expensive resorts and feature rain showerheads and glass bowl sinks. The hotel is located in northern Chaweng, which is a more relaxed and quiet area of the beach, although it's not as easy to swim here because there are sandbars at low tide. If you're looking to get to the bustling center, expect a 15-minute walk or five-minute motorcycle ride.

The Maryoo Hotel Samui (99/99 Mu 2, North Chaweng Rd., tel. 07/760-1102, www.maryoosamui.com, 2,700B), a modern midsize hotel near Chaweng Beach, has very clean, comfortable guest rooms and a big, beautiful swimming pool. There is also an average Thai restaurant and a spa on the property. This won't be the right choice for those looking for lots of personality, but those who want cleanliness and comfort at a reasonable price will find it a great value.

3,000-4,500B

Villa Nalinnadda (99/1-4 Mu 1, Maret, tel. 07/723-3131, www.nalinnadda.com, 3,500B) is a small luxury boutique hotel on Lamai Beach that seems like it was expressly designed for honeymoons and romantic getaways. All of the eight bright, airy guest rooms on the property face the ocean, they'll serve you breakfast in bed whenever you want it, and the guest rooms also come equipped with private whirlpool tubs. There's also a definite Greek Mediterranean feeling to the property, thanks to the bright white buildings, but you won't forget that you're still in Thailand. The beach it's on is very quiet, but if you travel down to the center of Lamai Beach, you can find some more action.

Over 4,500B

If you want to stay in a large resort hotel with lots of amenities and facilities as well as nicely appointed guest rooms, the **Centara Grand** (38/2 Mu 3, Chaweng Beach, tel. 07/723-0500, www.centarahotelsresorts.com, 6,500B) is a great choice on Chaweng Beach. The resort has more than 200 guest rooms, so although it doesn't quite feel secluded, there is plenty of pool space, a beautiful full-service spa, and bars and restaurants on the premises. There are also tennis courts and even a small Jim Thompson Thai Silk outlet. The guest rooms are all modern Thai with dark hardwood flooring and private balconies. The property has just undergone refreshing and renovation, so the guest rooms and grounds feel new and fresh despite the fact that the resort has been around for a while. Although it's quiet and peaceful on the grounds, just outside on Chaweng Beach it can get crowded and noisy, especially during high season.

Beluga Boutique Hotel (129/92 Mu 3, Lamai, tel. 07/731-0710, 6,000B) is a very small (14-room), adults-only resort on the beach at the far southern tip of Lamai. The new resort has modern, clean rooms, with contemporary decor and furnishings. It's not quite a five-star property, but because it is so small, the little stretch of beach in front of it feels much less crowded than in other, larger resorts. Facilities include a swimming pool between the resort and the beach, an on-site restaurant and lounge, and a small spa. If the resort feels too small, head out to the main area of Lamai, as there are plenty of places to eat and drink just a few minutes away by car. Almost all rooms have a view of the sea, too. No children under 14 are allowed.

Another pleasant, midrange resort in Lamai is **Rocky's Boutique Resort** (438/1 Mu 1, Lamai, tel. 07/723-3020, 6,000B). The very picturesque property is right on the beach, and perhaps the name "Rocky's" refers to the large boulders that surround it, a common topographical element in the area. Rooms are spotless, comfortable, and designed in a Thai-cum-Swiss-chalet style that defies the odds by looking nice. With nearly 50 rooms, the common grounds and facilities are just big enough for most guests. There is a beautiful swimming pool at the center of the resort, but no on-site fitness center (it's a five-minute drive away).

The Library (14/1 Mu 2, Chaweng Beach, tel. 07/742-2767, www.thelibrary.co.th, 12,600B) is centered on the property's immense, trendy library filled with books and magazines, but guests may find it hard to focus on anything other than the superb modern design of the resort. It's just too cool here. The buildings are white minimalist cubes, and the grounds are filled with modern sculpture. The best part is the red-tiled swimming pool. Inside the enormous guest rooms and suites, expect to find sleek wood furniture, lots of sunlight, and sparse decorations; they share the same clean, modern design as the rest of the resort. You'll still find the same types of amenities, such as a beachside restaurant and cozy lounge chairs on the beach, as you would in other similarly priced resorts.

Banyan Tree Samui (99/9 Mu 4, Lamai Beach, tel. 07/791-5333, www.banyantree. com, 18,000B) is a luxurious all-villa property in the northern part of Lamai Beach. The Banyan Tree Samui, which cascades down the side of a hill overlooking Lamai Bay, is understated and elegant, with some subtle Thai design elements throughout the dozens of structures that make up the property. Even basic villas have their own private swimming pools and private gardens. Complimentary golf cart service will take you down to the beach at the base of the resort. For those traveling with children, the property has a small kids' club and babysitting services.

WEST COAST
1,500-3,000B

The **Viva Vacation Resort** (19/4 Mu 3, Nathon Beach, tel. 07/748-5611, www.vivavacationresort.com, 2,500B) has huge, clean rooms and bungalows, lush, well-maintained grounds, and a pretty swimming pool. Rooms are nicely furnished and decorated, though picky travelers might find the Thai decor a bit over the top. Not a tragedy considering this is a three-star property and prices are more than reasonable. Because there are only a dozen rooms here, and it is in a less densely populated location, it's a nice spot for those who want to relax and enjoy the peace and quiet. Nathon Beach is close by and, while it isn't the most swimmable beach on the island, those looking to lounge in the sand or walk on the shore will find it suitable.

The **Sibaja Palms Sunset Beach Resort Apartment** (39/1 Nara Taling Ngam Rd., Taling Ngam, tel. 081/270-6872, www.sibajapalmssamui.com, 2,300B) is a small, midmarket resort with large rooms, called apartments on this property, and villas. Though the facilities are limited by the fact that there are fewer than a dozen rooms and villas here, there is a nice, large swimming pool and pretty garden area for guests to enjoy. Apartments, which are nicely furnished with typical Thai wooden furnishings, have kitchenettes but don't have separate rooms for sitting or dining. Villas have two floors. The fitness room, with its own *muay Thai* room, is a fun detail. The location feels a little remote to some; others find the relative lack of tourism in the immediate vicinity to be a plus.

Over 4,500B

The **Intercontinental Samui** (295 Mu 3, Taling Nam Beach, tel. 07/742-9100, www. starwoodhotels.com, 8,000B), a five-star resort on Taling Nam Beach, has every amenity a guest could want, including a beautifully decorated kids' club with daily activities, a spa, a variety of food and drink options, and seven swimming pools to choose from. Rooms are clean, comfortable, and well appointed, but like other properties in this chain, decor wise they are plain or even a little old-fashioned. Though some might like the fact that this resort is in a less-crowded part of Samui, if you want to get off the resort you will need to arrange transport; there are no big points of interest within walking or quick driving distance.

NORTH COAST
Under 1,500B

Though not right on the beach, **Cocooning Hotel and Tapas Bar** (6/11 Mu 1, Bo Phut Beach, tel. 07/742-7150, www.cocooninghotelsamui.com, 1,000B) is a lovely, intimate, well-designed guesthouse with some of the prettiest guest rooms you'll find on the island for the price. There are only a handful of guest rooms here, and each has its own color and design theme against a backdrop of white walls and modern concrete flooring. This is not a resort, and it's quite small, so the only amenities available are a very small swimming pool and a tapas bar serving drinks and light snacks. Still, the property has a very chic European feel to it, probably thanks to the French owner.

Ampha Place Hotel (67/59 Mu 1, Mae Nam, tel. 07/733-2129, www.samui-amphahotel.com, 1,200B) has cheap, clean guest rooms just 10 minutes on foot from Mae Nam Beach. Ampha Place is a no-frills property but isn't old or run-down. Guest rooms are small but surprisingly well equipped, have small balconies, and are accented with Thai decor. There is also a small but pretty swimming pool in the middle of the property.

While there are plenty of beach bungalows in the 400-500 baht range on Mae Nam Beach, **Moon Huts** (67/2 Mu 1, Mae Nam, tel. 07/742-5247, www.moonhutsamui.com, 500B) tend to be a little cleaner and nicer than the competition. At this price they won't deliver luxury, but you will get a private bath, fresh sheets, and a spotless guest room a short walk from the beach and the property's bar-restaurant. Nicer bungalows on the beach have air-conditioning instead of fans; expect to pay around 1,000 baht for these. There are also large two-bedroom family bungalows available.

Like other Ibis properties in Thailand and all over the world, **The Ibis Bophut** (197/1 Mu 1, Bo Phut Beach, tel. 02/659-2888, www.ibishotel.com, 1,400B) offers guests a good location and spotlessly clean, reliable guest rooms and common areas. Guest rooms at this large hotel are very small, but the bar, restaurant, and large pool area give guests plenty of other options for hanging out. There are also family rooms available with bunk beds for kids, although they are also small.

1,500-3,000B

A good location and reasonably priced guest rooms are what make **Samui Hacienda** (98/2/1 Mu 1, Bo Phut Beach, tel. 07/724-5943, www.samui-hacienda.com, 1,800B) such a good value. Guest rooms, many of which have beach views, are simple but clean and comfortable, and the whole property is well maintained. The design theme—a fusion of Mediterranean and Thai styles—surprisingly does not seem out of place in Bo Phut. There is a very small rooftop pool, not big enough to get any exercise but a wonderful place for a cocktail or just to cool off.

The guest rooms and villas at **The Waterfront Boutique Hotel** (71/2 Mu 1, Bo Phut Beach, tel. 07/742-7165, www.thewaterfrontbophut.com, 2,900B) are simple and unpretentious, and the setting right next to the beach, with the requisite coconut trees shading the sun, is as good as it gets. What sets this property apart is the relaxed environment, the friendly staff, and the great value for the money. There's a pool and also a small restaurant on the premises where you can enjoy a complimentary fresh-cooked breakfast and

Wi-Fi, but it's not quite luxurious enough to be a boutique hotel. It is, however, a very family-friendly place—there are larger suites available as well as babysitting services.

Over 4,500B

The ★ **Anantara Samui** (101/3 Bo Phut Bay, tel. 07/742-8300, www.anantara.com, 6,000B) has all the luxury, style, and generous Thai hospitality that has made Samui famous the world over. The grounds are perfectly manicured and filled with exotic details such as fire torches and reproductions of ancient sculptures. The pool area, with a large infinity pool that seems to spill out into the Gulf of Thailand, and the main lobby look like the grounds of a royal palace. The guest rooms are modern and luxurious, and there's also an indulgent spa and lots of great restaurants to eat and drink at. The staff is professional and friendly. If you're looking for a place to splash out, perhaps for a honeymoon or an anniversary, you will not be disappointed here. The Anantara offers lots of the typical activities and excursions, but they also have windsurfing lessons on Bo Phut Bay as well as sailboat rental.

Bo Phut Resort and Spa (12/12 Mu 1, Bo Phut Beach, tel. 07/724-5777, 7,000B) is a pretty, upscale resort on Bo Phut Beach. The decor of the property is classic Thai resort style, with high pitched roofs, lots of palm trees, and local art on the walls. The large rooms and villas on the property all have modern amenities including Wi-Fi, flat-screen TVs, and DVD players, what one would expect for a resort at this price. There's a kids' club with daily activities, and some activities for grown-ups as well. Though the resort is not secluded, the grounds are quiet and peaceful. If you want to enjoy some of Bo Phut's nightlife, you're only about 10 minutes from the center of Fisherman's Village.

The **Scent Hotel** (58/1 Mu 4, Bo Phut Beach, tel. 07/796-2198, www.thescenthotel.com, 6,000B), a high-end, intimate boutique hotel right on the beach, has beautifully furnished guest rooms with European or Asian decor (you can specify, depending on availability). Regardless of decor, guest rooms are spacious and many have balconies with enough space to dine. The common areas are not large, but all guest rooms open onto the property's pleasant beachfront infinity pool and are reminiscent of an old Chinese shophouse.

Napasai (65/10 Mu 10, Mae Nam Beach, tel. 07/742-9200, www.napasai.com, 10,000B), one of the Orient Express branded hotels, is also one of the island's most luxurious and indulgent properties. The villas and guest rooms are scattered among the surrounding hills and are spacious and private. Some also have kitchens where guests or staff can cook. Expansive common areas, including an infinity pool, a spa, two restaurants, and two bars, mean guests don't need to leave the property for anything if they don't want to.

Sila Evason Hideaway & Spa (9/10 Mu 5, Ban Plai Laem, Bo Phut Beach, tel. 07/724-5678, www.sixsenses.com, 17,000B) looks like it was built specifically with the jet-setting movie-star crowd in mind. The private thatched-roof villas come complete with personal butlers available to answer your every need. Each also has a small private dip pool and lounge area. And the views, which you can easily enjoy from the comfort of your bed, are amazing. The public parts of the property, including the large swimming pool and open-air restaurant, are equally swanky, although the style of the grounds and buildings is subdued, sleek, and modern.

The **Hansar Samui** (101/28 Mu 1, Bo Phut Beach, tel. 07/724-5511, www.hansarsamui.com, 6,300B), part of a small but up-and-coming chain of luxury hotels in Thailand, is a high-end property right on the beach in Bo Phut. The ethos of this chain seems to be upscale, international, and sophisticated, and those themes seem to run throughout the property. Rooms are clean, modern, and understated but chic—plenty of natural material and neutral colors. Some rooms have great views of the pool and ocean. The centerpiece of the modern resort is the large swimming pool, which overlooks the ocean. There is also a small fitness center.

Though a stay at the **W Retreat Koh Samui** (41/1 Mu 1, Mae Nam Beach, tel. 07/791-5999, www.starwoodhotels.com, 15,000B) doesn't come cheap, it's fast becoming a favorite jet-setter destination in Samui. Every accommodation is a stand-alone or semiattached villa with a private swimming pool, separate lounging space, and massive bathroom with oversized bathtub, so guests enjoy a level of privacy not typical in most resorts. If your private pool is boring, head to the common swimming pool or the semiprivate beach. There is also a fitness center, tennis court, and water sports center on the premises. The atmosphere all over the resort, like other Ws, feels a little like a lounge/nightclub, though the average guests who can afford to stay here are not in their twenties.

Food

Whatever you're in the mood for, you won't go hungry on Ko Samui. The island seems to have an inordinate number of restaurants for its size. Although there are plenty of uninspired, overpriced tourist restaurants, there are more and more excellent places to eat, whether you're looking for quick, inexpensive street food, international fare, or a special

Thai meal in a romantic setting overlooking the ocean. On Ko Samui, it's important to remember that the quality of the food sometimes has no relationship to the appearance of the restaurant. Some of the best meals to be found are at very casual places that almost look like holes-in-the-wall. Although you'll find the most restaurants on and near busy

Chaweng Beach, if you're looking for a place to enjoy a meal and watch the sunset, head to Nathon Beach on the west coast of the island.

MARKETS

The **Lamai Food Center,** about 2.5 kilometers (1.5 mi) from HinTa HinYai, in front of the Wat Lamai School, has a handful of small casual restaurants with great inexpensive Thai food. This is a very relaxed local spot, so expect great food but not a lot of amenities. Many of these restaurants stay open 'til the wee hours of the morning. If you're in the mood for some *kanom chin* (rice noodles with curry), try **Sophita** (tel. 08/6954-8861, 9am-3am daily, 40B). For simple but hearty *guay teow* or *khao mu dang* (red pork with rice), try **Chakangraw Noodle** (tel. 08/9868-8515, 10am-10pm daily, 40B). If you're in the mood for freshly made seafood, **Chaophraya Seafood** (tel. 07/741-8117 or 08/6345-9647, 11am-9pm daily, 80B) has excellent *gang thot kratiem* (extra-large fried shrimp with garlic and pepper).

Right near Chaweng Beach, close to the Island Resort and Chaweng Villa Resort, is a food center with different food vendors where you can find fresh fruit, the typical selection of noodles and rice dishes, and lots of seafood.

THAI

If you're near Lamai Beach, stop at **Sabiang Lae** (tel. 07/723-3082, 10am-10pm daily, 200B), between Lamai Beach and Ban Hua Thanon, for seafood Samui style. This casual open-air beachfront restaurant is a great place to watch the sunset and enjoy some *kung yai thot rad nam manao* (fried lobster with lime juice) and *yum sabiang lae* (spicy seafood salad).

Bang Po Seafood (Bang Po Beach, tel. 07/742-0010, 10am-10pm daily, 300B) on Bang Po Beach is another great seafood restaurant with a similar atmosphere to Sabiang Lae. This is a popular spot among international and Thai visitors to the island, perhaps because of the *kei ji* appetizer they offer for free. It's a delicious blend of shrimp paste and

coconut, and you won't find it anywhere in Bangkok.

Another great casual open-air spot for good, inexpensive food is **Sunset Restaurant** (Nathon 175/3, Mu 3, Tambon Ang Thong, tel. 07/742-1244, 4pm-10pm daily, 300B) on Nathon Beach. Although it's not right on the beach, as the name implies, it's a great place to watch the sunset overlooking Nathon pier, and the Thai food is fresh, fast, and cheap. Try the rice in coconut if you're looking for something hearty and not spicy; it's great comfort food. This is definitely a casual place to eat, so don't worry about showing up in flip-flops and a T-shirt.

K-Siri (4169 Mu 1, Bo Phut Ring Rd., no phone, 6pm-10pm daily, 150B), a modest restaurant serving Thai seafood, is the perfect spot for those looking for a place to eat that's basic and simple but doesn't skimp on quality ingredients or preparation. The open-air restaurant, just a short walk from the beach, is a step above a basic shophouse (they even serve wine!) but is definitely pleasant enough for a casual dinner.

FUSION AND INTERNATIONAL

If you're on Chaweng Beach for breakfast, head straight to **Akwa Guesthouse** (28/12 Chaweng Beach Rd., tel. 08/4660-0551, 7am-11pm daily, 300B). Its breakfast combos are generous and delicious; no tiny slices of toast and hot dogs masquerading as sausages here. Instead, you'll get real sausage, fresh bread, omelets, pancakes, and even hash browns. All of that comes on one plate if you order the Canadian breakfast. Their imported coffee is also excellent, and the bright colors and friendly staff will definitely help wake you up.

Poppies (Chaweng Beach, tel. 07/742-2419, www.poppiessamui.com, 6:30am-midnight daily, 600B) has become something of an island sensation in the past decade, thanks to the elegant setting at the resort of the same name, the beach view, and the excellent food. The restaurant serves Thai and international dishes, and both sides of the menu offer innovative interpretations of standard fare. Try the *kai pad met mamuang* (stir-fried chicken with cashew nuts) or the roast-duck spring rolls if you're looking for something familiar with a creative twist. Or try the ostrich in panang curry for something really unexpected. Poppies also has an extensive selection of seafood and grilled meats as well as a very good vegetarian menu. The vegetarian green curry with pumpkin is excellent and something you won't be able to find meatless in many places.

Top Ten (98 Mu 2, Chaweng Beach Rd., tel. 07/723-0235, www.toptenrestaurantsamui. com, 5pm-11pm daily, 400B), a nicely decorated, upscale modern restaurant, serves a mix of straight European flavors, fusion, and some standard Thai dishes, including a clever *tom yam* pasta. The restaurant wins on decor and service, and it's a great choice if you want to eat somewhere a little nicer than the typical Chaweng Beach restaurant.

Sala Thai (12/12, Mu 1, Tambon Mae Nam, tel. 07/742-5031 to 07/742-5038, 6pm-11pm daily, 700B) is another excellent choice for an upscale Thai meal. The restaurant is part of the Santiburi Resort but attracts plenty of people who aren't staying there. The setting—traditional Thai architecture, lily ponds, pathways lit with tiki torches, and a luxuriant garden—is about as romantic as it gets. The food is mostly traditional Thai cuisine, and it's all expertly prepared and presented. The *tom yam kung* is as good as you'll find anywhere, as are other classic dishes such as *kai phat* (stir-fried chicken) and *pha kung* (spicy shrimp salad).

The chef at **Zazen** (Zazen Boutique Resort and Spa, 177 Mu 1, Bo Phut Beach, tel. 07/742-5085, 5pm-11pm daily, 600B) mixes fresh local ingredients with foreign flavors to create interesting and innovative modern Thai and fusion cuisine. The elegant restaurant, with a nice view of the Gulf of Thailand, serves dishes such as five spices-marinated barracuda, sesame and wasabi-crusted shrimp, and *neua pla nam deng* (caramelized roasted fish) in addition to some traditional Thai and

European favorites. For dessert, the banana flambé in Mekhong whiskey is both entertaining and palate-pleasing.

Betelnut (43/4-5 Mu 3, Soi Colibri, Chaweng Beach, tel. 07/741-3370, 6pm-11pm daily, 700B) is a top contender for best restaurant on the island. The California-Thai fusion menu is filled with the dishes of crab cake, seared tuna, and duck breast you'll find at upscale international dining spots around the world. To spice things up a bit, the U.S.- and European-trained chef also features dishes such as New England clam chowder with green curry and softshell crab with mango and papaya salad. Although there are lots of culinary risks being taken in the kitchen, the food is too good to be gimmicky. The restaurant is light and airy, with plenty of modern art on the walls.

Another great choice for a special dinner on Chaweng Beach is **Eat Sense** (11 Mu 2, Chaweng Beach, tel. 07/741-4242, 11am-midnight daily, 700B). The upscale beachside restaurant has lots of seating with great views of the Gulf of Thailand, and there are plenty of little patios at different levels to make the large space feel a little more intimate. The cuisine is international, and there are lots of seafood dishes to choose from. The Thai food, which includes a variety of seafood dishes such as the classic *pla thot ta khrai* (fried whole fish with lemongrass, garlic, and lime juice) is definitely made for Western palates. If you're looking for something a little spicier, make sure to ask.

The cliff-top **Dr. Frogs** (103 Mu 3, Chaweng Beach Rd., tel. 07/741-3797, www. drfrogssamui.com, noon-2am daily, 400B), a Thai and Italian restaurant, has some of the nicest views on the island and for that reason alone is worth visiting for drinks or dinner. Food is well prepared and presented, and while their pizzas may not remind you of your vacation in Italy, considering the island location, they are pretty good. Pastas and seafood entrées are consistently delicious.

The dark wood furnishings, lounge music, and trendy patrons make ★ **Rice** (167/7 Mu 2, Chaweng Beach, tel.

KO SAMUI
FOOD

07/723-1934, www.ricesamui.com, 6pm-midnight daily, 400B) feel more like the type of Italian restaurant you'd find in a trendy city neighborhood instead of on the main strip in Chaweng Beach. The food is among the best European fare you'll find on Samui. In fact, the brick oven-baked pizza is unparalleled. Ditch the flip-flops, or you'll definitely feel underdressed.

The small, unpretentious, but well-put-together **Barracuda** (216/2 Mu 2, Soi 4, Mae Nam Beach Rd., tel. 07/724-7287 or 07/792-1663, www.barracuda-restaurant.com, 6pm-11pm daily, 400B) offers high-quality seafood dishes that take advantage of Thai flavors, such as lobster tortellini and salmon with a *tom yam* sauce, and other mostly Western fare. The interior feels more like a nice fish shack than a shophouse restaurant.

While combining Greek and Thai cuisine in one restaurant seems like a recipe for mediocrity, **Fi Kitchen & Bar** (75/1 Mu 1, Mae Nam Ring Rd., tel. 08/9607-2967, 6pm-11pm daily, 300B) pulls off the combo surprisingly well, and it's a fun, casual place to go, especially if you're craving Greek food. Fresh vegetables and lots of flavor seem to be the hallmarks of the Greek dishes, and the small stand-alone restaurant, which opened in early 2011, already has a following among expatriate and vacationing Greeks on Samui.

The sexy, shabby chic **Boudoir** (Soi 1, Mae Nam Beach, tel. 08/5783-1031, 6pm-midnight daily, 450B), offers casual French cuisine in a relaxing, fun atmosphere. This is a good place to go for inexpensive wine and cheese platters before dinner, although the full meals are also a great value.

Homesick for cheesecake, brownies, and a Western breakfast? Head to **Angela's Bakery and Café** (64/29 Mu 1, Mae Nam Beach, tel. 07/742-7396, 7am-3:30pm daily, 150B) for some of the best desserts and baked goods on the island. The very basic restaurant has been around for years, and it even has bagels and lox and sandwiches, although those looking for Thai food will find a few dishes.

For well-prepared, great-tasting vegetarian food, **Radiance** (Spa Samui Resort, 71/7 Mu 3, Maret, tel. 07/723-0855, 7am-10pm daily, 300B) is the best choice on the island and might even be the best in the country. The extensive menu has mostly meatless and vegan dishes made with lots of fresh fruits and vegetables, but it features a few fish and chicken meals, too. It can be difficult to find vegetarian versions of most Thai dishes, but here the kitchen can make just about anything, including *tom kha* (coconut soup) and *tom yam* (spicy, sour soup) without any meat products. Radiance also has a large breakfast menu featuring items such as French toast made with homemade whole-grain bread and veggie sausages. There's even a large selection of raw dishes for raw foodists. This is a casual place, with open-air seating on the spa's verdant grounds.

A Cajun restaurant in the middle of a tropical island in Southeast Asia seems a little strange, but when you enter **Coco Blues** (161/9 Mu 2, Chaweng Beach Rd., tel. 07/741-4354, 5pm-midnight daily, 300B) on Bo Phut Beach, it all makes sense. The spicy dishes, including blackened fish and Cajun crepes, taste just right in the heat, and the live blues music creates a decidedly comfortable atmosphere. The three-story restaurant opens onto the street and has New Orleans decor and vibe. If you've already eaten, drop in to listen to some music and have a draft beer or two.

For a casual beer and some barbecue, stop in to **Bill's Beach Bar** (near Hua Thanon Beach, just south of Lamai Beach, tel. 08/4778-9145, 9am-10pm daily). Imagine an open-air beach shack, add running water, a mix of Thai-, Australian-, and Western-style grilled meats, and plenty of foreigners, and you'll get a good idea of what to expect here. The bar holds a barbecue party every Sunday for just 100 baht per person.

A pretty beachside location, nice Mediterranean fare, and a relaxing atmosphere make **Ad Hoc Beach Cafe** (11/5 Mu 1, Bo Phut Beach, tel. 07/742-5380, noon-11:30pm daily, 450B) a perfect spot for a casual meal or a snack and cocktails while watching the sunset. The menu, mostly typical Italian dishes, is reliable and not too expensive, but it's the view that keeps people coming back.

★ **The Farmer** (1/26 Mu 4, Mae Nam Beach, tel. 07/744-7222, www.thefarmerrestaurantsamui.com, noon-11pm daily, 550B), surrounded by paddy fields with mountains in the background, is one of Samui's nicest new restaurants. The interior of the large open-air restaurant is upscale but understated, so it doesn't compete with the beautiful view outside. The menu, mostly European dishes but including some Thai classics, spotlights local and organic produce. It's definitely worth the taxi ride.

Information and Services

The regional **Tourism Authority of Thailand office** (TAT, 5 Talat Mai Rd., Surat Thani, tel. 07/728-2828) is located on the mainland in Surat Thani, but you can call either the office or the TAT hotline (1672, 8am-8pm daily) for information about ferry schedules and other travel-related issues.

Internet access is available at Internet cafés on most beaches. All large resorts and even many small guesthouses now offer Wi-Fi, too.

Transportation

GETTING THERE
Air
Charming **Samui Airport** is owned by **Bangkok Airways** (www.bangkokair.com), which runs as many as 17 flights per day during high season. Although Bangkok Airways has just opened the airport to **Thai Airways,** they are only running limited flights, mostly for international passengers connecting in Bangkok and traveling on to the island, but between the two, if you are booking even a few days in advance and are flexible with your travel times, you should be able to get a flight. The big exception to this is during high season, especially in December, when you should book as far in advance as possible. With limited competition, airfares to Samui from Bangkok are generally higher than for similar distances to other parts of the country, where budget airlines such as Nok Air can fly. Expect to pay 5,000-9,000 baht for a round-trip ticket to the island. The cheapest fares sell out quickly. From Bangkok, the flight is just over an hour.

Boat
If you have a little more time, it's easy to fly into Surat Thani on Nok Air or Air Asia and then take a fast boat to Samui. Flights to Surat Thani can cost as little as 3,000 baht round-trip with tax, and once you arrive at the Surat Thani airport, you can buy a combination bus-ferry ticket for around 300 baht that will take you from the airport to the pier, and then from the pier to the island. The **Pantip Ferry Company** (tel. 07/727-2906) has a booth in the Surat Thani airport. From the airport to the ferry pier is about 90 minutes; from the time you leave the airport, expect the whole trip to take about 4.5 hours to your hotel.

Bus or Train
You can also take a bus from Bangkok's Southern Bus Terminal or an overnight train from Hua Lamphong to Surat Thani (actually Phun Phin, about 16 kilometers [10 mi] outside downtown Surat Thani). If you are coming by train, you'll need to take a bus to the Donsak pier from the station, and then transfer to the ferry. Whatever time of day or night

you arrive, there will be touts selling combination bus-train tickets to Samui; they should cost no more than 300 baht.

If you are taking a government bus from Bangkok, the ride to Surat Thani is around 12 hours, but you'll then have to get from downtown Surat Thani to the pier. You can either take a local bus, which you can get at the bus station, or a taxi to Donsak pier. The better way may be to take a Samui express bus from Bangkok, using one of the private bus companies that leave from the Southern Bus Terminal. These buses will travel directly to the pier, and some include the ferry ride in the price. **Transportation Co.** (tel. 07/742-0765) and **Sopon Tours** (tel. 07/742-0175) both run VIP buses to the ferry, and fares are under 700 baht for the trip.

GETTING AROUND

Ko Samui has frequent *song thaew* that circle the island's main road from early morning into the evening. There are no fixed stops, so if you want a ride, just give the driver a wave and then hop in the back. When you want to get off, press the buzzer in the back (it's usually on the ceiling) and then pay your fare after you get off. Fares are set, and rides cost 20-60 baht if you are going from beach to beach. For trips from the pier to Chaweng, expect to pay 110 baht, less if you are traveling to a closer beach.

There are also plentiful **taxis** and **motorcycle taxis** on the popular beaches in the area. If you are staying somewhere more secluded, your guesthouse can call a taxi or motorcycle taxi for you.

Ko Pha-Ngan   เกาะพะงัน

If you're looking for a beautiful island with nice beaches that's cheap and full of folks who want to party all night long, this is the spot to pick. Although Ko Pha-Ngan is physically similar to Ko Samui, except that it's about half the size and has smaller sandy beaches instead of Samui's large, sweeping ones, and is just a short ferry trip away, it definitely feels a world apart. You won't see as much development here, or even any main roads. Instead, the island is rimmed by stretches of clean white sand, and the interior mountainous rainforest is peppered with inexpensive bungalows and, more and more, secluded resorts.

Although there is one long strip of coast on the west side of the island, which gives the added benefit of beautiful sunsets, many of the beaches on Ko Pha-Ngan are set in small coves backed by cliffs and thick forest. The physical landscapes are truly beautiful, and they are often the more secluded-feeling areas, but they can be really tough to access. Weather and tidal conditions permitting, you can take a longtail boat from one beach to another. Many of the roads leading to these beaches are

dirt roads; there are some 4WD vehicles on the island that can take you, and many visitors also rent motorcycles to get from one beach to another. If you go that route, be aware that some of the dirt roads can be treacherous on two wheels, especially if it has been raining.

In many ways, Ko Pha-Ngan is a breath of fresh air since it's so much less developed than other popular spots in the region. It tends to attract visitors such as young backpackers and aging hippies, all looking to enjoy the beauty of the region without spending a lot of money. For better or worse, the island has become something of an international party zone, probably thanks to the many young travelers who visit every year. During high season, the all-night full-moon parties have given way to half-moon parties and black-moon parties—any excuse to have a few drinks and dance around on the beach to music more fit for an urban rave than a tropical paradise. Don't bother wearing a watch, as the drinking tends to start as soon as the haze from the night before has cleared sufficiently to open a bottle of beer. If you're in the right mood, it can be a lot

Ko Pha-Ngan

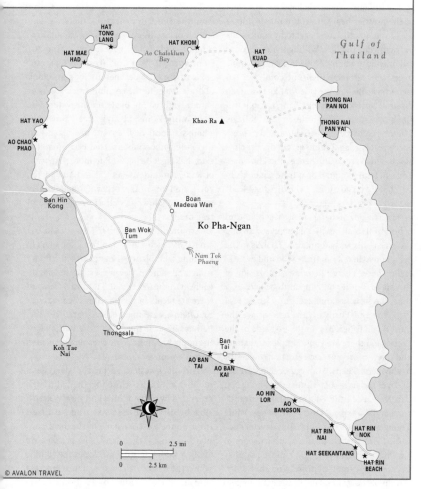

of fun, particularly because you can sleep your hangover off on one of the beautiful beaches come morning. If you're not into the scene, avoid Hat Rin, the island's party beach.

BEACHES AND ISLANDS

The beaches in the northern part of the island on **Ao Chaloklum Bay** are the least desirable on the island. The sand is darker and a little coarser, and the tides make it difficult to swim unless you're doing so at high tide. It's

also not a great place for snorkeling as most of the coral surrounding the bay is dead. It's not paradise, but it is home to a fishing village, so while you may not be able to enjoy the swimming too much, you will be able to hang out and watch the colorful longtail boats on the water. If you travel just a little east to **Hat Khom,** you'll find a prettier beach with some vibrant coral in relatively shallow water (great for snorkeling). This beach, however, is not easily swimmable at low tide either. **Hat**

Kuad, just to the west, is one of the island favorites. A wide swath of sand backed by green mountains and surrounded by a cove, it's one of the prettier beaches on the north side of the island. It's difficult to get to by land, so it's only crowded by those willing to take a longtail or endure a bumpy ride in a 4WD vehicle to get here. Although there's no coral, you can swim regardless of the tide thanks to a steep drop-off close to shore. **Hat Tong Lang** is in a small cove surrounded by leafy green foliage. There's a coral reef close to shore, and its presence creates a lagoon of sorts. This beach is also tough to access and hence calm and quiet. You can take a longtail boat from Chaloklum Bay, but if you go by land, the dirt road leading to the beach is pretty rough.

The east side of the island has just a handful of beautiful small beaches interspersed among the green hills and mountains. Thanks to the geography, there's a definite wild and natural feeling here. There's no coral on this side of the island, but if you happen to be awake in time, the sunrises are beautiful. **Thong Nai Pan Noi** and **Thong Nai Pan Yai** are the most popular beaches on the east side of the island, and there are some simple bungalows and a few more upscale resorts if you want to stay here. The two curved beaches are set in coves and have soft white sand. Thong Nai Pan Noi has a little village with restaurants, bars, and a few places to spend money, while Thong Nai Pan Yai is a little less developed.

Hat Rin Beach in the southern part of Ko Pha-Ngan is the island's most popular. Located on a small peninsula on the southern tip of the island, Hat Rin is actually two bays—**Hat Rin Nok** and **Hat Rin Nai** (also called Hat Rin Sunrise and Hat Rin Sunset, since the beaches face east and west, respectively). At the bottom of the peninsula is **Hat Seekantang,** a small, slightly quieter beach. All of the beaches on the peninsula have clean, light sand and clear water and are fringed with palm trees. Since they're so popular among travelers, there are plenty of bungalows and bars. Hat Rin Nok and Hat Rin Nai are home to the island's infamous full-moon parties, so

expect a lot of partying if you're hanging out or staying here.

Traveling up the west side of the island from the Hat Rin peninsula, there's a long stretch of beach broken only by an outcropping of verdant hills. Here you'll find **Ao Bangson, Ao Hin Lor, Ao Ban Kai,** and **Ao Ban Tai.** The beaches are long and look idyllic thanks to the coconut trees, views of Samui, and fishing boats on the water. The swimming is not always great, however. There's a coral reef just off the coast, and there are some sandbars that pop up at low tide, making it difficult to do more than walk or wade. Around Ao Ban Kai and Ao Ban Tai, you'll find lots of inexpensive to moderately priced bungalows as well as beach bars and restaurants.

Around the ferry pier at **Thongsala** is a stretch of beach more than five kilometers (3 mi) long with plenty of bungalows to choose from (and some of the cheapest on the island). Right at the beach, the land is mostly flat, and there are plenty of surrounding coconut trees that help create the tropical-paradise vibe. Perhaps because they're so close to the ferry, the bungalows tend to be cheaper and also to attract a younger crowd.

The upper western part of the island has a number of beaches close together, although separated by cliffs or hills and mostly accessible by dirt road. **Hat Yao** and **Ao Chao Phao** to the west are some of the most popular beaches on the island. The beaches are about a kilometer (0.6 mi) long, the sand is white, the western views spectacular, and the surrounding green hills an added bonus. Here you'll find a variety of accommodation options, from simple 200 baht-per-night bungalows with fans to more upscale small resorts.

Hat Mae Had is another beautiful white-sand beach fringed with coconut trees, but what really sets this beach apart is neighboring **Ko Ma,** a small island that's connected to the main island by a thin sandbar. The snorkeling around Ko Ma is great, as there is a lot of healthy coral and marinelife to look at, so it's also a popular dive site.

Full-Moon Parties

While it's tempting to think that celebrating the full moon by dancing out on the sand is part of some ancient Thai ritual, the truth is that it's a relatively new tradition and one that's primarily fueled by foreign visitors.

No one can agree on exactly how the tradition was started, but as the prevailing legend would have it, the full-moon parties that Ko Pha-Ngan has become famous for were started by a small group of backpackers who celebrated the full moon one night by throwing a party on Hat Rin. The party was such a success that on the night of the next full moon, they threw another party, and more visitors joined them, then another and another until the attendees packed the beach.

Whatever its origins, during peak season the full-moon parties on Hat Rin now attract thousands of partiers, and coming down to the beach for one of the outdoor all-night music-filled soirees is an unforgettable experience. There are DJs, fire-eaters, fireworks, and lots and lots of booze. The raves also tend to feature illicit drugs of various sorts and sometimes undercover police.

SPORTS AND RECREATION

If you're staying on Ko Pha-Ngan, expect to do quite a bit of **hiking,** unless you park yourself on the beach and don't leave 'til it's time to go home. Much of the island's interior is rugged, and some of it is rocky, so you'll need to be agile to get from one place to another. The island's highest peak is at **Khao Ra,** just over 600 meters (1,969 ft) above sea level. To hike there, start in the village of **Ban Madeua Wan** in the center of the island. The trail will take you past **Namtok Phaeng** and lead to the top of the mountain, where there's a viewpoint from which you can see the whole island. The trail is steep at times and not always clearly marked, so use caution when climbing, and expect to spend a couple of hours going and coming back if you are in good physical shape.

The west side of the island has some **coral reefs,** sometimes just a few hundred meters from the coastline. The water is generally very shallow until the reefs, so you'll be able to see the reefs without having to swim out too deep.

The best **diving** in the area is around **Ko Tao,** but the west side of **Ko Pha-Ngan** has some good diving, too. Most of the diving is relatively shallow, at around 15 meters (50 ft), but there's plentiful hard and soft coral to see as well as lots of colorful marinelife swimming around. Local dive companies also do daily trips to dive sites around the region.

ACCOMMODATIONS

Most of what you'll find on Ko Pha-Ngan are casual beach bungalows and midpriced small resorts. Unlike neighboring Ko Samui, the island isn't filled with luxurious amenities, although there are more small, high-end resorts opening every year. If you are on a tight budget and looking for simple accommodations, you'll be able to find something inexpensive and comfortable. If you want to get away from it all and enjoy a little luxury, there are a handful of resorts that are not in the middle of all of the action.

Coco Garden Bungalows (100/7 Mu 1, Bang Thai Beach, tel. 07/737-7721, www.co-cogardens.com, 400B) is as good a bungalow resort as you're going to find on the island. The small compound is right next to a beautiful strip of the beach, the bungalows are cute and well maintained, and the interiors are furnished in a simple Thai style. Only a handful of the bungalows come with air-conditioning, so if that's a priority, book early and make sure you confirm you are not in a fan-only guest room. There's a small, relaxed restaurant and bar on the premises serving inexpensive and well-made food and drink; if you're looking to enjoy some of the partying that goes on, you'll be close to the black-moon and half-moon parties on Hat Rin—but not so close that you won't be able to get some sleep if you want.

If you're on the island to enjoy the rugged

beauty and peace and quiet, the **Coconut Beach Bungalows** (Hat Khom Beach, Chaloklum, no phone, www.coconutbeach-phangan.com, 400B) on Hat Khom is an excellent choice. The bungalows are very simple and very cheap, and what they lack in amenities, such as hot water and air-conditioning, they make up for in the friendliness of the staff and the secluded, peaceful feeling that seems to permeate the area. The beach is good for snorkeling, and the staff has snorkel sets available. There is a small restaurant attached, but if you're looking for more action, it'll be tough to get there—you have to travel about 15 minutes on an unpaved road to get back to civilization (the bungalow will arrange to pick you up at the pier and take you back when you depart). Better to pack a bunch of books and enjoy their cold beer without having to leave.

Seaview Bungalows Thansadet (Thansadet Beach, no phone, www.seaview.thansadet.com, 400B) is an excellent choice for cheap, clean bungalows. Thansadet Beach, south of Thong Nai Pan, is small, rugged, and secluded and has beautiful clear water. Fan-cooled bungalows are very basic wooden structures but have comfortable beds and modern baths (albeit with cold water only). Although there isn't lots to do on the beach, there is a small restaurant on the property, and most people come just to relax anyway.

The rustic but comfortable **Sunset Cove Resort** (Ao Chao Phao, www.thaisunsetcove.com, 1,200B), on popular Ao Chao Phao on the west coast, has pretty, lush grounds, a great pool, and a fantastic location right on the beach. Guest rooms are clean, and though not opulent, are well coordinated and calming. Staff members are very friendly and helpful, and they set the tone everyone else at the resort seems to follow—happy and relaxed. There is a restaurant and bar on the property, but this is really more a place to chill out and have a few beers with friends while enjoying the view than to party.

Palita Lodge (119 Mu 6, Bang Thai Beach, tel. 07/737-5170, www.palitalodge.com, 2,000B) isn't a high-end resort but offers guests nearly every amenity that more expensive properties do, including a very pretty, well-maintained swimming pool as well as clean, stylish guest rooms with flat-screen TVs and minibars and spotless modern baths. The modern Thai style is subtle but consistent throughout the property. Palita Lodge is right on Hat Rin and in the middle of full-moon madness, and it tends to attract partygoers.

The Green Papaya Resort (64/8 Mu 8, Salad Beach, tel. 07/737-4230, www.greenpapayaresort.com, 4,600B) is a beautifully designed small resort on the northwestern part of the island. The property is filled with modern Thai furnishings, a beautiful pool overlooking the ocean, a couple of restaurants, and not much else to distract you from the scenery or the sunsets. Most of the accommodations are in new wooden bungalows with all the amenities you could want inside, including large sleek baths, DVD players, and minibars. There are also two-bedroom family villas on this property.

Another option for a bit of remote luxury is the **Panviman Resort** (22/1 Mu 5, Thong Nai Pan Noi Bay, Bantai, tel. 07/744-5100, 4,500B) on Bantai. Like the Santhiya, it's in a location that's well away from the crowds and the partying, and it has a beautiful pool, restaurants, and a bar to keep you fed, quaffed, and entertained. The guest rooms are done in a Thai style, and the baths are large, well equipped, and nicely designed. This is a great resort for families since there are a few large family villas that can accommodate more than two people comfortably. Some of the guest rooms and villas are in the hills, so when booking, make sure to take that into consideration; the hillside rooms have a nicer view, but you'll need to climb some stairs to get to them.

For a more upscale Ko Pha-Ngan experience, try the **Santhiya Resort & Spa** (22/7 Mu 5, Thong Nai Pan Yai, tel. 07/742-8999, www.santhiya.com, 10,000B), which opened in 2006 and has some of the nicest guest rooms on the island. The resort is done in a traditional Thai style, with plenty of carved woodwork and colorful textiles as well as

Detox Retreats

The colonic-irrigation trend is still popular in Thailand, and Ko Samui has more than a handful of spas offering the service as part of a multiday detox program. The programs vary from spa to spa, but in general, participants consume only water, fruit juice, special low-calorie shakes, and vitamin supplements for the duration. In addition to twice-daily colonics, the spas offer meditation, yoga classes, and massage.

Colonics have been viewed with skepticism by the traditional medical community, but there are thousands of people from across the globe who flock to Samui's spas every year for their detox programs, hoping to get a little healthier and maybe drop a few pounds in the process. Whether it works in the long term is up for debate, but people who've spent a week at one of the island's detox retreats say they come away feeling good.

Absolute Yoga, one of the upscale yoga studios in Bangkok, has a spa called **Absolute Yoga & The Love Kitchen** (Fisherman's Village, Bo Phut Beach, tel. 07/743-0290, www.absoluteyogasamui.com) offering a variety of programs from weekend detox retreats to 10-day intensive programs that include yoga, meditation, and colonics. Some of the programs involve juice fasting, but they also have programs where you dine on vegetarian food from its Love Kitchen. The programs run around 1,400 baht per day, which includes food and classes. If you're not interested in the detox regimen, you can buy an unlimited yoga pass for a week for just 1,500 baht. The resort itself is a charming, boutique-style small hotel with colorful but elegant guest rooms and a nice swimming pool.

The Spa Resorts (Lamai Beach, tel. 07/742-4666, www.thesparesorts.net) has a number of programs centered on detox and cleansing as well as meditation and yoga. The program runs around 1,500 baht per day, not including accommodations. The spa also has a basic bungalow resort with a nice swimming pool and gardens. The vegetarian menu at the spa is one of the best on the island.

luxuriant grounds. The guest rooms are all nestled in the cliffs surrounding the beach, and the views are beautiful, although it can be difficult to get from one place to another, especially if you're in one of the higher-level guest rooms or you're not agile. The grounds, in the middle of lush tropical foliage, have multiple swimming pools, including one with a waterfall. For those who want to stay out of the sun, there is also a fitness center and a library. The Santhiya offers reasonably priced guest transfers by catamaran or speedboat from Samui, which makes it considerably more convenient. The beach itself is not quite as smooth on your feet as others you'll find on the island, but if you're just there to sunbathe and kayak, it's not a problem.

FOOD

If you're looking for something authentically Thai, you'll probably be disappointed in the offerings on Ko Pha-Ngan. The island is so overrun by young Western travelers looking for pizza and falafel that it's nearly impossible

to find great Thai food. Western food varies from mediocre to pretty good, and most of the restaurants are around "Chicken Corner" in Hat Rin, the area's crossroads.

The street parallel to Hat Rin Beach is full of places advertising foreign food of all types, but **Fair House Restaurant & Bar** (119/1 Hat Rin Rd., 9am-10:30pm daily, 100B) has just about anything Western you could be missing. From potatoes (baked, mashed, or fried) to pasta dishes, steaks, bacon rolls, plus a wide selection of Thai options and even burritos, the menu here is massive, but the pizza is a winner. They also have some creative and appetizing salads on the menu (pumpkin-tofu), and drinks cover the rounds, from *lassis* to whiskey fruit shakes and cocktails. Try a carrot-honey *lassi*. The only downside to this casual spot is that you will have to endure season after season of the TV series *Friends*, although they sometimes play movies at nighttime.

In a location that's too convenient to be good, **Pla-Bla Restaurant** (Hat Rin Rd., 36 Mu 6, next to Sunrise Resort, 9:30am-11pm daily, 100B) actually does get patrons returning for their tasty and satisfying meals. Better known as the "Family Guy restaurant," they play episodes of the U.S. comedy series *Family Guy* continuously. The menu here is almost as extensive as Fair House's, with options for everyone. All of the following got seriously good reviews: shrimp pad thai, green curry chicken or seafood, and the *yam* salad with chicken (a Thai dish with plenty of chicken and a light, spicy dressing). For Western fare, the burgers and hot sandwiches are popular. The large drink selection, including alcoholic drinks and shakes, will quench any thirst. Besides the food, it seems that no matter what the nationality, the crowd drawn to "Family Guy" is a friendly sort, and it is an overall pleasant dining experience, especially after a day in the sun.

The baked goods alone will force you to peek into **Nira's Deli Sandwich Bar & Restaurant** (right off Hat Rin Rd., on the way to Chicken Corner, sit-down meals 7am-11pm, bakery and deli 24 hours, 200B), just a few meters off the main drag. If you can tear your eyes away from the food on display, you will see the build-your-own-sandwich board. What better for a place that has the best bread in town? (We suspect they supply all other restaurants offering "fresh bread.") The options range from spreads—cheese, hummus, even Mexican salsa—to more hearty fillings such as boiled egg, smoked salmon, and even turkey. The deli shares dining space with its full-service restaurant, offering Thai food as well as thin-crust individual pizzas baked in the oven just behind the counter. Whatever you fancy, they have a delicious breakfast menu, and you don't have to be a vegetarian to order the vegetarian sandwich (scrambled eggs with tomato, onion, and cheese on your choice of bread). Nira's opens early, making it a great option before a ferry trip or if your night runs into morning. In their fridges they have premade sandwiches and foods and usually squares of deep-dish pizza at the bakery. They also sell their hummus and salsa. Even with all the sweets that make you forget about any other food you ate, this place definitely has a healthy vibe; whole grains and fresh fruit juices such as carrot-ginger abound.

If you're craving Middle Eastern food, **Paprika Mediterranean Restaurant** (Chicken Corner, 11am-10:30pm daily, 150B) is as good as it gets. It's also why you'll hear mostly Hebrew chatter here. The service also sets this place apart, and they can pop out a delicious Israeli salad in three minutes. On Saturday they offer a special beef-tomato stew, but the hummus and falafel dishes are so good it can be difficult to order anything else. Paprika's also serves schnitzel (it comes out steaming hot) and *shawarma,* so everyone can be satisfied. There is Thai food on the menu, too, but it is quite possible nobody has ever tried it. Perhaps the true reason this place always has customers is its 80 baht deal: a full pita with falafel and hummus and a fruit shake. The best of both regions? Judge for yourself.

Palita Lodge (119 Mu 6, Hat Rin, tel. 07/737-5170, 8am-10pm daily, 150B) will make you wish your breakfast wasn't included in the cost of your accommodations. Its menu has seven different sets to choose from, such as eggs, porridge, or pancakes. Each set comes with a choice of hot drink (tea, chocolate, or fresh coffee), plus fresh fruit or juice. The fruit plate is a better option and very generous. If you want a traditional Thai breakfast, opt for the rice soup. There are also plenty of Thai and Western choices for lunch and dinner. It is a very pretty spot, a bit away from the main entrances to the beach, so it is surprisingly quiet without being out of the way. Digest afterward by their pool in the comfortable sun chairs.

The Lighthouse (Leela Beach, Hat Rin, 8am-11pm daily, 200B) gets an A for atmosphere. The isolated corner it is located on is an easy walk from the hedonistic side of Hat Rin Beach, but it feels like it is the opposite side of the island. Perched on the very southern tip of Ko Pha-Ngan, the panorama-windowed eating-lounging area looks straight out to sea. If you go by beach, you walk to the end and then follow a lovely boardwalk that wraps around the corner of the island. Come lounge in the hammock and admire the view over fruit shakes; it has an atmosphere that feels like an afternoon nap. The scenery is especially beautiful at sunset, but at any point during the day, the peaceful atmosphere (as well as any Thai massage) dissipates tension. It has the familiar menu with Western and Thai options along with very hearty breakfasts, from porridge to a Thai stuffed omelet. The Thai food is the cheapest option, and you aren't charged extra for picking a back-road location. They have a choice of salads, plus a more obscure Western taste that found its way to the menu: the cheese plate—four different types of cheese (including brie) with salad. Order this if it's to your liking, with a glass of 100B wine, and looking out at the ocean, you may decide you have achieved the pinnacle of all Euro-Asian ideals.

Far up the hill, **Sunsmile Restaurant and Guesthouse** (Hat Rin Beach, 8am-9:30pm daily, 100B) occupies a scenic spot overlooking Hat Rin Nok (Sunrise Beach). An everlasting breeze blows here. It definitely caters to backpackers, and you can either dine outside with the view or inside with a host of movies to choose from. It is a hike—at least a 10-minute walk up a heavily rutted rocky and sandy road—so if you need to escape and really just avoid people for a bit, this is the place. The curries and Thai food are very good deals. Western food is on the menu but is more limited. During full-moon party weeks, it can be fun to watch the party from a distance and still be able to hear the music. The rest of the month, it's one of the quietest places in all of Hat Rin.

TRANSPORTATION
Getting There

The closest airport to Ko Pha-Ngan is **Samui Airport** on Ko Samui, so if you want to spend as little time as possible getting to the beach, you can fly to the neighboring island and then take a ferryboat to Ko Pha-Ngan.

Since the island mostly attracts a younger crowd with tighter purse strings, most people arrive by boat from Surat Thani. If you're arriving in Surat Thani by air, you can buy a combination bus-ferry ticket right at the airport, and the whole trip should run around five hours. If you're coming to Surat Thani by train or bus from Bangkok, you'll need to make your way to the Donsak pier outside of town and then catch a ferry to Ko Pha-Ngan. The ferries that travel from Surat Thani to Samui then make their way to Ko Pha-Ngan; you'll spend another couple of hours on the ferry and pay an additional 150 baht on top of the Samui fare. There is no direct ferry to Ko Pha-Ngan from Surat Thani—you have to stop in Samui first.

Getting Around

Ko Pha-Ngan is less built up than Ko Samui but has some roads in place, and during the day there are *song thaew* running from the pier in Thongsala to other beaches. You should pay under 80 baht for most rides (unless you charter the *song thaew* to take you to a specific destination that is not on the route, in which case you'll need to negotiate a price). Many visitors also rent motorcycles or mountain bikes, both of which are available at most beaches. Expect to pay around 200 baht per day regardless of whether you're getting a pedal-powered or gas-powered bike.

Ko Tao means turtle island, although that's not so much about its shape (it looks more like a kidney bean) as the fact that the waters around the island used to be filled with sea turtles. They've since mostly moved on, but there's still lots of amazing marinelife to explore around Ko Tao. The waters surrounding the island are relatively shallow and have little current, except during monsoon season. In fact, the island is one of the best launching points for scuba diving in the Gulf of Thailand and a great place to do some snorkeling right off the beach. The island is full of dive shops and dive schools, so if you're looking to get PADI certified, this is a great place to pick—courses tend to be a little cheaper than the rest of the country, and you can really shop around for the dive instructor you feel most comfortable with. In fact, the island issues more PADI certificates than any other spot in Thailand and most other spots in the world. If you visit, you'll find bungalow resorts and a few up-market offerings, and they are mostly geared toward divers. Every resort, up-market or otherwise, has a dive shop attached.

Even if you're not into diving, Ko Tao is a beautiful little island to enjoy the scenery and the beaches, although you might feel a bit like the odd man out. The island itself is surrounded by some stretches of sandy shore surrounded by rocky promontories and backed by shady palm trees. The center of the island is mostly jungly rainforest, although there's enough development here that you'll be able to find a post office and a few places to spend your money. Getting around the island, however, can be a little tough. It's a great place for hiking, but the road system is not well developed. If you're not staying near Mae Had (on the island's west coast, where the ferry arrives and departs), expect a long and bumpy ride, especially if you're going across the island. Despite the challenging transport, don't write

off Ko Tao—its remoteness gives it a distinct *sabai* attitude.

BEACHES AND ISLANDS

For a clear stretch of sandy beach, **Sairee Beach,** closest to the ferry pier, is your best bet on the island. The nearly 3.5-kilometer (2 mi) beach faces west, so you not only get the view of the mainland but beautiful sunsets, too. This is the most populated beach on the island, and there is a good selection of accommodations and places to eat, although you could hardly call it overcrowded, even in high season. Since the island itself is so small—just a couple of kilometers across—it's a good base from which you can hike around the rest of the island. Just south of Sairee Beach and adjacent to it is **Mae Had,** where the ferry pier is located and probably the only part of the island that could ever legitimately be described as crowded or busy. The area right around the pier isn't optimal for relaxing, but to the south the beach gets nicer and there are some decent places to stay.

Aside from the long stretch of sand on Sairee Beach and Mae Had, the rest of Ko Tao is made up of about a dozen small bays on the north, east, and south of the island. Popular ones include **Hin Wong Bay** on the east coast and **Mango Bay** on the north coast. Both have spectacular views and excellent snorkeling and diving, but the beaches are often quite rocky.

Neighboring **Ko Nang Yuan,** just off the northeast coast of Ko Tao, is perhaps the coolest-looking island in the area. It's actually three separate small islands connected together by a thin stretch of sand you can walk across during low tide. The cluster of small islands also lends itself well to snorkeling and diving, as the interconnecting islands create three separate shallow bays that are mostly protected from strong currents. The beaches are also very shallow unless you walk out

Ko Tao

© AVALON TRAVEL

Beach, tel. 07/745-6868, 350B) cannot be beat. It's in a remote spot on the southwestern part of the island, so the only way to get there is either by boat taxi or a bumpy ride in a 4WD vehicle. Once you're there, the view to the Gulf of Thailand is gorgeous, as is the surrounding verdant scenery. The bungalows are very simple wooden shacks with mosquito netting and fans. There's a small restaurant that's open all day, and even Internet access, but no pool, and the spa has limited services. It's not a luxury choice, by any means, but if you're looking for that *Survivor* feeling on a budget, you'll be very satisfied here.

If you're just on the island to do some diving, **Khun Ying House** (15/19 Mu 1, Sairee Beach, tel. 08/0620-5527, 450B) is a cheap, clean, and comfortable hotel. The guest rooms are well maintained, although they aren't the most stylishly designed. Some have shared baths and fans, and you can use their kitchen facilities if you feel like cooking up a meal yourself. There are limited facilities here; it's definitely just a place to store your flippers and sleep.

Koh Tao Simple Life Resort (Sairee Beach, tel. 07/745-6142, www.kohtaosimplelliferesort.com, 1,500B) has a good location on popular Sairee Beach, a big swimming pool, a popular restaurant and bar serving Thai and Western food, and nicely furnished, stylish, modern guest rooms. Despite the name, though, it's not a luxury resort and really more like a well-run midsize hotel.

The **Mango Bay Grand Resort** (11/3 Mu 2, Mae Had, tel. 07/745-6097, www.kohtaomangobay.com, 1,500B) isn't quite grand, and it's not really a resort either, since there's no pool and limited facilities. Still, it's a great place because of its location and the clean and well-maintained bungalows perched on stilts on the rocks above the bay. The interiors of the bungalows are simple and clean, and each has comfortable beds and stunning views to the water. The interior design in the baths may cause you to wonder who picked the paint and tile colors, but everything is modern and works well despite the fact that it's not entirely

pretty far, making it a great place for families. If you're looking for something to do on land, the mountainous island is filled with boulders to climb and a couple of short hiking trails.

From Sairee Beach on Ko Tao you can charter a longtail boat to take you to Ko Nang Yuan for about 150 baht each way. During high season there are plenty of people going back and forth, so it won't be a problem to get a ride back to Ko Tao. During low season you should arrange a round-trip ride. There is also a ferry that runs from the main pier in Ko Tao once a day during high season; make sure to check at the pier for the current schedule and price. If you are coming from Ko Samui, you can take the ferry to Ko Tao, and then transfer to another boat (either a small ferry or longtail), but you may want to consider spending at least one night on Ko Tao if you're doing that, as you'll spend at least five hours traveling back and forth. There is one resort on the island, Three Paradise Islands, and if you're staying there, they'll help you arrange transport.

ACCOMMODATIONS

For simple, rustic, charming bungalows, the **Sai Thong Resort & Spa** (Mu 2, Sai Nuan fashionable. The snorkeling in the area is excellent when it's not monsoon season, and this alone might be reason to stay here. From the resort you can swim out to see excellent coral and other marinelife.

For small-resort luxury, the **Jamakhiri Spa & Resort** (19/1 Mu 3 Chalook, Ban Kao, tel. 07/745-6400, www.jamahkiri.com, 2,500B) is an exceptional property set on the rocks and just a few minutes' walk to the beach. The guest rooms are all large and well kept, with comfortable, modern Thai-style furnishings and hardwood floors. All have views to the Gulf of Thailand and large bay windows. There's a beautiful pool, a small spa, and even a fitness center, although unless it's pouring outside, there's really no reason to stay indoors. The resort seems to cascade down the rocks, which means there's quite a bit of walking involved if you're staying on one of the higher levels. As at many other secluded places on the island, you'll have to contend with difficult roads to reach the Jamakhiri, although the hotel will arrange transportation for you from the pier.

The small, upscale **Chintakiri Resort** (19/59 Mu 3 Chalook, Ban Kao, tel. 07/745-6391, www.chintakiriresort.com, 2,500B) has beautiful views of the Gulf of Thailand and clean, nicely furnished Thai-style bungalows. The property is built into the hills behind the beach on one of the island's southern bays near the Jamakhiri Spa & Resort, which makes for amazing views, lush landscaping, and a secluded feeling, but those with any mobility issues might have trouble getting up and down to their guest room. The infinity pool is not huge but also has a beautiful view, and since the property is so small, it rarely gets full.

Anankhira Boutique Villas (15/3 Mu 1, Sairee Beach, tel. 08/7719-7696, www.anankhira.com, 3,500B) is a little more luxurious than the typical Sairee Beach accommodations. Each of the charming thatched-roof villas has a big bedroom, large outdoor lounging area, and its own small plunge pool. The style, which management calls "ecoconscious," is rustic but very clean and well maintained. Those who want more space and privacy will find these an excellent value. The villas are not right on the beach, but they are a 10-minute walk away from the northern part of Sairee Beach.

If you want to stay on Ko Nang Yaun, the set of three islands joined by sandbars just off the coast of Ko Tao, your only choice is the **Three Paradise Island Resort,** sometimes also called the **Nang Yuan Island Dive Resort** (tel. 07/745-6088, www.nangyuan.com, 1,500B). The resort has accommodations scattered across the three islands, from simple fan bungalows to larger air-conditioned cottages. None of the options are luxurious, but there's a small restaurant and a dive shop, and staying on a private island might be worth giving up a few amenities.

FOOD

Hidden behind the Gym & Fitness is **Fitness Cafe** (35/42 Mu 1, Sairee Village, tel. 092/338-3273, 8:30am-6:30pm daily, 100B), a gem of a café bursting with healthy choices for all palates. Vegan, paleo, raw foodist, or any combination of the above will find something tasty and healthy to eat at Fitness Cafe, which focuses on dishes that use lots of fresh fruits and vegetables. The laid-back atmosphere is unpretentious and friendly. It also serves yummy organic coffee.

The Gallery Restaurant (10/29 Mu 1, Sairee Village, tel. 07/745-6547, 5:30am-11pm daily, 300B), a very cool Thai restaurant cum art gallery, is a favorite among tourists and long-staying residents, not just because of the atmosphere (the dining room is dark and loungy but very relaxed) but because the food is just so good. The menu offers straightforward Thai dishes including popular salads, curries, and soups, plus appetizers, yummy desserts, and a good selection of wine. Make a reservation, as this place is one of the most popular on the island.

Just across the way from The Gallery is **Jam's Boomerang** (28/3 Mu 1, Sairee Village, tel. 084/308-2663, 2pm-midnight daily, 200B), a very homey, very simple Thai restaurant. There are ready-to-eat dishes on the buffet, but you can also order just about any standard Thai dish that you want. The atmosphere, mostly outdoor seating and lots of bamboo, is cute. Jam's also offers cooking classes.

Despite your good intentions to eat only local food on vacation, you might find yourself seriously craving some Mexican while you're in Ko Tao. If you do, head to the **Taco Shack** (28/3 Mu 1, Sairee Village, tel. 083/176-2043, 11am-10pm daily, 150B) on Mae Had. Freshly made salsa, cold beer, tacos, and other Mexican favorites are on the menu. Food isn't entirely authentic, but considering the distance from Mexico, it does a very good job.

Whether you're detoxing after toxing, or just want to enjoy some fresh juice, visit **Living Juices** (27/4 Mu 1, Sairee Village, tel. 09/0171-5281, 11am-7pm daily, 150B) in Sairee. This unassuming little café offers fresh juices, plus smoothies and some raw and vegan snacks, including the house-made trail mix with goji berries and other fun treats.

Barracuda Restaurant and Bar (9/9 Mu 1, Sairee Village, tel. 08/0146-3267, 11am-11pm daily, 150B), an upscale Thai fusion restaurant, is regarded as one of the best places to eat on the island. Dishes such as shrimp in lemongrass served with spicy curry mayo, sticky barbecue ribs, and tequila and lime shrimp skewers have diners raving about the flavors. The atmosphere in the dining room is homey and casual, though it can be a bit on the pricey side, especially if you order wine. Seafood is the specialty here, but you can also get some vegetarian dishes.

TRANSPORTATION

The only way to get to Ko Tao is by boat, either from Chumphon on the mainland or from Ko Samui and Ko Pha-Ngan, using the normal ferries. A high-speed ferry from Chumphon or Samui takes just under two hours and costs around 550 baht; an overnight ride on a cargo boat takes six hours and costs half the price. There are a number of different companies offering ferry services, including **Lomprayah High Speed Ferries** (www.lomprayah.com), **Ko Jaroen Car Ferry** (tel. 07/758-0030), **Seatran Ferry** (tel. 02/240-2582, www.seatrandiscovery.com), **Songserm Express Boat** (tel. 02/280-8073, www.songserm-expressboat.com), and the **Talay Sub Cargo Night Boat** (tel. 07/743-0531), and the schedules change from year to year, but from neighboring islands there are at least two boats per day each way.

Southern Gulf of Thailand

Visit the lower southern Gulf of Thailand for idyllic islands, off-the-beaten-path beaches on the mainland, and some charming small historical cities where you can learn about the culture and history of the region.

White-sand beaches, coconut trees, and green rolling hills make the lower southern Gulf a top choice if you're looking for a beach vacation in Thailand. The region has plenty to offer that you won't find on the other side of the Kra Isthmus. The landscapes are not as dramatic as the karst cliffs that pepper Phuket, Krabi, and Trang, but thanks to an abundance of coconut trees and a softer, more rolling topography, the islands are greener and lusher. The resorts can be as posh as those on the Andaman coast, and at the cheaper end, the selection is better. The rainy season is much shorter, lasting from only mid-October to mid-December.

Though the mainland beaches north of Nakhon Si Thammarat aren't as slick and foreigner-friendly as the more popular beach spots, the natural landscape is mostly unmarred by development, and the area still retains the typically Thai culture that's often harder to see in more popular destinations.

The city of Nakhon Si Thammarat doesn't have enough attractions to draw huge crowds of foreign tourists, but it has plenty of temples to visit, and plenty of authentic Thai food to try. Visit Khanom and Sichon for their beaches, which still attract more locals than foreign visitors. Khao Sok National Park, closer to the Andaman Coast, has some beautiful waterfalls and plenty of opportunities to canoe.

South of Nakhon Si Thammarat, the coast along the Gulf of Thailand changes significantly. You'll still find stretches of beach and plenty of friendly people, but once you enter Songkhla Province, Islam begins to be more apparent. Hat Yai, the area's economic hub, attracts hordes of visitors, but mostly people from Malaysia, who come for shopping and to take advantage of Thailand's more permissive culture. This makes it a very interesting place to people-watch, if you happen to be passing through, although it's

Previous: boating off of Nakhon Si Thammarat; beaches of the Southern Gulf. **Above:** fishing boat off of Ko Samui.

Look for ★ to find recommended
sights, activities, dining, and lodging.

Highlights

★ **Khao Sok National Park:** At the country's wettest national park, you can see a variety of plant life, including the three-foot-wide *Rafflesia* (page 149).

★ **Nakhon Si Thammarat:** The coolest city you've never heard of is the center of Thai Buddhism, and it offers plenty of culture, great food, and not a lot of other travelers (page 150).

★ **Khanom and Sichon:** These are two relatively undiscovered beaches with clear, clean, warm water, soft sand, and friendly people (page 155).

Khanom's mellow beaches

Southern Gulf of Thailand

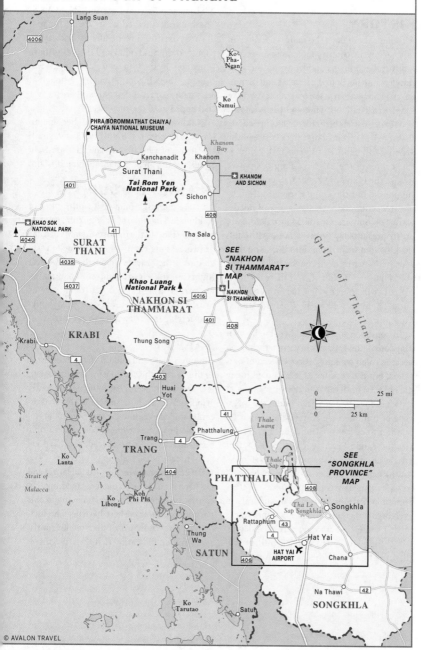

Lang Suan

4006

Ko Pha-Ngan

Ko Samui

PHRA BOROMMATHAT CHAIYA/
CHAIYA NATIONAL MUSEUM

Kanchanadit   Khanom

Khanom Bay

Surat Thani   KHANOM AND SICHON

Tai Rom Yen National Park

Sichon

401

408

KHAO SOK NATIONAL PARK

4040

SURAT THANI

4035

4037

Khao Luang National Park

41

NAKHON SI THAMMARAT

Tha Sala

SEE "NAKHON SI THAMMARAT" MAP

4016   NAKHON SI THAMMARAT

KRABI

Krabi

4

Thung Song

401   408

403

Huai Yot

41

Thale Luang

Trang

4

Phatthalung

404

TRANG

Ko Lanta

Thale Sap

PHATTHALUNG

SEE "SONGKHLA PROVINCE" MAP

Strait of Malacca

408

Ko Libong   Koh Phi Phi

Tha Le Sap Songkhla

Rattaphum   Songkhla

43

Hat Yai

4

Thung Wa

HAT YAI AIRPORT   Chana

406

SATUN

Na Thawi   42

Ko Tarutao   Satun   **SONGKHLA**

Gulf of Thailand

0   25 mi
0   25 km

© AVALON TRAVEL

probably not going to be a primary destination for most.

HISTORY

Although these days the mainland cities in this part of the country look more like semi-industrialized towns and transport hubs for travelers moving onto the beaches and islands, Surat Thani was once the seat of the Srivijaya Empire in Thailand. Though little is known about the lost empire, historians speculate that it existed from somewhere between the 3rd and 5th centuries to the 13th century. The center of the Srivijaya Empire's power was on the island of Sumatra, in present-day Indonesia, but the empire spread throughout the Indonesian archipelago and northward, encompassing the Malay Peninsula up to present-day Surat Thani. Although the kingdom was Hindu, Buddhist, and then Muslim, remains from the Surat Thani area are Mahayana Buddhist, and there are temple ruins in the city of Chaiya, outside of Surat Thani, as well as the Chaiya National Museum.

In some sense, Thailand became its own kingdom in the 13th century when the region became ruled by Thai people instead of outsiders, but the country as it is known today did not exist until the 20th century. Southeast Asia had for centuries been under the influence of innumerable empires bearing little relation to current national borders, and it was the Anglo-Siamese Treaty of 1909 that put the last pieces of the puzzle (at least in the south) together for the Kingdom of Siam. It was then that Siam got the provinces of Satun, Songkhla, Pattani, Narathiwat, and Yala in exchange for giving up claims to provinces farther south that are now part of Malaysia. While the country as a whole identifies with the Kingdoms of Sukhothai and Ayutthaya,

the south has always had a somewhat different history.

Since the Srivijaya period, Nakhon Si Thammarat emerged as its own kingdom of sorts, existing independently but paying tribute to the Sukhothai and then Ayutthaya Kingdoms. By the 18th century, the region was ruled by the Kingdom of Siam, although at least with respect to Songkhla, that rule was challenged until the 1909 treaty.

Nakhon Si Thammarat has become an important city for Buddhists, and you'll see plenty of *wats* if you visit. Just south, in Songkhla, the predominant religion is Islam.

PLANNING YOUR TIME

If you're planning on a visit to the cities of Nakhon Si Thammarat or Songkhla, you can easily see most of the important sights in a day or two, leaving plenty of extra time to relax on one of the beaches up north. With direct flights on Nok Air to Nakhon Si Thammarat, it's surprisingly easy to get to the city or nearby Songkhla without spending hours transferring from one place to another.

SAFETY

Although Islam and Buddhism have coexisted in this part of the country for centuries with few problems, sectarian violence currently gripping Yala, Pattani, and Narathiwat has recently spilled over into parts of Songkhla. Hat Yai, the province's capital, has had multiple bomb attacks in the past decade that have targeted hotels, pubs, and shopping centers. The violence so far has been limited to Hat Yai and has been very sporadic, but it's something that cannot be ignored if you're traveling to this part of the country. There have been no incidents, however, in any of the popular tourist spots and no indication that there is a threat of violence there.

Mainland Surat Thani สุราษฎร์ธานี

Surat Thani isn't a place most tourists end up spending too much time in, given the beautiful islands just offshore. It's more or less a run-of-the-mill city going about daily life despite the throngs of foreign visitors that pass through. But just outside the city is Chaiya, the former seat of the Srivijaya Empire, which has an excellent museum. There are also a couple of nearby national parks worth visiting if you are in the area.

TAI ROM YEN NATIONAL PARK
อุทยานแห่งชาติใต้ร่มเย็น

The **Tai Rom Yen National Park** (Amphoe Ban Na San, Surat Thani, tel. 07/734-4633, 8:30am-6pm daily, 400B), covering part of the Nakhon Si Thammarat mountain range, is covered in dense forest, with beautiful waterfalls to visit and well-marked trails for hiking. The 22-step **Dard Fa Waterfall** is the region's largest, and one of the levels is a 75-meter (246 ft) cliff drop. To get here, you must drive to the base of the trail at the park headquarters (once you enter the park you'll see signs), where you can also pick up a map to get to **Khao Nong,** the highest point in the province at over 1,370 meters (4,495 ft). In addition to the beautiful natural scenery, the park is also home to a couple of significant historical landmarks worth visiting. In the 1970s and 1980s, the area was a communist-rebel stronghold, and there are a couple of former hideout camps that can now be visited. There are bungalows and a canteen at the park headquarters near the Dard Fa Waterfall.

Transportation

From Surat Thani there's a direct bus that will take you to the entrance of the park on Route 4009. Ask for buses headed south toward the Phin Phun train station; the 15-minute trip should cost around 20 baht. Once you arrive, it is impossible to get around the park without transportation.

If you're driving, take Route 4009 south from Surat Thani about 24 kilometers (15 mi) to Ban Chiang Phra, then look for the signs for the national park.

★ KHAO SOK NATIONAL PARK
อุทยานแห่งชาติเขาสก

Khao Sok National Park (Mu 6, Phanom, tel. 07/739-5154, 8:30am-6pm daily, 400B) in Surat Thani Province is covered with rainforest, limestone cliffs, and lakes. It's the wettest national park in the country, thanks to an abundance of rain in the region, and it's also often referred to as the most beautiful. The frequent rainfall keeps the 285-square-mile park lush and green, and there is plentiful exotic flora, including palm trees, fig trees, lots of bamboo, and vine trees. There's also the *Rafflesia*. At nearly one meter (3 ft) wide, the flower is one of the largest in the world and is quite rare. You'll also find pitcher plants, which are large insect-eating plants shaped like pitchers to trap unsuspecting bugs. The big attractions here are hiking, canoeing, and mountain biking. You can canoe on **Chong Kaeb Khao Ka Loh** lake, the result of a dam built to generate hydroelectric power for the region, or explore the park's waterfalls and caves. Canoe rentals cost about 100 baht per hour.

Accommodations and Food

The park offers simple accommodations in dormitory-style rooms and very cool but basic floating huts near two of the ranger stations. The huts, which have beds but shared toilets, are only 400 baht per night but are popular with large tour groups and book up quickly; you must reserve your place in advance. The park's website (www.dnp.go.th) has instructions on reserving accommodations (click on "National Park Online Reservation" in the

English version of the site). Near the ranger station are also a couple of small restaurants that are open for breakfast, lunch, and dinner. These canteens serve only Thai food, but it is fresh and inexpensive.

Transportation

If you are coming from Surat Thani, you can take a bus to the park's entrance. The bus ride takes an hour and costs 70 baht, but they only run two a day—one in the morning and one in the afternoon (make sure to check at the bus station for current schedules). Once you are in the park, as with all national parks in Thailand, you will have a very difficult time getting around unless you either plan on hitching rides with other visitors or renting a car.

If you are driving on your own, the park's entrance is on Route 401, which runs east-west between Surat Thani and Takua Pa. The park is about 97 kilometers (60 mi) east of Surat Thani.

PHRA BOROMMATHAT CHAIYA AND THE CHAIYA NATIONAL MUSEUM

พระบรมธาตุไชยา และ พิพิธภัณฑ์
สถานแห่งชาติไชยา

Located about 48 kilometers (30 mi) north of the city, **Phra Borommathat Chaiya** is an ancient *chedi* said to house relics of the Buddha. The *chedi* itself is small but has amazingly detailed carvings. It was probably built around 1,200 years ago during the Srivijaya Empire. On the grounds you'll also find the **Chaiya National Museum** (Raksanorakit Rd., Tambon Wiang, Amphoe Chaiya, tel. 07/743-1066, 9am-4pm Wed.-Sun., 30B). This small gem of a museum has an excellent collection of prehistoric artifacts such as tools, pottery, and housewares found in the region as well as regional art from the 6th century to the present. Here you'll be able to see a large collection of Srivijaya art, mostly devotional figures of the Buddha, but also Hindu art such as sculptures of Vishnu from before Buddhism took hold in the region.

The museum also has a collection of items found in shipwrecks in the Gulf of Thailand, left by sailors from China and beyond.

Transportation

Chaiya is 48 kilometers (30 mi) north of Surat Thani on Route 41. To visit without a car, you can take one of the frequent *song thaew* that depart from Surat Thani's bus terminal during the day. The trip will take about 45 minutes and cost 50 baht.

Nakhon Si Thammarat Province
จังหวัดนครศรีธรรมราช

The Nakhon Si Thammarat region might just be one of the best untouristed places to visit in Thailand. The city is well organized, easy to navigate, and filled with museums and *wats*. The beaches have the clean, warm waters of the Gulf of Thailand but none of the crowds, and the inland national parks are filled with fertile rainforests and scores of waterfalls. There's also an airport with direct flights from Bangkok, and you can pick up a ticket for a song on Nok Air. Best of all, if you enjoying traveling to places where you're not likely to run into folks just like you, there are still very few Western travelers coming this way. The area is frequented by visitors from other parts of Thailand and Southeast Asia, however, so there are adequate accommodations and other tourism infrastructure.

★ NAKHON SI THAMMARAT
นครศรีธรรมราช

Nakhon Si Thammarat is one of the oldest cities in the country and has a great collection of interesting historical and cultural sights to visit. If you're looking for an urban break in a small city after soaking up the sun and sea, spend a day visiting the museums and religious buildings. As a whole, the city isn't beautiful. The newer parts suffer from a type of generic urbanization that seems to know no international boundaries. But in the older part of the city you'll find Wat Phra Mahathat, one of the oldest and largest *wats* in the country, and some charming streets to wander around.

Despite the charm and cultural significance, the city is not a typical tourist trap. There are a couple of Tourism Authority of Thailand offices (one in city hall and one near the Ta Chang market), but other than that, the city is pretty much oblivious to travelers. You won't find lots of signs in English or even lots of taxis. To get around, it's best to grab one of the visitor maps from your hotel or the TAT office and set out on foot.

Sights

Nakhon Si Thammarat is one of the oldest cities in the country, and although only fragments of the **Old City Wall** from the 13th century remain, they give a glimpse of what the city must have been like hundreds of years ago. The wall once enclosed the center of the city.

Located in such a historic city, the **Nakhon Si Thammarat National Museum** (Ratchadamnoen Rd., 9am-4pm Wed.-Sun., 30B) does a nice job of exhibiting artifacts from prehistory through modern times, many relating to Buddhism. You'll find exhibits of local crafts through the ages and also some excellent examples of fine art. The niello ware (engraved metalwork) pieces are worth extra time perusing. There are also some more fun exhibits in the museum's new wing on Thai life, marriage rituals, and local food. The museum is 2.4 kilometers (1.5 mi) out of the center of town, heading south on Ratchadamnoen Road. You can grab a local *song thaew* or public bus from the main road, which will cost about 10 baht.

Nearly every postcard you see in the city will have an image of the imposing *chedi* at **Wat Phra Mahathat Woramahawihan** (Ratchadamnoen Rd., 8am-4:30pm daily, 30B, museum 20B extra), which indicates how important the *wat* is to the city and the country. The original structure is believed to have been built between the 6th and 8th centuries, during the Srivijaya period, as a monastery and school. The ornately decorated *ubosot* (coronation hall), from the 18th-century Ayutthaya period, is relatively new, but the foundation of the large Phra Borom That Chedi is believed to have been built when the *wat* itself was founded. There is also a small museum on the premises with Buddhist reliquaries and other objects. While the historical significance may be difficult to grasp for someone unfamiliar with the spread of Buddhism in the region, the grounds themselves are quite stunning, and just wandering around for an hour or two is worth the time. The *wat* is 1.5 kilometers (1 mi) south of the center of town: Grab a local *song thaew* or public bus on Ratchadamnoen Road or, if the weather is good, walk.

The Nakhon Si Thammarat **Arts and Culture Center Rajabhat Institute** (Nakhon Si Thammarat-Phrom Khiri Rd., Hwy. 4016, 9am-4pm daily, free), 13 kilometers (8 mi) east of the center of town, has numerous archaeological exhibits of artifacts found in the region, including tools and other objects from the Srivijaya Empire. The center, which is unfortunately mostly signed in Thai, also preserves and catalogs local customs, languages, and literature.

Accommodations

Although the city has a lot to offer travelers, the accommodations have yet to catch up (or catch on), and you'll find very limited options in Nakhon Si Thammarat. If you're looking for a place to indulge in a little luxury, or even a charming guesthouse with decent facilities, you're out of luck. If you just want a clean and comfortable place to sleep, there are a few options.

The top-of-the-line hotel in the city is the **Twin Lotus Hotel** (97/8

Nakhon Si Thammarat

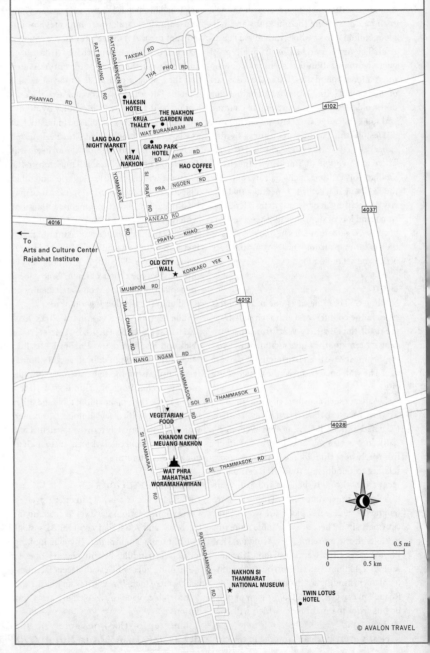

© AVALON TRAVEL

Pattanakarn-Kukwang Rd., tel. 07/532-3777, www.twinlotushotel.net, 1,500B). The guest rooms are spacious and well equipped, and the property is clean and maintained. Since it's a large city hotel, it's not a particularly interesting place to stay, however. Think beige curtains, Formica, and floral bedspreads. It does have a large pool, a fitness center, and other amenities you won't find anywhere else in the city. The hotel is not quite in the center of all of the action, so if you're looking for a place from which you can easily walk to all the sights, this may be a little far.

The **Thaksin Hotel** (1584/23 Si Prat Rd., tel. 07/534-2790 to 07/534-2794, www.thaksinhotel.com, 600B) and the **Grand Park Hotel** (1204/79 Pak Nakhon Rd., T. Klang, tel. 07/531-7666, www.grandparknakhon.com, 600B) are more central but still suffer from a lack of character that's even more pronounced in a city that's so culturally rich. Thaksin is a large, clean, modern place, just off of the main Ratchadamnoen Road and close to the train station. The guest rooms are well kept and comfortable, and the price is more than reasonable, but generic decor and a business-conference vibe make it more of a utility choice than anything else. The Grand Park Hotel is similar to the Thaksin—clean, large, comfortable, and generic.

The guest rooms at **The Nakhon Garden Inn** (1/4 Pak Nakhon Rd., tel. 07/534-4831, 700B) are set around a leafy courtyard. This property has perhaps the most character of all the places you'll find in the city, although it's definitely not as modern and tidy as the other options.

Food

Downstairs at the Robinson Ocean Department Store is the highly popular **Hao Coffee** (Robinson Ocean, Pak Panang Kukwang Rd., tel. 07/534-6563, 10:30am-8:30pm daily, 35-120B), and the **Ligor Bakery** next door, which offers a choice of cakes and pastries. There are plenty of seats, but these restaurants do get busy at lunchtime, especially on the weekend, although chances are you will be able to find a free table among the knickknacks and curios on display and get to try some of their acclaimed food. The English menu has many one-dish choices from just 35 baht, such as prawns in chili sauce or chicken with holy basil, 10 different types of fried rice, and a wide choice of larger meals featuring curries, *tom yam,* and the intriguing fried Chinese kale with shellfish

mountains of Nakhon Si Thammarat Province

sausage. There are 16 coffees and eight types of tea to choose from, along with fresh fruit juices and ice cream or desserts from the Ligor Bakery to finish. The *khao gluk gapee* (fried rice with shrimp paste) is just right for a light lunch, with a glass of the wonderfully sweet *nam makaam* (tamarind juice) on the side. There is also a Hao Coffee at Bavorn Bazaar, but they have no English menu. Neither location has English-speaking staff.

Set centrally in a large open-air *sala* at Bavorn Bazaar is **Krua Nakhon** (Bavorn Bazaar, off Ratchadamnoen Rd. near Thawang Junction, no phone, 6:30am-2pm daily, 25-100B), well known for the southern specialty *khanom chin*—a type of thin rice noodle served with dishes of fish curry, *kaeng tai pla* (fish-stomach curry), and vegetables. This is available in a small size for 1-2 people for 180 baht, or in a large size for five or more people for 250 baht. Also available is a selection of premade curries on rice for just 25 baht, and *khao yam*—another local dish of fried rice mixed with herbs, lemongrass, and pomelo. There's no menu, and English isn't spoken, so this really is a "choose and point" restaurant. A small shop at the back of the restaurant sells a small selection of local handicrafts and sweets, and the whole place is decorated with old farming and cooking implements, including a rather naughtily shaped coconut grinder.

Out toward Wat Mahathat you can find the spotlessly clean **Vegetarian Food** (496 Ratchadamnoen Rd., on the left about 300 meters (985 ft) before the Provincial Court, 7:30am-4pm daily, 40-80B) restaurant and store. Each day there is a choice of around 12 premade vegetarian stir-fries and curries, along with a selection of meat-free sausages and cutlets as side dishes. Everything here is free of animal products, so the curries are made with tofu or textured vegetable protein (TVP), and even the fish sauce contains absolutely no fish. Everything used to prepare the food is for sale, and each table has a price list in English of the TVP products for sale including fish balls, sausages, pig intestines, mock duck, and many others. There's no menu, and though the owner speaks English, the staff does not. They will provide a larger helping of food, however, for a few extra baht if you let them know you're hungry.

If you only go to one restaurant in Nakhon Si Thammarat, this is the one. Within walking distance of Wat Mahathat is the specialty ★ **Khanom Chin Meuang Nakhon** (23 Soi Panyum, left off Ratchadamnoen Rd. about 500 meters before the temple, tel. 07/534-2615, 7:30am-3:30pm daily, 25B), which serves mountains of freshly made *khanom chin* every day. There are a few premade curries named in English available, but the *khanom chin* is a bargain at just 50 baht for a set meal for two, or 100 baht for a meal for four. For the money, you'll get a basket of *khanom chin,* light fish curries with and without coconut milk, a sweet curry with tamarind and peanuts, a plate of local herbs with cucumber salad, fried morning glory, and pickled cabbage with bean sprouts on the side. Get a dish of the *kaeng tai pla* (fish-stomach curry) as well and experiment a little—add a little fish curry to your *khanom chin,* maybe a few spoonfuls of *kaeng tai pla,* tear up a few herbs, add some bean sprouts, mix it all up with some cucumber salad, and enjoy. It's the perfect place to come for lunch when visiting Wat Mahathat, especially if you finish with some *khanom jak* (shredded coconut with sugar wrapped in long thin palm leaves and slow grilled until it all caramelizes) from the stalls offering sweets outside.

In the area where most of the places to stay are situated, **Krua Thaley** (1204/29-30 Pak Nakhon Rd., opposite VDO Town video, next to Nakhon Garden Inn, tel. 07/534-6724 or 07/531-7180, 4pm-10pm daily, 50-250B) is locally recommended for its choice and quality of seafood. The mussels, crabs, prawns, oysters, clams, and fish are all on display, but in the kitchen they're transformed into dishes such as green mussels with hot and fragrant herb salad and steamed butterfish with Chinese plum sauce. The English menu has some cheaper simple Thai food, too, but there's a good chance there will be something in the pages of seafood offerings that will appeal. If not, every day there are also 12 specials on the board in Thai, though the owner may need to translate these as the staff does not speak English. The front of the restaurant is decorated with Buddha images, antiques, and collectibles and has a very "old Thai" feel to it, whereas the back room is a little farther from the road, and the trees and plants make for a different atmosphere. Recommendations here are the *tom yam kung* and the southern specialty *kaeng som pla grapong* (orange curry with flaky whitefish).

Around the area in front of the railroad station, the **Lang Dao Night Market** (Yommarat Rd., 4:30pm-9:30pm daily) has many stalls selling fresh fruit and cheap packet food for a few baht, but this is really the place to come for some proper local food. Pots of steaming curries almost line the road in places, and you can sit and eat a bowlful with rice for just 25 baht. It's definitely a place to experiment. Noodle stalls and *khao man kai* (chicken and rice) are easy to find, but do look out for the stall selling *hoi thot* (deep-fried shellfish wrapped in egg) for something a bit different. Walking food comes by way of *luk chin* stalls selling skewered fish balls, crab sticks, tofu, quail eggs in batter, and others that are grilled or deep-fried, depending on the stall, then drowned in a bag of spicy chili sauce. For dessert, try the exotic fruit in sickly sweet syrup, or the *bpatong goh* (deep-fried batter), maybe washed down with a bag of sugarcane juice. It's a great place to see what takes your fancy, but if you need to know exactly what you're eating, it's unlikely you'll find many people able to explain in English.

Transportation

The easiest and fastest way to get to the city is to fly to the **Nakhon Si Thammarat Airport** (598 Nakhon Si Thammarat Airport Rd., Pakpoon, Nakhon Si Thammarat, tel. 07/536-9325) from Bangkok, and there are a couple of carriers that have direct flights at least once per day.

If you're going by land, the city is about 800 kilometers (497 mi) south of Bangkok, so expect a long ride. By bus, it's about 12 hours from Bangkok. There are frequent buses, including an overnight bus that leaves from the Southern Bus Terminal in the early evening. Another option is to take the train from Bangkok's Hua Lamphong Station; there are a couple of direct trains that take a little over 14 hours.

★ KHANOM AND SICHON
ขนอม—สิชล

If you're in the area to enjoy the beaches, the two towns of **Khanom** and **Sichon,** in the northern part of the province, are where you want to be. Here you'll find miles of beautiful sandy beaches fringed with palm trees and surrounded by mangrove forests and occasional limestone cliffs. If you want to experience the country's physical beauty and feel like you're in a foreign country while you're doing it, this area is unrivaled. In fact, you'll hear from a lot of people that this is one of Thailand's undiscovered gems. The truth is, development is happening, just at a very slow pace. You won't find lots of resorts or tourist diversions compared to Samui, Phuket, or Krabi, but there are a handful of places to stay. You also won't find discos, go-go bars, or much evidence of the sex industry.

Although the beaches of Khanom and Sichon are adjacent to each other, for now you cannot go directly from one to the other on a paved path, as there is no road connecting them near the coast. From Khanom to Sichon (or vice versa) you'll have to get out onto the main highway and circle around, which takes about 45 minutes.

Beaches

Starting from Khanom at the northernmost part of the region, the first beach to visit is **Hat Na Dan,** a long stretch of clean, clear beach. Khanom's eastern border is the Gulf of Thailand, and unlike most of the coastline in the region, this beach is undisturbed by many promontories or cliffs. Although the area is referred to as **Khanom Bay,** most of the coastline isn't curved; it's just one long stretch of sea and sand for miles. This is the area's most popular beach, and it can get a little busy during weekends or holidays, although the crowds are nothing like you'll see in Samui.

At the bottom of Hat Na Dan is a small bay where you'll find **Hat Nai Pret** and then, separated by a grouping of boulders, **Hat Nai Phlao.** The gently curving coastline is what makes these beaches so attractive. To add to the charm, just around the beach are coconut plantations. The shore is rocky, though, so it's not the greatest place for swimming.

Just south of Hat Nai Phlao are **Ao Thong Yi** and **Ao Thong Yang,** two small secluded bays with excellent beaches for swimming, snorkeling, or just lying around and reading a novel. Ao Thong Yi has some coral just off the coast that's easy to view by swimming out. These beaches are quite isolated and a great place to go if you're looking for a bit of the desert-island feeling without having to trek out for miles. You'll be able to reach Ao Thong Yi from Hat Nai Phlao, but because of some mountains in the way, to get to Ao Thong Yang you can either travel by boat from Hat Nai Phlao or by road from Sichon in the south.

In Sichon, a small coastal town on the way to Nakhon Si Thammarat, there are a few beaches worth visiting. **Sichon Beach** and **Hat Hin Ngam** are beautiful and quiet, but there are lots of rocks on the shore, especially in Hat Hin Ngam. **Hat Piti** (also called Hat Ko Khao) has a smooth, sandy coast and also a few restaurants and resorts. Both Hat Nin Ngam and Hat Piti can be reached easily from Hat Sichon using the small service road that follows the coast.

Accommodations

There's not much in the way of five-star luxury in Sichon and Khanom since the area is still largely unknown by foreign visitors. There are a handful of modest, simple bungalows and small resorts that offer enough amenities and comfort for most travelers.

The basic white wooden bungalows at ★ **Sichon Cabana Beach Resort** (625 Mu 3, Hin Ngam Beach, Sichon, tel. 07/553-6055, www.sichoncabana.com, 550B) are clean and air-conditioned and even have simple private baths. The small resort fronts a beautiful stretch of beach, and the young manager, Palm, whose family has owned the resort for decades, also gives windsurfing lessons. There is a nice open-air restaurant on the beach and

Sichon's mellow beaches

plenty of chairs to lounge on if you're not windsurfing with Palm.

Next door, **Prasarnsook Villas** (Hin Ngam Beach, Sichon, tel. 07/553-6299, www.prasarnsookresort.com, 1,500B) is owned by the grandmother of the family, and the villas, which opened in 2008, are very nicely designed, spacious stand-alone structures with modern baths and small outdoor verandas. Depending on your budget, either choice is a great value for the money. Visitors here are mostly urban Thais on vacation, but staff members speak English and are happy to accommodate foreign guests.

The **Ekman Garden Resort** (39/2 Mu 5, Tumble Saopao, tel. 07/536-7566, www.ekmangarden.com, 1,200B) is a small family-run resort with clean, basic guest rooms and bungalows, a swimming pool, and a good location on the beach in Sichon. The sunny guest rooms are not luxurious, but they are well decorated, if simple, and have air-conditioning, comfortable beds, and modern baths. The wooden buildings and thatched roof give the resort a relaxed, unpretentious feeling, and it's family-friendly as well.

Set on a beautiful open stretch of coast is the **Khanom Golden Beach Hotel** (59/3 Mu 4, Nadan Beach, www.khanomgoldenbeach.com, tel. 07/532-6688, 1,200B). This large modern hotel is a great choice if you want hotel amenities (in fact, it's the only hotel in the area), and the guest rooms are clean and well maintained though not particularly interesting. There is also a nice beach bar and a swimming pool. This property tends to attract families, and there are plenty of little kids at the beach and pool.

The **Piti Resort** (Hat Piti, tel. 07/533-5301, 1,500B) is another clean, simple resort right on the beach in Sichon. The guest rooms feel a little more modern and less traditional but still have a basic budget feeling you'd expect for the price and considering the location. The resort also has a small swimming pool and a good inexpensive restaurant with lots of local dishes.

Khanom Hill Resort (60/1 Mu 8, Khanom Beach, tel. 07/552-9403, www.khanom.info, 2,500B) is set on a hill overlooking Khanom Beach, with bungalows and guest rooms dotting the hillside. The guest rooms vary from simple and clean to beautifully decorated with modern Thai touches and nicer-than-usual baths, depending on the rate. The newest guest rooms, which are across the road from the beach, are the nicest, and there's a small swimming pool on that side, but the older guest rooms have a better view of the water. There is direct beach access and a nice restaurant overlooking the water that serves Thai and Western food. Staff and management are friendly and helpful.

Aava Resort & Spa (28/3 Mu 6, Nadan Beach, tel. 07/530-0310, www.aavaresort.com, 2,500B), which opened in 2010, is the area's nicest resort. The minimalist Thai design and massive swimming pool seem almost out of place in otherwise sleepy Khanom, but those who enjoy flashpacking and off-the-beaten-path beaches will love it (as do, it appears, the Finnish, who seem to be most of the guests). The resort is set right on the beach, and there are a couple of high-end restaurants serving Thai and Western food.

Food

There is very limited food in the area, but all of the resorts and bungalows listed above have restaurants serving fresh, well-prepared Thai food, and all also have outdoor areas with beach views to enjoy your meals.

Halfway along the Nadan Beach Road, you will find **Taalkoo Beach Resort and Restaurant** (23/9 Mu 2, Nadan Beach, just south of Golden Beach Resort, tel. 07/552-8218, 7am-10pm, jantima_manajit@yahoo.com, 60-150B) right on the beach surrounded by its 42 bungalows. Sit inside on the heavy gnarled wooden chairs, or head for the veranda in the afternoon after the sun has passed behind the trees and sit with a clear view of the long, empty beach. The English menu is quite small, but the usual Thai stir-fries, *tom yam,* and curries are secondary to the choice of "by-weight" fresh fish and seafood. The fresh fish sold in this restaurant has a good reputation locally; the *yam tak-rai* (spicy lemongrass salad), *thot man kung* (deep-fried mashed prawns), and *pla lui suan* (fish with cashew nuts and lemongrass) make a great meal for two. The staff generally cannot speak English, but the manager will be able to help.

At the northernmost end of Hat Ko Khao, on the right where the road hits the beach, are 10 **food stalls** (Hat Ko Khao, no phone, 11am-8pm daily, 50-150B), all serving similar menus based on Isan food and grilled seafood. The food is great with *yam, larb, som tam, tom yam,* and sticky rice, but it's really the low-key atmosphere that appeals here. Small bamboo-roofed *salas* that look like they should've blown away years ago sit above the beach covering concrete seats or haphazard wooden benches, while a dilapidated jukebox plays Thai music at an unreasonably loud volume just far enough away so you don't really care. Get a bucket of ice and a bottle of something appropriate to pour over it, get a plate of the excellent *namtok mu* (marinated grilled pork salad with ground chilies) to start with, and prepare yourself for a slow afternoon grazing the menus—which will all be in Thai, and it's unlikely anyone will speak much English, but if you're not sure, just point.

Another Thai experience can be had at the Music Kitchen, or **Krua Dondtree** (Talaad Seeyaek, Khanom, tel. 08/6952-7835, 11am-11pm daily, 40-80B), where Isan food meets with country-and-western and 1970s easy-listening music. It's on the right about one kilometer (0.6 mi) north out of Khanom Town; look for the green-fronted *sala* 500 meters (1,640 ft) after the Honda dealer. There may not be many places in Thailand where you can eat your *som tam* accompanied by "Puff, the Magic Dragon" or "Tie a Yellow Ribbon," but this is definitely one of them. As well as *som tam, larb mu,* and *larb pla duk,* numerous kinds of *yam, namtok mu, tom yam kung,* and grilled meat and seafood, there is a daily specials board with another five dishes to supplement the small two-page menu. The specials

are not in English, however, and the owner does not speak English, so it might be easiest to ask for her most popular meal: *yam pak grut* (spicy local-vegetable salad) with *larb pet* (duck *larb*), another combination you're unlikely to see in many places.

The last restaurant on the beach road before Piti Resort is **Sichon Seafood** (Beach Rd., Hat Sichon, tel. 08/9586-9402, 7:30am-10pm daily, 80-250B), offering the basic Thai fare of curries, stir-fries, and *yam,* but specializing in seafood dishes such as grilled lobster, crab with plum sauce, and deep-fried sea bass with mango salad, which comes highly recommended. The open-air *sala* has a cozy feel with aged-wood tables, and a veranda projects over the rocky beach while remaining shaded from the afternoon sun. It's a nice place for a long, relaxed evening meal, possibly taking advantage of the wide range of local spirits on offer at the bar. Menus are in English, and a little English is spoken.

Positioned fairly centrally on Hat Hin Ngam is the **Prasarnsook Resort** (625/4 Hin Ngam Beach, tel. 07/553-6299 or 07/533-5601, 6:30am-9:30pm daily, www.prasarnsookresort.com, 50-250B), a fairly standard resort-based restaurant set in pleasant cultivated gardens and immediately overlooking the sea. The extensive menu runs from breakfasts, with a choice of Thai food, through more Western-oriented Thai food with cream or wine sauces, with fresh seafood being the most expensive of the options. That said, there are lots of choices around 80 baht. There are also five specials, in Thai only, on the otherwise English menu, but the restaurant manager will be able to explain them to you. The *kung gati jaan rorn* (prawns in coconut milk) is definitely worth a try, especially if you don't like your food too spicy. There's the choice of eating in the large, impressive *sala* or at one of the small tables on the beach itself.

Raan Nong Wee (Hin Ngam Beach, tel. 08/9287-1522, 10am-7pm daily, 30-100B) is at the southern end of Hat Hin Ngam just before the Isra Beach Resort (turn left at the bottom of the only small *soi* off the Beach Road down to Hat Hin Ngam). It is a place well worth hunting out. You can eat in the small *sala* in front of the owner's house, but it's more enjoyable to sit on a mat on the beach under the trees with a cold beer and a few choice plates of Isan food. There is only a Thai menu, and don't expect any English to be spoken, but all of the essentials are here—*som tam,* different kinds of *larb,* many different *yam* spicy salads, sticky rice, deep-fried fish cakes, grilled fish and other seafood, fried rice, and simple stir-fries. It's so cheap and delicious that you can get a selection of dishes, and then grab a table and get to chatting with the locals. A good choice for two people would be *som tam pla rah* (papaya salad), *yam wun sen pla muek* (spicy salad of squid and glass noodles), *thot man pla* (deep-fried fish cakes), and *pla duk yahng* (grilled catfish). Add a couple of Chang beers to keep the chilies under control.

Back in Sichon Town on the way to the main highway, opposite the police station, the **Kotone Restaurant** (6/1 Talaad Sichon, tel. 07/553-6259 or 07/553-5242, 7am-9pm daily, 35-150B) comes highly recommended by local people. A 15-page English menu gives ample choice among one-dish Thai food such as curries on rice and stir-fries for just 35 baht, soups, spicy *yam* salads, and other Isan food, along with southern curries such as *kaeng som pla* (orange curry with fish) and Massaman curry, lots of pork dishes that are the general specialty of this restaurant, and, of course, fresh local fish, crabs, and prawns. The particular specialty here is *khao mu kotone*—leg of pork cooked in the three-flavor "sweet, sour, and salt" style. Well-served tables are available outside on a decked area, inside at street level, or in an air-conditioned room on the upper floor, and the duty manager will help if your waitress doesn't speak English. Not surprisingly, this restaurant is so popular they have opened another one on the main highway, about two kilometers (1 mi) toward Khanom, called **Kotone Restaurant 2.**

Transportation

Sichon and Khanom are between Surat Thani and Nakhon Si Thammarat, and you can take a plane, car, bus, or train to either city and then make your way to your final destination. The cheapest and easiest way is to get to the bus station in Surat Thani or Nakhon Si Thammarat and take a bus for less than 100 baht. There are frequent buses (at least hourly 8am-6pm daily) to Sichon and Khanom from both Surat Thani and Nakhon Si Thammarat.

If you're driving, Sichon and Khanom are both off Highway 401, which you can access from either Surat Thani or Nakhon Si Thammarat.

KHAO LUANG NATIONAL PARK
อุทยานแห่งชาติเขาหลวง

Khao Luang National Park is named for Khao Luang mountain, at nearly 1,830 meters (6,004 ft) the highest mountain in southern Thailand. You can hike to the summit and back in two days if you hike 7-8 hours per day. You can also do the hike over three days and include a stay in **Kiriwong Village** (tel. 07/530-9010, 05/394-8286, or 08/1642-0081), which includes basic accommodations in the village and meals, for 1,500 baht per person. The views from the peak are spectacular—you'll be able to see the tropical cloud forest and the rest of the mountain range from above. The park is also home to more than 300 species of wild orchids, some of which aren't found anywhere else in the world.

This inland park is best known for its waterfalls, and there are 10 major falls in the 570-square-kilometer (220 sq mi) national park. The **Krung Ching waterfall** is one of the most spectacular, and there's also a nearby ranger substation and visitors center you can drive to, and then walk to the waterfall, just a few minutes away. To get here, take Route 4016 from Nakhon Si Thammarat until you reach the junction with Route 4140. Turn left onto 4140 until you reach Ban Rong Lek, where you'll turn right onto Route 4186 to Route 4188. Turn left on this road, and you'll find a sign for the visitors center after about six kilometers (4 mi).

If you're interested in staying in the park, there are bungalows for rent and campgrounds where you can pitch a tent. You must reserve accommodations in advance; check the park's website (www.dnp.go.th) for details.

For a real off-the-beaten-path experience, you can also base yourself in one of the neighboring villages. Kiriwong Village, at the base of Khao Luang in the southern part of the park, is not technically in the park but has become something of an ecotourism destination, and for good reason. The village's primary industry is growing fruit, but instead of clearing forests, the villagers have interspersed their mangosteen, jackfruit, and durian trees within the natural ecosystem. You can tour their organic *suam somron* garden or arrange a homestay with one of the village families. They've been taking in visitors from all over the world for years, so although you won't be in luxurious surroundings, you'll be comfortable, well taken care of, and get a chance to get to know some of the villagers. The **Thailand Community Based Tourism Institute** (tel. 07/530-9010, 05/394-8286, or 08/1642-0081) is a not-for-profit organization that arranges homestays and tours of the area as well as to other places in the region, many of which are once-in-a-lifetime opportunities.

Transportation

If you're driving to the park's main headquarters, take Route 4015 from Nakhon Si Thammarat for about 24 kilometers (15 mi) to Lansaka. Just past the town, you'll see a turnoff for the park headquarters.

You can also take a *song thaew* from Nakhon Si Thammarat that stops right after the turnoff on Route 4015.

Songkhla Province   จังหวัดสงขลา

Just north of the three southernmost provinces in Thailand, Songkhla Province is bordered on the east by the Gulf of Thailand and on the west by the state of Kedah in Malaysia. It was part of the Srivijaya Empire, then came under the rule of neighboring Nakhon Si Thammarat. It's in this part of the country that you'll feel the dominance of Buddhism give way to Islam, as evidenced in the mosques and attire of many of the people living in the province. Many people in Songkhla Province speak Yawi as their primary language instead of Thai, and although it may be difficult to discern, the Thai speakers here have a markedly different accent from their compatriots up north.

SONGKHLA
สงขลา

Bordered to the west by the large Tha Le Sap Songkhla lake and to the east by the Gulf of Thailand, the coastal city of Songkhla is surrounded by magnificent physical scenery.

Thanks to its location, it was once a thriving port city attracting merchants from Persia, the Arabian Peninsula, and India. Nowadays it's considerably sleepier, although you'll still find a thriving fishing industry and remnants from its trading past in the city's Sino-Portuguese architecture. This small city offers a great opportunity to observe urban life in Thailand and learn a bit about the culture and history of the southern region as well.

Sights

The city's old quarter, centered on Nang Ngam Road, has a collection of historic buildings and small shops selling everything from snacks to religious wares for monks. Although not vast, it's a nice area to wander around for a while.

The **Songkhla Zoo** (189 Mu 5, tel. 07/433-6268, 8am-6pm daily, 50B adults, 30B children) covers more than 140 hectares in the hills just outside of the city limits—it's almost necessary to rent a motorcycle to see the whole

Songkhla Province

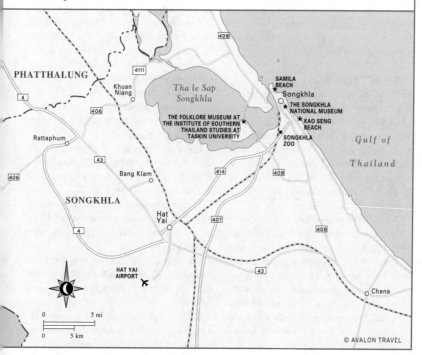

thing. Inside the confines you'll find a typical selection of animals that includes tigers, camels, primates, and bird species. This public zoo is also a breeding center for endangered tapirs—large mammals that look like a cross between a rhinoceros and an anteater. In addition to visiting the animals, you'll get a great view of the city from above.

The Folklore Museum at the Institute of Southern Thailand Studies at Taksin University (Ko Yo Hill, 9am-4pm Tues.-Fri., donation) has a wide collection of materials and exhibits on the culture of southern Thais. There are some exhibits on the history of the area in the museum, but the most interesting things to see are the exhibits relating to the everyday life of the people in this part of the country, featuring local art and handicrafts, shadow puppetry, and traditional medicines. The museum is worth visiting just

for its location: It's on the small Yo Island on Songkhla lake, one of the country's largest natural lakes, and the grounds are filled with local plants.

Housed in a sweeping Chinese-style mansion originally built by the deputy governor of Songkhla in 1878, **The Songkhla National Museum** (Vichianchom Rd., Bo Yang, tel. 07/431-1728, 9am-4pm Wed.-Sun., 30B) now displays a large collection of art and artifacts from the region from prehistoric times to the present. The small collection of prehistoric artifacts includes terra-cotta, pottery, and small beads. The Srivijayan collection has both Buddhist and Hindu art and illustrates the transition the kingdom made from one religion to another. The Dvaravati Buddhist art section has some beautiful examples of 16th- and 17th-century Buddhist imagery from the Nakhon Si Thammarat School of Art. In addition to the art based on the cultures of the region, the museum also houses a large collection of art from China along with some pieces (mostly ceramics) from Vietnam, Japan, and Europe, illustrating the region's former importance as a trading port.

Accommodations

As in the rest of the region, the accommodations in Songkhla aren't up to international standards. There are some large, generic hotels in the city with basic accommodations but no character, and just a couple of resorts on the water. As the area's charms and attractions become better known, this might change, but for now it's a challenge to find good places to stay in the city and environs.

The **Hat Kaew Resort** (163/1 Km. 5, Ching Ko, Singhanakhon, tel. 07/433-1058 to 07/433-1066, 1,200B) on Samila Beach is a large property with clean, comfortable guest rooms, a large swimming pool, and well-maintained grounds. If you're not looking for a five-star experience, this property will be more than adequate. The resort isn't full of local character, however—beige and floral prints seem to dominate the decor. It's also a popular place for conventions, thanks to the large banquet hall and meeting areas.

The **Pavilion Songkhla Hotel** (17 Palatha Rd., tel. 07/444-1850, www.pavilionhotels. com, 1,200B) is another large, generic hotel in the city. It's often bustling with organized tours, and the tour buses can be a little off-putting. But it is inexpensive and right in the city if you're looking for a place to stay while you set out to explore Songkhla.

Food

Coffee Peak (95/5 Somrong Junction, Songkhla-Natave Rd., tel. 07/431-4682, 11am-9pm daily, 100B) is a casual restaurant with a small outdoor seating area in town. In addition to coffee, the menu also offers a nice combination of Thai food and international dishes. This is not a restaurant that tries to please Western palates: International dishes are geared toward Thai tastes, so some items may not taste as you would expect them to, so it's best to stick with the Thai dishes and the delicious desserts.

Another great place for Thai food and coffee is **Crown Bakery** (38/1 Tai Ngam Rd., tel. 07/444-1305, 11am-8pm daily, 100B). The atmosphere is casual but is much more upscale than your typical noodle shop or shophouse eatery. The menu has typical Thai and Chinese-Thai dishes—there's no standout here, but everything is well prepared, and the atmosphere is nice.

If you don't mind trading atmosphere for taste, **Pajit Restaurant** (1/25 Saiburi Rd., tel. 07/432-1710, 11am-8pm daily, 40B) has excellent *guay teow* (traditional noodle soup). This is a typical shophouse with outdoor seating, mismatched dishes, and toilet-paper rolls for napkins—a very casual, inexpensive place for a quick meal.

For some Isan fare, stop at **Deeplee's** (211 Nakornnai Rd., tel. 08/9463-3874, 11am-10pm daily, 80B). You'll find *som tam, kai yang* (grilled chicken with smoky, spicy sauce), and sticky rice. The atmosphere is very local and casual, making it another great place for a quick, inexpensive meal. Another Isan restaurant, **Rotsab** (39/11 Mu 1, Pawong, tel. 07/433-4602, 11am-9pm daily, 100B), offers similar dishes but is a little larger and fancier. This spot is very popular with families and large groups in the evening.

Transportation

To get to Songkhla by rail or air, you'll have to arrive in neighboring Hat Yai and make your way the 30-something kilometers (19 mi) to Songkhla either by bus or by car. There are numerous daily buses between the cities. If you're taking the bus from Hat Yai, make your way to the city's main bus terminal to get to Songkhla.

HAT YAI
หาดใหญ่

Until the construction of a railroad line linking Thailand with Malaysia in the 20th century, Hat Yai was just a small village with nothing particularly special going on. When the railroad station came, the city seemed to develop around it, and while Songkhla is the provincial capital, neighboring Hat Yai has become the economic hub of the area and is a much more bustling, urban, industrialized city. If you spend time in Hat Yai, you might think that Songkhla got the better end of the deal, and that's probably an accurate assessment. Some southern Thais half-jokingly refer to Hat Yai as the ugliest city in Thailand. It's not so much the concrete buildings, traffic, and generic urban feeling in Hat Yai that makes it unappealing, but the seedy feeling the city seems to have. There's a lot of neon and plenty of nightclubs, and it's a big spot for visitors from neighboring countries. Unfortunately, it seems like most people are visiting the city as sex tourists. In Hat Yai there's no ambiguity about what's going on—you'll see plenty of massage parlors, strip clubs, and bordellos, and also plenty of people frequenting them. Use Hat Yai as a transit hub (since it's the southernmost airport currently connected to Bangkok) and spend your time in the regions outside of the city.

Sights

Just on the edge of Hat Yai is **Samila Beach,** a surprisingly quiet and uncrowded stretch of coast given its proximity to the center of the city (you can easily walk there from the main market in about 20 minutes). The water is shallow and fine for swimming, although you won't see many people swimming here, and it's not as beautiful as some of the beaches you'll find in Sichon and Khanom to the north. You'll also find Hat Yai's unofficial symbol on Samila Beach—a large sculpture of the Hindu goddess Mae Thorani as a mermaid.

About three kilometers (2 mi) south of Samila Beach is **Khao Seng Beach.** Like its neighbor, Khao Seng is relaxed and uncrowded. The shoreline has some very large rocks, one of which is said to have treasure buried beneath it. As the legend goes, a wealthy merchant was bringing some treasure to a *wat* in Nakhon Si Thammarat but had to stop on Khao Seng Beach. He left the treasure here under a large rock and promised that anyone who could move the rock would get the treasure. The Muslim fisherfolk at Kao Seng village ply the waters with colorfully painted Kolae boats, which you'll be able to see if you're at the beach.

Accommodations and Food

Selection is bleak in Hat Yai. If you've arrived late and need to spend the night before heading out, you'll have to choose among sometimes dicey-looking small hotels, guesthouses, and mediocre large hotels.

Laem Thong Hotel (46 Thamnoonvitti Rd., tel. 07/435-2301, 500B) isn't really stylish or modern, but it's well located in the city and doesn't seem to have too much brothel activity going on in the area. Guest rooms look like they haven't been updated in decades (nor has the lobby), but they do look like they were cleaned this morning. Another inexpensive guesthouse is **Cathay Guesthouse** (93/1 Niphat U-Thit 2 Rd., tel. 07/424-3815, 300B). Cathay is a longtime favorite of backpackers, so if you're craving some conversation in a language you're fluent in, you'll definitely find it at the hotel's downstairs café-restaurant. There's also plenty of tourist information available here. Guest rooms are pretty shabby, but you can't really complain for the price. The only drawback, which may be a showstopper for some, is the squat toilets.

The most reliable and nicest hotel in the city is the **Hotel Novotel Hat Yai Centara** (3 Sanehanusorn Rd., tel. 07/435-2222, 2,000B). You'll welcome the slightly generic, very clean guest rooms with crisp sheets and modern baths compared to the musty digs in the other large hotels in this area. The hotel also has a pool, a fitness center, and a good restaurant.

Transportation

Hat Yai is well served by **Hat Yai International Airport** (tel. 07/422-7131), with flights from Bangkok, Malaysia, and Singapore, a large train station, and buses from Bangkok's Southern Bus Terminal as well as surrounding localities. If you're planning to fly from Bangkok, Air Asia, Nok Air, and Thai Airways all have direct flights to Hat Yai.

The train station is one of the largest in the region, and there are five daily trains from Bangkok as well as daily trains from Butterworth in Malaysia if you happen to be coming from the south.

Background

The Landscape

Located in the center of the Southeast Asian peninsula, Thailand's irregular shape defies any easy analog in nature, but it has loosely been compared to the shape of an elephant's head, with the northern part of the country the animal's face and ears and the thinner southern part down the Malay Peninsula its trunk. The country is bordered by Burma to much of its western boundary, with the lower western boundary facing the Indian Ocean; by Burma and Laos in the north; and by Laos and Cambodia in the east. The Gulf of Thailand cuts a horseshoe shape into the lower central part of the country, and the far southern border is shared with Malaysia.

GEOGRAPHY

Thailand's peninsula stretches from the bottom of the central basin around Phitsanulok Province all the way to the Malay Peninsula. At its thinnest point, the narrow strip of land between the Gulf of Thailand and the Indian Ocean is known as the Kra Isthmus. Home to smaller mountain ranges that cut down the center of the peninsula and dramatic karst landscapes as well as the Indian Ocean, the region is one of the most beautiful in the country. It is in this region, primarily on the west coast, that you'll see many mangrove forests, where trees flourish in the muddy, salty water on the edge of the coast.

CLIMATE

The southern part of the country is essentially a tropical rainforest climate, with average temperatures around 30°C (86°F) throughout the year. Rainfall follows a similar pattern as in the rest of the country, although on

a slightly different schedule. December-May are the region's driest months, with little or no rainfall. Beginning in April, rainfall picks up, and the wet weather continues through November.

ENVIRONMENTAL ISSUES

Never-ending tourism that continues to grow year after year puts considerable strain on Thailand's islands. Waste management is continuing challenge, there is limited recycling, and most garbage is piled into landfills. Thailand's islands also routinely face water shortages. Popular and heavily visited islands have experimented with pipelines, desalination plants, and other methods to ensure an adequate water supply, but none have been without drawbacks. Pipelines are expensive and untenable for islands far from the mainland. Desalination is energy-intensive, and the by-product, water with a high saline content, may have an impact on sealife when it is discharged into the ocean. The islands are a huge tourist draw, and local and national governments are reluctant to place limits on the number of people who can visit, so water supply will continue to be a challenge.

The rapid economic growth that has propelled Thailand from a developing country to a middle-income country in the past few decades has also created air-quality issues. Air pollution has been one of the country's major challenges. As bad as it may look, the Thai government has done an amazing job cleaning up the air. Since air quality hit an all-time low in the 1980s, policies such as higher emissions standards for gas-powered vehicles and incentives to switch to natural gas-powered cars

---

Previous: one of hundreds of amphibian species in Thailand; typical jungle vegetation.

have been put in place to reduce pollution. Air quality in Thailand is now within acceptable limits when measured by U.S. Environmental Protection Agency standards, and nearly acceptable limits when measured by European Union standards.

Other environmental issues include deforestation, erosion, and rising sea levels.

Plants and Animals

Because Thailand is a tropical country stretching more than 1,900 kilometers (1,181 mi) over an area of over 823,000 square kilometers (317,762 sq mi) from north to south, it has an incredibly diverse range of flora and fauna in varied habitats.

Sadly, due to human ills such as poaching and deforestation, Thailand has a less diverse range of vegetation and animal life than it once did, although the government has taken steps in recent years to prevent further erosion of its natural environments. There are now over 100 protected national parks in Thailand, which provide endless opportunities for visitors to get an up-close look at the country's natural beauty.

TREES

It is estimated that about 25 percent of Thailand's land mass is covered with forest, with the UN's World Development Report ranking the country 44th in the world in terms of natural forest cover. Thailand's forests can be classified into two main types—evergreen and deciduous—with two basic types of deciduous forest: monsoon forest (with a dry season of three months or more) and rainforest (where rain falls at least nine months of the year).

Southern Thailand is predominantly a rainforest zone, but many of these forests overlap, with some zones featuring a mix of monsoon and rainforest vegetation. Other forests in this region consist of mangroves, freshwater swamps, and forested crags.

There are hundreds of tree species native to Thailand, with some of the best known including an array of fruit-producing varieties such as the widely popular rambutan and durian. Then there are rubber trees (*Hevea*

karst mountains in the Andaman region

brasiliensis), which are widespread in the south, the lovely floral frangipani (*Plumeria rubra*), the durable rattan—a climbing palm found deep in Thai rainforests used for furniture—and the much-utilized bamboo (*Bambusa vulgaris*). In fact, Thailand is believed to have more species of bamboo than any country outside China, and its wood has been used for centuries in everything from buildings and tools to weapons and cooking utensils. Two other highly sought-after trees are the rosewood (*Dalbergia cochinchinensis*) and teak (*Tectona grandis*), popular for use in fine furniture due to their durability and beauty, much to the detriment of the forests.

OTHER VEGETATION

Flowers have long played an important role in Thai society, used as offerings at temples or spirit houses, in festivals such as the annual Loi Krathong celebration, and even as food in certain dishes. It's not surprising then that the country has over 25,000 species of flowers; the best-known variety is the orchid, Thailand's national floral symbol. Botanists have found there are 17,500 species of orchid in the world, and 1,150 of those species originated in Thailand's forests. Today there are a number of orchid farms throughout the country, dedicated to the breeding and export of this highly coveted flower.

Given the diversity of Thai cuisine, it's only natural the country is also home to a wide range of herbs and plants. Among the most common are several varieties of basil, Kaffir lime, mint, pepper, chili, cumin, garlic, lemongrass, and ginger, many of which grow wild throughout the country, particularly in the mountainous north.

MAMMALS

Thailand is home to approximately 300 species of indigenous mammals, but most can be found in the country's national parks or wildlife sanctuaries, since poaching and development have drastically depleted their numbers in many areas of the country. These include tigers, leopards, elephants, bears, gaur (Indian

macaque

bison), banteng (wild cattle), serow (an Asiatic goat-antelope), deer, pangolins, gibbons, macaques, tapirs, dolphins, and dugongs (sea cows). Forty of Thailand's 300 mammal species, including the clouded leopard, Malayan tapir, tiger, Irrawaddy dolphin, *goral,* jungle cat, dusky langur, and pileated gibbon, are on a number of international endangered-species lists.

Although once highly revered, elephants today are treated with far less respect in Thailand. Few travelers will escape a trip to the country without witnessing an elephant walking down a city street, mahout (trainer) perched atop ready to accept a few baht from those who would like to feed the exhausted animal. Many domesticated Asian elephants have been born and raised in captivity, put to work in the logging industry in rural villages. Using elephants for jobs like this is now illegal in Thailand, so their owners have found work in the many tourist camps that offer rides to foreign visitors. A small number of wild elephants do remain, however—mostly in national parks now that their native habitat is dwindling. Ironically, for centuries elephants were highly valued creatures in Thailand, used in battle to fight the Burmese on many occasions. A white elephant is even featured on the flag of the Royal Thai Navy, and the Order of the White Elephant is one of the country's highest honors, bestowed by the king. Contrary to popular belief, white elephants are very rarely completely white, although the skin has to be very pale in certain areas for it to qualify as a genuine white elephant and thus a prized commodity.

Chances are that visitors will also encounter more than a few primates in Thailand, as there is no shortage of the crafty little fellows, whether they are hanging off the telephone lines, looking for handouts at temples, or stealing cameras from bewildered travelers. Species include white-handed *lar* and pileated gibbons, as well as different varieties of long- and short-tailed macaques and langurs. Many of these species are endangered and shouldn't be used as entertainment.

Traditional hunting and poaching for medicine have devastated Thailand's wildcat populations. The tiger is the largest and best-known of all Thailand's wildcats, with populations kept and bred in captivity by private collectors. The country's Western Forest Complex, which features 17,800 square kilometers (6,873 sq mi) of protected rainforest habitat, is currently home to 720 tigers, according to a study by Thailand's Department of National Parks, Wildlife, and Plant Conservation released in 2007. But Thailand's parks and wildlife reserves could hold up to 2,000 wild tigers, about three times their current level, if the government steps up efforts to control poaching.

Bears in Thailand don't fare much better. There are two species found in the country, the Asiatic black bear and the Malayan sun bear. The black bear is bigger, recognized by the white V on its neck, and found all over the country. The sun bear is smaller and more aggressive, commonly found in Thailand's southern region. Although prohibited by law, bear cubs are often taken from the wild as pets, while older bears are known to have been poached for their gallbladders and paws to be used in traditional Asian medicines.

REPTILES AND AMPHIBIANS

Thailand features around 313 reptiles and 107 amphibians, a population that includes 163 species of snakes, 85 of which are venomous. Among these are the common cobra (of which there are six subspecies), king cobra, banded krait (three species), Malayan viper, green viper, and Russell's pit viper. Thailand's largest snake is the reticulated python, which can grow to a length of 15 meters (49 ft) and is found in the rainforests of northern Thailand. There are also many lizards throughout the country, including geckos and black jungle monitors.

BIRDS

Bird-watchers will be kept busy in Thailand, given that the country is home to over 1,000 recorded resident and migrating species. Distribution varies according to geography and climate. Among the more predominant species are various types of partridge, quail, pheasant, fireback, duck, goose, woodpecker, barbet, hornbill, trogon, kingfisher, bee-eater, cuckoo, *malkoha,* parrot, parakeet, swiftlet, needletail, owl, frogmouth, dove, nightjar, pigeon, crane, crank, sandpiper, jacana, plover, gull, tern, kite, eagle, vulture, falcon, cormorant, broadbill, oriole, flycatcher, fantail, robin, forktail, starling, bulbul, warbler, babbler, laughing thrush, sunbird, and spiderhunter, to name a few. One of the best ways to go bird-watching is by heading to one of Thailand's national parks.

Hornbills and kingfishers are two of the most popular species due to their unique features. Thailand has 15 species of kingfishers, and most of them have bright plumage. Kingfishers typically perch in trees in an upright exposed posture, plunging into the water for food. Some species, such as the white-throated kingfisher, inhabit inland areas.

They're commonly seen around rice fields looking for lizards, frogs, and insects, and they will amaze even the most jaded of nature lovers, providing an absolutely stunning sight when the sunlight hits their shiny blue feathers. Hornbills, meanwhile, make their nests in holes in trees and are easily recognizable by their hooked beaks. Of the 54 species of hornbill worldwide, Thailand is home to 13 varieties. Hornbills are primarily frugivorous (fruit eaters), although they will take small reptiles, insects, and even other smaller birds when they are molting or rearing young.

Loss of habitat due to human development is the greatest threat to Thailand's birds. For instance, shrimp farms along the coast are robbing waterfowl of their intertidal diets, while the popularity of bird's nest soup has led to the overharvesting of swiftlet nests in the south. Of the country's roughly 1,000 bird species, about 30 are listed as being critically endangered, which means they face possible extinction within 50 years.

Serious bird-watchers will want to check with the Bird Conservation Society of Thailand (www.bcst.or.th), an excellent source of information on the latest sightings, tours, and data.

History

Thailand has long been a cosmopolitan kingdom that played an important role in international trade and worked to defend its existence against its neighbors. It should come as no surprise that they were able to use their well-practiced diplomatic skills to maintain their sovereignty even as most of their neighbors became de facto European colonies. Thailand's greatest challenge has not been maintaining its identity or becoming a major economic player; rather, it has struggled for almost 100 years with different interpretations of "progress," and particularly what that means for politics and governance.

WHO ARE THE THAI?

There is evidence of human activity in the mainland of Southeast Asia dating back 180,000 years. There are signs of civilization dating back at least 6,000 years, but the area did not see significant growth until the development of rice agriculture and bronze tools circa 2500 BC.

Some people believe that the Thai people were originally from southwestern China and migrated to Southeast Asia. Some people believe that they originated in Vietnam and spread north and west to China, India, and Burma, and then southwest to Laos and Thailand. Although the question is not entirely settled, it is known that they were influenced by the Chinese, both genetically and culturally. There were also significant Indian influences. By the 8th century AD, there were a number of related peoples who shared similar languages and cultures on the mainland of Southeast Asia. They were distinct from other groups on the mainland, particularly the Khmer, the Mon, and the Burmese. While many of them lived in what we now call Thailand, there were also settlements in Vietnam and the Malay Peninsula.

THAILAND? SIAM? IT'S COMPLICATED . . .

The larger discussion about the differences between ethnicity and nationality and how they are influenced by language is beyond the scope of this book. However, because of the way those ideas shaped Thailand's later history, some explanation is provided.

Tai is the language of many of the peoples who resided in Thailand, Vietnam, and Malaysia. The word itself means "free." The Tai written language is based on Mon and Khmer, but the spoken language is based on the Indian languages Sanskrit and Pali. We will refer to the language for the rest of this section as "Thai" in keeping with the modern convention.

The word *syam* is of Khmer origin and is first recorded in the 12th century in the temple complex at Angkor Wat. It means "dark brown" and refers to the Thai peoples who were vassals of the Khmer at that point. Even after the Thai peoples won their independence, that word endured as a descriptor for the people. Hence, "Siam" eventually became the name of the country in the 19th century.

However, like many modern nations, Thailand's borders have changed through the centuries. Further, multiple Thai kingdoms coexisted with each other at certain points. We will refer to the kingdoms by their names but the people of those kingdoms as "the Thai."

It should also be noted that for much of Thailand's modern history, there was significant migration from southern China, particularly during the 19th century. Although many eventually returned to China, a large population stayed, most of whom became assimilated into Siam's population. Thus, while the majority of Siam's population was indeed Thai-speaking, Chinese was a significant minority language.

EARLY KINGDOMS AND INFLUENCES
Ban Chiang

There are signs of a well-established stable civilization on the Khorat Plateau in northeast Thailand near Laos. It's believed that it was settled by 4000 BC. Although it is widely held that the Bronze Age did not begin until 3500-3000 BC and was confined to the civilizations in China and Mesopotamia, bronze and iron tools and utensils have been found at Ban Chiang dating back before that time. Elaborately decorated ceramic vessels, silk, stone, and glass beads as well as printed textiles dating to the same period have also been found here. Scholars are not in agreement about whether this indicates migration of an established civilization into Ban Chiang or whether the inhabitants developed these

skills while in Southeast Asia. However, it can be reasonably asserted that this provides evidence that these early inhabitants were involved in some trade. It has been theorized that Ban Chiang may have suffered from overfarming by 2000 BC, a development that might have necessitated the migration to the Chao Phraya River Valley.

Dvaravati

The Dvaravati period lasted from approximately the 1st century BC to the 11th century AD. During this time, the Mon people migrated from India through Burma into an area from northern Siam to the west half of the Chao Phraya River Valley. Most probably the area had already been exposed to Indian culture, particularly the idea of the divinity of kings, styles of art and architecture, political structures, and Hinduism, including Hindu literature.

Although little is known about this period, we do know that Buddhism came to Siam at this point. In addition to the Mon migration, there was also movement from the inhabitants of Tibet, Burma, and China into central and northern Thailand.

The Dvaravati kingdom disappears from history by the 11th century, possibly as a result of conflict with the powerful Khmer Empire. The Mon were assimilated into the larger Thai civilization, but they persist in modern times as an independent influence in Burma.

Srivijaya

Srivijaya was a Buddhist trading empire that arose in the 7th century. It overlapped in time with the Dvaravati but was centered in the Malay Peninsula and southern Thailand.

The wealth from their trade activities facilitated their patronage of Buddhist learning, and Srivijaya became known as a center of Buddhist scholarship. Mahayana Buddhism grew in importance in the empire during the next century.

Other kingdoms coveted their control of key positions, particularly the kingdoms of East Java and the Cholas of south India.

The Cholas attacked in 1025 and captured Srivijaya's maharaja. Srivijaya never recovered, and by 1286 what remained of it was conquered by the East-Javanese Singhasari king Kertanagara.

Khmer

The Khmer Empire was a Hindu kingdom established in the early 9th century in what is now northern Cambodia by Jayavarman II. It was the primary rival of the Thai kingdoms for centuries. During its primacy, it was the power center of Southeast Asia.

The Khmer city of Angkor Thom arose after 900. Filled with temples, palaces, and towers and protected by walls and moats, all decorated with details of Hindu deities, it rivaled both contemporary London and, more importantly, Paris.

Construction on the more famous Angkor Wat temple complex began in 879 but was completed under the patronage of Suryavarman II in the early 12th century. In addition, Suryavarman II also increased the holdings of the empire, extending it into Thailand, Burma, Malaysia, and Vietnam. He also established diplomatic relations with China in 1119.

Conflict with Vietnam in the late 12th century weakened the Khmer. Jayavarman VII repulsed them in 1181, and under his rule there was a brief revival of Angkor Wat and renewed conquest, but after his death the empire began to lose its holdings again. In 1431 they were sacked by Ayutthaya and were never again a regional force.

Lanna Thai

Lanna Thai was the dominant kingdom in northern Thailand 1259-1558. It was established during the reign of King Mengrai (1259-1317). The phrase lanna means "land of a million rice paddies." It made its capital first at Chiang Rai and then at Chiang Mai. A successful alliance with the southern kingdom of Sukhothai helped fend off both the Mongols in 1301 and then Ayutthaya in 1372.

Until the 15th century, Lanna was characterized by alternating periods of stability and unrest. The kingdom peaked under Tilokaracha (1441-1487), but soon after his death it was under constant threat from Burma until it finally fell to them in 1558.

Sukhothai

The word sukhothai means "dawn of happiness." The Sukhothai Kingdom was founded in 1238 by King Indraditya to defend against the Khmer empire. The kingdom was defined by Indraditya and his son Ramkhamhaeng. The latter ruled 1275-1317 and was not only a skilled military leader but also a savvy diplomat who established relations with Chiang Mai and Chiang Sen as well as China, Burma, India, and Ceylon (now Sri Lanka). Theravada Buddhism was the dominant religion of the Sukhothai Kingdom. The Thai alphabet was also created under Ramkhamhaeng in 1283. Sukhothai was known for its great works of art and architecture, including temples, palaces, and statues.

The kingdom declined after Ramkhamhaeng's death. By 1365, it came under the control of Ayutthaya.

Ayutthaya

Ayutthaya was founded by U Thong, later known as Ramathibodi I, in 1350. It was under Ayutthaya that much of modern Thailand was first united.

Within its first century, Ayutthaya established itself as a key player in Southeast Asia, first conquering Sukhothai, then Chiang Mai, and finally the Khmer Empire itself. For close to a century, they enjoyed a period of relative peace and great prosperity.

Portugal established relations with Ayutthaya in 1512. Relations were subsequently established with the Dutch in 1605, Great Britain in 1612, Denmark in 1621, and France in 1662.

Ayutthaya battled with Burma in 1538, 1549, 1563, and 1569. During the last conflict, the Ayutthaya prince Naresuan was taken as a long-term hostage of the Burmese and raised with their crown prince. The relationship between the two combined the worst of sibling and political rivalry. Nevertheless, Naresuan was asked to lead a mission into Ayutthaya territory for the Burmese. He turned against Burma and later killed the Burmese crown prince in hand-to-hand combat. Naresuan reigned over Ayutthaya from 1590 to 1605.

By the 18th century, Ayutthaya was a key participant in a robust trade network and was one of the most cosmopolitan cities in the world. The Siamese merchants were able to independently manage trade, but they frequently used royal commissioned ships.

Internal conflicts overall engrossed the government, and they missed the signs of the resurgent Burmese threat. As such, they were unable to stop the Burmese attack in 1767. The result was that Ayutthaya was destroyed. Thousands were killed, and many priceless artifacts and examples of architecture were lost forever.

Taksin and Thonburi

Taksin, a Sino-Siamese governor from Western Siam who rose to power through the military ranks, defended Ayutthaya against the Burmese, but when it was evident that Ayutthaya was going to fall, he gathered his followers and established a base near the Cambodian border. After the Burmese troops retreated, he retook the Thai plain. In addition to setting up an orderly government, he also distributed food to the starving, devastated population. He led an attack against the Burmese and defeated them in battle. Burma was subsequently invaded by China. Later, he and his generals expanded the territory of the kingdom into what is now Cambodia and Laos.

Taksin made the decision that it would be easier to build a new city at Thonburi than to rebuild Ayutthaya.

Taksin was revered for his salvation of the Thai people. His fall from power, and the rise of his general, Buddha Yodfa Chulaloke, also known as Chao Phraya Chakri, is a subject of controversy.

Taksin was not from the royal line or any of the aristocratic houses that sometimes supplied successors to the throne. Within 15 years of his ascension to the throne, Taksin is said to have demanded to be worshipped as a Buddha and to have meted out cruel and arbitrary punishments, including executions, for minor offenses.

According to most accounts, Chao Phraya Chakri was in the middle of a campaign in Cambodia when relations in Thonburi broke down and Taksin was overthrown. He returned to Thonburi, put the coup down, and then took power himself, eventually naming himself king. He ordered the execution of Taksin in 1782.

The Chakri Dynasty and Bangkok

Chao Phraya Chakri, later renamed Rama I, moved the capital to Bangkok. He repulsed another Burmese attack in 1785. From this point on, although there would be later hostilities with Burma, they would never again present a serious threat to the Thai. Once the Burmese were neutralized, Bangkok began to expand its borders. By the end of the First Reign, the kingdom included all of modern Laos and Cambodia and parts of Burma, Vietnam, Malaysia, and China.

The Bangkok court consciously cultivated what might be termed a "Buddhist" style of rule, inviting open discussion and attempting to deliver judgments based on dispassionate Buddhist ideals as opposed to human passions. At the same time, there was a tolerance for the other non-Buddhist religions and cultures represented by the inhabitants of the city. At this time, classics from other Asian countries were translated into Thai. The translations were not only in prose but in less elaborate language and thus more accessible to more readers.

Trade was purposefully revived in the First Reign, particularly with China. During the Second Reign (1809-1824), under Buddha Loetla Nabhalai, Rama I's eldest son, who ruled as Rama II, Bangkok maintained diplomatic relations with China, Vietnam, Burma, and Malaysia. It also received representatives from both Portugal and the East India Company.

A Problem with Succession

Succession to the throne did not follow the hard-and-fast rule of primogeniture; there was an election of sorts by the king's advisers and court. Rama II's older son Phra Maha Jessadarajachao, although not born to a queen, had a good claim on the throne, was experienced in state affairs, and was popular with some of the more traditional elements in the court. Another son, Mongkut, was Rama II's oldest son by his queen and was seen to have the intellect and character that a monarch required even at an early age. However, although he may have had a better technical claim, he was too young to have established the supporters at court his older brother had. Mongkut was in a monastery when his brother, now known as Rama III, became king.

King Rama IV's statue in Bangkok

While the First and Second Reigns saw the expansion and solidification of the Thai Kingdom, the Third Reign (1824-1851) saw rebellion from within and new opportunities from without. Most of these rebellions were put down, but they were a frequent characteristic of the Third Reign.

During this period, Bangkok strengthened relations both with the Chinese and the Chinese government. Trade became even more important to the Thai economy, as did Chinese immigrant labor. The new immigrants were hired both as tax farmers and paid laborers.

Bangkok began to increase contacts with the Western world, signing treaties with the British East India Company in 1826 and the United States in 1833.

Relations with Europe

After the founding of Singapore in 1819, the British believed that developing trade relations with the Malay Peninsula and Bangkok were vital to Singapore's success. However, most Europeans saw trade in Bangkok as byzantine and corrupt. The Thai realized how such a viewpoint could be used to justify military action against it.

By the middle of the 19th century, Western nations demanded more open trade, diplomatic relations, and extraterritorial legal protections for their nationals in Bangkok. In 1850 the American John Balestier and the Briton Sir James Brooke tried unsuccessfully to negotiate terms with Siam.

Rama III's health was failing, and his court knew that a succession fight was looming. They did not want to enter into any negotiations that might compromise a new monarch.

By the time Mongkut assumed the throne as Rama IV, European powers were willing to use force to obtain the terms they wanted. In 1855, Bangkok signed the Bowring Treaty. Siam was able to continue to control opium, gambling, alcohol, and the lottery, activities that were not within the purview of the treaty. While the Thai on the whole benefited, it did hurt the livelihoods of the Chinese minority that dominated trade.

Having seen the influence of the British in Burma and the French in Vietnam, Bangkok sought to limit one dominant influence by opening itself to multiple countries. The Thai not only played countries off each other but also exploited competing entities in the same country, particularly in Britain, France, and their colonial offshoots.

MODERN TIMES
Mongkut, Chulalongkorn, and Modernization

Mongkut's knowledge of Western methods and thought and his ability to meet European nations on their terms was invaluable. The Thai court understood that perceived corruption and the potentially negative impact it would have on international business was the reason Europe demanded changes and why Siam (and other countries) agreed in principle to open themselves to Western suggestions.

Official government business was conducted in the homes of the nobles in office. Justice could be biased and influenced by money and power sometimes more than by written law. Civil administration was influenced by nepotism, and officials received a cut of the business they helped facilitate and transact.

The government was neither transparent nor efficient. Branches of government performed multiple duties, including governance, taxation, raising troops, administering law, and sometimes most importantly, organizing labor for public works.

Had it simply been a monarch and his court in charge, Mongkut may have made all of the sweeping changes immediately demanded by Europe. However, there were enough vested interests in Bangkok's bureaucratic aristocracy that Mongkut could not simply declare change. His strategy was to move gradually toward them. Unfortunately, he died before he could complete those reforms.

Mongkut was succeeded by his son Chulalongkorn, who ruled as Rama V. He was educated by Western instructors (Anna Leonowens perhaps being the most famous) and continued his father's reforms.

In 1893, Siam was maneuvered out of Laos east of the Mekong by French manipulation and British inaction. It was a better fate than many in Asia, who were being colonized wholesale.

As part of the modernization initiative spurred by Chulalongkorn, much of Siam's landscape was changed to meet demands for rice production to feed other Asian countries. From the late 1850s to the turn of the 20th century, the volume of rice exported increased by a factor of 11, and the price of rice doubled. Thousands of households contributed by expanding the land they cultivated, clearing and planting new land, and utilizing more intensive farming methods.

Chinese immigration grew during this period. The new immigrants found work with established Sino-Siamese residents and as substitutes for Siamese corvée labor. Generally, this new population stayed in urban areas and found work in trade and government.

The dependence on Chinese immigrants for labor, combined with their large numbers, may have led to some of the beginnings of later mistrust. When trouble broke out, the government used force. The sugar tracts east of Bangkok were particularly vulnerable, and in 1870 Chinese miners almost won control of the town of Ranong during a riot. Further, in 1889, Chinese gangs battled each other in the center of Bangkok for three days. These episodes and others like them made the government fear that Chinese laborers could bring Bangkok to a standstill. After such a strike did in fact stop business in Bangkok for three days in June 1910, Rama V himself warned that "[the Chinese] influence is tremendous."

Nascent Nationalism

Vajiravudh succeeded his father as Rama VI. Like many of his brothers, he had been educated in Europe. It is not surprising, then, that his reign is remembered for taking the first steps toward defining the Thai "nation." But as so many other countries experienced during the early 20th century, the elite classes were beginning to embrace not only the idea of nationalism but also democratic or republican reforms. It can be said that the monarchy wanted to have it both ways: continued emphasis on hierarchy with limited reforms to serve the "national" interests. What Vajiravudh and his successors were to find was that Siam was progressively less willing to accept change in everything but its political institutions.

What was the Sixth Reign's idea of the nation? Ideally, it was the triumvirate of nation, religion, and monarch (*chat-satsana-phramahakasat*). The nation could be seen as composed of similar people who were unified in their desire for the good of the many. It was something that its members should be willing to defend even with their lives. Not surprisingly, during this period the issue of ethnicity assumed greater importance, as it did around the world.

Another worldwide phenomenon that touched the Thais at this time was xenophobia. If it is a common identity that is the primary unifier of those within the nation, those who are different can be a threat. Although Thailand was long home to different ethnic and language groups, the Chinese, by virtue of their numbers and importance in trade and bureaucracy, attracted the most negative attention. Rama VI himself wrote an infamous pamphlet called "The Jews of the East." In it he accused the Chinese of being disloyal, entitled, and overly reverential of wealth while clinging to their ethnic identity. Their relationship to Siam's economy was compared to "so many vampires who steadily suck dry an unfortunate victim's life blood."

This was one of the low points in Thai history. However, it's useful to examine it not only to understand internal Thai relations but also Siam's role in the larger world. As repugnant as it is to modern readers, anti-Semitism was a popular political and social orientation in early 20th-century Europe, particularly among the aristocratic elite. Further, the British and other European nations saw the Chinese as a commercial threat. By the 19th century, Europe had made so many breakthroughs in technology and conquest that they perceived themselves to be the ascendant leader into the future and China as the decadent symbol of a failed past. Many of the Thai nobility and royal family, including the king, would have been educated with these people from a young age, and it follows that many of them adapted this worldview to their special circumstances.

If his father and grandfather in many ways were the right monarchs for their times, Vajiravudh may have been the wrong one for his. His extravagance, suspected homosexuality, and Western style made him seem in some ways too foreign to many of the people he governed, which is ironic given his promotion of national unity. He also seemed at times more interested in the arts than affairs of state. Further, he appointed some of his favorites, many of whom came from the common class, to positions of importance in his cabinet. This was a break with the precedent his father had established in which his well-educated uncles and brothers would normally have filled the majority of the top posts. Although many questioned the motivations behind these appointments, they helped to establish an example that was later used in subsequent reigns to allow commoners access to government positions.

The country was still smarting over its 1893 territorial losses when World War I broke out. Many of Vajiravudh's advisers opposed his decision to declare war on Germany and send a token force to fight for the Allies (which included Great Britain and France) in 1917. However, this ended up yielding important rewards. Not only was Siam able to alter its treaties with Britain and France to its advantage, but it also earned a seat at the Treaty of Versailles and became a founding member of the League of Nations.

Those achievements are best appreciated in hindsight. Post-World War I contemporaries found Vajiravudh increasingly more a burden than an asset to Thailand. He was not the first extravagant ruler, but in light of the post-World War I economic depression, his continued lavish expenditures did nothing to endear him to a populace that was already beginning to question the utility of an absolute monarchy.

After the war, the demand for rice and silver, two of Bangkok's primary exports, declined. The steps taken to address the falloff led to deficits and borrowing. In addition, some of the promises the royal family had made in the years before the war were beginning to look thin. Although education was a stated priority, it took only 3 percent of the budget; 23 percent went to military spending and more than 10 percent to royal expenditures under the auspices of the Privy Purse and the Ministry of the Palace.

Political tensions were rising, and nationalism began to take hold in Southeast Asia. While the Malay and Lao populations in Bangkok were easily controlled, the larger and more influential Chinese were not. They were angered over Japanese activities in China and staged anti-Japanese boycotts and protests. Bangkok also became a focus of Vietnamese, Lao, Cambodian, and Burmese nationalist activity against their European colonizers. The Thai government was sympathetic, but they were leery about alienating the European nations.

Thai students who returned from abroad—particularly France—were increasingly dissatisfied with Bangkok's progress toward modernization. Two such student leaders, Pridi Phanomyong and Plaek Phibun Songkhram, were to play important roles later in Thai history.

The End of Absolute Rule

Vajiravudh died in 1925 only days after his queen gave birth to a girl. He was succeeded by his youngest brother, Prajadhipok. Prajadhipok was the youngest of Chulalongkorn's sons and the second youngest of all of Chulalongkorn's children. Because of his birth order, it had been unlikely that he would inherit the throne. He chose a military

career and earned commissions in both the British and Thai armies. By 1925, however, many of his older brothers had died, and he was the logical successor.

Before his death, King Vajiravudh had realized that the government needed to be ready for democracy, but he advised caution and a slow course. The Advisory Committee of the Privy Council was established in 1927. That experiment ended as the economic situation improved and criticism of the government subsided. However, nascent activity among students and "resident aliens" continued.

Prajadhipok was initially heralded as a reformer who would finally bring the political reforms for which the Thais had been agitating. Initially, he removed Vajiravudh's favorites from office and announced that his government was considering economic and political reforms with the express purpose of gaining the population's favor. However, the only concrete actions he took were toward uniting the court and trying to create a check against an imprudent monarch. He created both a Supreme Council of State and a Privy Council, but he filled both bodies with members of the royal family. As a contemporary Thai journalist observed, these bodies were more likely to create legislation that would benefit the upper classes from which they drew their members rather than the population at large.

Prajadhipok had only been on the throne for seven years when the bloodless coup replaced an absolutist with a constitutional monarchy. While he has been accused of being too incremental and not sensitive to the needs of the overall population, the coup clearly reflects forces that had been building for decades.

The immediate instigators were a group of young students who met in 1927 in Paris and agreed to the principles of moving to a constitutional monarchy and using the state as an instrument to initiate economic and social progress for all. Among this group of idealistic young students was Plaek Phibun Songkhram, a student in one of the military colleges, and Pridi Phanomyong, a gifted law student. These two would later be archrivals, but for now they were unified in their desire to bring Thailand into the future.

There were two primary forces in this group. The first studied the political philosophy popular in Europe. Their central belief was that the state could be a positive force for change. The other group was disgruntled by the growing feeling that the Thai government was, for all its lip service to progress, still more concerned with the upper class than the majority of the country.

The press, both popular and underground, was critical of the absolutist monarchy. By the early 1920s their position had evolved from criticism to advocacy for reforms: independence, public safety, economic planning, equal rights, and universal education.

Finally, even the business community saw the current system of government as a hindrance to the economy, especially as the country suffered through the Great Depression. When business leaders petitioned for the government to take measures to improve the economy, they were met with skepticism. While modern-day readers may find that surprising, in the 1920s and 1930s such economic planning was seen as dangerously reminiscent of the communist Soviet Union's central economic planning.

While the coup may have been inevitable, Prajadhipok's government's reaction to the economic conditions exacerbated frustration with the status quo. The government chose to balance the budget by cutting the funds of officials, reducing spending on education, and raising taxes. When corruption was discovered in several parts of the government, penalties were limited to the lower ranks. When even the upper ranks of the government began to take exception to official policies, the response became reactionary. Criticism was firmly discouraged, and some transgressions were punishable by death or deportation. The regime also closed certain newspapers and threatened critical journalists.

In 1932 the People's Party had attracted about 100 members, many of whom were in the military. By the morning on June 24, 1932, the party had arrested the commander of the royal guard and members of the royal family and declared that the era of absolute monarchy was over. There was one shooting episode, but no one was killed. People from all walks of life throughout Thailand welcomed the announcement. For his part, Prajadhipok had decided against resistance in favor of cooperating with the People's Party.

Both Prajadhipok and the People's Party decided that they would be more successful working together, at least publicly. The People's Party took some of the king's former senior officials into their Assembly, and the constitution was drafted to include a greater role for the king than they had originally planned. Most importantly, it was arranged that the king would present the constitution as if he and his advisers had drafted it themselves.

Most popular histories assert that the reason Prajadhipok ultimately abdicated in 1935 was that he felt he was powerless to effect changes to the constitution that would counter some of the autocratic tendencies of the new government. In reality, the king and the rest of the royal family were deeply concerned that the new government was going to heed popular calls to confiscate royal property and use it to revive the economy. Because of these concerns, he encouraged a coup in May 1933. The reaction was a countercoup in June 1933. When it was clear the royalists had lost the struggle, the king called for amnesty, despite implications that he had funded and helped to organize the initial coup and the following response. By the end of 1933, there were 230 people who had been arrested, 23 had been killed, two members of the military had been executed, and one prince had been sentenced to life in prison.

By 1935 the king had left Thailand for Europe, ostensibly to receive medical treatment. Once away, he refused to sign legislation that would reduce the spending power of the king as well as the royal prerogative. In reply to appeals for his return, he demanded changes to augment the king's power and role, including the power to veto legislation and appoint members of the Assembly. By March 1935, Prajadhipok abdicated, leaving Thailand without a monarch.

Militarism Versus Reform

The designated heir was Prince Ananda Mahidol, a nephew of Prajadhipok. As the young prince was only 10 years old and studying abroad, he would not be a factor in Siam's politics for at least a decade. The power vacuum this created was filled both by the military and intellectuals, led by Phibun and Pridi, respectively. Phibun took control and at this point changed the name of the country to Thailand.

Phibun and his supporters were openly enamored with the strength of the militant nationalism espoused by Italy, Germany, and Japan. Further, the Thai felt a kinship with the Japanese as their two countries were the only ones in Asia that had escaped European colonization during the 19th century. Despite this, he did not have any desire to enter a war between the Allied and Axis powers and strove to keep balance between the two interests in Thailand. However, once France capitulated to Germany in 1941, Phibun took the opportunity to snatch back the parts of French Cambodia that had been lost in 1893. Japan sweetened the deal with Thailand by giving them territory to the north and east of their borders.

Thailand's entry into World War II on the side of the Japanese was complicated. On one hand, Phibun was hopeful that if Japan could use Thailand as a base, they would be able to gain back more "lost" territory. Indeed, they did gain territory from Burma and Malaya in 1943. On the other hand, resisting the Japanese would have been disastrous. After Japan's initial request to use Thailand as a base in December 1941, Phibun's aides attempted to delay giving an answer for a day. When Thailand was invaded at nine different points on the same day that the Japanese infamously struck at Pearl Harbor, however, the Thais felt they had no choice but to comply with the Japanese terms.

Initially, Phibun imagined that Thailand could be a partner with Japan that would throw off the hated European colonialists. However, it quickly became apparent that the Japanese saw Thailand as an occupied country and not an ally. They forced the Thai government to make "loans" to them and used their supplies for their war effort.

The war alienated the civil leaders, such as Pridi, from the militaristic followers of Phibun. Nevertheless, when it was apparent by 1943 that Japan would not be victorious, both factions began to make contacts with the Allies to undermine the Japanese. They were joined by Seni Pramoj, a member of the royal family who was serving as the ambassador to the United States and had refused to serve the notice of war to the U.S. government. These efforts came together in the Seri Thai (Free Thai) movement.

By 1944, Pridi's civilian group took power from Phibun, in part to improve their chances with the Allies after the foreseeable Axis loss. This maneuver did in fact help the Thais when the British and French, indignant over the manner in which the Thais had taken advantage of their weaknesses during the war, demanded retribution. The United States, which had never officially been at war with Thailand, instead insisted that it be treated as an enemy-occupied state. After Pramoj was invited to return to Thailand as prime minister, the British were convinced to settle for a compensation of rice and the return to prewar boundaries. These negotiations were the beginning of the strong ties between the United States and Thailand.

Progress, Stability, and the Cold War

Although most scholars now agree that Thailand could have suffered far worse at the end of World War II, contemporary Thais were unsatisfied with both the reparations and the loss of territory. Inflation and the disorganized new government contributed to their discontent.

Nonetheless, Pridi's government was able to craft a constitution in May 1946 that created a bicameral legislature. The House of Representatives was elected by popular vote, and the Senate was elected by the House of Representatives. In the 1946 election, Pridi's party, the Constitutional Front, and the Cooperation Party won a majority of the seats in the lower house and thus were able to fill the upper house. Thailand seemed to be well on its way toward political stability.

The mysterious death of King Ananda, who ruled as Rama VIII, forced another change in power. Ananda was found dead of a gunshot wound in his bedroom in 1946. To this day, a definitive ruling on whether Ananda was murdered, committed suicide, or accidentally shot himself has not been made. Rumors began to circulate that Pridi had been responsible for his death, perhaps in order to turn Thailand into a republic. Although most now agree that this was not what happened, Pridi resigned, and Phibun returned to power through two coups in 1947 and 1948. The throne went to Bhumibol Adulyadej as Rama IX, the current king.

The militaristic Phibun was well positioned to take advantage of the burgeoning Cold War and the genuine rise of communism in Asia. His government became a valuable asset to the United States. Thailand became the recipient of millions of dollars in U.S. aid, both to the economy and to the military.

Phibun's second period of control was marked by instability as elements within the military attempted to push him out of power. Several attempted coups were followed by mass arrests as Phibun attempted to purge dissident elements within the military that seemed to threaten his power base the most. The constitution was altered in 1949 and then suspended in 1951. Thailand returned to the 1932 version that stipulated only one legislative house and allowed the government to appoint half its members. Not surprisingly, the majority of the appointed members were from the military.

The government validated the suspension of the 1949 constitution with the fear of communist assault. The Phibun government returned to the anti-Chinese policies it had employed in the 1930s and married them to the anticommunist sentiment of the 1950s. The harassment of the Chinese included making arrests, closing Chinese schools, and banning Chinese organizations. As crackdowns on suspected communists became more aggressive, the United States was impressed and rewarded Thailand with increasing amounts of economic and military aid.

As of 1951, Phibun was sharing power with two other military strongmen. General Phao Siyanon was the director of the police, and General Sarit Thanarat was the commander of the Bangkok battalion. It was an uneasy triumvirate, and Phibun knew he was vulnerable, especially to the younger and more ruthless Sarit. He was able to maintain his power, however, in part because Phao and Sarit were locked in a struggle with each other and individually too weak to remove Phibun.

By 1955 it was clear that Sarit had more support among the military leadership than Phibun or Phao. In desperation, Phibun attempted to engender allegiance from the people. He stated that he wanted to make a present of *prachathipatai,* or democracy, to the Thai people. He encouraged open criticism of the government both in public forums and in the press. He also ended many of his anti-Chinese policies and promised to give municipal governments more power.

The 1957 election disappointed most interested parties in Thailand. The party Phibun and Phao founded, the Seri Manangkhasila, just barely won a majority. Even those results were called into question, particularly by Sarit. Many students were outraged at the outcome as well and protested the fraudulent results. At this point, Phibun called a state of emergency and effectively ended the experiment with democracy.

Phibun's Thailand could hardly be called a

democracy. Even if the 1957 election and his later reforms had been above reproach, a true democracy requires more than attempted reforms and a questionable election. Further, many of his reforms were undone by his successors after he was forced from power in a bloodless 1957 coup. Thailand needed to maintain a semblance of a democratic state, however, for the sake of their American patrons.

On assuming power, Sarit dissolved parliament. The ouster of Phibun was approved by the royal family, who had disapproved of Phibun's policies since the 1930s. Sarit briefly relinquished control to his deputy Thanom Kittikachorn so he could receive medical treatment, but when he returned to Thailand in 1958, he began to rule in earnest. He suspended the constitution, citing the "experiments" up to that point a failure that had not improved the lives of the Thai people. He also shut down over a dozen newspapers and jailed those who were critical of the government, including academics, students, labor leaders, journalists, and legislators.

The strategy Sarit used to validate his regime was a return to the proto-nationalist policy of nation-religion-king. If Sarit embodied the nation, he needed to ensure that the other two mechanisms were visible and beloved. Sarit encouraged the king and queen to tour Thailand and serve as unofficial ambassadors of Thailand abroad. He also moved the administration of the monasteries to a body friendly to his government and employed the monks to advocate for government programs. This was a controversial tactic. Many felt that it disgraced and even corrupted the religious orders.

In spite of these criticisms, many remember the 1960s as a period of political stability and economic development. The staunchly anticommunist Sarit nonetheless instituted a series of economic plans with the objective of increasing employment and modernizing the country. Spending on education was increased, and irrigation, electrification, and sanitation projects were initiated, some of which was partially funded by the United States.

The Vietnam War and escalating communist activities in Southeast Asia provided the justification for Thailand's continued anticommunist policies. When the Americans stationed troops in Thailand in 1962, the government claimed it was a sign of their commitment to protecting Thailand from communism. U.S. aid continued to grow, as did U.S. tourism. This continued presence exposed Thais not only to American culture but also to American values.

There was a peaceful transition of power in 1963 when Sarit died and his deputy Thanom succeeded him. He continued Sarit's domestic and international policies. His priorities were maintaining the political stability that had been established under Sarit, continuing economic development and using that to help raise the standard of living for all Thais, and protecting the country from both domestic and regional communist threats.

Thanom's primary departure from his predecessor was his acceleration toward a democratic government. In addition to directing the newly appointed Constituent Assembly to draft a constitution, he also relaxed restrictions on the media. Reaction within the government was mixed; some saw this as an opportunity to increase popular support, but others worried that party politics would create openings that communists could exploit.

The constitution was decreed in 1968, the same year political parties were legalized. However, Thailand remained under martial law. Not surprisingly, the general election in February 1969 gave Thanom's United Thai People's Party the majority of the seats in the parliament.

The Thai economy grew at an unprecedented rate of 8 percent per year during the 1960s and 1970s. Much of that can be directly traced to military aid from the United States. Loans as well as foreign investment from the United States, Japan, and Taiwan also increased the foreign-exchange rate during this period.

Thailand was increasingly preoccupied with Laos. Thanom's government worried that a victory by the Pathet Lao would make Thailand vulnerable to a communist attack. Part of their strategy to address Laos was to strengthen their ties with the United States and allow it to use Thailand as a base of operations against North Vietnam. By 1968, more than 45,000 American troops and 500 fighter planes were stationed in Thailand. This was in addition to a contingent of Thai soldiers who were sent to South Vietnam.

When the Johnson administration made the decision in 1968 to stop bombing Vietnam and included no plans for Laos, Thanom's government was deeply concerned that this would allow the Pathet Lao to achieve victory. While they continued to maintain a close relationship with the United States, they also remained involved in South Vietnam and Laos.

Activities in and near Malaysia were also a cause for concern. There were communist and Muslim insurgents on both sides of the Thai-Malaysian border, some of whom were agitating for separation from Thailand. Further, while Thanom's government had begun a campaign to improve the standard of living, conditions in the northeast lagged behind the rest of the country. Opposition groups exploited these complaints to advocate for a change in government. Thanom's reaction was to conflate most dissent with communism, thus demeaning legitimate criticism.

By 1971, Thanom decided that the experiment with parliamentary democracy had been a failure and launched a coup against his own government. Once again, the constitution was suspended and Thailand was ruled by martial law. Power was now held by the National Executive Council, which included Thanom as prime minister and Field Marshal Praphat Charusathian as his deputy prime minister. Narong Kittikachorn, Thanom's son and Praphat's son-in-law, rounded out the council.

Between martial law, dependence on the United States, increased Japanese investment, and the obvious corruption of the military leaders, many groups were disenchanted with Thanom. They were particularly nervous about Narong's appointment. In light of the cooling relations between Thanom and the king, many were genuinely concerned that Thanom was making a move to overthrow the king and replace the monarchy with a "republican" dynasty. Dissenters included students, labor, civilian bureaucrats, and even rival factions in the military.

When Thanom published a new constitution in December 1972 that created a fully appointed legislative body that drew two-thirds of its membership from the military and the police, the opposition movement grew. By June 1973, labor and students were holding public protests against Thanom's government and demanded a democratic constitution and parliamentary elections. After eleven students were arrested for handing out opposition pamphlets, demonstrators took to the streets in increasing numbers. On October 13, more than 250,000 people, many of them students, gathered at the Bangkok Democracy Memorial to demand a more democratic government. Troops opened fire on the crowd the next day, killing at least 75 people, and then occupied Thammasat University.

The king, who had been increasingly dissatisfied with Thanom, summoned him and his council and compelled them to resign. The king allowed them to leave rather than forcing them to stand trial. After consulting with the student leaders, he appointed Sanya Dharmasakti, the rector of Thammasat University and someone known to be sympathetic to the student demands, as interim prime minister.

The constitution of 1974 created a fully elected lower house and required an election to be held within 120 days. During this period, no overwhelmingly favored party or leader appeared. Instead, 42 officially sanctioned political parties ran for the 269 seats, and most did not have a well-organized platform, ideology, or reform package to offer. Further, only 47 percent of the eligible population participated in the election held in January 1975.

These problems were not the result of corruption but rather inexperience.

If the student groups had expected a left-leaning government, they were disappointed. The vast majority of the seats went to center and right-of-center parties. Of those, no one held a clear majority. Seni Pramoj of the Democrat Party was able to put together a weak coalition, but his government only lasted one month. His brother Kukrit Pramoj, the leader of the more conservative Social Action Party, created a more secure coalition. While Kukrit's government proposed reforms to give municipalities more power in financial planning, he was unable to overcome the status quo, and those measures failed.

The change in internal affairs, combined with the shift in regional politics, increased the criticism of U.S. presence and influence. Many were concerned that the United States was responsible for an increase in the severity of crackdowns on communists and other government critics. Further, they felt the relationship with the United States was alienating them from their neighbors. The government, for its part, did not want to do anything that would discourage the flow of international aid and investment.

Between 1975 and 1976, a total of 27,000 American troops left Thailand. When the United States used the Ban U Tapao base for a rescue operation in Cambodia, however, without first obtaining permission, the Thais saw it as an insult to their sovereignty, and anti-American demonstrations were held in Bangkok.

Thailand's diplomacy with the new communist regimes in South Vietnam, Laos, and Cambodia were initially unproductive. In 1975, however, they were able to both reestablish diplomatic ties with the Chinese as well as become an active participant in the Association of Southeast Asian Nations (ASEAN) in technical and economic regional planning.

Growing Unrest

While Thai politicians of this period did not always make the best choices, it is not entirely fair to blame them for the unrest of the 1970s. Population growth and economic changes also contributed to the instability.

Although the United States continued to invest in the Thai economy, the end of the Vietnam War meant a sharp decrease in the amount. Further, although the Thai economy continued to grow at an impressive rate, the population grew more quickly. In 1960 there were 26 million Thais; by 1970 there were 34 million. In addition, agricultural gains, particularly in rice, were made not through increased productivity but increased land use. By the mid-1970s, there was little uncultivated arable land. As farming became a less attractive option for the population, migration to the urban areas exploded in the 1960s and 1970s, in some cities by as much as 250 percent. By 1980 the population of Bangkok-Thonburi reached 4.5 million.

Conditions in Thailand were already more favorable to business than labor. The large youthful population meant a large labor pool. Many recent university graduates found themselves without jobs, and many of those with jobs found themselves working for lower wages and longer hours.

The fear of communism persisted, and as frustrated opposition groups increased the volume and frequency of their complaints, they found themselves more vulnerable to accusations of communism, even in more moderate circles. As those groups grew more radicalized, right-wing support and paramilitary groups arose, including the Nawa Phon (New Force), the Red Gaurs (Red Bulls), and the Luk Sua Chaoban (Village Tiger Cubs/Scouts). By the mid-1970s, membership in those groups totaled close to 100,000. As right- and left-wing groups clashed, political arrests and assassinations became more commonplace.

In this atmosphere, it followed that many media outlets became sensationalized. Many of the organizations that arose after a relaxation of the censorship laws were known more for circulating rumors than accurately reporting or analyzing current events. While there were also reputable news agencies, it was very easy to find publications that reinforced what one already believed.

After attempting to curb the corruption of the military, Kukrit was pushed out of power. He was replaced by his brother Seni as the head of a right-wing government after bloodshed during the 1976 election season left 30 dead. With so many tempers running high, it may only have been a matter of time before an event pushed Thailand to a breaking point.

In August 1976, Praphat briefly returned from Taiwan. As angry as many leftist groups were, they were outraged when Thanom himself returned in September. Some say he snuck in disguised as a monk, others that he was expressing his desire to join a monastery.

By the first days of October, factional discontent was at the highest point it had ever been. When a right-wing newspaper altered a picture to make it appear that students were burning a member of the royal family in effigy, right-wing radio stations called for the death of students and communists. On October 6, paramilitary groups and the police attacked student activists at Thammasat University. Over 400 students were brutally murdered, hundreds wounded, and thousands arrested.

The military assumed power once again and established the National Administrative Reform Council. The council chose Thanin Kraivichien to lead the new government. A staunchly anticommunist former judge, he quickly earned a reputation for being harsher and more reactionary than his military predecessors. The government reinstated martial law, censored the media, and purged the universities of dissidents. Many felt he went too far, and by October 1977 he was replaced by Kriangsak Chomanan. Kriangsak, in comparison to his predecessor, was more moderate. He gave amnesty to the students who had been tried after the October 1976 riots and gave the press more freedom. He also showed openness to labor and increased the minimum wage in 1978 and 1979.

Perhaps most importantly, he published a constitution at the end of 1978 and allowed for an election in 1979. The House of Representatives would be popularly elected but the Senate would be appointed. The Senate had the power to block any House of Representatives legislation that affected national security and financial and economic matters. Further, neither the prime minister nor the cabinet was required to be popularly elected.

In 1979, the Thai government supported remnants of the Khmer Rouge, perceiving them as a necessary counterweight to the communist elements in Southeast Asia, particularly Vietnam. This support continued in spite of the regime's well-publicized atrocities in part because the numbers of Cambodian and Lao refugees only added to the destabilization the government had been working to keep under control.

"Premocracy"

The unforeseen oil crisis in the late 1970s forced the most dramatic changes. Inflation reduced the standard of living in Bangkok, and government inaction delayed the implementation of policies that were meant to help farmers. The announcement of a rise in energy prices generated protests on a scale similar to what had been seen in 1973. Kriangsak resigned, and in March 1980 General Prem Tinsulanonda became prime minister.

Prem lent credibility to his term by resigning from the military and appointing civilians to his cabinet. In addition, he cultivated the support of the royal family. Such support was critical to his ability to put down an attempted coup in 1981 by younger military officers.

Although Prem was able to remain in power, unrest persisted within the government, the military, and the economy. Although not as radical as they were in the 1970s, students remained both dissatisfied and politically active. Civilian political parties were also gaining strength, in large part because the population was disenchanted with the failures of previous military regimes.

These challenges were overcome within the first three years of Prem's term in power, and the rest of his tenure was seen by many as a model of stability and prosperity.

Prem's control of Thailand (1981-1988) marked a period of partial democracy referred to sometimes as "Premocracy." While the defense, interior, finance, and foreign ministries were held by men from the military and trusted technocrats, less-important ministries were held by elected parliamentarians. Elections were held during this period, and the parliament was a functional body. Some other generals followed Prem's example and resigned their commissions to legitimize their own service in the parliament.

Although dissent was less dramatic in the 1980s than it had been in the previous decade, political persecution continued, particularly in rural areas. The Internal Security Operations Command, in conjunction with the Village Scouts and the Red Gaurs, dealt ruthlessly with rural activists, quietly executing many.

Part of the Prem government's relative longevity can be explained through its strategic investments in alleviating poverty. The poorest villages, most of which were concentrated in the northeast, benefited from programs to improve water supplies, irrigation, electricity, and soil quality as well as to build schools and roads. (Another reason to create roads for the poorer villages: It allowed the army easier access to areas that were known centers of dissident activity.) While these programs improved the quality of life for the poorest citizens, overall inequality persisted.

The new infrastructure made it possible for the rural population to connect to the cities, both physically and culturally. The roads made possible the growth of bus and motorcycle manufacture. By the mid-1990s over 60 percent of all households owned a motorcycle. The motorcycle was used by everyone, whether it was going to market, taking children to faraway schools, or getting farmers to work.

Electricity in rural areas led the way for another important acquisition: the television. By 1990, almost every Thai household, rural and urban, owned a television set. This was a boon not only for the consumer but for the government. In comparison to print media, censorship of television and radio was much simpler: All television and radio stations were controlled by government or military figures. Not only could they control what news would be broadcast, they could also set the terms for the cultural messages. A popular theme in many of the programs was the middle-class family, prospering and maintaining their values despite the temptations of an outside world that included nepotism, violence, and corruption.

Under Prem's government, Thailand began to export more finished products than raw materials. In the 1980s, agriculture accounted for close to half its exports, but by the 1990s those products accounted for about 10 percent. As an example, in 1978 the top export was tapioca, followed by rice. In 2001 the top export was computer parts, followed by garments and motor cars; rice was seventh on the list.

Although internal and international groups had been calling for a change to export manufacturing since the mid-1970s, it wasn't until the early 1980s that business could force the shift. As U.S. investments tapered down and the price of oil increased again, the economy suffered. By 1984 a banking crisis developed, and the business community and economic reformers used this as an opportunity to facilitate the shift to manufacturing. Tariffs and taxes were revised to encourage investment in the manufacturing sector.

Between 1984 and 1989, the annual increase in exports was 24 percent. Because Japan had allowed the yen to rise against the U.S. dollar and dollar-backed currencies such as the baht, the value of exports to Japan tripled in worth at the same time. Japan, along with Korea, Taiwan, and Hong Kong, found it less expensive to operate in Thailand and began opening factories at an unprecedented rate. By the mid-1990s a new

Japanese factory was opening in Thailand every three days.

Tourism grew in the same years. Between the mid-1970s and 2000, annual tourism grew from the hundreds of thousands to 12 million. The sex industry, which had grown during the Vietnam War, was now marketed to tourists.

Unsteady Footing

In 1988, Prem bowed to public pressure and moved to the Privy Council. The election of 1988 brought to power General Chatichai Choonhavan. Chatichai's power base came not from the military but from regional businesspeople, particularly those in the northeast. He alienated both the military and established bureaucrats by moving important cabinet functions to elected legislators and reducing the military budget. By this time, aid from the United States had ended, and the military elite perceived this as a direct threat to their livelihood.

When stories of bribes connected to infrastructure projects surfaced in 1989, the press criticized Chatichai's government and called them the "buffet cabinet." The middle class soured on Chatichai, and by 1991 he was removed from power by the military.

Anand Panyarachun, a foreign-service official and later businessman, was picked to be the interim prime minister. Anand's cabinet consisted of technocrats who drew up liberal business reforms that were eagerly received by the middle class and urban businesspeople.

The warm relations were short-lived. The faction that came to power as a solution to the retail politics of its predecessor did nothing to curb their own excesses in public. When lucrative telecommunications contracts were called into question (including one awarded to Thaksin Shinawatra, a future prime minister), even Anand could not support them. As international governments began to discourage tourism to Thailand because of its new leadership, the business community was eager for an alternative.

The publication of the military junta's constitution sparked a prodemocracy movement reminiscent of the 1973-1976 period. The king's attempts to soothe the divisions were successful for a short time. Despite earlier promises, General Suchinda Kraprayun assumed power after the 1992 election and filled his cabinet with military leaders and well-known money politicians.

By May, the middle class had had enough and supported the prodemocracy demonstrations. On May 17, about 200,000 people protested in Bangkok, including many from the middle class. Though jokingly called the "mobile phone mob," protestors also included migrants, workers, and students. Similar demonstrations were held throughout the provinces.

Suchinda declared that the demonstrations were an attack against "nation, religion, and king," and he unleashed fully armed soldiers onto the crowds. The violence continued for three days, and the government was unable to stop domestic and international news outlets from broadcasting images from the crackdown. Estimates of the death toll are between 40 and hundreds. On May 20 the king intervened and demanded a halt to the violence. Suchinda resigned.

Immediately after the crisis, a career in the military was seen as a liability for the first time in Thai history. Some were publicly harassed or even refused medical treatment. Thousands lost their positions in government and business. However, they refused to give up the idea that they were not only entitled but required to participate in politics, if only to ensure national security.

Anand returned to power until the election of September 1992. The election was won by the "Angels" (civilian political parties) only after the "Devils" (supporters of the military and money politicians) threw their support to the Democrat Party's candidate, Chuan Leekpai.

Those who hoped for reforms were disappointed. Momentum for reform faded after the end of the violence and assurances that middle class and business prosperity was no longer threatened. The government failed to take substantive action on education reform, decentralizing government functions, or loosening controls on the media.

Rural areas felt increasingly compromised. The Forestry Department announced the creation of new national parks where hill tribes and peasants traditionally lived. Businesspeople and politicians used their connections to obtain land for commercial development. The people who lost access to the land launched protests. In 1994, almost 1,000 individual protests were held over land rights.

Banharn Silpa-archa was elected in 1995. The majority of his support came from the provinces. His government ignored signs that the economic boom was ending and instead focused on repaying political favors with cabinet positions. After his government fell in 1996, he was succeeded by Chavalit Yongchaiyudh. Chavalit promised to stop the impending financial collapse, but he lacked both the people and the political power to do so. By 1997 the value of the baht fell from 25 to the U.S. dollar to 56.

Most agreed that the economic failure was the result of political failure, and many protested to demand the constitution drafted in 1995-1996 be passed. The constitution curbed military power, liberalized the press, reduced the power of the Senate, and attempted to control corruption at the voting booth and in office.

Chavalit was forced to resign in 1997, and Chuan returned to replace him. By 1998, his government concluded an agreement with the International Monetary Fund (IMF) to bail out the economy. The US$17.2 billion aid package included the provision that revenues exceed expenditures by 60 million baht. It also required high taxes and interest rates.

The effects of the collapse were devastating. Between 1996 and 1998, the rate of suicides increased 40 percent, and the number of abandoned children grew. The use of child labor remained stable; because that number had been decreasing in recent years, this was a negative indicator of the finances of the citizenry.

The IMF program was condemned in Thailand. The baht stabilized at 40 to the U.S. dollar, but the austerity program was politically and financially ineffective. Confronted with business collapse, social misery, and international criticism, the IMF backed away from the austerity program in 1998. The Thai government launched a stimulus program, and by 2002 the economy began to recover.

Big Money Politics

Thaksin Shinawatra, the wealthy telecommunications businessman, formed the Thai Rak Thai (TRT, "Thai Love Thai") political party. In 2001 the TRT was the overwhelming victor and won 300 of the 500 seats in the House of Representatives.

In many ways, the Thaksin administration combined the nationalism of the 1930s with the adoration of international finance of the 1990s and 2000s. Instead of a military strongman, Thaksin strove to be the "CEO premier." His first priority was the economy. His government's goal was not to return Thailand to 1997 levels but to earn First World economic standing. He methodically identified which sectors of the economy required intervention and at what levels.

Thaksin centralized power not by force but by corporate-style intimidation. By routinely emptying and then reappointing governmental bodies, he made clear the need to remain loyal. Additionally, he set up consultative bodies that effectively substituted his ministries.

Thaksin was not above force and intimidation, however. His campaign against the methamphetamine drug trade, although touted as a success, cost 2,700 lives and was criticized by the king. Once again, media content was censored, whether through official decree or unofficial favors and intimidation. Individual critics, nongovernmental organizations, and regional groups were harshly attacked, but now the term "anarchist" replaced "communist."

Whereas Phibun wanted to define "Thai," Thaksin wanted to prepare the Thais to take their place on the world stage. He increased the usage of the Thai flag, going so far as to use Phibun's phrase "unite the Thai blood-flesh-lineage-race" underneath the flag on every bus in Thailand.

While Thaksin weakened corrupt tit-for-tat politics, he replaced it with a big-party model that required big money and, by extension, big business.

Thaksin's Demise

Thaksin, though undeniably popular among the electorate, especially the rural working class, was not as popular among those in the existing power structure of Thailand, which included royalists, some members of the military, and some big business interests. Much of the so-called Bangkok elite were not supporters, either.

The catalyst for broader anti-Thaksin sentiment came when Thaksin's family sold their interest in Shincorp, the country's largest mobile phone company, to Singapore's investment arm for US$1.9 billion. Thaksin's detractors saw it as a slap in the face to Thailand's sovereignty and just another way that Thaksin was squeezing money out of Thailand for his own gain. Demonstrations in Bangkok, which had begun in small numbers by a group calling itself the People's

Alliance for Democracy (PAD), ballooned into protests involving thousands of people. In protest of Thaksin's actions, two of his cabinet members resigned from their positions, and in February 2006 Thaksin responded by dissolving parliament and calling a snap election.

The Democrat Party boycotted the election, and Thai Rak Thai won a majority of seats in parliament. Thaksin said that he would not accept the position of prime minister, but he would continue as caretaker prime minister until new elections were held. The election was invalidated in May following an investigation into vote-rigging allegations, and this effectively returned Thaksin and his TRT party to the seat of power.

In September 2006, while Thaksin was out of the country, General Sonthi Boonyaratglin, then Commander-in-Chief of the Royal Thai Army, deposed Thaksin in a bloodless coup and martial law was declared again. The constitution was once again abolished and a retired general, Surayud Chulanon, was installed as a temporary prime minister.

Since the Coup

On September 22, 2006, Chamlong Srimuang, a core member of the PAD, who had also

Citizens decorated tanks with flowers after the 2006 coup.

helped bring down General Suchinda in 1992, said "not once in Thai history have Thais been so divided. Nothing but a coup could have remedied such a situation."

But the country has remained divided since 2006, and although the coup was bloodless, the numerous events of civil unrest since have not been without loss of life.

Thailand's first democratic elections since the military coup were held in December 2007. Although Thaksin's Thai Rak Thai party had been banned from participating in the elections, a new party, Phak Palang Prachachon (the People's Power Party), allied with Thaksin Shinawatra and probably financially supported by him, too, won a majority of seats in parliament. The new prime minister, Samak Sundaravej, was largely regarded as a Thaksin proxy. In January of 2008, Thaksin returned to Thailand after 17 months and it looked as though the coup might be forgotten and Thailand might pick up where it left off in 2006.

But the PAD and Thailand's Democrat Party, long the opposition party to TRT, were not satisfied with the results and over the course of the next nine months, thousands of protesters took to the streets once again, breaking into Government House and intermittently closing down government offices across the country.

A court decision in September of 2008, which kicked Samak out of office for conflict of interest stemming from his paid participation in a cooking show, seemed to quiet things down for a while, but his replacement, Somchai Wongsawat, Thaksin's brother-in-law, was perhaps even more controversial and incendiary. He was removed from office less than two months later. During his short tenure, the PAD managed to take over Bangkok's international airport, halting flights for more than a week, stranding passengers from all over the world, and disrupting trade in and out of Thailand.

When the dust had settled, the PPP and affiliated parties were dissolved by the Constitutional Court, leaving the once minority Democrat Party in power for the first time in history.

Having been disenfranchised during the 2006 coup and then again after the 2007 elections did not sit well with thousands of mostly rural, less-affluent Thais who had supported Thaksin and the parties later affiliated with him. They took to the streets after the Democrats came into power in 2008 and while the PAD had worn yellow shirts, this group wore red and thus became known to the world as the red shirts.

In 2009, anti-government protesters stormed a meeting of regional leaders in Pattaya, resulting in Songkran festivities effectively being cancelled in Bangkok until the following week.

By March 2010, things had gotten much worse as red shirts began gathering in central Bangkok. Numbers of red shirts in the Rajaprasong area continued to grow for weeks with little military or police intervention. Protesters, who demanded that the current prime minister step down and new elections be called immediately, shut down roads, burned tires, and forced businesses to close. Bombs in central Bangkok killed bystanders, and sporadic clashes between military and protesters resulted in more deaths of innocent people.

On April 10, 2010, conflicts exploded out on the streets, including on typically tourist-filled Khao San Road, where protesters clashed with army/police resulting in deaths and injuries (including to tourists). The escalating conflict finally came to a head on May 19, when security forces stormed areas where red shirts had gathered, resulting in more bloodshed. According to Human Rights Watch, between March and May of 2010, at least 90 people were killed and at least 2,000 injured in clashes between security forces and anti-government protesters.

Thaksin's Return?

When democratic elections were held in 2011, the Pheu Thai Party, the successor to Thaksin's Thai Rak Thai party, fronted

Yingluck Shinawatra, Thaksin's younger sister, as its party head. Pheu Thai won a majority of seats in parliament, and she became Thailand's 28th prime minister and first female prime minister on August 5, 2011.

During the campaign, Yingluck made no secret of the fact that she continued to take counsel from her older brother, and many of her populist policies, including support for the country's rural poor, can be seen as a continuation of where Thaksin left off. Yet she has proven to be popular in her own right. One of her platforms during the campaign was reconciliation after years of political upheaval.

But attempts by her party to push through an amnesty bill in 2013 met with intense public outcry, followed by drawn-out public protests even after the bill was pulled. As a result, Yingluck was forced to dissolve her government and call elections. After the Democrat Party refused to participate in elections, Yingluck Shinawatra and nine of her cabinet ministers were removed from office on May 7, 2014, after a controversial court ruling regarding misconduct over the transfer of a senior security officer. Less than two weeks later, the Thai military stepped in, establishing martial law and dissolving the constitution.

Government

In 1932 Thailand was changed from an absolute monarchy to a constitutional monarchy, allowing the king to remain as head of state but stripping him of his absolute governing powers. Although the king has had some executive legislative powers in the successive constitutions that have followed since the end of the absolute monarchy, he holds tremendous moral sway over the population. Generally the king has remained quiet on political matters, though after more than 60 years on the throne, he is perceived as a moral leader by the people. It could be said that his opinions can affect the direction that his country takes, and there is a certain degree of reassurance present when major governmental changes are made with royal assent. The king's silence during the 2008 political turmoil has been variously interpreted, but there has frankly been little vigorous discussion of it outside of a few international publications. Lèse-majesté, which makes it a crime to criticize the king, has been used as a political weapon by various parties and has had the (perhaps) unintended consequence of stifling debate and conversation.

After nearly a decade of political tumult, the populist Phea Thai Party fronted Yingluck Shinawatra in 2011. The party won a majority of seats in parliament and Yingluck became

Thailand's 28th prime minister and first female prime minister on August 5, 2011. She was removed from office in May 2014, after a Thai court held that she had abused her power in transferring a government employee from one position to another.

ORGANIZATION

The executive branch essentially consists of the king, the prime minister, and the other ministers, who do not necessarily have to be elected members of parliament. The Council of Ministers, or cabinet, is in day-to-day control of the government and all of its activities, except those of parliament itself and the separate entity of the courts and judicial system, and they meet regularly to establish government policy and prepare budgets for due consideration by parliament. Along with their deputies, the ministers head their respective departments and give policy direction to the permanent agency officials who supervise the actual work done by regular employees of the agency.

The legislative branch, otherwise known as parliament or the National Assembly, has the primary responsibility of adopting laws to regulate Thai society, although all bills must be signed into law by the king. It consists of two bodies, the Senate and the House of Representatives, each with its own secondary responsibilities and duties.

The Senate consists of 150 members, 74 of whom are appointed by a subcommittee of the Electoral Commission from around 500 applicants across all professions, and 76 of whom are democratically elected to represent the 76 provinces of Thailand. They consider laws and bills previously approved in the lower House of Representatives, inspect and control the administration of state affairs, as well as approve or remove people in higher positions of power.

The House of Representatives contains 480 seats, with 400 of these occupied by members of parliament democratically elected from electoral constituencies, and 80 on the basis of proportional party-list from groupings of votes in the provinces. One party will sit in sole majority, or in coalition with other parties, with opposition coming from any parties not elected to power. The House selects a prime minister from its members to administer state affairs and have the general duties of approving legislation to be brought in front of the Senate, inspecting and controlling the administration of state affairs and expenditure, and to be a representative of the people.

The direct administration of Bangkok and Pattaya comes under elected governors, while appointed governors administer the other 74 provinces, with these being broken down into districts, subdistricts, and villages for purposes of local management. At the village level, a mayor (*pu yai ban*) will be elected by the people subject to approval by the central government, and often the mayor is the first contact for settlement of minor disputes within the community before the matter is brought to the attention of the higher authorities.

POLITICAL PARTIES

As of 2014, the dominant political party in Thailand is Pheu Thai, the third iteration of Thaksin Shinawatra's Thai Rak Thai party. The People's Power Party, which was formed after Thai Rak Thai was dissolved, was itself dissolved in late 2008 by Thailand's Constitutional Court after it found electoral fraud and other misdeeds by members. Despite questions about Thaksin's administration, Thai Rak Thai attracted a great deal of support among the people due to its populist policies, including debt suspension and universal health care for the poor and low-cost housing for those with low incomes, as well as the prospering economy under his leadership.

Government House, where the country's parliament meets

As demonstrated during subsequent elections, its successor parties continued to retain that support.

The People's Power Party won a considerable amount of support from fans of Thaksin in the 2007 election, though this was still insufficient for them to take an outright majority. Their coalition partners were smaller parties receiving 2-10 percent of total votes each, and most of them had similar election platforms of populist policies, with conservative and royalist ideals at heart. The Royalist People's Party, Thais United National Development Party, and Neutral Democrats Party were formed mostly by former allies of Thaksin, which is reflected in them having very similar standpoints to the People's Power Party. The For the Motherland Party was formed by a mixture of Thaksin's opponents and supporters and had a much more central manifesto of policies, with a slogan of "Bring happiness and well-being to the people." Thai Nation Party has more history than the other parties and had previously joined a coalition with Thai Rak Thai in 2001, but fiercely opposed them in later years. There had been talk of mergers between some of these parties prior to the election, so the coalition was not too surprising in some ways, but the Thai Nation Party in particular found themselves heavily criticized by their voters when they joined the coalition in apparent defiance of their stated position against Thaksin and his cohorts.

The Democrat Party, once the sole party in opposition to the PPP, became the ruling party in the wake of the 2008 airport siege. Though they shared the common populist policies and royalist conservative ideologies of many other parties, they have remained steadfast in opposing much of what Thaksin stands for, and what he has been accused of. In doing so they have won the support of areas of the country that did not directly benefit from Thaksin's policies, such as Bangkok and the south, but have alienated voters in the poorer north and northeast.

In the July 2011 elections, Pheu Thai won a decisive victory, taking 265 of the House of Representatives' 500 seats, even more than their predecessor party took in 2007. Party head Yingluck Shinawatra, Thaksin Shinawatra's younger sister, became prime minister in August 2011. She was removed from office in 2014. A caretaker government is in place until the country moves forward with new elections.

POLITICAL ISSUES

Though there were clearly problems within the political processes at work in Thailand prior to the September 2006 coup, the army's action was met with mixed responses from within Thailand and some condemnation from the international community. As democracy had been upheld in Thailand since the events of Black May in 1992, it was felt that a step backward had been taken.

The United Nations raised concerns over human rights, and the United States, United Kingdom, European Union, Australia, Malaysia, and New Zealand all voiced their misgivings. Others, such as Japan and South Korea, looked more to a successful resolution and a return to democracy, and China seemed almost unconcerned.

With the return to a democratically elected government in 2007, Thailand had once again become a part of the international community, with previously suspended aid being recommenced and diplomatic relations being reestablished. However, the People's Alliance for Democracy's seizure of the airport, the implicit support the Democrat Party took from them in taking power, and the continued sometimes violent civil unrest have once again caused people to question the country's ability to govern itself in a democratic manner.

Yingluck's main platform during her campaign was reconciliation, and there is no arguing that her party enjoys far more popular support than the opposition. However, Yingluck was ousted in May 2014. Political divisions in Thailand continue, with no elected government in place and no clear path to democratic elections.

Internal problems also remain, most

notably in the deep south, where thousands have died since the early 2000s. Political measures taken by previous governments have been considered ineffective, and military actions have sometimes been considered brutal, but the conflict is no closer to being resolved.

JUDICIAL AND PENAL SYSTEMS

The Courts of First Instance deal with all legal matters in Thailand, with civil, criminal, and provincial courts adjudicating on general matters, issues involving juveniles and family concerns, and specialized areas such as bankruptcy and tax. Bangkok has many district courts dealing with criminal cases and three main civil courts, including municipal courts that handle only minor cases that can be dealt with quickly. All other provinces have at least one provincial court that will exercise unlimited jurisdiction, and all cases in the province are considered there. At least one judge will sit on a case with no supporting jury, though in some matters a quorum of up to four judges may be established depending on the severity and complexity of the case.

Each region also has a Court of Appeal, and a quorum of three judges including one chief justice will hear every case. The next and last step is for a case to be referred to the Supreme Court, where again a quorum of three judges will sit, with the president of the Supreme Court playing a personal role in some judicial matters.

It is widely accepted that any custodial sentence in Thailand is a very unpleasant experience, and the bookshelves of airports will usually have a few firsthand accounts of the treatment that can be expected. The notorious Bang Kwang jail, or Bangkok Hilton, houses a number of long-term foreign prisoners who often came to be there as a result of drug offenses, sometimes with sentences of over 50 years. In a typical jail they would live alongside Thai murderers and drug dealers who have avoided the death sentence, which is often meted out but usually commuted except in severe or high-profile cases.

Policing at the local level varies. Thailand has recently been at the center of some internationally coordinated arrests, and there is no doubt that the very highest standards of policing can be seen in the country. It also should be recognized that the average salary for a local police officer is relatively low, and that stories of on-the-spot fines or outright bribes being offered and taken are common. Consequently it can seem that crimes of almost any level can be paid off with a substantial donation to the police or, where appropriate, even to the victim's family themselves.

Though this does little to encourage a sense of justice being done, it does mean that it is possible to pay for minor misdemeanors to be overlooked. Police officers in tourist areas have understood this for many years, and travelers faced with the official 50,000 baht fine and deportation or even a jail sentence for a small drug bust might prefer to take the option of a large cash fine. However, unsuccessfully attempting to bribe a police officer would probably have very dire consequences, and this course of action is not recommended.

People and Culture

Current estimates place the population of Thailand at around 67 million people, with 31 percent of those living in urban areas and the remainder in poorer, rural areas around the country. The area around Bangkok officially contains some 10 million residents, and the city itself claims to be home to around 6 million, making it by far the most populous place in Thailand and well ahead of Chiang Mai, which has around 250,000 city inhabitants and 1.3 million in the surrounding province.

The population is split almost evenly between men and women, though the spread widens in the older population, with 55 percent of over-65s being female. This is reflected in mean life expectancies. Men live an average 70.2 years; women generally outlive them by nearly half a decade to 75 years. During their lives, average women will give birth to 1.64 children, providing for a rate of population growth of just 0.663 percent. This has declined dramatically from 3.1 percent in 1960, particularly in the last few years. For now, nearly 25 percent of the population is under age 15, but decreasing birthrates will age the population in due course.

Though the average annual wage is officially quoted as 250,000 baht, the legal minimum wage can be as low as 55,000 baht per year. In addition, the fact that the minimum legal wage is not always paid results in unskilled workers in impoverished regions working full days of heavy labor for as little as 100 baht per day. Officially, 10 percent of the population lives in poverty and just 2 percent are classed as unemployed, and there are currently no standard government subsidies to help them.

IMMIGRATION

Since Thailand became a country in its own right as Siam in the 13th century, the almost-constant battles over borders with its neighbors and easy integration of the vanquished has resulted in a healthy ethnic mix. At present, 75 percent of the population consider themselves to be of Thai descent, 14 percent of Chinese heritage, and 11 percent as the "others" who have come to live here for reasons of profession or trade, choice or lifestyle, or as refugees from war.

The Indians were the first visitors from distant countries who settled here in the 1st century AD as merchants and to spread the word of the Buddhist religion, and the next major influx was in the 13th century when Chinese from Yunnan fled the danger of the Mongol Empire and settled under the protection of the Siamese king. But these migrations were nothing compared to the numbers of Chinese who started to arrive in ever-larger numbers in the 18th century, until by the 1920s over 100,000 were settling each year, and stricter immigration laws had to be introduced. Nowadays, migrant workers come from Burma, China, Cambodia, and Laos to work in factories, agriculture, and domestically with around 1.3 million working legally and up to 700,000 working without permits.

The wars in Southeast Asia from the 1960s led to large-scale issues with refugees, with 600,000 Cambodians, 320,000 Lao, and 158,000 Vietnamese being displaced and seeking asylum in Thailand. Nearly all of these people were eventually repatriated or settled in other countries, but a small number still remain in Thailand. More recently, the refugees from persecution have been arriving from Burma, with nearly 150,000 of the Karen people currently living long term in refugee camps near the Burmese border. These people are part of a larger group of ethnic minorities that live in Thailand, including the various hill tribes in the north of the country whose somewhat nomadic lifestyle has been restricted by both tighter border controls and an unwelcoming attitude from some of Thailand's neighboring countries.

Thais do choose to migrate from Thailand; this practice essentially started in the 1970s when professionals could earn much higher salaries in more developed countries such as the United States, continuing through the 1980s when skilled workers were attracted by the opportunities available in the oil regions of the Middle East. More recently the draw has been for Thai people at all levels to work in the prospering industrialized countries in Southeast Asia, with Taiwan particularly attracting professionals, semiskilled workers in fields such as transport, and even unskilled workers as domestic help. Large Thai communities have developed outside Thailand, most notably in Los Angeles, which has a Thai population of around 200,000 and is jokingly referred to as "the 77th province of Thailand."

YOUNG THAIS

All Thais now receive free education for 12 years, with nine years' attendance being compulsory, and this has resulted in literacy levels of 15-year-olds improving from 71 percent in 1960 to 92 percent in 2012. University education is not individually subsidized apart from some scholarships that are offered, and it remains prohibitively expensive for many, with associated costs of 150,000 baht each year. Nevertheless, around 12 percent of students go on to complete the four years minimum for a graduate degree, which is almost an essential requirement for any progressive career in the social sciences or business. These lines of work account for some 37 percent of usual employment, with industry accounting for around 14 percent and the remaining 49 percent associated with agriculture.

Income levels depend greatly on qualifications, so young unskilled workers can expect to receive as little as 3,500 baht per month, skilled workers maybe up to 5,000 baht; police and teachers start at 6,500 baht, whereas a new graduate could realistically earn 8,000 baht, or more in Bangkok. However, employment in the capital brings the problem of higher living costs—the minimum apartment rental is around 5,000 baht per month, compared to less than 2,000 baht in the rural towns. Alternatively, nearly every Thai male has the chance to enter the armed forces either as a volunteer or as a conscript to make up the numbers, although this is only really a viable long-term career path for commissioned officers.

Young people are particularly at risk from untimely deaths in inopportune ways, as motorcycle accidents account for over 30 deaths and 400 injuries every day, with most of these being young males; 1.3 percent of the population has HIV or AIDS and is under the age of 25, resulting in around 50,000 deaths every year. These figures have reduced greatly following government campaigns in the past, and now the government is looking at other problems that may affect youth. Alcohol advertising has essentially been banned, and sales are becoming more restricted, which has also been the case with cigarettes. Additionally, the war on drugs has recently been resurrected, with the main target being the cheap methamphetamine from Burma and Cambodia called *yah bah,* which is becoming increasingly available and popular.

THE CHANGE OF PEOPLE

Since the years after World War II, Thailand has seen a rapid increase in economic development and a corresponding decline in the "traditional" way of life. Financial aid from the United States started in the 1950s and helped to accelerate economic development, but this led to an increase in people leaving their home villages and migrating to the urban areas to work. An eventual effect of the rapid economic growth was a greater reliance on money and not on the produce of the land, and a corresponding increase in personal debt.

Tourism started to bring different influences in the 1960s, which also saw the heightened presence of American troops in certain parts of the country, further shaping the development of the country. They both generated income in different ways and amounts than ever before, with tourism becoming a vital part of Thailand's economy over the next 30 years.

This had a profound effect on the seaside villages that had lived on fishing the waters for hundreds of years and were now finding their homes being quickly transformed. People who had led very simple lives and were deeply reserved in many ways were suddenly exposed to the money and behavior of a significantly different group of people: foreign tourists.

RELIGION

Buddhism has played a significant role in Thailand since the 6th century and pervades the history and culture of the country. Today, Theravada Buddhism, which came into Thailand through Sri Lanka during the Sukhothai period, is by far the dominant religion, and more than 90 percent of the population of Thailand call themselves Buddhists. Although Thailand considers itself a pluralistic society and there are large numbers of Thai Muslims as well as citizens of other religions, Buddhism still plays a major role in everyday life. The Thai calendar begins at the time of the Buddha's life, 543 years before the Western calendar (i.e., the year 2011 is 2554 by the Thai calendar). Although Thais move seamlessly between the two systems, all official documents are dated using the Buddhist calendar. Monks are allowed free passage on public transportation, and there are even seats reserved on most buses, trains, and boats for them. In Bangkok, you'll notice many people, from executive to laborer, wearing Buddhist amulets. No matter where you are in Thailand, you're never far from a Buddhist temple, called a *wat* in Thai. There are thousands, ranging from simple structures to ornately decorated compounds, and *wats* serve not only as places of devotion or worship but also to house the particular order's resident monks. In fact, most Thai Buddhist men will ordain as monks at some point in their lives and spend a month or more living as a monk.

Monks rely on the community to care for them. Walk the streets any morning before 6am and you're likely to see orange-robed monks walking barefoot, carrying their alms bowls. You'll also see residents going to their doors to offer food, water, and other necessities to the monks. This concept of "merit-making" through good deeds, be it feeding a monk or contributing to a *wat* or helping a stranger, is a very important concept in Thai Buddhism.

But Thailand isn't an entirely Buddhist country, and the second-largest religious group, representing about 5 percent of the population, are Muslims. Though Thai Muslims live all over the country, the four southernmost provinces have the highest concentration, with more than 70 percent of the population. Most Thai Muslims are Sunni and are originally Malay, with their own language and cultural identity. The southernmost provinces were once known as the Kingdom of Pattani, and this part of the Thai population, known to some as Yawi, was historically more connected with neighboring Malaysia than with Thailand. Over the past 500 years, the region has alternately been under the control of Thailand (then Siam) and revolting against it.

After a period of calm, violence in the deep south of Thailand has continued since 2001. Although the violence is often connected to Muslim separatist groups, it is still not clear who is leading them and what the specific aims are. Thailand's seemingly monolithic and inflexible Buddhist identity and the central government's seeming inability to grapple with difficult cultural, religious, and social issues that this large minority population presents have only exacerbated the problem, according to some pundits.

Art and Architecture

Throughout Thailand's long and diverse history, art has always played a key role in society, providing outlets for worship, educating the masses on Buddhist values, or glorifying national achievements. By looking at the country's varied artistic and architectural forms, one can trace Thai history back through the ages, with two major sources of inspiration playing a continuous role—religion and monarchy—while a diverse mix of foreign influences have also slipped in. Even the tiniest temple in a rural village is often home to a wealth of artistic treasures, such as priceless Buddhist sculptures and murals depicting deeply entrenched religious beliefs.

Indeed, temples were the main source of art in Thailand for about 800 years, as every royal court made it a priority to build these ubiquitous religious structures to enshrine Buddha statues. The walls were decorated with murals, intricate wood carvings, and lacquer works, reflecting the complex court culture with its heavy Indian influences. Today, the nucleus of Thai art is Bangkok, where several quality museums feature classic and contemporary art from Thailand and abroad, while Chiang Mai is becoming a major center for the arts in its own right, highlighted by collections of Lanna pieces from past and present depicting the unique culture of the region.

MAJOR ART PERIODS
Mon Dvaravati

The Mon Dvaravati period is particularly notable as it planted the first artistic seed in Thailand, influencing the various styles that would later emerge. Dvaravati art was the product of the Mon communities that ruled Thailand from the 7th to 11th centuries, prior to the arrival of the Khmers. Most art forms produced during this period were sculptures made of stone, terra-cotta, bronze,

and stucco, influenced by Hinayana and Mahayana Buddhist and Hindu religious subjects. Perhaps the most distinctive Dvaravati sculpture is the Wheel of Law, a symbol of the Buddha's first sermon erected on high pillars that is still today placed in temple compounds. Fine examples of Dvaravati art can be found in Bangkok's National Museum and the Jim Thompson Museum.

Sukhothai

One of the most prominent Thai kingdoms was Sukhothai, established in 1238. Its art was heavily influenced by Theravada Buddhism, merging human form with the spiritual. Buddha images and ceramics were the most popular art forms, and sculptures were characterized by elegant bodies and slender, oval faces. Emphasizing the spiritual aspect of Buddha by leaving out anatomical details, the effect was enhanced by casting images in metal, as opposed to carving them. Brick and stucco Buddha images can still be found in the ruins of the Sukhothai Historical Park, while many examples of art from this period were moved to the National Museum in Bangkok.

Ayutthaya

An era spanning 400 years, 1351-1767, the Ayutthaya Kingdom spawned a wide variety of art forms, influenced by everyone from the Khmers and Chinese to the Japanese and Europeans, a by-product of mid-16th-century trade and diplomacy. The early Ayutthaya period reflects Dvaravati and Lopburi influences, featuring Buddha images carved primarily of stone, while paintings featured only red, black, and white coloring, with rows of juxtaposed Buddhas. Due to the destruction and pilfering of the Ayutthaya Kingdom by the Burmese, few artifacts of this period remain, but some examples of Ayutthaya art can be found at the National Museum in Bangkok as well as Wat Rajaburana in Ayutthaya.

Lanna

In the 15th century, the northern region of Thailand began to flourish, referred to as the Lanna era. This was the golden age of Chiang Mai, when King Tilokaraja ruled and great emphasis was placed on the arts. The word *lanna* translates as "land of one million rice fields," and its art is characterized by Burmese, Lao, and Sukhothai influences but boasts a distinct identity all its own. Lanna people were considered a gentle and sweet group—a stereotype that remains today. Many works are based on the artists' natural surroundings, featuring paintings of flowers, leaves, and outdoor scenes. Lanna murals depict cultural traditions, including ceremonies, festivals, and regular activities in the village, as well as religious dharma images. Local artisans are today keeping the Lanna tradition alive by creating reproductions; workshops and retailers can be found throughout Chiang Mai.

Rattanakosin

The Rattanakosin period—also referred to as the Bangkok era—was born with the Chakri Dynasty that still rules today, founded after the collapse of Ayutthaya in 1767. Art from this era is characterized by two themes, the promotion of the classical Siamese traditions under the reigns of three kings—Ramas I, II, and III—followed by the rule of Rama IV, when Western elements found their way into Thai art. Initially the art scene during the Bangkok era was focused on salvaging what was left from the pillaged war-ravaged areas, and new pieces of art continued in this vein. Later, however, ornamentation became a dominating factor, and images became more realistic. Murals began to flourish, as did the ornamentation of temples with gilded colorful images, statues, and intricate designs. For the best examples of art from the early Rattanakosin period, visit Wat Phra Kaew and the Grand Palace in Bangkok.

Contemporary Art

Interestingly, the father of modern Thai art is actually a foreigner, an Italian sculptor named Corrado Feroci who was invited to Thailand by Rama VI in 1924. Feroci created bronze statues of Thailand's past heroes and in 1933 was asked to establish an institute of fine arts to instruct a new generation of artists in modern art. The school eventually became a university and was called the Silpakorn (Fine Arts) University, and Feroci's own name was changed to Silpa Bhirasri. He remained in Thailand until his death in 1962. With the introduction of modern art, painters began experimenting with impressionism and a bit of cubism. Today, Thailand's contemporary art scene is centered in Bangkok, with an increasing variety of works available on the market. Although many younger artists have departed from the religious themes of the past, there are still some who remain influenced by traditional Buddhist values, hence they tend to be more popular among the general public. Much to the dismay of the traditionalists there are some Thai artists breaking away from these norms by addressing more controversial issues in their work, often stirring up public controversy in the process.

FAMOUS THAI ARTISTS

While few Thai artists have made a name for themselves on the international stage, there are several notable individuals who led the Thai art scene into uncharted territory, such as Angkarn Kalayanapongsa (born 1926) and Misiem Yipintsoi (1906-1988). Chakrabhand Posayakrit (born 1943) was also a groundbreaking artist, painting portraits that interpret classical themes in soft colors. Montien Boonma (1953-2000) was one of the only Thai artists to create a buzz overseas, his works appearing in many international exhibitions. Works by Montien reflect sections of Thai life that have undergone rapid change, using local materials and motifs in an incredibly unique style. Most Thais will also recognize the name Chalermchai Kositpipat (born 1955), Thailand's most successful painter today. The Chiang Rai native's works have been exhibited worldwide, and he is known for his innovative use of Buddha images in his art that often raise eyebrows. Some say he has lost his confrontational edge, but nonetheless he is still admired by many high-profile clients, including King Bhumibol Adulyadej.

ARCHITECTURE

Fabulous teak mansions built high on stilts, golden palaces, colorful *wats*, and even quaint rows of shophouses built by Chinese immigrants are all major hues on Thailand's architectural palette. The country's history is heavily imprinted on its wide-ranging architectural gems, allowing for a developmental history of Thai society to be traced back in time. Because Thailand's capital kept changing locations throughout the ages, there are several key areas that are home to some of the country's key architectural highlights; however, contemporary architecture is mainly found in forward-thinking Bangkok.

Sukhothai

The Sukhothai period (13th-14th centuries) is regarded as the apex of Thai culture, advancing major achievements in architecture. During this period the mainstays of Thai temples were developed, including the *phra chedi* (stupa), *bot* (where Buddha image is enshrined), and *prasat* (castle). Khmer elements abound, while the Mons—dominant from the 6th to 9th centuries—also provided Theravada Buddhist influences. Sukhothai-era houses and palaces built of wood have long since vanished, but ruins of stone and brick temples in the Sukhothai Historical Park—a UNESCO World Heritage Site—remain to provide evidence of the period's distinctive architecture.

Ayutthaya

Architecture of the Ayutthaya period (14th-18th centuries) was largely an extension of the Sukhothai style, but while Sukhothai laid the groundwork, Ayutthaya was the golden age. In a rich and powerful city renowned for its military might, buildings erected during this period took on a royal grandeur of sorts, with golden temples and glittering palaces becoming a mainstay. During the Ayutthaya period there was also a Khmer revival, when kings built a number of neo-Khmer-style temples and edifices. During the 13th-15th centuries the influence of the Chinese appeared in the form of kilned ceramic roof tiles and mother-of-pearl inlay, while in the 16th-17th centuries European styles slipped in with the arrival of foreign diplomats and high-ranking officials. Much of the ancient city's architecture was destroyed in 1767 when Ayutthaya was sacked by the Burmese; however, ruins of the ancient city remain and have been designated a UNESCO World Heritage Site.

Rattanakosin

For most travelers to Bangkok, their first views of historical Thai architecture come courtesy of Wat Phra Kaew and the Grand Palace, two attractions that have shaped the architectural image of the country in the world's eye. Indeed, the Rattanakosin period is the most diverse of all Thailand's eras in terms of architecture, given that it began with the founding of Bangkok in 1782 and continues today. Much like the earlier art of this era, architecture was designed to mirror the dominant styles of the former capital Ayutthaya in the wake of its destruction. This meant incorporating Khmer (such as Wat Arun), Chinese, and a few Western elements into temples and palaces.

Traditional Thai styles began to decline around 1900, when buildings increasingly took on European forms. For craftspeople to be considered masters of their trade they were required to learn Western techniques, hence the concepts of Frank Lloyd Wright and Ludwig Mies van der Rohe were embraced by local architects. Neoclassical elements were incorporated, a fine example of this being Wat Benchamabophit (Marble Temple) in Bangkok, which was erected for King Chulalongkorn in 1900 and designed by his half brother, Prince Naris. A few decades later, art deco became a key style, evident in buildings such as the Hua Lamphong Train Station and those along Ratchadamnoen Avenue.

Starting a few decades ago, when Bangkok's urban center really began to grow, a feeling of "anything goes" appears to have emerged, with elements of modernism, Greek revival, Bauhaus, sophisticated Chinese, and native Thai styles all mashed together into eclectic designs that are often quite eye-catching but occasionally quite garish. Today's urban architecture has few features to distinguish it from that of any other major international city, with glassy high-rises, ritzy condominiums, and flashy shopping malls becoming the norm. That said, many government buildings and universities have been built combining Thai styles with sensible contemporary design for a pleasing effect.

Traditional Thai structures can still be found throughout the country, and even the simplest building with uniquely Thai elements can be a great source of beauty. There are elegant classic wooden houses on stilts with curved roofs, Malay-inspired buildings in the south, "raft" homes over the river, Chinese shophouses, and Sino-Portuguese buildings in areas such as Phuket. It is in this diversity that Thailand's architectural beauty can be found, a stark contrast to the glittering high-rises that are becoming the mainstay in the capital.

Essentials

Getting There

AIR

Thailand is served by two large international airports: **Suvarnabhumi Airport** (tel. 02/132-1888, www.suvarnabhumiairport.com) just outside of Bangkok, and **Phuket International Airport** (tel. 07/632-7230 to 07/632-7237, http://phuketairportthai.com) on the island of Phuket on the Andaman coast. There is also a budget airport in Bangkok, **Don Mueang Airport** (tel. 02/535-1111, http://donmueangairportthai.com) which serves regional budget carriers including Air Asia. There are also four other smaller airports in the country that have limited international flights. If you are flying from North America or Europe, you'll most likely land in Suvarnabhumi first regardless of your destination, as the Phuket airport and other smaller international airports only serve direct international flights from parts of Asia as well as limited seasonal charter flights from Europe. Once you've landed in Bangkok, you can transfer to a flight going to one of more than a dozen regional airports around the country, including Phuket, Krabi, Ko Samui, and Surat Thani. If you are traveling during high season, though, you may not have to change planes in Bangkok as some Asian cities have direct flights to Phuket and Samui.

The **Airports of Thailand Public Company Limited** (AOT, http://airportthai.co.th) runs most of the airports, and its website has information about the larger ones. Some airports, such as the Samui Airport, are not part of AOT. To access information about the Samui Airport, visit the website for **Bangkok Airways** (www.bangkokair.com), as they are owned by the same company.

Carriers

If you are coming from the United States, there are currently no direct flight to Bangkok, so you'll have to change planes in Europe, the Gulf, or another Asian city before making your way to Bangkok. In that case, the shortest flight combination is about 17 hours from New York, but many routes will take more than 20 hours. If you're not flying from a major hub in the United States, add an additional flight and at least another couple of hours.

Bangkok's airport is a major hub for long-haul flights, so if you are visiting Thailand from another part of Asia, from Europe, or from Australia, there are plentiful options. All major regional carriers, including **Singapore Airlines** (www.singaporeair.com) and **Cathay Pacific** (www.cathaypacific.com), have multiple daily flights to Bangkok.

Don't forget to check the regional budget carriers, too. **Air Asia** (www.airasia.com) has many daily flights to Bangkok from Singapore, Malaysia, Indonesia, Hong Kong, Macao, India, Cambodia, Vietnam, Taiwan, Burma, and some cities in China. Their long-haul budget airline, **Air Asia X,** offers flights from Australia, New Zealand, and Europe through Malaysia. Check **Nok Air** (www.nokair.com) for flights from Vietnam, **Jet Airways** (www.jetairways.com) from major Indian cities, **Jetstar** (www.jetstar.com) from Australia, and **Tiger Airways** (www.tigerairways.com) from Singapore. These flights will arrive in Don Muang, though, not Suvarnabhumi.

Costs and Booking

A round-trip ticket from North America to Bangkok costs from US$1,100-1,500, as of early 2014, but prices can vary wildly depending on the route and time of year you are traveling, and how far in advance you book your flight. Although all of the major travel websites will show you flights to Bangkok, remember that you can sometimes find better prices and schedules by visiting the websites of individual airlines directly, and that even the major websites such as **Kayak** (www.kayak.com), **Priceline** (www.priceline.com), **Travelocity** (www.travelocity.com), and **Expedia** (www.expedia.com) cannot book flights for all of the airlines you may want to travel on. Deals such as **Cathay Pacific's All Asia Pass,** which allows you to fly to Hong Kong then add an additional four destinations, including Bangkok, for a fixed fee, are a great bargain, especially if you are combining a trip to Thailand with some regional travel, but it won't show up on the travel websites. This is a very popular product, and it has some time restrictions and is only offered during some parts of the year, so you have to book it through Cathay Pacific (www.cathaypacific.com) or through a travel agent well in advance of your trip.

Since you'll probably have a stopover anyway, another option is to consider flying into Singapore, Malaysia, Korea, Japan, or another destination in Asia, then purchasing a separate ticket to Thailand. This involves a little more planning but can sometimes result in a cheaper overall price, especially if you are flying into one of the cities served by the regional budget airlines. For example, flights from cities such as Singapore and Kuala Lumpur can routinely be found for under US$100 on Air Asia.

Checking In

For international flights, make sure to reconfirm your flight a few days in advance. In addition, sign up for notifications by email or mobile phone so you'll find out immediately if there have been any changes to your schedule. Especially if you are flying from a busy U.S. airport, make sure to give yourself plenty of time to check in. With stringent security protocols and the requirement at some airports that you bring your checked baggage through the security screening process after check-in, allowing three hours is not excessive. You may end up hanging around in the terminal for a while, but it's better than risking missing a flight for your vacation.

Passengers on international carriers are typically allowed two checked bags on flights from North America to Asian destinations,

Phuket International Airport

but make sure you check with your airline before you pack. That same rule applies to carry-on baggage, although regional carriers are more generous with their rules on how many bags you can bring in the cabin. Regional budget airlines, however, will charge a modest fee per checked bag, and it's much cheaper, and easier, to pay the fee online when you book your ticket versus at the airport when you are checking in. Restrictions on liquids are essentially uniform across the globe, so know what you are allowed to bring on board with you by checking the website for the Transportation Security Administration (www.tsa.gov). You can use its rules as a guide for the rules airports in other countries will apply, but always check with individual carriers for additional regulations.

Insurance

There are many types of travel insurance, covering everything from unforeseen events that result in missed flights to medical treatment when you are abroad to lump-sum payments to designees should you be killed or maimed while traveling. Flight insurance will cover you for accidents and flight cancellations, meaning that you will be repaid the amount of money you've spent on your vacation if your flight is canceled or if you miss it due to sickness or injury. While this can come in handy if you are flying with a charter company or taking a cruise, for many people it is just a waste of money. Most international carriers, with the exception of budget carrires, will allow you to reschedule even nonrefundable tickets, and generally you won't be required to put down a deposit for accommodations in Thailand (though you may be charged a one-night cancellation fee). Agents will try to persuade you that the policy is worth the US$50 or more for the peace of mind, but it's probably better to save that extra cash unless you absolutely cannot afford the costs of canceling a trip.

LAND

If you are already in Southeast Asia, you can enter Thailand by bus or train at one of the border crossings with Malaysia, Cambodia, and Laos (currently you cannot enter Thailand through Burma). There are no buses that cross from one border to another; instead, you'll have to get to a border stop, such as Poi Pet for Cambodia or Nong Khai for Laos, cross the border on foot, and board another domestic bus. This can be time-consuming and cumbersome, but thousands of backpackers and other travelers have worn these paths smooth and flat before you. If you are doubtful about whether a crossing is possible, check the Internet for information, but always contact the embassy of the country you are trying to enter to confirm whatever you read.

If you are traveling from Singapore or Malaysia, there is train service linking these countries to Thailand. From Singapore, you'll have to change trains twice, but you can buy one ticket that will take you all the way. **The Man in Seat 61** (www.seat61.com/thailand) has the best description of the process as well as up-to-date information on schedules and prices.

SEA

There aren't many opportunities to enter Thailand by sea; however, you can do it if you are coming from Langkawi Island in Malaysia. There are frequent ferries (www.langkawi-ferry.com) from this island that will deposit you in the town of Satun in southern Thailand, from where you can continue your travels.

FROM BANGKOK
Airport

Bangkok is served by the country's main international airport, Suvarnabhumi Airport, 25 kilometers (16 mi) outside of the city center. Suvarnabhumi Airport was built to replace the outdated Don Muang Airport in 2006, and now Don Muang serves the region's budget airlines. If you are flying out of Bangkok on a domestic flight, make sure you check which airport you're leaving from.

Even with Don Muang taking up some of the slack, Suvarnabhumi is one of the busiest airports in Asia, handling up to 40 million passengers per year through one domestic and one international terminal. Generally, check-in and security lines move quickly and efficiently, but you can get caught up at immigration processing. Make sure to allow plenty of time to get through. Wait times can be as long as 45 minutes. Once you're in, there's plenty of food and shopping in the international terminal to keep you busy, although there aren't a lot of comfortable places to just sit and relax.

Taxis from the Airport

Assuming it's not rush hour, the fastest, cheapest way to get to the city center is to take a metered taxi. The airport arrival area is a little confusing, with throngs of people from all over the world pouring out into a cramped area filled with waiting friends, family, and tour guides. You have to go down to level 1 to get to the taxi stand, where you line up and tell the attendant your destination. The attendants are generally helpful and have a list of popular destinations in Thai and English in case you can't get your message across adequately. You'll then be directed to the next available taxi; you must pay 50 baht in addition to the meter fare as well as any tolls (luggage is free). To the city center, expect the full fare to run 250-350 baht, depending on traffic. Unless you have time to kill and want to save the equivalent of US$2, ask the driver to take the *thang-duan*, or highway. Drivers will usually ask you to pay tolls as you go, and if you forgot to get small bills at the airport, toll booths can usually break large bills. Sometimes taxis will try to negotiate the fare instead of using the meter. This will never work in your favor, and if one tries to push the point, ask to be returned to the airport (that's usually enough to get them to turn on the meter). As you're making your way to the taxi line, you may be asked if you want a private taxi or limo instead. Do not accept a ride from anyone other than a metered taxi in the official taxi line staffed by airport workers. You'll end up at your destination, but you'll pay three or four times the going rate.

Airport Express Train

The **airport rail link** opened in 2010 and offers express service to central Bangkok for 150 baht, which is a great option if there is traffic and you don't have too much luggage. Board the train in the basement of the arrivals terminal. From there, take either an express train to Makkasan Station and switch to the local line for two stops to connect with Bangkok's Skytrain at Phaya Thai Station, or walk across the street to the Petchaburi subway station. If you are just in Bangkok for a night, but want to head to the capital to check it out, you can leave your luggage at the airport and get in quickly by express train.

Airport Buses

There are four public bus lines that run between the airport and the city, making intermittent stops and terminating in Silom, Bang Lamphu, Sukhumvit, and Hua Lamphong Railroad Station. You have to take a free bus from the terminal to the airport bus depot (you can catch the bus on level 2 and level 4), then switch to the shuttle, which costs 150 baht per person and can take a couple of hours, depending on your destination. Unfortunately for the environment, it's about the same price and much faster to take a taxi if you're traveling with someone else. Buses run 5am-midnight.

Train

Bangkok has two major train stations, Hua Lamphong and Bangkok Thonburi (sometimes referred to as Bangkok Noi Station), served by the State Railway of Thailand (www.railway.co.th); all international trains terminate at Thonburi. **Hua Lamphong** (445 Rongmuang Rd., tel. 02/220-4334), on the edge of Chinatown, is easily accessible by subway. **Bangkok Noi Station** (Rot Fai

Road, Thonburi), right across the river from Ko Rattanakosin, serves as a terminating station for trains coming in from Kanchanaburi. There is no direct public transportation except for public ferry to the Rot Fai pier. All of the stations remain open all day and night.

Bus

There are three main bus stations in Bangkok where long-distance buses depart and arrive: the **Northern Terminal** (Khampeng Phet Rd., tel. 02/936-2852-66), near Chatuchak Weekend Market, serving destinations in the north and northeast; the **Eastern Terminal** (on Sukhumvit Soi 40, tel. 02/391-2504), serving eastern destinations; and the **Southern Terminal** (Borom Rat Chonnani Rd., tel. 02/391-2504), across the river in Pinklao, serving southern and western destinations. Buses depart and arrive at these stations at all hours of the day and night.

Accommodations

If you are just transiting through Bangkok and need a place to stay overnight, the easiest option is to pick one of the many hotels around the airport (assuming you are flying in and out of Suvarnabhumi Airport). **Novotel Bangkok Suvarnabhumi Airport** (Mu 1, Suvarnabhumi Airport, 02/131-1111, www.novotel.com, 3,500B) is the only hotel on the airport premises. It is a modern, clean, and comfortable four-star hotel. There is a pretty swimming pool, a small spa, and a fitness center—everything you'll need if you are there waiting for your next flight. Its 24-hour flexi rate allows you to check in at any time day or night and pay for just one night, so long as you check out within a 24-hour period. Another option is to get a hotel near the airport. There are scores of cheap choices and as they are catering to mostly transit passengers, almost all include pickup and drop-off, at any hour, at the airport. A much cheaper option is **Lilac Relax-Residence Bangkok Airport Hotel** (100 Soi Lat Krabang 7, On Nut Lat Krabang Rd., 02/734-4337, www.lilac-suvarnabhumi. com, 1,500B). Rooms in this small property

are clean, comfortable, modern, purple, and just big enough.

Getting Around Bangkok
Skytrain and Subway

Given the sheer size of Bangkok and its heat and humidity, it is not advisable to try to walk from one neighborhood to another, especially if you have very limited time in the city. In the past decade, city authorities have opened both an elevated train, referred to as the **Skytrain** or **BTS** (tel. 02/617-7600, www.bts.co.th), with two lines, and a single-line subway system, called the **MRT** (tel. 02/612-2444, www.mrta. co.th). Both are efficient, modern, and inexpensive, and if you ever have a choice between a taxi and the Skytrain or subway, opt for public transportation.

Ferries

The Chao Phraya is served by a **public ferry system** that runs up and down the river, stopping at various piers on either side along the way. If you're taking the Skytrain, you can connect to the ferry at the Taksin Bridge stop, which is Central pier. Just follow the signs for the pier when you exit the station. There are five different types of commuter boats running along the river, all run by the **Chao Phraya Express Boat Company** (www. chaophrayaexpressboat.com). The company website offers clear schedules and maps for each pier on the river.

Canal Boats

There are also **commuter boats** plying some of the major canals in Bangkok, although the service seems to be declining every year. One major convenient route that's still running is along the Saen Saep Canal, which runs right next to Petchaburi Road and goes as far west as the Golden Mount near Democracy Monument and past Sukhumvit Soi 71 to the east. Canal boats are a little more of an adventure than riverboats. During rush hour they can be very crowded, and they're smaller and move faster. Boats run about 6am-8:30pm and cost 9-13 baht per ride.

Taxis

Metered taxis come in a variety of crazy colors, from bright orange to purple to green, but they are all clearly marked, and you won't be able to miss them. If they're available, you'll see a brightly lit red sign on the passenger side of the windshield; just wave one down. On any major road there will be plentiful taxis available, unless it's pouring rain or right around rush hour. Metered fares start at 35 baht, and getting across town should run you no more than 80 baht unless traffic is really bad (though it often is).

Buses

Under the right circumstances, taking a **city bus** in Bangkok is convenient and inexpensive. Under the wrong circumstances, it's confusing, time-consuming, and a little scary. The city buses, administered by the **Bangkok Metropolitan Transportation Authority** (BMTA, www.bmta.co.th/en), cover all of Bangkok and even out into surrounding provinces, so you can get from any place in the city to another by public bus. Bus stops are marked with signs and often have small benches and covered waiting areas. If you are standing at the stop, a bus will not necessarily stop for you unless you wave it down. Fares are 7-22 baht, depending on the distance and the type of bus.

Getting Around

AIR

Thailand has many regional airports served by national airlines and competing low-cost carriers. If you are short on time and don't mind the extra expense, this is the best way to travel around the country. **Thai Airways** (www.thaiairways.com), the country's flagship carrier, has flights to the Andaman coast, Isan, and the north. **Bangkok Airways** (www.bangkokair.com) serves Ko Samui, Sukhothai, Krabi, and other traditionally tourist destinations. But do not forget the budget airlines. Small ones seem to pop up all the time, but two are reliable and popular. **Nok Air** (www.nokair.com) is partially owned by Thai Airways, and **Air Asia** (www.airasia.com) is one of the largest budget carriers in Asia. Both have extensive schedules to popular destinations such as Phuket (between the two there are more than a dozen daily flights) and limited flights to less-popular places. None of the budget airlines show up on any of the travel websites, so you have to book through their websites, by phone, or at the airport. Luckily both have very user-friendly websites. Nok Air even lets you book by phone (call 1318 or 02/900-9955) and then pay for and pick up your ticket at a 7-Eleven. This will only work for flights scheduled more than 24 hours in advance, but it will really come in handy if you are having trouble using a credit card on the Internet.

TRAIN

Thailand has an extensive railroad system serving all parts of the country. The train system is run by the **State Railway of Thailand** (www.railway.co.th) and you'll find schedules and fares on the website. Seats are available in first through third class, depending on the route, and range anywhere from plush and comfortable air-conditioned cars with snacks and beverages served to your seat to wooden benches, open windows, and café cars serving local beer and inexpensive Thai dishes. Sleepers likewise run the gamut, but even the second-class sleepers are quite comfortable (you'll even get freshly laundered sheets and blankets). This is a great way to get to see the country and meet people, but it's definitely not the fastest way to travel (buses are routinely faster).

You cannot book train tickets on the Internet. You'll need to go either to the train station in person or stop in at any travel agent (you will pay a small fee for this service). If you are planning on traveling on a weekend or around a national holiday, you must book well in advance (especially if you are taking an overnight train and want a sleeper). Tickets will often sell out days or even weeks in advance of popular travel dates.

BUS

Thailand is covered by an extensive network of interregional, regional, and local buses, and it is possible to get almost anywhere in the country via bus if you're willing to spend the time navigating the system. From Bangkok and other major cities, there are frequent air-conditioned buses (sometimes referred to as **VIP buses**) where you'll be guaranteed a comfortable reclining seat on an express route. If you are traveling to a popular destination, it may be as easy as that. To get to more far-flung areas, you'll generally need to take a bus to the closest big city and then switch to a local or interregional bus for the rest of your journey. A ticket on a standard bus, which may be the only option, depending on where you are going, does not guarantee you a seat, and buses can get packed. You may find yourself standing for hours or smashed up against the windshield as the bus speeds along a highway.

Unfortunately there is no central repository for bus schedules and routes, and they can change. Although there is plenty of information available on the Internet, the best bet is to contact someone at your final destination who will be able to advise you on the best route possible.

The main bus company, with routes from Bangkok to all parts of the country and back, is **The Transport Co.** (www.transport.co.th). The website lists all of the routes, fares, and schedules to and from Bangkok.

TAXI

You will find taxis in most of the major cities and popular destinations in the country, though you most likely will not find them in

A vendor at a train station hawks food to travelers.

rural areas or less-affluent places. In Bangkok, taxis are generally reasonable and easy to find. A trip anywhere in the city should run less than 150 baht (sometimes significantly less, as the meter starts at 35 baht). In places such as Phuket, finding a metered taxi is nearly impossible, and local taxis charge exorbitant rates to take you from one part of the island to another.

SONG THAEW

For short trips between neighboring villages (or even between neighborhoods in Bangkok), these vehicles—essentially pickup trucks with seats in the back and roofs overhead—are a common and easy option. They usually run specific routes and will stop to pick up and discharge passengers along the way for anywhere from 5 baht, depending on the length of the journey. Schedules aren't posted, nor are prices or routes, or even stops. They may seem totally inaccessible, but any local person will know the route and be able to direct you. When in doubt you can just say *"song thaew bai* [destination]" and someone will point you in the right direction.

CARS

Thailand's major road system is exceptionally well maintained and relatively easy to navigate. Driving in Bangkok is probably not a good idea unless you're really comfortable navigating confusing streets, dealing with informal rules that often seem completely at odds with what you learned in driving school, and sitting in traffic for hours.

Outside Bangkok, driving is perhaps the best way to cover a lot of ground and see the country at the same time (you'll beat the buses and the trains). If you are traveling with small children, it is unfortunately also the only way to guarantee that you are even going to get a seat belt. For very small children, bring a car seat with you or buy one at one of the high-end department stores before you hit the road. The larger **Central Department Stores** will have them in stock, as will the department stores in **Siam Paragon, Central World Plaza,** and **Emporium** in Bangkok. Outside Bangkok you may not be able to find one easily, and their availability at car rental agencies is limited. If you are coming from North America, remember that in Thailand, your steering wheel is on the right and you must drive on the left.

Rental Agencies

All of the major agencies, including **Avis** (www.avis.com), **National** (www.nationalcar.com), and **Hertz** (www.hertz.com), have locations in Samui, Phuket, and Bangkok. Prices are typically US$50-100 per day, with a slight discount if you rent by the week. Most international agencies will require that renters be at least 25 years old. There are also local rental-car companies, and prices may be significantly cheaper if you choose one of these. Make sure you understand the insurance you are getting, however, as you may be liable for any damage to the vehicle.

Legal Requirements

You must hold a valid driver's license from your home country to drive in Thailand. An international driver's license is not required unless you are going to be in the country for an extended period of time. Make sure you carry your passport or a copy of it if you are driving. If you get pulled over, the officer will require it, and you'll save yourself a trip to the police station if you have it with you.

Road Rules

Speed limits are expressed in kilometers, as are speedometers. On the highway the speed limit is generally 80 kilometers per hour (just under 50 mph) to 120 kilometers per hour (about 75 mph). On nonhighway roads outside of cities and towns it's 80 kilometers per hour. In cities and towns it is usually 60 kilometers per hour (35 mph). Seat belts are required for both the driver and the front-seat passenger. Although this law is routinely broken, it's best to stay within the bounds of the law if you are driving in a foreign country (not to mention the safety issues). **Drunk driving** is a serious offense in Thailand, and a blood alcohol level of 0.05 percent is all that is required to land you in jail. Remember that local beer is significantly stronger than the average North American brew. At 6.4 percent, one Chang Beer, especially if it's a large one, is probably enough to keep you off the road for an hour or two at least.

Remember that you **pass on the right** and slower vehicles stay in the left lane.

Though most of the signs and rules of the road are technically the same as the rest of the world, the **informal rules of the road** are probably a lot different than you are used to and might not make sense if you didn't grow up driving in Thailand. Suffice it to say that other drivers may (and probably will) do things you are not expecting, such as changing into your lane with less than a meter to spare or turning without signaling. The best way to handle this is to drive cautiously, watch out for other drivers, and keep a *sabai* attitude.

Gas Stations

On major roads and on highways there are plenty of gas stations, some open 24 hours (especially on highways). In smaller village areas, gas stations may close as early as 7pm, so keep an eye on your tank if you are driving to more remote areas. You can get diesel, leaded, and unleaded gas, but most of the newer cars run on unleaded. If you are in doubt, the gas station attendant will know the right mix. Gas is relatively inexpensive in Thailand. It is sold by the liter and recently has run around 33 baht per liter, which equals around US$2.25 per gallon.

Parking

Street parking in quieter beach towns is pretty relaxed, but in more crowded parts of Samui and Phuket, it's going to be challenging to figure out the Thai street signs enough to discern the rules. But, it is relatively easy to find an inexpensive parking lot wherever you are headed. All major malls, hospitals, hotels, and many larger restaurants offer parking, often with valet service. If you are parking your car in a lot, do not be surprised to see other cars lining the drive and blocking each other. This is normal and drivers are expected to leave their cars in neutral without engaging the emergency brake (obviously this does not apply on any sort of grade) so they can be pushed out of the way if necessary.

In less densely populated areas, parking is considerably easier, and there are generally parking lots at larger hotels and restaurants if street parking is unavailable.

Motorcycles

Motorcycles are very common in Thailand. If you are driving or even a passenger in a car, it is your responsibility to watch out for them. Motorcycle drivers will often straddle lanes, pass between cars, cross highways, and do all sorts of unanticipated things. Be aware that there are always motorcycles on the road, and sometimes they are difficult to see in your side and rearview mirrors. If you are on a major highway, it is not unheard of to see someone

Gas stations are common on major roads and highways.

on a bike attempting to cross perpendicularly in front of you, and there are plenty of motorcycle fatalities every year. If you are opening the door of a car or a taxi, look behind you beforehand. Motorcycles have been known to snake in and out of parked cars, and a quickly opened door can lead to disaster.

Renting a motorcycle outside Bangkok is probably easier than buying a can of soda. You will need your passport and cash; it's almost unheard of to be asked for a license. Sometimes rental agencies will hold your passport as collateral, and other times they will ask for a deposit of 500-1,000 baht. If you are asked to leave your passport, make sure you keep a copy of it as well as the rental receipt in case you are pulled over. Expect to pay 200-300 baht per day. In smaller areas, the rental shops have even been known to lend out a bike without asking for anything in return. You are required by law to wear a helmet, and the police are generally quick to pull over foreigners without them.

The helmets you get with a rental bike are

sometimes little more than plastic hats with chin straps. Ask for the best helmet available, and if no good ones are forthcoming, consider heading to the nearest Tesco or Big C to buy one.

Most of the bikes available are 100-125 cc semiautomatic scooters, which means that you have to shift gears with your foot but do not need to engage a clutch to do so. That part is easy enough, but do not consider riding a bike unless you know what you are doing. Motorcycles are often the cheapest, easiest, and most fun way to get around, but there are accidents and even deaths every year by foreigners who are overconfident and think that just because everyone in the country is doing it, they can, too. Yes, it's true that in any small village you'll probably see 12-year-old girls in their school uniforms piled three on a bike, sipping sodas, talking on mobile phones, and navigating these machines in their bare feet. That doesn't make it safe or easy. Motorcycles are a part of daily life, especially in rural areas, and the kids you see riding them probably literally grew up doing so. Even they are not immune—hundreds of Thais are involved in serious motorcycle accidents every year.

Maps and GPS

Detailed road maps of Thailand are available at bookstores in Bangkok, but it can be difficult to find ones that have place names translated into English. **Nelles Maps** and **Michelin** have maps that are generally available at **Bookazine** and **Kinokuniya** in Bangkok, but you won't be able to find them at local gas stations.

You can get a GPS system in a rental car if you are renting from one of the larger agencies. If you have a smartphone with GPS, you can also use that for navigation (make your life easier by unlocking your phone before you visit and popping a local SIM card with a data plan in it once you arrive; you can get them at 7-Eleven). In very remote areas, connection times can be slow, so maps will not load quickly (this is separate from the satellite navigation).

Roads and Highways

Thailand has a highway system running all the way north from the edge of Malaysia and linking nearly all major cities. Multilane major highways and tollways are generally in excellent condition, well signed, and fast. These are noted as "Highway" and almost always have a single-digit identifier (such as

Wear a helmet if you're traveling by moped.

Highway 4). Secondary roadways are usually identified with a two-digit number or a four-digit number and are referred to here as "Route." Usually these branch off larger roads and are usually in good condition, although they can be considerably smaller than the 4-5 lanes drivers on the largest highways enjoy. When the secondary roads pass through urban areas, they will also function as large Main Streets, with plenty of commerce lining them and plenty of traffic during normal rush hours. Roads denoted with three-digit numbers are of varying quality, including dirt or country roads. These can be particularly difficult to navigate in rain in areas prone to flooding, and even in the best conditions, it's very slow going.

Traffic

Outside of certain very popular beach areas in Samui and Phuket, traffic on the beaches and islands will be relatively light. Just like home, though, it tends to be worse on Friday afternoons before long weekends, and on the last Friday of the month, which is payday for many folks.

If you are driving somewhere on a schedule, make sure to ask a local person how long it will take. Between traffic and secondary roads, the drive might take a lot longer than you've estimated.

Visas and Officialdom

Thailand has an easy tourist visa process if you hold a passport from one of the 71 countries the kingdom has deemed eligible for a **visa waiver on arrival.** Countries include the United States, Canada, most European countries, many countries in Asia and the Middle East, and some countries in South America (check www.thaiembdc.org for the complete list). If you are entering from one of these countries, you get a free visa waiver at the airport when you arrive.

After you pick up your bags at the airport, you'll stand in line at the immigration counters, where you will be asked to hand over your passport and arrival card and have your photo taken. Fill out your **arrival card** before you reach the counter. Immigration officials are generally patient, but if there is a long line or someone has had a bad day, you may be sent all the way to the back of the line if you show up empty-handed. If you did not get an arrival card on the plane, there are desks stocked full of the white-and-blue sheets. After your passport has been scanned and you've been photographed, you'll be given an automatic 15-30-day tourist visa waiver (depending on your passport—visitors from most countries, including the United States, Canada, and EU countries, get 30-day visas) and part of the arrival card will be stapled inside your passport. Do not lose it—you need it to leave the country, and if you don't have it when exiting, at the very least you will have to fill out forms and paperwork, which can take upward of an hour.

If you are staying in the country for longer than the visa waiver permits, you can get an automatic **30-day extension** by visiting one of the Immigration offices in the country and paying a 1,900 baht fee.

You can also opt to apply for a 60-day tourist visa before you arrive if you know you'll be in Thailand for a while. You will pay a fee (US$40), but it's less hassle than having to extend your visa once you are here. Note that if you want to exit and reenter the country, you will need a multiple entry visa, and you will pay an additional US$40 per entry.

Do not overstay your visa. If you happen to be picked up by the police or even stopped for a minor traffic infraction, you will be thrown in jail until you are deported. That scenario may be unlikely, but when you leave the country you will be fined heavily by immigration.

Under current rules, the first day of an overstay is free, but each day after that results in a 500 baht fine, up to 20,000 baht. You will be required to pay this fine at the airport or other border before you can leave.

If you are planning on staying in Thailand for more than a couple of months, you must contact the Thai consulate or embassy in your home country. Thailand used to have a very permissive system whereby you could just leave the country at one of the many land border crossings for a few minutes and return in order to refresh your tourist visa for another 30 days. But in recent years the government has cracked down on these border runs. The rules continue to change, so be sure to check for the most recent policies.

STUDENT AND WORK VISAS

Students wishing to do study-abroad programs in Thailand must obtain a **student visa.** Although the process is straightforward, you must make arrangements with an accredited school in the country first, as they will need to provide documentation to the Thai consulate or embassy in order to obtain the visa. In addition to the major universities, which all offer foreign exchange or other study-abroad programs, there are some language schools that are accredited and can support an application for a student visa.

Obtaining a **work visa** if you are planning on teaching English in Thailand is also relatively easy. You must have a job before you can apply for the visa, and your employer will generally walk you through the process and paperwork (although not all schools will pay the visa costs for you). Many people wishing to work as teachers in Thailand arrive in the country on tourist visas and proceed with their job search once in the country. There are many teaching opportunities in the country, for varying levels of pay, in rural and urban areas, and for teachers of various skills. There are scores of websites that cater to teachers in Thailand; it's wise to do some research first.

THAI EMBASSIES AND CONSULATES

In the United States, the **Royal Thai Embassy** (www.thaiembdc.org) is located in Washington DC. There are three main consulates, in Los Angeles, New York, and Chicago, and an additional 13 offices of honorary consuls in Montgomery, Alabama; Denver, Colorado; Coral Gables, Florida; Atlanta, Georgia; Honolulu, Hawaii; Leawood, Kansas; New Orleans, Louisiana; Boston, Massachusetts; Broken Arrow, Oklahoma; Portland, Oregon; Dallas, Texas; El Paso, Texas; and Houston, Texas. The main consulates can process all visa applications, but if you are closer to an honorary consul, call the office to see whether it might be able to help you. The honorary consuls are generally far less busy than the full consulate offices, and you may have a faster turnaround.

FOREIGN EMBASSIES IN THAILAND

You should know the location and contact information of the embassy of your home country in Thailand, as this is where you will be able to find information about voting as a citizen abroad, register the birth of a citizen in Thailand, replace a lost or stolen passport, seek legal advice if you've been arrested, help arrange a medevac if necessary, or, in worst-case scenarios, notify families of deaths of citizens abroad. Remember that while your embassy is there to help you and can assist you or refer you to assistance, it is not able to get citizens released from police custody, pay medical bills, or help you return home. All embassies are located in Bangkok, though some countries have smaller offices in other parts of the country, too. To contact your embassy or consulate in Thailand, visit the following: **U.S. Embassy** (American Citizen Services, 95 Wireless Rd., Bangkok, tel. 02/205-4049, bangkok.usembassy.gov); **Australian Embassy** (37 S. Sathorn Rd., Bangkok, tel. 02/344-6300, www.thailand.embassy.gov.au); **British Embassy** (14 Wireless Rd., Bangkok, tel. 02/305-8333, www.gov.

uk/government/world/thailand); **Canadian Embassy** (15th Fl., Abdulrahim Pl., 990 Rama IV Rd., tel. 02/636-0540, www.canadainternational.gc.ca/thailand-thailande/index).

CUSTOMS

Customs regulations in Thailand limit the amount of goods you may bring into the country. If you stopped at a duty-free shop before entering the country, remember that you are limited to two cartons of cigarettes and one liter of alcohol. Generally you can bring in personal electronics, including laptops, cameras, and video cameras, but customs may charge you duties on anything over 80,000 baht. This rule does not seem to be applied to travelers who are not bringing in loads of equipment (click on "Travelers" in the English version of www.customs.go.th). You are generally not permitted to bring plants or animals into the country, but there are some exceptions that change over time. If you have any doubts, call the **Agricultural Regulatory Division** (tel. 02/579-1581).

When you are leaving the country, remember that you must report cash that you have in baht over 50,000 baht. You can also be stopped if you are exporting counterfeit goods or any art or artifacts of questionable provenance. There is still a significant trade in sculptures, carvings, and other artwork that is considered the property of the nation and rightfully belongs inside the country. Do not attempt to leave the country with anything that you have been told is an authentic piece from a ruin, temple, or other cultural heritage site.

POLICE

Thailand is generally a very safe place for tourists but (comparatively) wealthy tourists are sometimes targets for property crimes. Dial **1155** from any phone in Thailand if you need assistance. This is a special **tourist police** number set up with the Tourism Authority of Thailand to help visitors; they will be able to assist you in English. In certain heavily touristed areas, including **Pattaya,** the tourist police have set up kiosks where you can walk up and ask for help.

There are scores of anecdotal stories about minor corruption among police officers in Thailand. Generally these stories revolve around the payment of 100-200B to avoid a traffic ticket; rarely are there "shakedowns" of foreigners, especially those who are otherwise avoiding any trouble.

The **Thai Royal Police** wear dark-brown uniforms and mostly patrol on motorcycles. If you are approached by a police officer, be respectful and courteous and provide any information and documentation you are asked for. You are required by law to carry your passport with you at all times, and you may be asked to produce this.

Recreation

TOURS

There are hundreds of travel agencies and tour companies on the beaches and islands of Phuket and Ko Samui. Most tours are very similar to one another, with most companies offering hotel pick-ups, similar itineraries, and provided snacks and meals. Understandably, it can be very difficult to distinguish among the different offerings. Price can play a role, but it gets more complicated by the fact that tours are almost exclusively sold through resellers. Resellers are a third-party business that buy tickets from tour companies, then resell to consumers. Resellers include hotel concierges and travel agencies, and they often mark up the original price substantially. Expensive tours are not necessarily high-end ones. You may show up and find that others paid half of what you did.

One tip for getting the best price is to ask

Visiting *Wats*

Most *wats* are active Buddhist temples. Part of each temple's income is from visitor donations, but their purpose isn't to be a tourist attraction but rather a place for meditation and devotion. Generally there are no posted hours, but you can visit any time there's someone there to let you in. Most of the time you can just walk into the complex at any hour and wander around, although some of the buildings might be locked. Since Buddhist monks are supposed to abstain from unnecessary worldly items, there are usually no telephones in temples.

what the differences are among different tours. Does one offer a bigger boat? A more relaxed or unique schedule? Another tip is to shop around. Since resellers sell the same tours, you may get lucky and find someone offering a better price.

If you're taking a boat-based tour, know that boat accidents happen. At least once a year there is a fatal accident on an island-hopping tours in the Ko Samui or Phuket areas. Tour operators are subject to regulations, but speedy or reckless boat drivers can make these trips dangerous. All that doesn't mean you shouldn't go on a tour, as there are some amazing things to see here. Before you book a tour, read reviews online (on sites like TripAdvisor.com) and ask for personal recommendations from friends, if possible. When you get to Thailand, ask your hotel for recommendations, and ask whether there have been any recent accidents or incidents involving local tour companies. On the tour, wear your life jacket at all times, and if something doesn't seem right on the boat, don't be afraid to speak up. Safety regulations are even more important on diving trips, so be sure to book your diving tour with a PADI-certified company.

NATIONAL PARKS

Thailand has more than its share of national parks, many of which cover not only mainland nature areas but also swaths of sea and some of the islands off the coast.

Accommodations and Food

Many parks provide camping and bungalow facilities. The campsites often offer tent rentals, baths with cold-water showers, and even small canteen restaurants serving up more than decent local Thai food at reasonable prices.

The national parks also rent out simple bungalows that have baths with cold-water showers, and some even have air-conditioning. Beds are provided but generally not linens, so you'll have to bring your own sheets.

If your priorities are exploring the natural wonders of Thailand, or you even just want to enjoy a beautiful beach or island without the feeling of too much development around you, staying in one of the parks is an excellent option. It's also very budget-friendly. Pitching a tent will cost around 100 baht per night, and renting one of the bungalows often costs less than 1,000 baht per night.

During low season, it's possible to walk out to one of the park stations and ask if there are bungalows available, but even then there are times when the bungalows are booked solid for weeks. If you're interested in staying at one of the national parks, make sure to book a bungalow as far in advance as possible. You can book up to 60 days in advance, and in order to reserve a spot, the national parks department requires that you pay in full before you arrive. To do that from abroad, you'll have to make a wire transfer to the National Park, Wildlife and Plant Conservation Department. Although the process can seem a little daunting, they've laid out the bank codes you'll need to use (www.dnp.go.th/parkreserve/howtoreservation_4.asp?lg=2). Once you've confirmed that there's an available bungalow and transferred the funds, you must email reserve@dnp.go.th and dnp_tourist@yahoo.com with the confirmation information.

Hours and Admission Fees

All national parks are open 8:30am-6pm daily. The entry fee for foreigners is 200-400 baht.

Transportation

You may find that the mainland parks lack many well-marked hiking trails, and when they are marked, they are often only a couple of kilometers long. Since there are so few trails, it's also seemingly impossible to get around the parks without wheels of your own. It is not advisable to arrive at a national park without transportation. There is generally no public transportation within a park, sights are kilometers apart, and it's difficult even to get a trail map once you arrive. Many parks have large main roads cutting through them, making driving a convenient, if not very environmentally friendly, way to cover a lot of ground. But once away from the roads, you'll find the parks peppered with amazing waterfalls, beautiful scenery, and wildlife.

Thais who visit national parks (and this is the vast majority of visitors) are usually not hikers. Most visitors drive from parking lot to parking lot to see waterfalls and viewpoints, and that's really how the parks are designed to be used. Information centers rarely have trail maps available, and when they do, they are usually not in English.

Accommodations

Accommodations in Thailand run the gamut from guesthouses with shared baths for as little as 100-200 baht per night to amazingly posh and spacious five-star resorts. If you are not traveling during high season, you generally do not need to book ahead unless you have your heart set on a particular property in a particular location. Unless otherwise noted, the prices listed in this book are based on high-season rates for a double-occupancy room.

During high season, especially in late December-early January, it can be very difficult to find a decent place to sleep in heavily touristed beach areas. There is really no low season for tourism in Thailand, but you can expect rates to be substantially lower than those noted in this book if you are not traveling during high season.

Unfortunately, there is no universal rating system for accommodations in Thailand, and the use of any amount of stars by a property is an arbitrary distinction that may have no relation to your expectations. Purported three- and four-star properties seem to be the worst offenders. Make sure to understand what you are getting for your money. Look at websites such as Agoda.com or TripAdvisor.com for reviews and read as many as you can to adjust your expectations.

GUESTHOUSES

Guesthouse is the common term for small locally owned and operated accommodations, typically in an urban area. These are the cheapest lodgings you'll find in the country, and there is no rating system for them. At a minimum, you'll get a bed and a fan with a shared bath, although some guesthouses have private facilities and air-conditioning. Sometimes, rooms do not have windows. Many also have attached cafés or small restaurants, but you should call in advance if you have any doubts about the level of amenities available. Generally, guesthouses do not have dormitory-style lodgings; these are commonly referred to as hostels.

BUNGALOWS AND CABINS

Bungalow is perhaps the most widely used term in the hospitality industry in Thailand,

and the word can mean nearly anything. Generally, bungalows are freestanding accommodations and are almost always at or near a beach. Other than that, anything goes. Some bungalows are literally four walls tacked together with a corrugated roof and a squat toilet. You'll also find bungalows as large as small apartments, with air-conditioning, cable or satellite TV, minibars, luxurious baths, and charming thatched roofs.

Occasionally you'll see **cabins** offered for rent, especially in or near national parks. These are also generally freestanding and follow the same rules (or lack thereof) as bungalows.

HOTELS

Hotels are found in almost all price ranges, from 300 baht in small urban areas to upward of 6,000 baht in certain parts of Phuket and Samui. All hotels offer private baths, and most have minibars, TVs, air-conditioning, and some sort of food available on the premises. More expensive hotels have swimming pools, room service, and concierge services.

RESORTS

Any property calling itself a resort will have a swimming pool and some amount of property surrounding the accommodations. Resorts also generally have restaurants or bars on the premises. More expensive resorts, and those run by international chains, almost always have sports facilities such as tennis courts or fitness centers, organized activities, and plenty of space to wander and relax.

SERVICED APARTMENTS

Serviced apartments typically have rooms and suites larger than the average hotel room, sometimes with multiple bedrooms plus a living room, and a small kitchen. Service can be more limited than in a hotel, so for example housekeeping may clean three times per week instead of every day. These are usually intended for long-staying guests or families and can be a great value depending on the size of your party and your needs. Though serviced apartments are rarer on the beaches and islands, you can find them in parts of Phuket.

ESSENTIALS
FOOD

Food

Walk down any main street in any city or town in the country and you'll notice that there is food everywhere. From little streetside vendors selling all sorts of snacks to sit-down restaurants, you cannot go hungry in Thailand. Food is very important here—the average citizen of the Kingdom eats out 13 times per week. That's almost two meals per day. Fortunately there is a lot to choose from.

Although Thai food is far more complex and varied than you may be used to if you've eaten at a Thai restaurant in your home country, there are some predominant flavors. First, you'll probably notice that food in the Kingdom can be really spicy, and the liberal use of chili peppers is common. But it's not just the heat that distinguishes the cuisine but rather a subtle mix of flavors such as cilantro, galangal (similar to ginger), lemongrass, lime juice, fish sauce, coconut milk, and, oftentimes, peanuts.

Thailand has four regional cuisines—northern, northeastern, central, and southern—and each has its own specific flavors and specialties in addition to the common themes throughout.

The country has also integrated many Western foods into its daily menu, albeit with a slight twist. In larger cities you'll find plenty of hot dogs and sausages being served by street vendors alongside *mu ping* and *sai crock Isan*. There's also Thai pizza, which is a little sweeter than the food by the same name in Italy. It's also served with toppings such as corn and spicy shrimp.

THE FOUR REGIONS

Northern Thailand is where you'll find lots of soups, a predominance of sour and bitter flavors, and generally richer dishes such as *khao soi*—flat egg noodles served with rich, meat-based curry soup—as well as sticky rice, which is eaten by rolling it into balls in your hand, instead of the fluffier version.

Northeast Thailand is known for its *som tam*, the spicy papaya salad that has made its way from the humble plains of Isan to virtually every corner of the country. In this region you will find a predominance of spicy food, many salads (called *som*), grilled meats, and, of course, sticky rice.

Central Thailand is known for its fragrant *hom mali* rice, similar in flavor and texture to jasmine rice, often eaten with spicy coconut milk-based curry. You'll also find coconut milk in dishes such as *tom kar gai* and even in the *tom yam kung*.

In the south, you'll find a cuisine less like that of the rest of the country. Here's where you'll see dishes influenced by Indian cuisine, including the use of turmeric and the delicious pancake-like roti, served plain, sweet, or with savory curries. Curry dishes can be quite hot here, and you'll often see platters and plates of raw vegetables and herbs served at the table to complement the spice. You'll also see a dish called *khao yum* unlike anything you'll find anywhere else. This is essentially a rice salad served with numerous chopped and shredded vegetables as well as ground spices.

THE MOST TYPICAL THAI FOODS

One dish you'll find everywhere is *guay teow,* noodle soup, which probably originated in China but has become a staple in Thailand. While noodle soup may sound boring, you can find it prepared in infinite ways, from a simple bowl of beef broth and large, flat rice noodles to a sweet and spicy bowl of *guay teow tom yum*. Other common foods you'll find nearly everywhere in the country include *khao phad,* which is a fried rice dish, and many regional dishes such as *som tam, tom yam kung,* and many curries.

MEALS

Thailand's love affair with food ensures that you can generally eat whenever you want without worrying about offending anyone. **Breakfast** is available anytime from 7am onward. For locals, this may consist of a bowl of *jok* with crispy fried cruller slices, a soft-boiled egg, cilantro, and slivers of ginger or

a plate of Phad Thai

Restaurants

Thailand is full of places to eat, from restaurants to street stalls, and you'll easily find meals and snacks in any urban area or tourist destination. Be aware that your expectations of what constitutes a restaurant may be different than those here. In smaller towns, the fanciest restaurant you'll find will usually be a fan-cooled shophouse with plastic chairs for seats and limited restroom facilities. These shops, which probably make up the majority of food places in the country (including in major cities and many tourist areas), aren't always spotlessly clean by Western standards, and some visitors may be put off by the way they look. Many of the suggestions in this book are just those types of local restaurants, but we've tried our best to adjust expectations by indicating what you'll expect inside. If you come across a restaurant falling into this category, don't dismiss it. This really is where you'll find the freshest and best-prepared food in the country. It also happens to be the cheapest food (apart from street food), and meals will usually cost around 50 baht with a soda.

In Bangkok, Phuket, and Ko Samui, you will be able to find a good selection of air-conditioned sit-down restaurants that probably look a lot like what you're used to at home. When warranted by quality of food or convenience, we've included these places, and if you can't tell from the description, you should be able to tell from the prices listed; these types of restaurants are usually at least twice as expensive as the shophouses.

some noodles, although lots of people will take a more Western-style coffee and baked item instead, and you'll find plenty of street vendors in big cities selling sweet waffles and other more familiar breakfast treats. A Thai breakfast meal will cost 20-40 baht, but you may pay more for Western fare. If you are in the mood for a substantial Western breakfast, you'll have to hit one of the larger hotels or Irish or English pubs (if you are in Bangkok or Phuket), where you should be able to find what you are looking for.

Lunch is generally eaten 11am-2pm. If it's a workday and you happen to be in a city around this time, you'll notice throngs of people coming out of their offices for their afternoon meal—it's almost unheard of to pack a lunch. And why would you? Chances are there's plenty to choose from. During the week, lunch is often a social event, and casual restaurants and the tables of street vendors will be full of work colleagues or groups of college students taking a break and enjoying a meal together. If you're eating from a street vendor (and everyone does, from CEOs to domestic workers), expect to pay around 35-40 baht per dish. You may pay double, triple, or quadruple that if you're in an air-conditioned sit-down spot.

Dinner is as important as lunch, and you'll also find popular street-food areas packed full of families and friends from around 7pm onward. In larger cities you'll be able to find a meal in a restaurant anywhere from 6pm to midnight, but places in more rural or less populated areas will probably close earlier.

Snacking is nearly a national pastime. If you drop into anyone's office, you'll probably see a little corner set aside just for snacks, which can range from grilled fish balls to cookies to traditional *khanom thai*. You'll also find food vendors around throughout the day, in case the mood strikes you.

Conduct and Customs

SOCIAL BEHAVIOR
The *Wai*

You can't go more than 10 minutes in Thailand without noticing people putting their hands together in a prayer-like motion and bowing their heads at each other. Though this isn't a totally casual greeting, it is a sign of respect and will almost always be used to greet elders, teachers, bosses, and even hotel guests. The *wai* is an important social gesture and, for a Thai person, the absence of a *wai* when otherwise called for can be taken as a serious breach of norms. As a foreigner you won't necessarily be expected to use it in business situations where it would otherwise be appropriate (a handshake is fine), but if you are visiting someone's home and meet their parents, or are talking to a monk, or engaged in some other activity of that nature, make sure to *wai* as a greeting.

Daily Conduct

Another thing you'll notice immediately upon arriving (well, maybe once you leave the airport) is the general level of politeness in the country. The use of polite particles *ka* and *kap* is near universal: People will greet you when you walk into a restaurant or step into a taxi, and when someone bumps into you on a crowded street or even in a nightclub, chances are they'll say "excuse me" or apologize with a smile. A *mai pen rai* attitude, which loosely translates as "no worries," pervades casual social interactions, and acting aggressive and impatient will generally get you nowhere fast.

Although it's difficult to make generalizations, and exceptions always occur, the Thais are extremely friendly, social, and curious people, especially when it comes to foreigners. Don't be surprised if the taxi driver you just met wants to know whether you're married, how many children you have, and even your salary. There's no offense meant; this is just friendly banter, and you should take the opportunity to ask questions about the other person's life, too.

Although it might seem counterintuitive if you've ever seen a Thai go-go bar, people in the country are usually reserved and conservative in their behavior in public. "Conformist" may be too strong a word, but there is a propensity to behave in a manner that does not rock the boat. Very strange behavior or dress can make people very uncomfortable, although they may be too polite to express that discomfort to you.

Etiquette

There are few etiquette rules you'll need to remember when visiting, other than general politeness and respect. There are a couple of important ones, however. Do not criticize the monarchy. Although in small circles of close friends you will be able to have such a discussion, most people will take great offense. The king is generally revered, and in any case it is illegal to speak out against him. Twice a day, at 8am and 6pm, the national anthem is played on loudspeakers in all cities. Do as those around you do and stop where you are until the music is finished. If you are seeing a movie in a cinema, you are required to stand when the brief show about the king is played.

Also refrain from pointing your feet at anyone, especially at a Buddha in a temple, and don't touch anyone except little children on the head. Finally, you are expected to give your seat up to a monk if you are riding on public transportation, and there are even some specially reserved seats for them in trains and boats. Women are not allowed to touch monks, or vice versa, but the onus will fall on you to get out of the way if contact seems imminent.

Public Displays of Affection

In general, Thais are very affectionate in public but not in a sexual manner. It's quite common to see two girls, even in their teens, holding hands, parents hugging and kissing kids, and friends with their arms around each other. What is not common is seeing people hugging and kissing in a nonplatonic way.

Travel Tips

WHAT TO TAKE

You can find nearly everything you need in Thailand at a reasonable price, including international health and beauty products, so don't waste space in your luggage for shampoo or other toiletries. In general, pack as lightly as you can; your ability to explore the country will be limited if you're weighed down by baggage.

Thailand is a casual country, but people are generally quite style-conscious. If you don't want to stand out too much, don't disregard fashion sense just because you're on vacation. When **visiting temples** you will be expected to dress more modestly. That means no shorts for men and women, and no sleeveless tops for women. If you haven't planned ahead, most temples offer one-size-fits-all cloaks for rent. In some **Bangkok restaurants and nightclubs,** you'll be refused entry if you're wearing anything that looks too casual. On the beaches and islands, dress codes are much more lax. If you're traveling during the **rainy season,** consider bringing a lightweight rain jacket with a hood.

Thailand is on a **220-volt system,** so if you're traveling from North America, you'll need to bring a voltage converter for any appliances. Most mobile phones, laptop computers, and cameras can be charged on any voltage between 110 and 220.

ACCESS FOR TRAVELERS WITH DISABILITIES

Thailand is unfortunately an extremely difficult place to get around if you have difficulty walking. Although some (not all) of the high-end accommodations are wheelchair-accessible, sidewalks are often torn up or uneven and lack curb cuts, and using public transportation or even crossing major streets requires that you climb stairs. Likewise, museums and *wats* will often require some climbing of stairs. In rural areas you may not even find sidewalks, making navigating a wheelchair almost impossible.

There are several organizations that promote and facilitate accessible travel. Although there is no specific information about travel in Thailand available through any of these organizations, they can offer general tips and strategies. The most well known is **The Society for Accessible Travel and Hospitality** (www.sath.org).

TRAVELING WITH CHILDREN

Thailand is a great place to take your kids, thanks to plenty of outdoor activities, friendly people, and of course, the elephants. Thais are very friendly toward children and, except as noted in the entries for a couple of resorts, most places you'll want to go are appropriate for children. Challenges for parents, though, include getting around and keeping kids cool in the hot weather and keeping children safe in vehicles.

Sightseeing

All sightseeing and other activities listed in this book are open to people of all ages, the only exception being the diving sights. Particularly child-appealing sights are noted, but bear in mind that kids can have shorter attention spans than grown-ups, of course, and four-hour museum tours may be difficult for them (and as a consequence, for you) to bear. Depending on your child's age, take advantage of the inexpensive child-care options available in the country if there are some sights you can't miss but don't want to take them along.

Restaurants

Especially in more casual restaurants and eating spots, children are more than welcome, and you may even find the proprietors making a fuss about them, in a positive way. You may also notice that kids in the country are less restricted than you may be used to. It's not uncommon for a parent to let their child wander around a bit in a restaurant. Other guests and waitstaff will general keep an eye out, though obviously you are responsible for your kids.

You won't find special meals or menus for children except in some of the more upscale resorts. But if your child wants something particular, or can't tolerate spicy food at all, the chef will generally be more than happy to whip up something special. They may even suggest it or just bring it to the table. A great dish for kids is pad thai, since it's soft, mild, and not spicy. Since many Thai restaurants in popular beach areas also serve some Western food, you can almost always get French fries and spaghetti. If your kids are really picky, there's always international chain food as a last resort. All major cities and resort areas have at least a McDonald's in the area.

Transport, Accommodations, and Supplies

Although Thailand is very child-friendly, it's not necessarily child-safe, and you should bear that in mind as you are traveling from place to place. Many taxis do not have seat belts in the back, and it can be difficult to find a car seat. If you are traveling with a small child, try to bring your own car seat so that you know your child will be secure when you leave the airport. If you're traveling by airplane, even on budget carriers, your child will probably get some extra attention and a coloring book or some other toy to keep them occupied. The national trains will probably be the object of much fascination and have plenty of places to explore, though you should keep a careful eye on them as they can be dangerous, too.

Children under 12 almost always stay free if they are sleeping in their parents' room. If you need a cot or crib, you may be charged an extra fee, however, and some hotels do charge extra for small children, so make sure to contact them ahead of time so you don't have an argument on check-in. Almost all larger hotels have babysitting services. Generally, the more you are paying for the room, the more likely you are to get a babysitter who speaks English.

You should be able to find baby formula at almost any 7-Eleven, but it may not be the brand you're used to, so stock up before leaving. The same goes for baby food, as most Thai babies don't grow up on canned or bottled food. Local brand diapers are available at many 7-Elevens and all major hypermarket or large supermarkets. Western brand diapers are nearly impossible to find outside of Bangkok.

Nightlife

There are certain areas of the country, including Soi Bangla in Phuket, that are notoriously known for go-go bars and prostitution. Even walking through those places during the day will probably expose your children to things you don't want them to see. If you have kids old enough to understand what's going on, bear this in mind when planning your trip. There are plenty of family-friendly spots where you won't see sexpats or prostitutes, though, so long as you know what to look out for.

WOMEN TRAVELING ALONE

Thailand is generally an easy and safe place to travel if you are a lone woman. You may get a bit of unwanted attention from both locals and other travelers, but it usually stops at attempts at small talk and offers of drinks. The good news is that it's really easy to meet other travelers if you want to find other people to tour around with. Once people get to Thailand, they tend to pick up the local vibe and get friendlier and more open.

Restrooms

Restrooms in Thailand can present a challenge for those who are only used to Western-style sit-down toilets. Though sit-down toilets are very common, squat toilets are also quite common. For many Western travelers these present some particular challenges, and you may have to face them if you need to use a restroom at a public park, roadside gas station, or even perhaps a small restaurant. There are no tried-and-true tricks to get you through this if you're not used to using one; just be aware that at one point in your trip, you'll probably have to. Often these toilets do not have a flush handle. Instead, there will be a bucket of water and a smaller pail—you have to pour a few cups of water directly into the bowl to wash everything down.

Sit-down or squat toilet aside, you may notice a couple of additional confusing things about the restrooms you encounter in Thailand. The first thing you'll see is a water sprayer, and that's used exactly as you'd expect. The second is a waste bin next to the toilet. That's for toilet paper, as the plumbing infrastructure can't handle paper waste (except in most Western-oriented high-end hotels and restaurants). Make sure not to flush your paper. Also, it's wise to carry a small pack of tissues with you, as many public restrooms will not have toilet paper available.

In the women's room, if you encounter a line, people usually line up in front of individual toilet stalls instead of in one line. It's confusing and doesn't seem to be very fair, but that's what everyone does.

In the men's rooms of some nightclubs, you may come across something even stranger—the urinal neck rub. There are men working in the restrooms whose job it is to give massages. The first time you saddle up to a urinal and feel someone rubbing your neck, it will probably come as a total shock, and you can ask politely that they stop. Don't worry, though, it's all on the up-and-up, and the most you'll be asked for is a small tip.

Common Sense and Safety

If you are traveling alone, whether male or female, you must use common sense. Just because everyone in Thailand is friendly and laid-back doesn't mean you are always safe. Make sure you aren't in areas where no one else is around, especially late at night. Do not go for walks on the beach alone at night. In Bangkok, make sure you know where you are going if you're out late. Getting lost after clubbing can be a nightmare, worse so if you are worried about your physical safety.

Property crimes occur all over the world, and purse snatchings and muggings, though rare, can happen. Do not keep a lot of money on your person (better to take only what you need for the day from one of the thousands of ATMs in the country). If you have to hit an ATM late at night, find a 7-Eleven. Most have ATMs right outside and, since they are open all night, you can be assured that someone will be around. Also make sure to keep your bag close to your body, especially if you are walking in areas with lots of pedestrian and motorcycle traffic. This isn't just to safeguard you from getting your purse snatched; motorcycle drivers weave in and out of foot traffic, too, and getting your bag snagged on a passing bike can lead to serious injury for you or the driver.

In 2010, violent civil unrest spread to some of the most touristed areas of Bangkok, including Khao San Road. Though there was ample warning that protesters would be in these neighborhoods, many travelers did not change their plans, and some were caught up in the melee (some were seriously injured). Take any warning seriously, and avoid any area where there may be civil unrest. Outbreaks of violence can occur without warning.

Staying in Touch

Make sure to give your itinerary and the contact information at your hotel to someone back home, and check in frequently. There are Internet cafés in all but the most remote parts of the country. They are cheap and easy to find; use them. Also consider buying a mobile phone if you don't have a tri-band or quad-band phone with a removable SIM card already. If you are arriving in Bangkok, you can pick up a used one for as cheap as US$25 at MBK, then purchase a SIM card either there or at a 7-Eleven. These are prepaid phones, so all you have to do is buy a refill card for as little as 30 baht. Text messages to the United States are very inexpensive, and calls can be as little as six baht per minute.

Harassment and Violence

Thai culture does not really condone or encourage aggressive behavior toward strangers, but some do not feel that normal social rules apply to travelers. Usually it's as innocent as a catcall or a comment about your body. Once in a while it can be a little more offensive. If someone says something to you, just ignore it and walk away. If you are in a crowded area, you have nothing to worry about.

Rape and violence are rare, but there have been attacks on female travelers in the past.

You must exercise normal precautions, the same ones you'd exercise at home. If you feel like someone is following you, immediately find other people. You may not be able to communicate the problem, but you can either just say "police" or stay with them until you are safe. Don't brush off an uncomfortable feeling out of embarrassment.

GAY AND LESBIAN TRAVELERS

Whether because of the large population of out gays and transsexuals or because of the generally permissive culture, Thailand is a very comfortable place for people of any sexual orientation to travel. There are numerous clubs and neighborhoods in all major tourist destinations that are either completely gay or mixed, and in general, no one at any "straight" club will bat an eye if a same-sex couple enters.

Remember, however, that public displays of affection of a sexual nature are not appropriate regardless of sexual orientation.

Health and Safety

In major urban areas and popular tourist destinations on the coast, you'll find easy access to medical treatment and other emergency services, but in more rural areas, services can vary widely. Currently there is no nationwide EMS system in Thailand. If you are involved in an accident in Bangkok, the **Narenthorn Center,** a division of the Ministry of Public Health, has a **hotline number, 1699,** and is connected to a network of hospitals and ambulances and can dispatch emergency medical services quickly. The national number for the **police is 191,** but you probably will not get someone on the phone who speaks English. To ensure you get someone on the phone you can communicate with, call **1155, the tourist police hotline.** For nonurgent care, ask to be taken to a hospital, called a *rung paya ban* in Thai. There are also numerous privately run

small clinics set up in urban and tourist areas that you can visit for minor health problems.

By Western standards, the cost of health care in Thailand is exceptionally inexpensive, and the quality of care at private hospitals in big cities is on par with what you will find at home. Many of the larger private hospitals in Bangkok have excellent, clean, modern facilities. Doctors are routinely fluent in multiple languages, and many have studied at top universities across the country and around the world. An emergency room visit, even at one of these hospitals, will cost as little as 5,000 baht. Scheduled appointments with specialists are generally under 1,000 baht, meaning the complete cost of treatment will oftentimes be even less than the co-payment or deductible on your insurance back home. In fact, scores of patients from countries with national insurance programs travel specifically to Thailand for treatment they might otherwise have to wait months for back home, and each year perhaps thousands of people from around the globe come for cosmetic and other elective procedures; there are numerous websites dedicated to this topic.

BEFORE YOU GO

Before arriving in Thailand, as in any foreign country, make sure your medical information is current and you have sufficient supplies of any necessary prescription drugs. Carry a copy of your prescription with any drugs you are carrying in case you need a refill or to prove that the substance was legally obtained. Pharmacies and hospitals will normally have most common prescription drugs, but they are often named differently in different countries. If there is a chance you'll need something while you are here, make sure you know not only the brand name of your medication but the generic name as well.

Health Insurance

Check with your health insurance provider at home to determine whether you are covered in foreign countries and, if so, the extent of your coverage. There are numerous companies that provide health insurance for travelers and expatriates, including **Bupa** (www.bupa-intl.com) and **Travel Guard** (www.travelguard.com). If disaster strikes and you need to be transported home for treatment, not all policies will cover the cost, which can run in the tens of thousands of dollars, so look at the fine print on the policies.

If your health insurance policy already covers you for medevac and emergencies abroad, you are probably wasting your money buying any additional coverage. Even if there is a high deductible, remember that medical care is very inexpensive in Thailand.

Vaccinations

Check with your doctor, but most advise that the only vaccination you'll need for Thailand (assuming you are traveling in developed areas for a short period of time and not working in the health profession) is **hepatitis A,** a viral liver disease that is easily transmissible but also easily preventable. The **Centers for Disease Control and Prevention** (CDC) in the United States recommends that travelers to most countries outside North American and Europe get this vaccine. The vaccine is a series of two shots and should ideally be started about a month before you travel.

Malaria

Malaria is a very serious, sometimes fatal, disease transmitted by mosquitoes. Although it is extremely rare in most parts of the country, there is some malaria risk if you are traveling in rural, remote areas on the borders of Burma, Laos, and Cambodia. The CDC is currently recommending that you take prophylactic antimalarial drugs if you are going to be traveling in these areas and also recommends that you purchase them at home instead of abroad. There is no malaria on Phuket or Samui or in any of the most popular tourist beach areas. Antimalarial drugs are strong drugs with difficult side effects and should be handled accordingly, despite the fact that you may be able to buy them over the counter in some parts of Southeast Asia. Know where you are traveling and determine whether there is a risk of malaria before you arrive, and talk to your doctor about which antimalarial you should take. Side effects of even the most commonly prescribed drugs can be harsh and include not only stomachaches and nausea but vivid dreams, anxiety, and in rare cases, seizures or even fatal heart disturbances.

If you haven't seen a doctor in your home country but are considering traveling to a possible malaria zone when you are here, all of the major hospitals in Bangkok that cater to tourists (B&H, Bumrungrad, and Samitivej) have travel specialists who will advise you whether an antimalarial is appropriate and, if so, prescribe it to you. Do not take matters into your own hands by doing research on the Internet and stopping in at a local pharmacy. Also, check the CDC website (wwwn.cdc.gov/travel/

destinationthailand.aspx) for any changes in recommendations.

HEALTH MAINTENANCE

Most minor health issues can be addressed at a local pharmacy, and pharmacists in Thailand can dispense drugs that are often prescription-only back home, including antibiotics and antiviral medications. **Boots** (www.bootsthai.com) has many English-speaking pharmacists and a 24-hour hotline (tel. 800/200-444) that you can call if you want to find the closest location. In smaller towns, most pharmacists do not speak English.

If you are arriving in any populated area, don't worry too much about bringing common first-aid items with you. Any drugstore or pharmacy will have bandage strips, antiseptic cream, antidiarrheal treatments, and acetaminophen—the generic form of Tylenol, called paracetamol in Thailand. It will probably be cheaper than if you bought it back home. If you just need some pain reliever, every 7-Eleven and mom-and-pop shop will carry paracetamol, often in tear-off strips costing just a few baht per pill.

HEALTH ISSUES
Allergies

People with allergies to peanuts and shellfish may encounter serious difficulties in Thailand. Those are very common ingredients and, although most food preparation is hygienic, there is no guaranteeing that cross-contamination will not occur or that you will adequately be able to communicate the importance of avoiding such ingredients. Also, many prepared foods have warnings that they may contain traces of peanuts.

Bug Bites

Insects, especially mosquitoes, are common in Thailand, and aside from the inconvenience, they can pose a serious health threat. Aside from malaria, certain types of mosquitoes also carry **dengue fever,** a flu-like, debilitating, rarely fatal disease found in many parts of the world where mosquitoes are common.

Pharmacies are available in all major cities.

While malaria is almost never seen outside of rural areas, dengue outbreaks seem to occur annually even in Bangkok, and everyone who lives in the city knows someone who's had the disease. There is currently no vaccine for dengue; the only way to prevent the disease is to avoid mosquito bites. Despite questions about the long-term safety of using a DEET-based bug repellent, this is probably your best bet, and you can find plenty of options at drugstores in the country. Apply bug repellent liberally on both your skin and your clothing and reapply as directed according to the brand you are using. You can further reduce the risk of getting bitten by wearing long pants and sleeves, although this may be difficult to pull off if you are going to the beach. Although dengue-carrying mosquitoes generally bite during the day (just after sunrise and before dusk seem to be the most common times), you should make sure wherever you are sleeping has been mosquito-proofed or that you have a mosquito net. Dengue symptoms include fever, headaches, and muscle pains and should be treated immediately.

Heatstroke and Dehydration

If you are coming from North America, the temperature in Thailand, even during the cool season, may be hotter than the summers you're used to. Many travelers make the mistake of thinking they are immune to the effects of heat and sun and end up dehydrated, uncomfortable, or worse. Children and those over age 60 are even more susceptible. It may seem like common sense, but know your limits and pay attention to signals your body is sending you, as well as the condition of the people you are traveling with. If you aren't particularly physically active or used to the heat, walking around for hours on end in the hot sun will wear you down quickly, leaving you exhausted and cranky—not a great way to vacation. Make sure you drink lots of water. Bottled water is sold in virtually every corner of the country for little money; take advantage of the convenience and don't worry about lugging it around with you unless you will be in parts of the country that don't have any commerce.

Avoid heat exhaustion by avoiding strenuous activity during the hottest parts of the day and taking frequent breaks. It's probably not wise to go on a walking tour of Bangkok at 1pm, so plan your daily itineraries with temperature and sun patterns in mind. Outside activities are best done in the early part of the day and the later afternoon. Visiting museums and shopping malls and doing other indoor activities are great at midday, when the air-conditioning will be most appreciated. Also, take a cue from the locals: You'll probably notice that most people waiting to cross the street will find a shady spot, even if it's three meters (10 ft) from the curb, or walk slowly during the hottest parts of the day. There's a reason for that.

If you feel dizzy, get yourself to a cool place immediately and drink some water. If you begin to feel disoriented or confused, or have a rapid heartbeat or shortness of breath, you may be suffering from heatstroke and should seek immediate medical treatment. If you are traveling with children, pay especially close attention to how they are feeling and make sure they drink a lot of water. They may not be able to express that they are feeling the effects of the sun, but crankiness, short tempers, and fatigue are good clues that some rest and cooling down are in order.

Sexually Transmitted Diseases

Thailand did a laudable job in the 1990s of increasing public awareness and reducing the incidences of sexually transmitted diseases, including HIV/AIDS. But the 2006 UNAIDS Report noted that prevention awareness, specifically regarding HIV/AIDS, had "dropped off the radar screen," leaving a whole generation of Thais uninformed and unable to protect themselves. Although there are conflicting statistics, HIV/AIDS may once again be on the rise. If you are engaging in sexual activity while you are here, you must protect yourself. Condoms are commonly available everywhere in supermarkets and convenience stores and are inexpensive and prominently displayed.

In Thailand it is sometimes difficult to tell whether someone is a commercial sex worker. If you meet someone in a bar, especially if that person approached you first, odds are higher that this is not the first time he or she has ever done that. It is best to avoid pickups or one-night stands entirely.

Sun Exposure

Depending on where you are coming from, the sun in Thailand may be considerably stronger than what you're used to. That, amplified by the fact that you will probably be spending more time outside on vacation than you would during a normal day at work or home, means you have to use sunscreen even if you're not hanging out by the pool or on the beach. Larger chain drugstores, including **Watsons** and **Boots,** carry a range of sunscreen products for face and body. At these stores you are likely to find products that use the same SPF rating system used in the United States, so unless you have a particular favorite brand, skip packing the big bottle from back home. For your face, you will find international brands such as L'Oréal and Garnier with SPF 50, using Mexoryl as the active ingredient, for significantly cheaper than you will find anywhere else.

Traveler's Diarrhea

This is the most common traveler's ailment and is usually caused by contaminated food or drink. Conservative guidelines insist that travelers not buy food or beverages from street vendors, but the cost of that precaution is high. Thailand's food culture is difficult to access without eating food that has been prepared on the street or in places that may not seem as clean as you are used to back home. It is a shame to miss out on the experience, although if your immune system or health is already compromised and the consequences of getting a stomach bug could be severe for you, you should. If you decide to eat street food nonetheless, do not throw precaution completely to the wind. Fresh ingredients that have been prepared to order at high temperatures are the safest bets. Look for vendors who are busy, so you know the ingredients aren't sitting around for too long. Order foods that must be boiled, stir-fried, or deep-fried, and avoid any of the outdoor buffets where large pots of various foods are sitting out for extended periods of time.

Although some people will argue that the tap water in some cities is potable, virtually every person in the country, across age, education, and socioeconomic boundaries, drinks bottled water, and you should do the same—it is inexpensive and easy to find everywhere. At street stalls you may be wary of water served from pitchers, but look carefully and you'll notice that it's been decanted from industrial-sized bottles of purified water. You may also be served water that is slightly tan or brown in color. The color comes from boiling the water with a few tea leaves, and it's fine to drink.

If you should come down with diarrhea, most cases are mild and only last for a day or two. Drink plenty of fluids and rest. More severe cases can be treated with a combination of antibiotics and antidiarrheal drugs. Before you depart, ask your doctor for a prescription of antibiotics to treat diarrhea, should it become necessary. Azithromycin and ciprofloxacin are currently recommended, but that may change; your doctor will know best and will also give you instructions on when you should take them. You can pick up antidiarrheal drugs, such as Imodium, in Thailand if necessary, but you might want to bring some from home if you want to make sure you have them should illness strike before you can pick some up.

If you have symptoms that last longer than a few days, or are accompanied by fever, chills, severe pain, and/or bloody stools, seek medical treatment.

CRIME

Thailand is generally a very safe country. Violent crimes against strangers are rare, and the type of gun violence seen in other parts of the world is virtually unheard of. But while some make the mistake of painting the kingdom as an idyllic, peaceful place populated only by benevolent people, that's not entirely true, either, and a scan of the local papers will reveal that terrible crimes occur here, too. As it relates to travelers, there have been some notable crimes in recent years, including the rape and murder of a female tourist on Samui, shootings of tourists in Pai and Kanchanaburi, and continued violence in Pattaya. You must be mindful of your safety, even if the country feels idyllic and peaceful. If you are a woman traveling alone, always be aware of your surroundings. If you are involved in an argument or altercation with someone, particularly if alcohol consumption is involved, do everything you can to de-escalate the situation, including apologizing even if you do not think you are at fault. Bar fights involving travelers have occasionally turned fatal.

Petty Theft and Scams

Petty crimes and scams against foreigners are also common. Most of the people you meet and interact with will be kind and generous, but there are certainly taxi and *tuk tuk* drivers and others who will try to rip you off, more frequently in big cities and tourist areas. You can easily protect yourself from property crimes by leaving most of your valuables at home and safeguarding things such as digital cameras and computers. If your hotel room does not have a safe (or you don't feel confident in it), ask at the front desk whether they have a safe you can leave items in, and get a receipt for whatever you leave. If you're staying at a bungalow or inexpensive guesthouse and neither of those strategies is an option, do not flash money or valuables around, and do not leave them strewn about your room. Carry only as much cash as you need. There are ATMs all over the country (except in very off-the-beaten-path locations), and there is no need to have large sums of money with you.

Pickpocketing, especially in crowded markets, is not uncommon, but luckily it's easily avoidable if you follow the same common-sense guidelines you would in any other part of the world. Don't walk around with your bag open or wallet in a place it can easily be taken. If you are going to be in a crowded area, do not bring lots of bags with you. Walking around a market with a big backpack is asking for trouble. It is difficult to stay aware of your belongings when you have many of them.

The most common tourist scams are probably just inflated prices for transportation (and, unfortunately, Airports of Thailand sets the precedent for this from the moment you walk off the plane by trying to steer travelers toward their overpriced limo service instead of regular meter taxis). Unscrupulous taxi drivers will sometimes refuse to turn on the meter and try to negotiate inflated prices if they see that you are a foreigner. Your best defense is knowing how much things should cost. If a driver refuses to turn on the meter, just tell them you are getting out of the taxi and look for another one. Do not try to negotiate; an honest driver is bound to come along soon. This rule doesn't apply if it's pouring rain or you're headed somewhere really out of the city.

Rarely you will get a driver who will insist on taking you to the wrong place. Sometimes this is a mistake, but it may be because you've asked to go to a particular restaurant and the driver will get a commission if you go to another one. If a driver tells you that the place you want to go to is closed, the traffic is bad, or the place he's suggesting is better, just repeat your destination. If the driver insists, get out of the taxi.

Drugs

All illicit drugs are illegal in Thailand, although use of some drugs, especially marijuana, is not all that uncommon. You'll likely notice it on some islands and beach areas, being used as though it were totally legal. Locals may "know the ropes" and understand what they can get away with without raising the ire of the police, but those rules do not apply to foreign visitors. After all the movies and documentaries about foreigners getting arrested with drugs in Thailand, you'd have to be pretty stupid to have drugs on you in Thailand, as the consequences for being caught with large amounts of drugs, or even small amounts of hard drugs, are extreme. Drug dealers may face execution or life imprisonment, and your embassy won't be able to do much to help you.

Information and Services

MONEY
Currency

The Thai currency is the **baht**, and bills come in denominations of 1,000, 500, 100, 50, 20, and occasionally, an old 10B note, although these are no longer printed. Common coins are 10B, 5B, 2B, and 1B. Baht are broken up into satang; 100 satang equals one baht. There are no one-satang coins in circulation—in fact, the only ones you'll see are 25 satang and 50 satang. Most prices are expressed in baht, although in the supermarket you will come across items (for some reason often the ones on sale) with baht and satang pricing, and this is expressed as, for example, B|25.50.

You must carry small bills with you in Thailand, so make sure to keep an ample supply of 20B and 100B bills (50s are harder to come by) in your wallet. Cab drivers will almost never have change for anything larger than a 100B bill, nor should they, considering that most only earn a few hundred baht per day. Two ways to make sure you have some smaller bills: When you withdraw money from an ATM, don't request amounts in even thousands. ATMs will dispense 100B bills, so if you take out 1,900B, you'll get at least four 100B notes. Also, 7-Elevens and other large convenience stores can always break a 1,000B note, so it might be worth it to buy that 9B bottle of water to keep some small bills in your pocket.

Exchange Rates

As of early 2014, the Thai baht was about 32 to the U.S. dollar and 45 to the euro. Most bank websites have currency conversion charts; if you can't find one, try www.oanda.com or www.xe.com. Note that these will give you interbank rates, not the amount you'll get as a regular banking consumer, which will most definitely be less favorable regardless of whether you are buying or selling. To make sure you get the best rate, do not bring dollars or travelers checks to exchange when you arrive. Use your ATM card and withdraw in baht. Although the Thai bank will charge you a fee and your bank may, too, you will most likely get the best rate available.

ATMs

In Phuket, Samui, and almost anywhere else, you will easily be able to find an ATM where you can withdraw from your home bank account if you're on the Cirrus, Plus, or Maestro network or have a debit card with a Visa logo on it. All major-bank ATMs will also prompt you to select English as the interface language, so you won't be guessing. One confusing thing for most travelers is that many Thai banks have cash-deposit machines and statement-update printers that look very much like ATMs. If you find yourself in front of one of these, look to your left or right; they are almost always next to normal ATMs. Also, the other machines will say "Deposit" or "Passbook Update" on them. When you're asked to select the account, remember that "current account" is the same as "checking account."

Most ATMs will dispense 10,000-20,000 baht maximum per transaction, depending on the limit you've set with your bank at home. Make sure you contact your bank and credit card companies before you travel to let them know you will be in Thailand, or else your transactions may be blocked to protect against potential fraud. If you try unsuccessfully to withdraw cash from the same bank three times, the Thai ATM may confiscate your card. This can really be a drag, as bank policy generally requires that the card is sent back to your home bank, even if you're here. If you are having trouble withdrawing money, don't keep hitting buttons in hopes it will work. Figure out what's wrong and try again. Don't try a third time at the same bank; look for another bank's ATM.

Changing Money

Most money changers are run by major banks in Thailand, or else you can go into most large branches to exchange money. Rates are posted, as are any fees or percentages that the bank will charge you. Some but not all banks will require a passport to change currency, so it's best to bring it with you.

Banks

All urban areas in Thailand have at least one bank, and in cities such as Bangkok or Phuket there are scores and scores, often in very convenient places such as inside malls, in stand-alone department stores, or next to any of the large hypermarkets such as Carrefour, Tesco, or Big C. Banking hours vary tremendously, with smaller banks in quieter areas open 9am-3:30pm during the work week, and in big cities some stay open as late as 10pm and over the weekend. Some of the larger banks, including **Kasikorn Bank** (www.kasikornbank.com), **Siam Commercial Bank** (www.scb.co.th), **Bank of Ayudhya** (www.krungsri.com), **Bangkok Bank** (www.bangkokbank.com), and **United Overseas Bank** (www.uob.co.th), have websites with English content where you can find information about currency exchange and locations of branches.

Bank Transfers and Wiring Money

If you need cash in a pinch, there are numerous **Western Union** (www.westernunion.com) offices in Thailand; check the website for locations, but also check fees and exchange rates to understand the cost of the cash.

Travelers Checks

You can exchange travelers checks at major banks, foreign-exchange booths, and even some large hotels, although the fees you pay to both purchase them and change them can be significant when you add them up. In Thailand, the base fee is 150 baht per check.

Credit Cards

Visa and MasterCard credit and debit cards are accepted in larger hotels and department stores; American Express less so. In general, cash is king in Thailand, and even at larger restaurants and some hotels you may be asked to pay with the real thing. If you're purchasing something expensive, such as jewelry, you may pay an additional 2-3 percent if you pay with plastic. Note that you'll probably also be charged a transaction fee by your credit card company at home (usually a percentage of the charge) if you buy anything in foreign

Most ATMs have an English-language option.

currency. Some larger shops and duty-free stores will give you the option of charging your purchase in dollars or euros. Ask about the exchange rate, and if it's favorable, this may be the best option for you. If you don't often travel, remember that if you're using your credit card in a foreign country, you need to alert your credit card company beforehand. Otherwise, you may risk having your card denied as the company tries to track you down.

VAT

The value-added tax, or VAT, is 7 percent in Thailand; everything you spend money on will be subject to it. All shops list prices for goods inclusive of the VAT, but restaurants and hotels generally add the VAT on afterward. Travelers are entitled to a refund when they leave the country by air, assuming each item purchased is more than 2,000 baht, total purchases exceed 5,000 baht, you buy them from a participating store (you'll see a sign in the window), fill out all the necessary paperwork when you make the purchase, and take the goods out of the country within 60 days. To claim your refund, you will need to take your paperwork, passport, and the goods you've purchased to one of the customs officers at the airport you are departing from. Do this before check-in, as you will need to show your purchases to the officer. Once you've gone through these steps, you can get a cash or credit card refund on the spot, minus a 100 baht fee. The Revenue Department has a web page dedicated to understanding the VAT refund process (www.rd.go.th/vrt/engindex.html); make sure to check it if you are making a large purchase.

Bargaining

While some people will tell you that bargaining is done everywhere in Thailand, that's not really the case. Bargaining is frequent in areas where many tourists shop, but it would be totally out of place to bargain for a bowl of noodles from a street vendor or a bag of fresh fruit at a neighborhood wet market. If you are shopping in a tourist market, be aware that you should bargain, because prices are sometimes inflated as much as double, particularly in markets or street-shopping areas in places such as Phat Phong in Bangkok, Patong Beach in Phuket, or the markets in Chiang Mai. Bargaining is an art and not a science, so there are no hard-and-fast rules. It's best to know how much you are willing to pay for something before you start the process, and be prepared to walk away politely if you can't agree on a price.

Tipping

Tipping practices are often confusing in Thailand for foreigners. If you're eating at a street stall or very casual restaurant, tipping is not expected. On the other end of the spectrum, nicer restaurants in large cities will often automatically add a 10 percent service charge to the bill, though it's not always clear that this actually gets to the server and isn't pocketed by management or the owners. When you get your bill, always ask if service is included, and then decide whether you want to leave an additional tip. Many people will just round off the bill to the nearest even number, and only in very touristy places will you be expected to tip.

COMMUNICATIONS AND MEDIA
Mail

Thailand Post (www.thailandpost.com) has locations across the country, although there are no guarantees you'll find someone who can speak English if you need to ask questions and cannot communicate in Thai. Stamps are difficult to find outside the post office, though your hotel or guesthouse can often sell you some. Mailboxes are painted red and usually have two slots, one for local mail and one for everything else. If you are sending something within Thailand, service is generally quick, inexpensive, and reliable. If you are sending heavy or bulky items from Thailand abroad, postage can be very expensive and take weeks to arrive. It's better to plan on bringing everything back with you. If you need to send something express, there are **FedEx** (www.fedex.com) and **DHL** offices in Bangkok that do express worldwide shipping.

Telephone

Mobile phones are so common in Thailand that it might be difficult to find a pay phone if you want to call home—or anywhere else, for that matter. If you do, note that long-distance pay phones are generally not coin-operated. You need to purchase a phone card first at a convenience store, but you'll need to know what type or color phone booth you need the phone card for, as there are a number of different companies. Yes, it's confusing. Look for phone booths near convenience stores; at least you can point to what you need.

Nearly all hotels have in-room phones, although most guesthouses don't, and many bungalows don't, either. If you use one, your calls will be marked up sometimes double. If you really need to be in touch with people by telephone, the best bet is to pick up an inexpensive mobile phone and buy prepaid cards. Long-distance rates run as low as 6 baht per minute to the United States and Europe.

Thailand's country code is 66, and inside the country regional area codes are prefaced with a 0 and have one additional digit followed by a seven-digit number—0x/xxx-xxxx. Mobile phones begin with 08 followed by an eight-digit number. You always have to dial the area code, so if you're in Bangkok and you're calling another Bangkok telephone, you must dial 02 first. If you are calling Thailand from outside the country, dial the international access number used in the country you are in, plus the country code (66), and then drop the leading 0, whether calling a fixed line or a mobile phone.

To make international calls from Thailand, you must dial 001, 006, 007, 008, or 009 first, then the country code and phone number. Why so many choices? 001 is the official number, but the others offer cheaper rates. Just know that you'll almost always get routed over a VoIP line, and there may be a noticeable lag.

There are a number of venues throughout Thailand that have multiple phone numbers. These numbers are formatted differently throughout the book. For example, if there are 10 different sequential phone numbers—02/222-2000 through 02/222-2009—the phone number will be formatted as "tel. 02/222-2000 to 02/222-2009."

Mobile Phones

Calls from a mobile phone are cheap in Thailand and get even cheaper when the three largest providers, **AIS, DTAC,** and **True,** get into price wars, sometimes an annual occurrence. When that happens, calls can drop below 1 baht per minute. As in most parts of the world except the United States, you do not pay for incoming calls or text messages. If you have an unlocked tri-band or quad-band mobile phone and can remove your SIM card (ask your mobile service provider before you leave on vacation), bring it with you and buy a prepaid SIM when you arrive. This is the cheapest and easiest way to communicate when you are here. You can also pick up a new or used phone in Thailand, often for a lot cheaper than you'd find at home. All cities have mobile-phone stores that sell unlocked phones, and there are many secondhand phones available if you want to save some cash. Remember to have the seller test the phone for you so you know it works before you walk away with it. Renting a phone before you leave home or at the airport is generally far more expensive than buying a new phone of your own and should be considered only if you cannot go a few hours without mobile communication or do not have time to pick up a phone on your own.

SIM cards and the prepaid cards for the three largest mobile service providers can be found in any convenience store. Note that they sometimes sell their SIM cards under promotional names, such as Happy for DTAC or One Two Call for AIS. However, if you just ask for a SIM from one of the three, you should get what you want. It can be a little confusing to refill or top up your prepaid account, but usually the friendly clerks at any 7-Eleven will walk you through it or even do it for you.

Internet Access

The Internet has penetrated even into the smallest urban areas in Thailand, and even many rural areas. There are still some Internet cafés, though nowadays you'll see more and more places with free Wi-Fi that expect you to bring your own hardware.

Generally, Internet cafés in Thailand are either packed full of tourists on months-long sojourns or packed full of local teenagers playing computer games. Crime is pretty rare in either scenario, but keep an eye on your belongings anyway. It's easy to get distracted when you're writing home, and with all the commotion going on around you, you may just lose something valuable.

English-Language Press

In addition to wide availability of *The International New York Times* in larger hotels, Thailand has two daily English-language newspapers, the *Bangkok Post* (www.bangkokpost.net) and the *Nation* (www.nationmultimedia.com). Although you won't find them in remote or rural areas, you will find them virtually everywhere else. You can also check them out online while you are visiting. If you're curious about what's making headlines in Thailand, check the website a few times before you visit.

In every place where large numbers of English speakers travel, there are small and not-so-small weekly and monthly publications catering to them or the advertisers who want their attention. At any hotel you'll find a stack of them, but you may not find them all that useful. Content is often dictated by the advertisers, so it's hard to trust the food and hotel reviews.

Websites

More and more content about Thailand is available on the web every day, including tourist guides, expat forums where long-term foreign residents gripe about the difficulties of living in a foreign country, and personal travelogues. Spend some time surfing when you're planning your trip, and at the very least make sure to look at the **Tourism Authority of Thailand** website (www.tourismthailand.org) for specific information about the destinations you're planning to visit.

MAPS

While we've included as many helpful maps as possible in this edition, you'll still probably find yourself traveling into uncharted territory, especially if you are exploring some of the off-the-beaten-path recommendations. When you arrive at the airport, you'll be able to get reasonable tourist maps for free, or you can drop into one of the English-language bookstores in Bangkok to find more comprehensive road maps. **Google Maps** uses both Thai and English scripts in its Thailand maps, and it is a great resource both for planning and once you are here. Spelling can be a little bit challenging, so you may have to try a few different variations of the location you're trying to map before you hit it. An excellent mapping resource available online is www.mapguidethailand.com. You can sort by province and search by any number of different things, including *wats,* beaches, and restaurants. The database does not cover everything but is surprisingly comprehensive, and the maps generated are very detailed.

WEIGHTS, MEASURES, ELECTRICITY, AND TIME ZONES

Thailand uses the metric system. See the conversion chart in the back of this book if you're on the U.S. or Imperial system, but remember a few easy rules—a meter is about the same as a yard, a kilogram is just over two pounds (2.2 to be more precise), and a kilometer is 0.6 mile. This is probably as much as you need to know while you're traveling here.

The current for household electricity is 220 volts. Plugs are either two-pronged flat or two-pronged round, like those in the United States and Japan. But just because the appliances you bring from home will plug into most sockets in Thailand without an adapter doesn't mean you should do it. If you are coming from North America, you're on a 110-volt system, and most appliances don't like change. Many an innocent hair dryer has melted, and more than a couple of small fires have been started by making this mistake. If you need to plug something in from home, you'll need a converter to drop the voltage down. Fortunately, most electronics with built-in batteries can take multiple voltages, so chances are you can easily charge your computer or phone. Check the charger or, if in doubt, the manufacturer's website. Note that all Mac laptops and virtually all other laptops are mutlivoltage, and many phones are, too.

All of Thailand falls under one time zone, UTC+7. Thailand does not use daylight saving time and so, November-March, is 15 hours ahead of Pacific standard time, 12 hours ahead of Eastern standard time, and six hours ahead of Central European time.

Resources

Glossary

cha yen: iced tea

chedi: pagoda

chofa: spire-like ornamentations that adorn temple roofs

darma: rule of Buddhism

gaeng or kaeng: curry

gai: chicken

gai yang: grilled chicken with smoky, spicy sauce

guay teow: traditional noodle soup

hat: beach

khai: eggs

khan toke: the formal northern meal in which various dishes are shared and hands are used

khanom chin: thin rice noodles with curry

khanom Thai: coconut puddings scented with jasmine and other unexpected flavors

khao: mountain

khao phad: fried rice

khao soi: soft noodles in sweet, savory rich yellow curry, covered with crispy fried noodles and usually served with chicken or beef

khlong: canal

ko: island

mahout: elephant trainer

mai pen rai: no worries

mai phet: not spicy

mu or moo: pork

muay Thai: Thai boxing

naga: sacred snake

nam phrik: spicy dips served with a selection of fresh vegetables

nam tok: marinated meat salad with sliced grilled beef or pork

pad thai: stir-fried noodles with peanut sauce

ped: duck

phra that: relic of the Buddha

prang: tower

prasat: castle

Ramakien: the Thai version of the Ramayana

roti: pancake-like cooked dough, served with either sweet or savory fillings or dishes

sabai: to be relaxed or comfortable

sala: pavilion or sitting area

samlor: rickshaw-like bicycles

satay: grilled meat

soi: side street

som tam: shredded green papaya salad, with fresh long beans, tomatoes, dried shrimp, peanuts, lime juice, fish sauce, garlic, palm sugar, and chilies

song thaew: pick-up trucks with benches in the back that essentially serve as a cross between a bus (they usually run on fixed routes) and a taxi (you hail one down and just climb in)

tambon: community

tom yam kung: spicy, aromatic soup with shrimp

tuk tuk: three-wheeled motorcycle taxis

ubosot: coronation hall

wai: gesture of greeting and a sign of respect where people put their hands together in a prayerlike motion and bow their heads at each other

wat: temple

wiharn: Buddhist assembly hall

yam som o: pomelo salad with shrimp

Thai Phrasebook

Unless you are staying exclusively in five-star resorts that cater to English-speaking foreigners, you'll notice pretty quickly that most people in Thailand speak little English. English-language studies are compulsory for all students, but even most college graduates do not speak English at any level of fluency. That fact, coupled with a different writing system, makes Thailand a bit of a challenge at best and frustrating at worst. Expect communication problems – after all, you are traveling in a foreign country. Of course, the language barrier is also a great opportunity. Although it's a travel cliché, it's still a sweet experience when little children come up to you to practice saying "hello," and students of all ages will usually be happy to try out a little English on willing foreigners, although they may be too shy to engage you first. If you are looking to spend an extended period of time here, there are plenty of places you can teach English, either on a volunteer or paid basis.

The Thai language, with its confusing tones and difficult-to-decipher writing system, is too difficult to master before taking a vacation. But learning a few words and phrases will make all the difference, especially words and phrases such as "hello" and "thank you." No one in Thailand will expect that you speak the language fluently as a vacationer, so a little bit of Thai will go a long way in terms of breaking the ice. You'll find that people across the country will react positively to any effort you make (even if that positive reaction involves a little bit of laughter).

The Thai alphabet has 44 consonants, more than 20 vowel forms, and four tone marks. The alphabet was invented by King Ramkhamhaeng in the 13th century and was undoubtedly influenced by the Khmer alphabet in use at the time. That may not help too much in understanding what the letters mean; many foreigners find the script difficult. If you're just here on vacation, you won't have the time to do much more than familiarize yourself with the way it looks, but if you want to learn the language, you'll need to master Thai script.

PRONUNCIATION AND TRANSLITERATION

Thai is a tonal language with five tones – low, high, mid, rising, and falling – and a the meaning of a word varies depending on how it is pronounced. Say the name *Bob* out loud as if you were yelling at your little brother, then as though you were picking up the phone and wondering if Bob was on the other line. To speakers of nontonal languages, Bob is Bob, although you've intonated the word differently in different contexts. To speakers of tonal languages, the first pronunciation and the second can mean completely different things. Tones are identified in Thai script through the use of different consonants, vowels, and tone marks, depending on the tone being expressed, but as Thai script can take months of study to master, your best bet is to memorize a few basic expressions and try them out when you arrive. Listen carefully to the way native speakers say common phrases (you'll hear plenty of hellos and thank yous) and do your best to imitate them.

A tonal language also presents another challenge for visitors, as tones are impossible to replicate with the paltry 26-letter Roman alphabet. The word *khao*, for example, means white, mountain, rice, news, he or she, knee, and to enter, depending on which tone you're using and whether the vowel is long or short. Using the Latin alphabet to transliterate Thai words is just a rough approximation, which is why Thai speakers will often misunderstand you or find your pronunciation of a word incomprehensible despite the fact that you are pronouncing it exactly the way it is spelled in Roman letters. This is also why you'll see Thai words spelled in English in so many different ways – *Petchaburi* and *Petburi* or *ko* and *koh* are just two common examples.

We've used the Thai Royal Institute system of transliteration in this book, as it is the official system and the one used to translate place names on road signs and other notices. This system isn't perfect – it ignores tones and vowel length completely – but it's the least complicated and doesn't require that you learn a new system of tone marks; it's an imperfect compromise but the best one for someone visiting Thailand for vacation.

In the case of proper names of sights, restaurants, shops, and lodging, we've used either whatever spelling is approved by the Tourism Authority, what is printed on commonly available maps, what the business goes by, or what is printed on Thai street signs, whether or not it is consistent with the Thai Royal Institute system.

MASCULINE AND FEMININE PARTICLES

Even if you can't make out many Thai words, you will notice that nearly everyone you speak with ends their sentences with either *ka* or *kap*. These are polite particles meant to convey respect, but in truth they are used nearly universally and regardless of whether you are speaking with your boss or the teenage cashier at 7-Eleven. Which one you use depends not on what you are saying or who you are speaking to, but your gender. Women always end their sentences with *ka*, men with *kap*, and you should be particularly careful about making sure you do too. You'll probably notice that the polite particles are also used on their own, meaning the equivalent in English of "OK," "go on," or "yes."

BASIC AND COURTEOUS EXPRESSIONS

Remember that everything you say should end with a polite particle. Here we've listed *sawadee* as hello, but you would almost never hear that phrase spoken without a *ka* or *kap* following it.

Hello/Goodbye *Sawadee*
How are you? *Sabai dee mai?*
I'm well. How are you? *Sabai dee. Sabai dee mai?*
OK; good. *Dee.*
Not OK; bad. *Mai sabai.*
Thank you. *Khopkhun.*
You're welcome/no worries. *Mai pen rai.*
yes *chai*
no (depending on context) *mai chai*
I don't know. *Mai ru.*
Just a moment. *Sak khru.*
Excuse me. *Khothot.*
Pleased to meet you. *Yindi thi dai ruchak.*
What is your name? *Chue arai?/Khun chue arai?*
Do you speak English? *Phut phasa Angkrit dai mai?*
I don't speak Thai. *Phut phasa Thai mai dai.*
I don't understand. *Mai khaochai.*
How do you say . . . in Thai? *Riak… wa arai nai phasa Thai?*
My name is . . . *Chan chue…* (female)/ *Phom chue…* (male)
Would you like . . . ? *Ao… mai?*
Let's go to . . . *Pai… kan thoe.*

TERMS OF ADDRESS

I (female) *chan*
I (female, very formal) *de chan*
I (male) *phom*
I (male, very formal) *kra phom*
you (formal) *khun*
you (very formal, to show high respect) *than*
you (familiar) *khun*
he/him *khao*
she/her *khao*
we/us *rao*
you (plural) *phuak khun*
they/them *phuak khao*

Mr./Sir *khun* or *khun phu chai* (very
formal, used to address someone who
has a higher position than you)

Mrs./Madam *khun* or *khun phu ying*
(very formal, used to address someone
who has a higher position than you)

Miss/young woman *khun* or *nong* (Nong
translates as "younger brother" or
"younger sister." It is used to address
an unknown person who looks younger
than you.)

wife *phan ra ra*

husband *sa mee*

friend *phuean*

sweetheart *wan jai*

boyfriend/girlfriend *fan*

son *luk chai*

daughter *luk sao*

older brother/sister *phee*

older brother *phee chai*

older sister *phee sao*

younger brother/sister *nong*

younger brother *nong chai*

younger sister *nong sao*

father *pho*

mother *mae*

grandfather (father's side) *khun pu* or
pu

grandfather (mother's side) *khun ta*
or *ta*

grandmother (father's side) *khun ya*
or *ya*

grandmother (mother's side) *khun yai*
or *yai*

TRANSPORTATION

Where is . . . ? *. . . yu thinai?*
How far is it to . . . ? *Pai . . . ik klai mai?*
from . . . to . . . *chak . . . pai . . .*
Where is the way to . . . ? *. . . pai thang
nai?*
the bus station *sathani khonsong/
khonsong*
the bus stop *pai rotme*
Where is this bus going? *Rotme khan ni
pai nai?*
the taxi stand *pai taxi*
the train station *sathani rotfai*

the boat *ruea*
the airport *sanambin*
I'd like a ticket to . . . *Kho tua pai . . .*
first (second) class *chan nueng (song)*
round-trip *pai klap*
reservation *chong*
Stop here, please. *Yut thi ni.*
the entrance *thangkhao*
the exit *thang-ok*
the ticket office *thi khai tua*
near *klai* (rising tone)
very near *klai mak*
far *klai*
very far *klai mak*
to; toward *pai*
by; through (as in, I am going by/
through Chiang Mai on my way to
Pai) *pai thang*
from *chak*
turn right *liao khwa*
turn left *liao sai*
right side *dan khwa*
left side *dan sai*
straight ahead *trong pai*
in front *dan na/khang na*
beside *dan khang/khang*
behind *dan lang/lang*
the corner *hua mum*
the stoplight/traffic light *fai yut/
sanyan fai charachon*
right here *thi ni*
somewhere *sak thi*
street; road *thanon*
highway *thangluang*
bridge *saphan*
toll way/toll charge *thangduan/kha
phan thang*
address *thiyu*
north *nuea*
south *tai*
east *tawan-ok*
west *tawantok*

ACCOMMODATIONS

hotel *rongraem*
Is there a room available? *Mi hong wang
mai?*
May I see it? *Kho du dai mai?*

What is the rate? *Rakha thaorai?*

Is there something cheaper? *Mi rakha thuk kwa ni mai?*

single room *hong diao*

double room *hong khu*

double bed *tiang diao* (king-size)

twin bed *tiang khu*

with private bath *mi hongnam suantua*

hot water *nam un*

shower *fakbua*

towels *phachettua*

soap *sabu*

toilet paper *thit chu*

blanket *pha hom*

sheets *pha pu tiang*

air-conditioned *ae* (air)

fan *phatlom*

key *kunchae*

manager *phuchatkan*

FOOD

I'm hungry. *Chan hio.* (female)/*Phom hio.* (male)

I'm thirsty. *Chan hio nam.* (female)/*Phom hio nam.* (male)

menu *menu*

to order food/order *sang ahan/raikan ahan*

glass *kaeo*

fork *som*

knife *mit*

spoon *chon*

napkin *pha chet pak*

soft drink *nam-atlom*

coffee/hot coffee/iced coffee *kafae/ kafae ron/kafae yen*

tea/hot tea/iced tea *cha/cha ron/cha yen*

lime juice *nam manao*

bottled water *nam khuat*

beer *bia*

juice *nam phonlamai*

sugar *namtan*

snack *khanom*

breakfast *ahan chao*

lunch *ahan thiang*

dinner *ahan kham*

The check, please. *Chek bin* or *Kep ngoen duai.*

eggs *khai*

fruit *phonlamai*

pineapple *sapparot*

guava *farang*

watermelon *taeng mo*

rose apple *chomphu*

papaya *malako*

coconut *maphrao*

lime *manao*

durian *thurian*

jackfruit *khanun*

mango *mamuang*

fish *pla*

shrimp *kung*

chicken *gai*

beef *nuea*

pork *mu*

fried *thot*

grilled *ping/yang*

barbecue *babikhio*

not spicy *mai phet*

(prepared with) one chili *prik nung met*

SHOPPING

money *ngoen/tang*

bank *thanakhan*

Do you accept credit cards? *Rap bat khredit mai?*

How much does it cost? *Rakha thaorai?/ Ki baht?*

expensive *phaeng*

cheap *thuk*

more *mak kwa/mak khuen*

less *noi kwa/noi long*

a little *nitnoi*

too much *mak pai*

HEALTH

Help me, please. *Chuai duai.*

I am sick. *Mai sabai.*

Call a doctor. *Tho tam mo./Riak mo.*

Take me to . . . *Pha chan* (female)/*Pha phom* (male) *pai thi . . .*

hospital *rongphayaban*

drugstore/pharmacy *ran khai ya*

pain *puat*

fever *khai* (rising tone)
headache *puathua*
stomachache *puatthong*
burn *mai*
cramp *ta khrio*
nausea *khluen sai*
vomiting *achian/uak*
diarrhea *thongsia*
antibiotic *ya patichiwana*
pill; tablet *ya met*
acetaminophen/paracetamol *ya kae
  puat*
cream *ya tha*
birth-control pills *ya khumkamnoet*
condoms *thung yang anamai*
toothbrush *praengsifan*
toothpaste *yasifan*
dentist *mo fan*
toothache *puat fan*

POST OFFICE AND COMMUNICATIONS

long-distance telephone *thorasap
  thang klai*
I would like to call . . . *Chan/phom yak
  tho pai thi. . .*
collect/collect call *kep ngoen plaithang/
  thorasap riak kep ngoen plaithang*
credit card *bat khredit*
post office *praisani*
by air mail *air mail/chotmai thang akat*
letter *chotmai*
stamp *sataem*
postcard *postcard/praisaniyabat*
registered/certified *longthabian*
money order *thananat*
box; package *khlong*
tape *tape*

AT THE BORDER

border *chaidaen*
customs *sunlakakon*
immigration *dan truat khon khao muang*
arrival card *bat khakhao*
inspection *kan truat/chut truat*
passport *passport/nangsuedoenthang*
profession *achip*
insurance *prakanphai*

driver's license *bai khapkhi*

AT THE GAS STATION

gas station *pam nam man*
gasoline *namman*
unleaded *rai san takua*
full *tem thueng*
tire *yang rotyon/yang*
air *air/khrueang prap-akat*
water *nam*
oil change *plian namman*
grease *charabi*
My . . . doesn't work *. . . sia /. . . mai
  thamngan*
battery *battery*
radiator *monam*
alternator *alternator/dai charge/dai
  panfai*
generator *generator/khrueang panfai*
tow truck *rot lak*
repair shop *ran som*

VERBS

to buy *sue*
to eat *kin*
to climb *pin*
to make *tham*
to go *pai*
to walk *doen*
to love *rak*
to work *thamngan*
to want *tongkan*
to need *tongkan/champen*
to read *an*
to write *khian*
to repair *som*
to stop *yut*
to get off (the bus) *long (rot me)*
to arrive *ma thueng*
to stay (remain) *yu (thi)*
to stay (sleep) *yu thi*
to leave *ok chak*
to look at *mong thi*
to look for *mong ha*
to give *hai*
to carry *thue/hio*
to have *mi*
to come *ma*

NUMBERS

zero *sun*
one *nueng*
two *song*
three *sam*
four *si*
five *ha*
six *hok*
seven *jed*
eight *paed*
nine *kao*
10 *sip*
11 *sip et*
12 *sip song*
13 *sip sam*
14 *sip si*
15 *sip ha*
16 *sip hok*
17 *sip jed*
18 *sip paed*
19 *sip kao*
20 *yisip*
21 *yisip et*
30 *samsip*
100 *nueng roi*
101 *nueng roi et*
200 *song roi*
1,000 *nueng phan*
10,000 *nueng muen*
100,000 *nueng saen*
1,000,000 *nueng lan*
one-half *khrueng*

TIME

What time is it? *Wela thaorai laeo?/Ki mong?*
It's one o'clock *Nueng nalika.*
It's four in the afternoon. *Sip hok nalika.*
It's midnight. *Thiang khuen.*
one minute *nueng nathi*
one hour *nueng chuamong*

DAYS, MONTHS, AND SEASONS

Monday *Wan Chan*
Tuesday *Wan Angkhan*
Wednesday *Wan Phut*
Thursday *Wan Pharuehatsabodi/Wan Pharue Hat*
Friday *Wan Suk*
Saturday *Wan Sao*
Sunday *Wan Athit*
January *Mokkarakhom*
February *Kumphaphan*
March *Minakhom*
April *Mesayon*
May *Phruetsaphakhom*
June *Mithunayon*
July *Karakadakhom*
August *Singhakhom*
September *Kanyayon*
October *Tulakhom*
November *Phruetsa Chi Ka Yon*
December *Thanwakhom*
today *wanni*
yesterday *muea wan*
tomorrow *phrungni*
a week *nueng sapda*
a month *nueng duean*
after *lang*
before *kon*
rainy season *ruedu fon*
cool season *ruedu nao*
hot/warm season *ruedu ron*

Suggested Reading

ART AND ARCHITECTURE

Gosling, Betty. *Origins of Thai Art.* Trumbull, CT: Weatherhill, 2004. An accessible early history of Thai art, Gosling's book is full of beautiful photographs of building details and sculptures to illustrate the history she lays out.

Kerlogue, Fiona. *Arts of Southeast Asia.* London: Thames & Hudson, 2004. This small, nicely illustrated, and easy-to-read book offers a basic overview of the history of art across the region. Although not specifically focused on Thailand, the information provided is essential to putting the art and artifacts in the country into a broader context.

Poshyananda, Apinan. *Modern Art in Thailand: Nineteenth and Twentieth Centuries.* Singapore: Oxford University Press, 1992. Although most books on art in Thailand focus on the distant past, Poshyananda explains the different influences on modern art in a comprehensive manner.

Ringis, Rita. *Thai Temples and Thai Murals.* Singapore: Oxford University Press, 1990. For those interested in more than a cursory tour of Thailand's scores of temples, this book offers an excellent overview of temple architecture and mural work. There are also in-depth descriptions of some of the most popular temples in the country.

Woodward, Hiram. *The Art and Architecture of Thailand: From Prehistoric Times through the Thirteenth Century.* Boston: Brill Academic Publishers, 2005. Woodward's book provides the first comprehensive survey of art in Thailand through the 13th century. The book is academic in nature and offers a sociohistorical view of art history. Those with an interest in archaeology will find it very useful.

HISTORY

Baker, Christopher, and Pasuk Phongpaichit. *A History of Thailand.* Cambridge, MA: Cambridge University Press, 2005. This is one of the few books that offers a modern history of the kingdom; it tracks the economic, political, and social changes in Thailand over the past 300 years.

Handley, Paul M. *The King Never Smiles.* New Haven, CT: Yale University Press, 2006. Banned in Thailand before it even hit the shelves, Handley's biography of King Bhumibol tells the story of how Thailand's current king came to power and how he has created an important role for the monarchy over the past 60 years. Handley, a former journalist based in Bangkok for over a decade, offers a well-researched though controversial look at the king's life and reign.

Higham, Charles. *The Archaeology of Mainland Southeast Asia: From 10,000 b.c. to the fall of Angkor.* Cambridge, MA: Cambridge University Press, 1989. Respected archaeologist Charles Higham takes readers through the region's early social history using archaeological evidence found in Southeast Asia. For those planning to visit any of the major Khmer archaeological sites, such as Phanom Rung or Phimai, this book offers in-depth (albeit dense and academic) information to complement a visit.

Somers Heidhues, Mary. *Southeast Asia: A Concise History.* London: Thames & Hudson, 2001. This is an easy and quick general overview of the history of the region for those looking for an understanding of Southeast Asia without devoting hours to study.

Tarling, Nicholas. *The Cambridge History of Southeast Asia,* Vols. I and II. Cambridge, MA: Cambridge University Press, 2000. These two volumes offer a comprehensive social and political history of the region as a whole, which is essential to adequately understand the history of Thailand.

Wyatt, David K. *Thailand: A Short History.* New Haven, CT: Yale University Press, 2003.

CULTURE
Cornwel-Smith, Philip, and John Goss. *Very Thai.* Bangkok: River Books Press, 2006. Explains lots of seemingly quirky Thai cultural behaviors, including the obsession with tiny napkins.

Ziv, Daniel, Guy Sharett, and Sasa Kralj. *Bangkok Inside Out.* Jakarta: Equinox Publishing, 2004. This thoughtful, irreverent, and honest book explains all of the quirky, seemingly inconsistent pieces of the capital city without relying on clichés or judgmental descriptions. It's full of great photos too.

Internet Resources

There is tons of information about Thailand on the Internet, and no one should plan a trip here without taking advantage of some of the excellent resources available. The biggest annoyance is the many websites without original content whose sole purpose is to direct you to hotel or tour booking agencies. You'll know pretty quickly if you've stumbled onto one of these. Below is a list of reliable websites with informative, original content.

TRAVEL INFORMATION
Travel Authority of Thailand
www.tourismthailand.org
The Travel Authority of Thailand (TAT) may not offer the most objective view of the country's destinations, their destination guide covers every province in the country and has basic, reliable information. You may not want to plan your whole trip around what the tourism authority is saying, but this is a very good place to start your Internet research. The website also provides a calendar of events across

the country and often highlights quirky or otherwise unknown destinations.

Bangkok Tourism Division
www.bangkoktourist.com
The Bangkok Tourism Division also has a website full of tourism information for visitors to the capital city. The site is not as slick as the TAT website, but the information is generally accurate and the coverage of wats is extensive.

TRIP PRACTICALITIES
U.S. State Department
www.travel.state.gov/travel
Make sure to check the U.S. State Department's website for basic information about Thailand and any updates on safety, especially in the southernmost provinces.

Centers for Disease Control
www.cdc.gov/travel
Check out the Centers for Disease Control travel website for country-specific health

information, including updates on recommended vaccinations and medications.

BLOGS

There are a handful of good blogs on travel and life in Thailand worth spending some time perusing. Since blog content changes so frequently and is often out of date within months, search for blogs on travel in Thailand when planning your trip to find travelogues of people who've recently been here.

Austin Bush Photography
www.austinbushphotography.com
Austin Bush's photography site has an excellent food blog with beautiful pictures of mostly casual restaurants, food stalls, and markets across the country and is a must read for foodies visiting Thailand.

Bangkok Pundit
http://bangkokpundit.blogspot.com
This blog sometimes feels a little too insider-oriented for first-time visitors to Thailand, but it does offer a unique and sometimes funny perspective on current events and politics.

Promoting Thai Culture
www.richardbarrow.com
Resident expat Richard Barrow posts blog entries about travel around Bangkok, Thai culture, and a weekly piece about food in Thailand. His posts are usually in-depth and accompanied by great photos.

Index

List of Maps

MAP SYMBOLS

≡≡≡	Expressway	○	City/Town	✈	Airport	♪	Golf Course
──	Primary Road	◉	State Capital	✗	Airfield	P	Parking Area
──	Secondary Road	⊛	National Capital	▲	Mountain	⬟	Archaeological Site
------	Unpaved Road	★	Point of Interest	✦	Unique Natural Feature	⌖	Church
──	Feature Trail	•	Accommodation			⛽	Gas Station
- - - -	Other Trail	▼	Restaurant/Bar	🌿	Waterfall	∞	Glacier
··········	Ferry	■	Other Location	♠	Park	▨	Mangrove
≡≡≡	Pedestrian Walkway	Λ	Campground	⬛	Trailhead	∽	Reef
▬▬▬	Stairs			✗	Skiing Area	▱	Swamp

CONVERSION TABLES

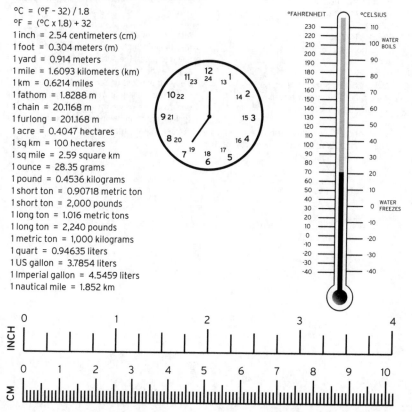

°C = (°F - 32) / 1.8
°F = (°C x 1.8) + 32
1 inch = 2.54 centimeters (cm)
1 foot = 0.304 meters (m)
1 yard = 0.914 meters
1 mile = 1.6093 kilometers (km)
1 km = 0.6214 miles
1 fathom = 1.8288 m
1 chain = 20.1168 m
1 furlong = 201.168 m
1 acre = 0.4047 hectares
1 sq km = 100 hectares
1 sq mile = 2.59 square km
1 ounce = 28.35 grams
1 pound = 0.4536 kilograms
1 short ton = 0.90718 metric ton
1 short ton = 2,000 pounds
1 long ton = 1.016 metric tons
1 long ton = 2,240 pounds
1 metric ton = 1,000 kilograms
1 quart = 0.94635 liters
1 US gallon = 3.7854 liters
1 Imperial gallon = 4.5459 liters
1 nautical mile = 1.852 km

MOON PHUKET & KO SAMUI
Avalon Travel
a member of the Perseus Books Group
1700 Fourth Street
Berkeley, CA 94710, USA
www.moon.com

Editor: Leah Gordon
Series Manager: Kathryn Ettinger
Copy Editor: Alissa Cyphers
Graphics Coordinator: Darren Alessi
Production Coordinator: Darren Alessi
Cover Design: Faceout Studios, Charles Brock
Moon Logo: Tim McGrath
Map Editor: Albert Angulo
Cartographers: Albert Angulo,
  Stephanie Poulain
Indexer: Rachel Kuhn

ISBN-13: 978-1-61238-914-1
ISSN: 2374-1503

Printing History
1st Edition – November 2014
5 4 3 2 1

Text © 2014 by Suzanne Nam.
Maps © 2014 by Avalon Travel.
All rights reserved.

Front cover photo: Ko Roi, Andaman Sea © Zach
  Holmes / Alamy

Printed in Canada by Friesens